Sedulo curavi humanas
actiones non ridere,
non lugere, neque detestari
sed intelligere.

I have made a ceaseless
effort not to ridicule,
not to bewail, nor to scorn human
   actions,
but to understand them.

Baruch Spinoza

Es gibt eine zarte Empirie, die sich
mit dem Gegenstand innigst identisch
macht, und dadurch zur eigentlichen
Theorie wird.

Das Allgemeine und das Besondere
fallen zusammen; das Besondere ist
das Allgemeine, unter verschiedene
Bedingungen erscheinend.

Wilhelm Meisters Wanderjahre
"Betrachtungen im Sinne der Wan-
derer" 565, 569

There is a delicate form of the empirical which identifies itself so intimately
with its object that it thereby becomes
theory.

The general and the particular converge; the particular is the general,
appearing under various conditions.

Wilhelm Meister's Journeyman Years
"Thoughts in the Mind of the Journeyman" Nos. 565, 569

Johann Wolfgang von Goethe (1829)

SEQUENCE ORGANIZATION IN INTERACTION

Much of our daily lives is spent talking to one another, in both ordinary conversation and more specialized settings such as meetings, interviews, classrooms, and courtrooms. It is largely through conversation that the major institutions of our society – economy, religion, politics, family, and law – are implemented. This is the first in a new series of books by Emanuel Schegloff introducing the findings and theories of conversation analysis. Together, the volumes in the series when published will constitute a complete and authoritative "primer" in the subject. The topic of this first volume is "sequence organization" – the ways in which turns-at-talk are ordered and combined to make actions take place in conversation, such as requests, offers, complaints, and announcements. Containing many examples from real-life conversations, this volume will be invaluable to anyone interested in human interaction and the workings of conversation.

EMANUEL A. SCHEGLOFF is Distinguished Professor of Sociology and Applied Linguistics at the University of California, Los Angeles. He has previously published *Interaction and Grammar* (co-edited with Elinor Ochs and Sandra Thompson, Cambridge University Press, 1996).

Video and audio examples of some of the interactions discussed in this book can be found at www.cambridge.org/9780521825726

Sequence Organization in Interaction

A Primer in Conversation Analysis I

EMANUEL A. SCHEGLOFF

CAMBRIDGE
UNIVERSITY PRESS

CAMBRIDGE
UNIVERSITY PRESS

University Printing House, Cambridge CB2 8BS, United Kingdom

Published in the United States of America by Cambridge University Press, New York

Cambridge University Press is part of the University of Cambridge.

It furthers the University's mission by disseminating knowledge in the pursuit of
education, learning and research at the highest international levels of excellence.

www.cambridge.org
Information on this title: www.cambridge.org/9780521532792

© Emanuel A. Schegloff 2007

First published 2007

A catalogue record for this publication is available from the British Library

ISBN 978-0-521-82572-6 Hardback
ISBN 978-0-521-53279-2 Paperback

Contents

Preface	*page* xi	
Acknowledgments	xvi	
1.	Introduction to sequence organization	1
	Capsule review 1: turns	3
	Capsule review 2: actions	7
2.	The adjacency pair as the unit for sequence construction	13
	Adjacency, nextness, contiguity, progressivity	14
	Alternative second pair parts	16
	Counters	16
	Relevance rules and negative observations	19
	Upshot	21
3.	Minimal, two-turn adjacency pair sequences	22
4.	Pre-expansion	28
	Pre-invitation	29
	Pre-offer	34
	Pre-announcement and other pre-telling	37
	A different kind of type-specific pre-sequence: the pre-pre	44
	Generic pre-sequence: the summons–answer sequence	48
	Multiple pre-expansions	53
5.	The organization of preference/dispreference	58
	Preferred and dispreferred responses: the terms	58
	Preferred and dispreferred responses: the practices and features	63
	Mitigation	64
	Elaboration	65
	Default	66
	Positioning	67

Multiple preferences   73

Type conformity   78

Summary remarks on preferred and dispreferred second pair parts   81

Preferred and dispreferred first pair parts   81

6. Insert expansion   97

Post-first insert expansion   100

Capsule review 3: repair   100

Pre-second insert expansion   106

Expansion of expansions   109

The extent of expansions   111

7. Post-expansion   115

Minimal post-expansion: sequence-closing thirds   118

"Oh"   118

"Okay"   120

Assessment   123

Composites   127

Post-completion musings, or postmortems   142

Non-minimal post-expansion   148

Other-initiated repair   149

Disagreement-implicated other-initiated repair   151

Topicalization   155

Rejecting/challenging/disagreeing with the second pair part   159

First pair part reworkings post-expansion   162

8. Topic-proffering sequences: a distinctive adjacency pair sequence
structure   169

9. Sequence-closing sequences   181

Unilateral and foreshortened sequence endings   181

Dedicated sequence-closing sequences   186

10. Sequences of sequences   195

Reciprocal or exchange sequences   195

Action-type sequence series   207

Successive parts of a course of action   213

Other relations between sequences of sequences: multi-part tellings   215

11. Retro-sequences 217

12. Some variations in sequence organization 220
     Sequence-closing thirds 221
     Distinctive sequence and expansion types 223
     Preference organization 225

13. Sequence as practice 231
     Non-canonical forms 231
     Incidental sequences 237
     Interactional projects, thematic threads, committed lines, etc. 244
     Sequence as practice: the bottom line 249

14. Summary and Applications 251

     Appendix 1: Conversation-analytic transcript symbols 265
     Appendix 2: Transcript of a telephone call 270
     References 287
     Index 294

Preface

Past and future

A primer, we are told by the *Shorter Oxford English Dictionary* (Onions, 1980:1,670), is "a small introductory book on any subject." Some ten years ago, amidst a mixture of encouragement and pestering by colleagues, I set about writing a primer in conversation analysis. I had been teaching a two-term course called "Conversational Structures" to classes of both undergraduate and graduate students for over twenty years by then, and more abbreviated courses to one or the other of these cohorts for several years before that. I had a fairly secure sense of what needed doing and how to get it done. Surely that could be transferred from the lecture hall and discussion room to the pages of a book.

The first term of my course took up three main subjects. First, we discussed what was meant by the term "conversation" in ordinary, informal talk, and what we would mean by it for the purposes of inquiry, and what, furthermore, might be meant by "*structures* of conversation." This ordinarily pro forma "introduction to the course" grew over time to three seventy-five-minute lectures, and sometimes part of a fourth. Second, we undertook a rough introduction to turn-taking in conversation – how people get to talk and for how long and with what consequences. For all its roughness, participants found themselves grappling with details of everyday conduct they had never before registered as "things" at all, let alone with the kind of care that was asked of them; let alone the consequentiality they were invited to see in them; let alone doing this for three to four weeks. And third, we turned our attention to stretches of talk that seemed to hang together, a stretch that seemed to constitute a unit in its own right, over and above the turns at talk that composed it; we called these "sequences," and we spent the last four to five weeks of the term elucidating and explicating how they were put together, what we could call their organization – "sequence organization."

When I set about drafting the primer in conversation analysis, I began, for reasons I no longer remember, by writing up the chapter on sequence organization. By the time I was done, it ran to some 275 pages! And this was just sequence organization! And the course I have described in the preceding paragraph was just the first of two! And I never ended up covering the subject matter by the end of the second of those terms! "A small introductory book on any subject," indeed!

This is that "chapter," somewhat revised and slightly expanded in the intervening ten years, and grown into a "book," with its parts now "chapters" in their own right. But you, the reader, are invited to register their less formal character – as "sections," perhaps, with less discontinuity between them than is often the case with "chapters." The book is meant to amount to a single, sustained presentation of a single organization of practices, and is meant to take its place in the company of others (also "chapters" grown into "books," each offering a single, sustained presentation of a single organization of practices), among which it was not meant to be the first, though it is the first to appear. The full introduction to this "set of primers" will be found elsewhere, but I hope the engagement with sequence organization will not suffer on that account.

The epigraph which Gene Lerner chose for the volume that he edited under the title *Conversation Analysis: Studies from the First Generation* was taken from a lecture by my colleague Harvey Sacks. He said:

> Basically what I have to sell is the sorts of work I can do. I don't have to sell its theoretical underpinnings, its hopes for the future, its methodological elegance, its theoretical scope, or anything else. I have to sell what I can do, and the interestingness of my findings.   (Sacks, 1992b: 3)

These were among the first sentences in the first lecture of the first course that Sacks taught at the Irvine campus of the University of California, after having moved there from UCLA, and that is not immaterial to their tenor; they were his first self-presentation. They are informed as well by Sacks' understanding of the then-current position of conversation analysis in the academic social sciences. They were meant (in my understanding, at least) to ground appreciation of this work – both on campus and in the wider academic community – not in abstract theoretical or methodological debates divorced from actual work, but rather in exemplary displays of what this work could do, and its "interestingness." If that could be established, the theoretical and methodological discussions could follow; if not, they would not matter anyway.

More than thirty-six years have passed since that time. In this primer, and the other primers that are meant to accompany it, I want to put forward all the things Sacks disclaimed, as well as what he put on offer; and not only what *he* put on offer, but some of what *other* members of the conversation-analytic community have put on offer. I do so in the hope of fostering the growth of that community, fostering a continuing rise in the scope, rigor, robustness, and perceptiveness of the community's research and teaching, and fostering growth in the accessibility of this work to those who have pursuits of their own, but find conversation-analytic work possibly relevant to those pursuits, or of such "interestingness" as to command their attention, whether relevant to their own pursuits or not.

Of the three epigraphs that introduce this work, the first is meant to represent its moral and political stance; the second embodies its theoretical aspiration; and the third declares one of its methodological premises and points of departure.

Substance

Whatever their other characteristics, it appears that all societies and sub-units of them have as a central resource for their integration an organization of interaction – an organization of interaction informed by the use of language. This awkward phrasing is meant to include signing communities and monastic orders in which vows of silence constrain the conduct of interaction. Though language in the conventional or vernacular sense may not be used there, conduct is informed by language via the specific renunciation of its use. When societies undergo the upheaval of massive transformation of their macro-structures – of economy, polity, and social organization – what remains largely untouched is this robust structuring of the coming together, co-mingling and interaction of members of the society. And despite the much-celebrated diversity of language, culture, mores, etc. among human communities, people crossing over from one to another can virtually always make do, even if at a relatively unsophisticated level of interaction.

What is this web of practices that is so deeply rooted that it can transcend linguistic and cultural diversity – indeed, that is the natural ecological niche for language and the arena in which the diversity of cultures as well as their commonalities are enacted? What is this web of practices that serves as the infrastructure of social institutions in the same way that a system of transportation serves as the infrastructure for an economy, that is so transparent that it is opaque, whose omnipresence and centrality make it a – if not *the* – core root of sociality itself?[1]

Surely a preface is no place to take up such questions with any seriousness and depth, let alone with empirical evidence that might show the claims to be not theoretical conjectures, but empirically grounded reports of the results of careful and systematic observation of the naturally occurring data of interaction in a variety of naturally occurring contexts. What follow, then, are thumbnail sketches of what so far appear to be generic orders of organization in talk-in-interaction – the term I will prefer to "conversation" so as to circumvent the connotation of triviality that has come often to be attached to the latter term, and to broaden the scope of what we mean to be

---

[1] Some of these features are taken up in Schegloff (2006 frth).

dealing with to interactional settings that clearly fall outside the common sense meaning of "conversation."

By "generic orders of organization," I mean the various organizations of practice that deal with the various generic organizational contingencies of talk-in-interaction without which it cannot proceed in an orderly way:

(1) the "turn-taking" problem: who should talk next and when should they do so? How does this affect the construction and understanding of the turns themselves?

(2) the "action-formation" problem: how are the resources of the language, the body, the environment of the interaction, and position *in* the interaction fashioned into conformations designed to be, and to be recognizable by recipients as, particular actions – actions like requesting, inviting, granting, complaining, agreeing, telling, noticing, rejecting, and so on – in a class of unknown size?

(3) the "sequence-organizational" problem: how are successive turns formed up to be "coherent" with the prior turn (or *some* prior turn), and what is the nature of that coherence?

(4) the "trouble" problem: how to deal with trouble in speaking, hearing and/or understanding the talk so that the interaction does not freeze in place when trouble arises, that intersubjectivity is maintained or restored, and that the turn and sequence and activity can progress to possible completion?

(5) the word-selection problem: how do the components that get selected as the elements of a turn get selected, and how does that selection inform and shape the understanding achieved by the turn's recipients?

(6) the overall structural organization problem: how does the overall composition of an occasion of interaction get structured, what are those structures, and how does placement in the overall structure inform the construction and understanding of the talk as turns, as sequences, etc.?

The organizations of practice addressed to these issues – turn organization and turn-*taking* organization, sequence organization, the organization of repair, the organization of word selection, overall structural organization, and others, in the options which they shape and the practices they make available – constitute a spate of interaction recognizable as "conversation," as "interview," as "meeting," as "lecturing," as "giving a speech," as "interrogation," etc. (what we call "speech-exchange systems," Sacks et al., 1974:729–31), and as particular, here-and-now-with-these-participants instances of these.

What makes an interaction is not just the juxtaposition of bodies. What mediates and organizes the conduct of the parties is not a structureless, featureless, transparent medium. The composition of a turn-at-talk – whether it be of single words, phrases, clauses or sentences – is shaped in part by the contingencies of turn production imposed by a turn-taking organization that will have other participants empowered or required or allowed to talk next, at points in the turn's development not wholly under the speaker's control. Particular courses of action implemented through turns-at-talk (like request sequences, complaint sequences, storytelling sequences, news-conveying sequences, etc.) implicate certain ways of understanding what is being said that render meaningful and consequential selection between apparently equivalent expressions: the delay of a turn's start by 0.2 second or less, and the like. How one says what one says can depend on who the other is, and, of all the persons and categories which could be used to characterize "the other," which one(s) have been made relevant at that moment in the talk, or can be made relevant by constructing the same "sayable" this way or that. And so on. (see Schegloff [2004b, 2006 frth]).

Each of the generic organizations of practice mentioned in the preceding three paragraphs will be the topic of one of the component primers in this set, the whole of which is meant (its size to the contrary notwithstanding) to constitute a primer in conversation analysis. None is fully understandable without the others. No one of them can have its beginning understood without having already absorbed its ending, so each should be re-begun after completion. But one has to start somewhere – both in the reading and in the writing. The writing begins here with "sequence organization"; for now, the reading starts here as well.

Acknowledgments

This work was first drafted in 1995, and has been used in my teaching and circulated informally since that time. The version presented here has benefited from a year at the Center for Advanced Study in the Behavioral Sciences in 1998–99, the awarding of a John Simon Guggenheim Fellowship for the same year, and time freed up by a sabbatical leave during the 2004–05 academic year.

I want to acknowledge from the outset my indebtedness to colleagues, friends, students, and students of my students who have contributed insightful listening, gentle and detailed suggestions, and/or supportive environments and collegiality that almost certainly are even more important to bringing this book to completion than I am aware of: the late Bob Alford, Galina Bolden, Herb Clark, Maria Egbert, Chuck and Candy Goodwin, John Heritage, Leslie Jarmon, Irene Koshik, Gene Lerner, Steve Levinson, Geoff Raymond, Jeff Robinson, Federico Rossano, Andy Roth, Neil Smelser, Tanya Stivers, an anonymous reviewer for Cambridge University Press, and several generations of undergraduate and graduate students whose reactions to my presentation of these materials in lectures, in discussion groups, and in earlier drafts of the present manuscript, gave me guidance on how to make it better.

No acknowledgment would suffice to capture what I learned from, and shared with, my intellectual comrade and best friend Harvey Sacks. The work we did together was the apotheosis of collaboration in inquiry – years of an altogether unique experience. Who knows where we would be in this work had he not died in 1975. Nor would any acknowledgment suffice to capture the patience, endurance, and support of my wife, Myra. Who knows where *I* would be in this work without it and without her.

1 Introduction to sequence organization

One of the most fundamental organizations of practice for talk-in-interaction is the organization of turn-taking. For there to be the possibility of responsiveness – of one participant being able to show that what they are saying and doing is responsive to what another has said and done – one party needs to talk after the other, and, it turns out, they have to talk singly. It is the organization of the practices of turn-taking that is the resource relied upon by parties to talk-in-interaction to achieve these outcomes routinely: they talk singly – that is, one at a time; and each participant's talk is inspectable, and is inspected, by co-participants to see how it stands to the one that preceded, what sort of response it has accorded the preceding turn. The organization of turn-taking requires a book of its own; all we can give it here is a capsule review, which will appear below. Suffice it to say that the turn-taking organization for conversation works extremely effectively, and produces long stretches of turns-at-talk that follow one another with minimized gap and overlap between them.

A moment's observation and reflection should suggest, however, that turns do not follow one another like identical beads on a string. They have some organization and "shape" to them, aside from their organization as single turns and as series-of-turns (that is, as turns starting with a back-connection and ending with a forward one). One might say that they seem to be grouped in batches or clumps, one bunch seeming to "hang together" or cohere, and then another, and another, etc.

The most common tendency is to think of these clumps as topical, the turns hanging together because they are somehow "about" the same thing. It turns out that such a claim is more complicated than it initially seems to be, although we must leave for treatment elsewhere what these complications are (Schegloff, 1990:51–53). Whatever may be the case about topics and topicality, it is important to register that a great deal of talk-in-interaction – perhaps most of it – is better examined with respect to *action* than with respect to *topicality*, more for what it is *doing* than for what it is *about*. An utterance like "Would somebody like some more ice tea" – as in Extract (1.01) – is better understood as "doing an offer" than as "about ice tea," as can be seen in the response to it, which does not do further talk about iced tea, but accepts an alternative to what has been offered. (Digitized audio or video files of the data are available at the following website: http://www.cambridge.org/9780521532792; transcription symbols are explained in Appendix 1.)

```
(1.01) Virginia, 11:16-19
1  Mom:  = ˙hhh Whooh! It is so hot tuhnight. *Would somebody like
2        some more ice tea. ((* = voice fades throughout TCU))
3        (0.8)
4  Wes:  Uh(b)- (0.4) I('ll) take some more ice.
```

When we think of clumps of turns in "action" terms, we are dealing with courses of action – with sequences of actions that have some shape or trajectory to them, that is, with what we will call "sequence organization" or "the organization of sequences." Because much of what Conversation Analysis is concerned with is "*sequential* organization," we would do well to take a moment to get our terms sorted out, and be clear on the difference between "sequential organization" and "sequence organization" as they are used here.

"Sequential organization" is the more general term. We use it to refer to any kind of organization which concerns the relative positioning of utterances or actions. So turn-taking is a type of sequential organization because it concerns the relative ordering of speakers, of turn-constructional units, and of different types of utterance. Overall structural organization is a type of sequential organization; by reference to its shape, some types of actions/utterances are positioned early in a conversation (e.g., greetings) and others late in conversations (e.g., arrangement-making, farewells).

"Sequence organization" is another type of sequential organization. Its scope is the organization of courses of action enacted through turns-at-talk – coherent, orderly, meaningful successions or "sequences" of actions or "moves." Sequences are the vehicle for getting some activity accomplished.

Just as parties to talk-in-interaction monitor the talk-in-a-turn in the course of its production for such key features as where it might be possibly complete and whether someone is being selected as next speaker (and, if so, who), so they monitor and analyze it for what action or actions its speaker might be doing with it. One basic and omnirelevant issue for the participants for any bit of talk-in-interaction is "why that now" (Schegloff and Sacks, 1973:299), and the key issue in that regard is what is being done by that (whatever the "that" is). And the parties monitor for action for the same reason they monitor for the other features we investigate; namely, because the action that a speaker might be doing in or with an utterance may have implications for what action should or might be done in the next turn as a response to it. If it is doing a request, it may make a granting or a declining relevant next; if it is doing an assessment, it may make an agreement or a disagreement relevant next; if it is doing a complaint, it may make an apology relevant next, or an account, or a denial, or a counter-complaint, or a remedy, etc.

So each turn – actually, each turn-constructional unit – can be inspected by co-participants to see what action(s) may be being done through it. And all *series* of turns can be inspected or tracked (by the parties and by us) to see what course(s) of action may be being progressively enacted through them, what possible responses may be being made relevant, what outcomes are being pursued, what "sequences" are being constructed or enacted or projected. That is, sequences of turns are not haphazard but have a shape or structure, and can be tracked for where they came from, what is being done through them, and where they might be going.

In this book, we will be asking whether there are any general patterns or general practices which can be isolated and described through which sequences – courses of action implemented through talk – get organized. Across all the different kinds of actions which people do through talk, are there any sorts of general patterns or structures *which they use* (and which we can describe) to co-produce and track an orderly stretch of talk and other conduct in which some course of action gets initiated, worked through, and brought to closure? If so, we will call them "sequences," and we will call their organization "sequence organization."

Before going much further, we need to be sure we share some basic understandings of what is meant here by terms such as "turns," "turn-constructional units" (or "TCUs"), and "turn-taking" on the one hand, and by "action(s)," and particular types of action, on the other. To that end, the next few pages are set aside for two "capsule reviews" – brief and highly concentrated reviews of these two domains which figure centrally in the concerns of this book, each of which is meant to be the topic of its own installment in the larger project of which this book is a part.

Capsule review 1: turns

Actions accomplished by talking get done in turns-at-talk. What are the features of this environment for talking/acting-in-interaction? And how are the opportunities for action through talk distributed among parties to interaction? That is, from the point of view of a participant, how does one come to have a turn and, with it, the opportunity and obligation to act?

The building blocks out of which turns are fashioned we call turn-constructional units, or TCUs. Grammar is one key organizational resource in building and recognizing TCUs; for English and many other languages (so far we know of no exceptions), the basic shapes that TCUs take are sentences or clauses more generally, phrases, and lexical items. A second organizational resource shaping TCUs is grounded in the phonetic realization of the talk, most familiarly, in intonational "packaging." A third – and criterial – feature of a TCU is that it constitutes a recognizable action in context; that is, at that juncture of that episode of interaction, with those participants, in that place, etc. A speaker beginning to talk in a turn has the right and obligation to produce one TCU, which may realize one or more actions.

As a speaker approaches the possible completion of a first TCU in a turn, transition to a next speaker can become relevant; if acted upon, the transition to a next speaker is accomplished just after the possible completion of the TCU-in-progress. Accordingly, we speak of the span that begins with the imminence of possible completion as the "transition-relevance place." Note: it is not that speaker transition necessarily occurs there; it is that transition to a next speaker becomes *possibly relevant* there.

Speakers often produce turns composed of more than one TCU. There are various ways this can come to pass which cannot be taken up here. Suffice it to say that if a speaker talks past a possible completion of the first TCU in a turn, whether by extending that TCU past its possible completion or by starting another TCU, whether in the face of beginning of talk by another or clear of such overlapping talk, then at the next occurrence of imminent possible TCU completion transition to a next speaker again becomes relevant.

But how does a party to the interaction come to be in the position of a speaker beginning to talk in a turn in the first place? There are two main ways. First, a just-prior speaker can have selected them as next speaker by addressing them with a turn whose action requires a responsive action next – for example, with a question that makes an answer relevant next, with a complaint which makes relevant next an apology, or excuse, or denial, or remedy, etc. Second, if no one has been so selected by a/the prior speaker, then anyone can self-select to take the next turn and does that by starting to fashion a first TCU in the turn-space they thereby claim; the first one to do so gets the turn. There is a good deal more to be said about this, but this will suffice for our purposes.

There are two features of turn-taking and turn organization that are most salient for readers to have a firm grasp of for our purposes. First, the TCU as a unit of conduct – readers should be alert to the TCU composition of a turn, to where a TCU is projectably coming to imminent possible completion, and what action or actions the TCU is recognizably implementing; and, second, that feature of a TCU that serves to select someone as next speaker (that is, that action), and what sort of responses that action makes relevant for that next speaker to do. It is these two features that, taken together, compose the central organizing format for sequences – the adjacency pair.

Here is one exchange to exemplify some of the points just discussed. Vivian and Shane (seated to the left) are hosting Nancy and Michael for a chicken dinner, and are recording it for use in a college course. Vivian has prepared the meal, and her boyfriend Shane has been teasing her by

complaining about this or that claimed inadequacy. In this exchange, he is
doing this again.

```
(1.02) Chicken Dinner, 4:28-5:06
 1                    (1.1)
 2    Sha:      Ah can't- Ah can't[get this thing ↓mashed.
 3    Viv:                         [Aa-ow.
 4                    (1.2)
 5    Nan:      You[do that too:? tih yer pota]toes,
 6    Sha:         [This one's hard ezza rock.]
 7    Sha:      ↑Ye[ah.
 8    Viv:         [It i:[s?
 9    Sha:               [B't this thing- is ↑ha:rd.
10                    (0.3)
11    Viv:      It's not do:ne? th'potato?
12    Sha:      Ah don't think so,
13                    (2.2)
14    Nan: →    Seems done t'me how 'bout you Mi[chael,]
15    Sha:                                     [Alri' ]who
16              cooked this mea:l.
17    Mic: →    'hh Little ↓bit'v e-it e-ih-ih of it isn'done.
18    Sha:      Th'ts ri:ght.
19                    (1.2)
```

The exchange starts with a complaint by Shane at line 2; Nancy tries to
divert the exchange into "shared ways of eating potatoes," but Shane is
insistent at lines 6 and 9, and Vivian is taken in by the ruse at lines 8 and
11. After Shane reinforces (at line 12) Vivian's concern that the potatoes
are "not done," insufficiently cooked (at line 11), Nancy joins in at line 14.
Notice here the following exemplars of matters taken up in the preceding
paragraphs: a) Nancy's turn is composed of two TCUs: "seems done t'me,"
and "how 'bout you Michael"; b) each of these is a grammatically possibly
complete construction, and each does a recognizable action (the intonational
contour of the first TCU is not clearly "final" for reasons we cannot take up
here, except to note that it anticipates and projects another TCU to come);
c) the first of these TCUs is addressed to the question Vivian has asked at line
11 – it answers that question in a fashion designed specifically to disagree
with, or contest, the answer previously given by Shane, and reassures Vivian
that the potato has been properly cooked; d) the second TCU is addressed
to Michael – designed as a question that makes an answer relevant next, it
selects its addressee as next speaker and the appropriate action: answering
the question. It is also designed to put Michael on the spot – having to side
with either his friend Shane or his partner Nancy and their host Vivian, a
fix which he tries to finesse with questionable success.

Here is one more exchange to consolidate some of the points just discussed – this one a bit more complicated than the last.

```
(1.03) Virginia, 1:6-16
1            (3.2)
2   Mom:     (C'n)we have the blessi-ih-buh-Wesley
3            would you ask the blessi[ng¿ please¿
4   Wes:                             [Ahright.
5            (0.2)
6   Wes:     Heavenly fahther give us thankful hearts
7            (fuh) these an' all the blessings °ahmen.
8            (.)
9   Vir:     >°Ahmen.<
10           (2.0)
```

This family has just sat down at the dinner table – Mom at its head; to her right, eldest child Wesley, in his mid- to late twenties; to his right his fiancée, Prudence; to Mom's left, youngest child, Virginia, 14; and, to her left off camera, middle child, Beth, 18, a college student videotaping the meal for a course assignment, and therefore minimizing her own active participation.

At line 2, Mom, on her own initiative (that is, self-selecting for next turn) produces a TCU (a sentential one) almost to completion. It initially appears (both on the page and in the video) to be a request for someone to say grace, but closer examination suggests that it was designed and understood as announcing the imminent saying of grace (by Mom) so that others might assume the appropriate posture and demeanor. As she begins her turn, Mom does not look at anyone at the table to whom "Can we have the blessing" might be being addressed as a request; rather she begins lowering her head to assume the appropriate posture for grace, and Wesley, looking at her and seeing this, lowers his own head to assume the same posture. As he does this, and as Mom reaches the fully lowered positioning of her head, on the "i-[ng]" sound of her utterance, she aborts the articulation of its potentially final sound, thereby preventing its reaching possible completion. In its place, she looks up and over to Wesley, and she produces a variant version of the utterance; it is now addressed specifically to Wesley (not only by visual targeting but by addressing him by name), who raises his head and orients it and his eyes toward Mom, showing that he has registered her targeting him as recipient, and displaying his alignment with that move (Goodwin, 1979, 1980, 1981). Her redone version of the TCU is now overtly fashioned as a *request* to him ("would you," "please") to do the actual "asking" of the blessing. So Mom has now produced a possibly complete turn, one addressed to a particular recipient, one which makes relevant a particular kind of response by that targeted recipient.

Wesley's response comes in two parts. The first part, at line 4, is apparently a possibly complete turn in its own right (of the lexical sort). It comes at just the place in the articulation of "blessi-[ng]" at which Mom, in her first version of this TCU, had cut it off, and begun its redoing; as well, it can be noted, the intonation contour at this point in the revised version of her utterance is hearable as possible completion. Wesley's initial response is a "compliance token." First, we can note that he does not reply to Mom's utterance as a question with a "yes," although her turn had the form of a "yes/no" question. What he does is to display his *understanding of it as a request*, and to betoken his *acceptance* of the request. This betokening is not itself the satisfaction of the request, however; it is only a commitment to provide that satisfaction. The "ahright" is not, then, the possible completion of the turn, for the action it does projects more to come. Then, at lines 6–7, Wesley provides the action requested by Mom; note here that the performance of this action is done in talk, but it is talk very different in character than the "ahright." What he does at lines 6–7 is equivalent to passing the salt, had that been Mom's request. That is, the "ahright" gives an undertaking that he will deliver what has been requested; lines 6–7 is that delivery; it just happens that what had been requested in this instance was something to be articulated, to be performed, and so its delivery is done through talk.

The rest of this volume will be full of such turns: one making some sort of response relevant next, another providing such a response – although not always in the next turn, and not always involving separate commitments to deliver the response on the one hand and actual delivery of the response on the other.

Capsule review 2: actions

When we talk about "actions" getting done through turns-at-talk, what kinds of actions are we talking about? How do we determine what action or actions is/are getting done in/by some TCU? How do we know we are right in so characterizing a TCU's action(s)? Good questions all, which will need separate treatment in a work entirely given over to what we can call "action formation"; that is, what the practices of talk and other conduct are which have as an outcome the production of a recognizable action X; that is, that can be shown to have been recognized by co-participants as that action by virtue of the practices that produced it. Here we can at best provide an orientation to this sort of issue.

What sort of actions are we talking about? Well, in discussing the preceding data extracts we had occasion to refer to asking, answering, disagreeing, offering, contesting, requesting, teasing, finessing, complying, performing, noticing, promising, and so forth. And the pages to follow will feature inviting, announcing, telling, complaining, agreeing, and so forth. Two observations about these terms and what they are meant to name will be useful to register here.

First, not all the actions that demonstrably get done by a TCU can be referred to by common vernacular terms like the ones listed above. Unlike

the other main analytic stance concerned with characterizing actions –
speech act theory of the sort primarily associated with the names of John
Austin and John Searle (Austin, 1962, 1979; Searle, 1969, 1975, 1976;
Searle and Vanderveken, 1985) – we do not begin with classes or categories
of action named by terms like the above and deconstruct them analytically
into the conceptual components that make some particular act an instance
of that class.

Instead of starting out from the outcome action (e.g., What would make
something a promise?), we start from an observation about how some bit
of talk was done, and ask: What could someone be doing by talking in
this way? What does that bit of talk appear designed to do? What is the
action that it is a practice for? We try to ground our answer to this sort
of question by showing that it is *that* action which *co-participants in the
interaction* took to be what was getting done, as revealed in/by the response
they make to it. And if, in the data with which we began, co-participants
did *not* treat it as the sort of action we (as analysts) made it out to be, then
we need to look to other data where that practice is being deployed and see
if in that instance – or in those instances – it was understood to be doing
the action we took it to be. If we find that, then we have strong grounds
for a claim that in the instance we began with, the co-participants failed to
understand correctly what the speaker was doing or, at least, that they acted
as if they failed to understand it. So the first observation is that we start
not from the names of types of action, not from *classes* of actions, but from
singular bits of data, each in its embedding context, and seek out what – in
that instance – the speaker appeared to be doing, and what in the talk and
other conduct underwrote or conveyed that that was what was being done.
Often proceeding in this way yields analyses of bits of data as "a request"
or "an invitation" that are far removed from what we ordinarily think of as
an instance of a request or an invitation.

Second, proceeding in this way can lead us to discover actions that have
no vernacular name, that speech act theory could not ordinarily undertake
to analyze. For example, sometimes one party does an utterance which
agrees with another (so there is one way of characterizing it – agreeing);
indeed, more than agreeing, this party's utterance seems to confirm what
another has said (so there is another way of characterizing it – confirming),
and yet we notice that, instead of using the most common way of doing
the "confirming" version of "agreeing" – for example, by "that's right" –
they repeat the thing that they are agreeing with, indeed, that they are confirming. Could they be doing something else by doing it in that way? If
one follows this trail of inquiry, one can find new things, new actions, that
we did not previously know people did. And, even though there is no separate term for this action (at least not in English), and therefore presumably
no special concept of it, the conduct of the parties makes it clear that they
understand something different by it than they understand by a conventional

confirmation, "that's right," or a conventional agreement, "yes, I think so too." We cannot continue this search here; the outcome can be found in Schegloff, 1996a.

Because this book is about sequence organization and not about action formation, it will not be possible on each occasion of characterizing the action a TCU is doing, and thereby perhaps what a sequence is doing, to present an analysis that will underwrite that characterization; that will be the task of another volume. But it is important for readers to understand at least this much about our use of the terms that name actions.

One additional point will figure importantly in the undertaking which follows, and that is that a single TCU can embody more than one action, and, indeed, some actions which a TCU implements are the vehicle by which other actions are implemented. In all three of the extracts examined so far, questions figure centrally, but in each of them more is being done than questioning or requesting information. In Extract (1.01), Mom's question is not (only) asking, it is offering; in (1.03), Mom's question is requesting, but not information. And in (1.02), Nancy's question to Michael serves to pose a dilemma which moves him to give other than a straightforward "answer," and provide instead some support to each "side."

With these resources made explicit, we can now return to the central pre-occupation of this book – sequence organization. Before taking our brief detour, we had posed the question, Are there any general patterns or general practices which can be isolated and described through which sequences – courses of action implemented through talk – get organized? If so, we will call them "sequences," and we will call their organization "sequence organization." We now return to address this question.

One very large set of sequence types seems to be organized around a basic unit of sequence construction, the *adjacency pair*. Most of this book will be concerned with this resource for talk-in-interaction, and its expansions and deployments. There *are* sequence organizations not based on adjacency pairs – for example, some forms of storytelling and other "telling" sequences (pp. 41–44), some forms of topic talk (although adjacency pairs may figure in such talk, even when not supplying its underlying organization, see below, at pp. 169–80), what will be discussed under the rubric "retro-sequences" in Chapter 11 below, and quite possibly other ones not yet described, perhaps because the settings in which they figure have been less studied (or not studied at all). But a very broad range of sequences in talk-in-interaction does appear to be produced by reference to the practices of adjacency pair organization, which therefore appears to serve as a resource for *sequence* construction comparable to the way turn-constructional units serve as a resource for *turn* construction.

In the closing paragraphs of the Preface, our ambition in this work was described as getting at the organization of "courses of action implemented through turns-at-talk." Both parts of that phrase are consequential: the turn-at-talk is being examined for the *actions* being implemented in it and the *relationship(s) between those actions*, on the one hand; and, on the other, the focus is on actions that are implemented through *turns-at-talk*. But, of course, not all actions are implemented through talk. How do actions not implemented through talk figure in this undertaking? How do they figure in adjacency pair organization?

Perhaps the most important sequence organization *not* basically organized by the adjacency pairs is that organized by other ongoing courses of actions which take the form, not of talking, but of other physical activity. That is, a very large domain of what we mean by "action(s)" refers to things done with the hands, as in Extracts (1.04) and (1.05), in both of which we see things being passed at the dinner table:

```
(1.04) Chicken Dinner, 3:15-32
 1 Viv:       ↑ˈhu:hh
 2            (0.3
 3 Sha:       °Goo[d.°
 4 Mic:  →        [Butter please,
 5            (0.2)
 6 Sha:       Good.
 7 Viv:       Sha:ne,
 8 Mic:       ↑ (Oh ey adda way)
 9 Sha:       eh hu[h  huh  hih   hih   hih-]hee-yee hee-ee ]    [aah=
10 Nan:           [eh-heh-hih-hih-hnh-hnh]h n h-h_n_h hnh]-hn[h
12 Sha:       =aah aah
13            (0.5)                  ⌉  Shane
14 Sh?:       °ˈhhh°                 |  passes
14            (.)                    |  butter
15 Sha:       (Hih       ).          |    to
16 Mic:       ha-ha.                 ⌋  Michael
17 Sha:       (Hih       ).
18            (2.3)
```

```
(1.05) Housemates
video only; no talk in this extract except a bit of laughter
```

Another large domain refers to things done with the feet, as in Extract (1.06), where what is at stake is who is going to move closer to where the other one is; and yet another large domain involves things done with the head and torso, as in Extract (1.07), where a new sequence start is launched with a summons ("Hey"), which attracts first the eyes of the targeted recipient (which it does as the word "like" is said) and then a stable postural commitment (at "telephone"), and so forth.

```
(1.06) US, 3:10-23
 1 Mik:       Jim wasn' home, [°(when y'wen over there)]
```

```
 2 Vic:                              [I  didn' go  by  theh. ]=
 3 Vic:          =I [left my garbage pail in iz [hallway.=
 4 Car:            [Vi:c,                        [
 5 Car:                                      [Vic(tuh),
 6 Vic:          =Yeh?
 7 Car:  →       C'mmere fer a minnit.
 8               (0.7)
 9 Vic:  →       Y'come [he:re.
10 Car:                 [You c'co[me ba:ck,
11 Car:                          [please?
12 Vic:          I haftuh go t'the bathroom.=
13 Car:          =Oh.
14              (3.5)
```

```
(1.07) Chinese Dinner, 11:11-17
1  John:       Well I'd like to (wring his throat).
2              (0.8)
3  Don:  →     Hey would you like a Trent'n::, a Trent'n
4              telephone directory.
5              (0.2)
6   Don:       We-wuh- we got fo' . . .
```

Some "sequences of action" may not involve any talk at all (indeed, do not require another person at all). Some may have talk going on but not concerning ongoing other courses of action. Some may involve talk organized to be complementary to courses of action being otherwise implemented, and thereby be organized by the structure of the physical activity they are complementary to. Sometimes the course of action being realized in talk is "functionally" quite distinct from that being realized in other ways, and yet each has some consequences for the other. Sometimes an action done in talk gets as its response one not done in talk, as in Extract (1.04), where the request for the butter is spoken, but its delivery is not accompanied by talk; or, conversely, sometimes an action not done in talk gets as its response something done by talk.

There is, of course, a by-now substantial literature describing the organization of bodily action, a great deal of it focused on work settings, but there is not yet a broad framework for capturing in the participants' terms the sequential organization that orders the courses of action of single participants, let alone the coordinated conduct of several. There is, therefore, no reliable empirical basis for treating physically realized actions as being in principle organized in adjacency pair terms, and this matter will, therefore, not have a place on our agenda. On the other hand, there are exchanges which at least initially appear to map onto adjacency pair organization: either an initial utterance being done in talk and a responsive action being physically embodied, as in Extract (1.04), or an initial move being made non-vocally, and being responded to with talk. These we shall take as at least potentially relevant to our central preoccupation, although we will not give them any special attention.

Our examination of adjacency pair-based sequences will be organized as follows. First, we will spell out the main features of the basic minimal form of the adjacency pair, and the minimal sequence which it can constitute (pp. 13–27). Second, we will explicate some of the ways in which sequences can expand well beyond the minimal, two-turn sequence which the adjacency pair itself constitutes – pre-expansions (pp. 28–57), insert expansions (pp. 97–114), and post-expansions (pp. 115–68), yielding extensive stretches of talk which nonetheless must be understood as built on the armature of a single adjacency pair, and therefore needing to be understood as expansions of it. In the course of describing these expansions, we will examine a key feature of adjacency pairs – their "preference" structure (pp. 58–96). Third, we will take up larger sequence structures to which adjacency pairs can give rise and of which they may be building-blocks – such as topic-proffering sequences (pp. 169–80), sequence-closing sequences (pp. 181–94), and sequences of sequences (pp. 195–216). Fourth, we will touch on some respects in which sequences and the practices which give rise to them can vary in particular contexts (pp. 220–30), and can be flexibly deployed in ways that give rise to non-canonical forms (pp. 231–250). At the end (pp. 251–64), we will take up some suggestions for using the materials that have been presented so that they can become part of the reader's analytic resources, ready to be activated by the data you, the reader, have occasion to examine.

2 The adjacency pair as the unit for sequence construction

We begin with the most elementary features of adjacency pairs and their basic mode of operation.

In its minimal, basic unexpanded form an adjacency pair is characterized by certain features.[1] It is:

(a) composed of two turns
(b) by different speakers
(c) adjacently placed; that is, one after the other
(d) these two turns are relatively ordered; that is, they are differentiated into "first pair parts" (FPPs, or Fs for short) and "second pair parts" (SPPs, or Ss for short). First pair parts are utterance types such as question, request, offer, invitation, announcement, etc. – types which *initiate* some exchange. Second pair parts are utterance types such as answer, grant, reject, accept, decline, agree/disagree, acknowledge, etc. – types which are *responsive* to the action of a prior turn (though not everything which is responsive to something else is an S). Besides being differentiated into Fs and Ss, the components of an adjacency pair are
(e) pair-type related; that is, not every second pair part can properly follow any first pair part. Adjacency pairs compose pair *types*; types are exchanges such as greeting–greeting, question–answer, offer–accept/decline, and the like. To compose an adjacency pair, the FPP and SPP come from the same pair type. Consider such FPPs as "Hello," or "Do you know what time it is?," or "Would you like a cup of coffee?" and such SPPs as "Hi," or "Four o'clock," or "No, thanks." Parties to talk-in-interaction do not just pick some SPP to respond to an FPP; that would yield such absurdities as "Hello," "No, thanks," or "Would you like a cup of coffee?," "Hi." The components of adjacency pairs

---

[1] Schegloff and Sacks (1973:295–96). A major resource on the adjacency pair may be found in the Sacks lectures for spring 1972 (Sacks, 1992b: 521–69); another early treatment is Schegloff (1968). Jefferson and Schenkein (1978) take a different view of what the minimal unexpanded unit of sequence organization is and what should be treated as expanded. What they treat as "unexpanded" is what will be later treated here as "minimally post-expanded," and involves the addition of a third turn. The Jefferson and Schenkein analysis is compelling for the data which they examine, but those data represent but one configuration of sequence organization, through which a particular kind of interactional dynamic is pursued. The account offered here is designed for different goals and, in particular, for more extended and general scope. It should be compatible with the Jefferson and Schenkein account for sequences of the type they address.

are "typologized" not only into first and second pair parts, but into the *pair types* which they can partially compose: greeting–greeting ("Hello," "Hi"), question–answer ("Do you know what time it is?", "Four o'clock"), offer–accept/decline ("Would you like a cup of coffee?", "No, thanks," if it is declined).

The basic practice or rule of operation, then, by which the minimal form of the adjacency pair is produced is: given the recognizable production of a first pair part, on its first possible completion its speaker should stop, a next speaker should start (often someone selected as next speaker by the FPP), and should produce a second pair part of the same pair type. The product of this practice and these features may be represented schematically in a very simple transcript diagram:

A   First Pair Part
B   Second Pair Part

None of these features – (a)–(e) above and the basic rule of operation – is rigid or invariant, and they all require some elaboration. As part of their exploitation as a resource for sequence construction, adjacency pair-based sequences can come to have more than two turns (though still two basic parts), they can be separated by intervening talk (what will be discussed later as insert expansions), they can on occasion be articulated by the same speaker as a way of conveying two "voices" (though this use relies on the basic property that Fs and Ss are produced by different speakers), some utterance types can be used as both Fs and Ss (for example, complaint can be used to initiate a sequence but also in response to an inquiry; an offer can be an FPP but also a response to a complaint) and, under specified circumstances, as both Fs and Ss at the same time (as when someone asks you to repeat your question, and you do – thereby doing both an S in granting their request and an F, since in doing so you re-ask your question), etc. In the next several pages, we take up a number of observations about the minimal, basic unit, the adjacency pair, which elaborate its features and explore some of its flexibility.

Adjacency, nextness, contiguity, progressivity

Among the most pervasively relevant features in the organization of talk-and-other-conduct-in-interaction is the relationship of adjacency or "nextness." The default relationship between the components of most kinds of organization is that each should come next after the prior. In articulating a turn-constructional unit, each element – each word, for example – should come next after the one before; in fact, at a smaller level of granularity, each syllable – indeed, each sound – should come next after the one before it.

So also with the several turn-constructional units that compose a multi-unit turn; so also with the consecutive turns that compose a spate of talk; so also with the turns that compose a sequence, etc. Moving from some element to a hearably-next-one with nothing intervening is the embodiment of, and the measure of, progressivity. Should something intervene between some element and what is hearable as a/the next one due – should something violate or interfere with their contiguity, whether next sound, next word, or next turn – it will be heard as qualifying the progressivity of the talk, and will be examined for its import, for what understanding should be accorded it. Each next element of such a progression can be inspected to find how it reaffirms the understanding-so-far of what has preceded, or favors one or more of the several such understandings that are being entertained, or how it requires reconfiguration of that understanding. For our purposes in this book, what will matter most is the relationship between successive turns; and what matters most immediately is the difference between the adjacent turns relationship on the one hand and adjacency pairs on the other.

The relationship of adjacency or "nextness" between turns is central to the ways in which talk-in-interaction is organized and understood. Next turns are understood by co-participants to display their speaker's understanding of the just-prior turn and to embody an action responsive to the just-prior turn so understood (unless the turn has been marked as addressing something other than just-prior turn). This is in large measure because of the way turn-taking for conversation works; namely, one turn at a time – and, specifically, exclusively *next turn* allocation.[2] That is, as each turn comes to possible completion and transition to another speaker becomes possibly relevant, it is transition to a *next* speaker that is at issue. If the turn is to be allocated by the current speaker selecting someone, it is *next* speaker that is being selected; and if no selection by just-ending speaker is done and another participant self-selects, it is for the *next turn* that they are self-selecting. However this contingency is handled, each participant has to have been attending to the just-ongoing-about-to-be-possibly-complete turn to determine (a) if he or she has been selected as next speaker, or (b) if *anyone* has been selected as next speaker in order to determine whether they can properly self-select as next speaker, and (c) what action(s) are implicated by the just-ending turn, relative to which any next turn will be understood. Each next turn, then, is examined for the understanding of the prior turn which it displays, and the kind of response which it embodies, and this is endemic to the organization of conversation without respect to adjacency pairs. The

---

[2] Note that this discussion is focused on conversation in particular. Because different organizations of turn-taking can characterize different speech-exchange systems (Sacks et al., 1974:701 n. 11, 729–31), anything that is grounded in turn-taking organization may vary with differences in the turn-taking organization. It is a matter for empirical inquiry, therefore, how the matters taken up in the text are appropriately described in non-conversational settings of talk-in-interaction, for example, in courtrooms-in-session, in traditional classrooms, etc.

adjacency relationship taken up in this paragraph operates most powerfully *backwards*, each turn displaying its speaker's understanding of the prior.

The *adjacency pair* relationship is a further organization of turns, over and above the effects which sequential organization invests in adjacency per se. Adjacency pair organization has (in addition to the backwards import just described) a powerful *prospective* operation. A first pair part projects a prospective relevance, and not only a retrospective understanding. It makes relevant a limited set of possible second pair parts, and thereby sets some of the terms by which a next turn will be understood – as, for example, being responsive to the constraints of the first pair part or not. And, as we shall see, the adjacency pair relationship invests a specially indicative import in the relationship of contiguity between first and second pair parts. Even if they are in adjacent turns – that is, no turn intervenes between them – other sorts of elements may be counted as obstructing or violating their contiguity, with considerable interactional import being attached to such a positioning.

Alternative second pair parts

Most adjacency pair types have alternative types of second pair part, a matter to be discussed in Chapter 5 under the rubric "preference organization." But some sequence types (a very few) seem to have only one type of second pair part. The prototypes here are greetings and farewells or terminal exchanges ("bye byes"). Although there may be a variety of greeting forms with which to respond ("Hello," "Hi," "Hiya," "Howyadoin," etc.), and a responder may have a favorite or signature, or aim to return the same as was received (or different), these are not alternative *types* of response; they all reciprocate the greeting. And the same is the case for terminal exchanges ("Bye," "Seeya," "Ciao," "Cheers," "Later," etc.). Actually, with great regularity greetings and their responses are done with the same form ("Hi," "Hi"), as are farewells ("Bye," "Bye"), and we may note that, where there are not alternative *types* of SPP, the actual SPP utterance frequently is not different from the FPP (at least in its lexical composition). But, with very few exceptions, there *are* alternative types of SPP with which to respond to an FPP.

Counters

There are alternatives to doing an appropriate SPP next after an FPP, and they will be taken up as part of our discussion of sequence expansion (and in particular, insert expansion, in Chapter 6). Virtually all such alternatives to an SPP in next turn are understood as deferring the doing of an SPP until a bit later, and are done in the service of a later SPP. But there is one alternative to an SPP in next turn whose effect is quite different, and it requires mention at this point. That next turn is the "counter"; that is, before (or without) responding with an SPP to the just completed FPP, the same FPP (or a closely related modification of it) is redirected to the one who just did it.

A familiar experience may exemplify this tack anecdotally, before a display of more determinate empirical instances. Readers may recall emerging with a companion from some entertainment or cultural event – a movie, performance, exhibit, etc. – especially one testing the boundaries of familiarity, and asking, "Well, what did you think?" or "How did you like it?" and getting back not an answer, but instead, "How did *you* like it?" or "What did *you* think?" or just "How about *you*?" These are counters; they do not serve to *defer* the answering of the question (though the one doing the counter may end up answering later nonetheless); they *replace* it with a question of their own. They thus reverse the direction of the sequence and its flow; they reverse the direction of constraint.

Here are several empirical instances. In the first, a mother and her child of just over a year and a half are looking at a children's picture book together:

```
(2.01) Tarplee, 1991:1
1  Chi: F →     What's this
2  Mom: Fcnt→   er::m (.) yo[u   t]ell me: what is it
3  Chi:                     [°() °]
4             (1.0)
5  Chi: S →    z:e:bra
6  Mom:        zebra:: ye:s
```

In line 1, the child has asked a question (an FPP), but in the next turn the mother does neither an answer nor a form of turn which projects later answering of the question. Rather, she redirects the same question back to its asker, for its asker to answer. Nor does she herself answer the question later.

The second instance is taken from a psychotherapeutic session:

```
(2.02) Scheflen, 1961:114, as adapted in Peyrot, 1994:17
1  Pat: F →    Do you think I'm insane now.
2  Doc: Fcnt→  Do you think so?
3  Pat: S →    No, of course not.
4  Doc:        But I think you are.
```

In this exchange, the doctor does end up answering (at line 4) the question which the patient asked, and so his redirecting it to the patient and getting an answer (at lines 2–3) ends up having only deferred the answer, and inserted one question–answer exchange inside another. But, following the sequence, as the participants did, in real time, when the doctor's question was asked at line 2, it did not project a later answer. It redirected the question, and could easily have been used to launch a line of inquiry by the doctor (e.g., at line

4, "Why not," etc., or "Why did you ask me then?," etc.). Again, then, the counter reverses the direction of the sequence.

In the third instance, Vic is a janitor/custodian, socializing with buddies in a local used-furniture store. His wife Carol comes to the door and "calls him" (lines 4–5).

```
(2.03) US, 3:10-23 (previously appeared as [1.06])
 1 Mik:          Jim wasn' home, [°(when y'wen over there)]
 2 Vic:                          [ I  didn'  go   by   theh.]=
 3 Vic:          =I [left my garbage pail in iz [hallway.=
 4 Car:             [Vi:c,                      [
 5 Car:                                          [Vic(tuh),
 6 Vic:          =Yeh?
 7 Car: F →      C'mmere fer a minnit.
 8               (0.7)
 9 Vic: Fcnt→    Y'come [he:re.  [please?
10 Car:                 [You c'co[me ba:ck,
11 Vic:          I haftuh go t'the bathroom.=
12 Car:          =Oh.
13              (3.5)
```

When Vic responds from a distance (line 6), Carol asks him to detach himself from his friends and come closer (line 7); this is a first pair part – a request. What it requests is a physically realized action, not one implemented by an utterance (though it is not uncommon that, when such a requested action is done next by the recipient of the request, it is accompanied by some utterance – for example, a compliance token such as "sure"). Such requested physically enacted actions are under the same constraints as talk-embodied ones would be: the first pair part makes relevant the occurrence of an appropriate second pair part, which should come "next." In this episode, however, what comes next is not Vic's compliance with the request, not the projected second pair part, but rather a counter; he reverses the sequence (line 9), and makes Carol the recipient of the same request she had directed to him.

In the fourth instance, Tony has called his ex-wife Marsha about the return of their teenage son Joey, who ordinarily lives with him, after the son's holiday visit to his mother in a city some four hundred miles away.

```
(2.04) MDE-MTRAC: 60-1/2, 1
 1               ring
 2 Mar:          Hello:?
 3 Ton:          Hi: Marsha?
 4 Mar:          Ye:ah.
 5 Ton:          How are you.
 6 Mar:          Fi::ne.
 7               (0.2)
 8 Mar: F →      Did Joey get home yet?
 9 Ton: Fcnt→    Well I wz wondering when 'e left.
```

```
10                      (0.2)
11   Mar:               `hhh Uh:(d) did Oh:.h Yer not in on what
12                      ha:ppen'.(hh)(d)
13   Ton:               No(h)o=
14   Mar: S →           =He's flying.
15                          (0.2)
16                          ((continues))
```

In this exchange, Marsha's question to Tony at line 8 is not followed by an answer, even though an answer may be understood to be conveyed by implication in the following turn. Instead of answering, Tony asks his own question, a version of the same question but as seen from the point of view of the destination of a trip rather than from its point of origin. In effect, then, this is a counter to Marsha's question, and it is Marsha who ends up answering, not Tony (nor does Tony answer later). Here again, the counter reverses the direction of the sequence, and it reverses the direction of constraint.

What does that mean, "reverses the direction of constraint"? In order to make clear what is meant by "reversing the direction of constraint," we need to take up what we call "relevance rules," because the adjacency pair is one main locus of relevance rules, one place in talk-in-interaction where they have a specially notable bearing. Because this is an important topic in its own right, we will linger on it a bit, but the discussion will come back to the sense of "reversing the direction of constraint."

Relevance rules and negative observations

The organization of turn-taking provides a way (for co-participants and for us as external observers) to say non-trivially that someone in particular is not speaking, when in fact *no one at all* is speaking. It is by virtue of a "rule" or "practice" having been invoked or activated which makes it relevant for that particular "someone" to be talking. Even though no one is talking, it is the relevance introduced by a prior speaker having selected someone as next speaker that makes *that* person be specifically singled out as not talking, even when there is general silence.

But this is just a special case of a much more general issue, one concerning what we will call "negative observations." There is an indefinitely large and extendable number of things that have not been said, of events that have not happened, of persons who are not speaking, of actions that are not being performed by someone who *is* speaking. This paragraph has not so far reported who won the American Presidential election in 1992, or 1988, or . . ., etc. Any asserted observation of an absence is at risk of being but one of a virtual infinity of absent occurrences or activities, and in that sense a *trivial* observation or assertion (however true). For the noting of an absence to be *non*-trivial, we need a "relevance rule" that makes it relevant for something to happen or be done or be mentioned, etc. Then, if it does not happen (or is not done or is not mentioned, etc.), it is "missing" in a different sense than the sense in which everything that does not happen is missing, and with a different import. We can then speak of it as a "noticable absence" or an "official absence" or a "relevant absence." Negative observations imply relevant absences, and relevant absences imply relevance rules. Noticing that someone in particular is not speaking constitutes a claim of sorts that this is a relevant absence (as set against the non-speaking of everyone else), and turns on some relevance rule that makes it so – such as a prior speaker having selected the noticed one as next speaker. The turn-taking organization, then, constitutes (among other things) a set of relevance rules.

Adjacency pair organization is also a major locus of relevance rules. What relates first and second pair parts can be termed a relationship of "conditional relevance." "First" and "second" do not refer merely to the order in which these turns *happen to* occur; they refer to design features of these turn types and sequential positions. The very feature of "first-ness" sets up the relevance of something else to follow; it projects the relevance of a "second." It is the occurrence of a first pair part that makes some types of second pair part relevant next; that relevance is conditioned by the FPP. If such a second pair part is produced next, it is heard as *responsive to* the first pair part which preceded. If such a second pair part is not produced next, its non-occurrence is as much an event as its occurrence would have been. It is, so to speak, noticeably, officially, consequentially, absent. The relevance of some turn type which can be a second pair part is conditional on the occurrence of a first pair part from the same pair type. Often enough, the person who can be observed (relevantly) to be "not talking" (by reference to the turn-taking rules) can be heard as well to be "not answering" when their "non-talking" follows a prior utterance which was a question. Thus, the silence in a room can nonetheless often be characterized (and, in the first instance, *heard*) specifically for *who is not talking*, and *what kind of talk they are not doing*. The first of these is furnished by turn-taking organization, the second by adjacency pair organization, and specifically by hearing to be missing the kind of second pair part (or *some* kind of second pair part) made relevant by a just-preceding first pair part.

But relevance rules contribute not only to how silences get heard, but also to how the talk itself gets heard. Just as not talking after a question can thus be "not answering," so a great variety of talk after a question invites hearing as, and does get heard as, "answering" (even if, on occasion, "answering indirectly"). Academic inquiry is sometimes puzzled by how some apparently semantically unrelated talk gets heard as an answer, especially when trying to build the "artificial intelligence" for computers to answer questions "naturally" or to recognize answers. (For example, how can "It's raining" – or even "Isn't it raining?" – be a recognizable answer to "Are we going to the game?") What is critical here is that the action which some talk is doing can be grounded in its *position*, not just its *composition* – not just the words that compose it, but its placement after a question. Talk after a question invites hearing for how it could be answering, and invites it from those who can bring all the particulars of the setting to bear, rather than by some general rules of interpretation. Just as the questioner presents a puzzle of sorts to its recipient, so does the one who responds; that challenge is, "how is this an answer?" and "what answer is it?" At the same time, doing something which is analyzable/recognizable as a relevant second pair part is its speaker's way of showing an understanding that the prior turn was the sort of first pair part for which this is a relevant second. Doing something which can be an answer displays an understanding of the prior turn as a possible question.

Adjacency pairs organize with special potency these relevance rules, which can imbue the talk following a first pair part with its sense or meaning, and can imbue the *absence* of talk with sense or meaning or import as well. Given, via the turn-taking organization, that the absence of talk can be an event in its own right, the adjacency pair's relevance rules infuse it with a specifiable action import. The first pair part thus sets powerful constraints of action (what the recipient should do) and of interpretation (how what the recipient does should be understood) on the moments just following it. Relevance rules are a key part of the glue that binds actions together into coherent sequences.

The earlier observation that counters following first pair parts "reverse the direction of constraint" should now be more readily accessible. The recipient of some first pair part is put under certain constraints by it – either to do a relevant second pair part, or be heard as "not doing" such a relevant second pair part. We will see in Chapter 6 that recipients of first pair parts are not without resources for dealing with these constraints. But for now we should notice that "counters" take the very constraints that were just cast on the *recipient* of the first pair part and shift them back onto its *speaker*; they "reverse the direction of constraint."

Upshot

What relevance rules do, then, is to set the initial terms for conduct and interpretation in the next moments following their invocation. They do not *define* those next moments and what occurs in them; virtually nothing in interaction is that unilateral. But it is by reference to a first pair part that what follows gets selected, done, and understood. The first pair part casts a web of meaning and interpretation which informs the surrounding talk. But "surrounding talk" can include more than just second pair parts. As we bring under examination more of the sequences which can grow out of adjacency pairs, we will see how much more, and where.

3 Minimal, two-turn adjacency pair sequences

Although adjacency pair organization provides a resource for the construction of sequences of various sizes, an adjacency pair in its basic, minimal two-turn form can itself constitute the whole of a sequence.[1]

Minimal adjacency pair sequences are common, and virtually formulaic, in the opening and closing sections of conversations and other types of episodes of talk-in-interaction.[2]

In openings, for example, greetings and "how-are-you" sequences may run off as minimal adjacency pairs, as in Extracts (3.01) and (3.02) (previously Extract [2.04]) respectively:

```
(3.01) TG, 1:01—04
1                     ring
2    Ava:             H'llo:?
3    Bee: F →         hHi:,
4    Ava: S →         Hi:?
5    Bee:             hHowuh you:?

(3.02) MDE-MTRAC 60-1/2,1 (previously 2.04)
1                     ring
2    Mar:             Hello:?
3    Ton:             Hi: Marsha?
4    Mar:             Ye:ah.
5    Ton: F →         How are you.
6    Mar: S →         Fi::ne.
7                     (0.2)
8    Mar:             Did Joey get home yet?
9    Ton:             Well I wz wondering when 'e left.
```

[1] Some students of talk-in-interaction take the basic minimal size of a sequence to be *three* turns (Coulthard, 1977; Sinclair and Coulthard, 1975; among others). From this point of view, two-turn sequences are elliptical; they are missing something, ordinarily their third turn – a view which may reflect its origin in the study of classroom interaction. The discussion in the text which follows, and the numerous exemplars which are displayed there, are meant to ground the claim that the basic, minimal form of a sequence is *two* turns, and that sequences composed of more are expansions. On the former view, it is the absence of a third turn in a two-turn sequence which requires explanation. On the latter view, it is the presence of additional turns in sequences longer than two turns which requires analytic accounting.

[2] In what follows, single instances of such sequences stand proxy for vast numbers of virtually identical recurrences which it would be redundant to reproduce – although some of these sequence types may, of course, also occur in more-than-two-turn versions.

In Extract (3.01), the "Hello" at line 2 does not serve as a greeting but as a response to the summons embodied in the ring of the phone. Bee's greeting at line 3 is what initiates the greeting exchange, the return greeting at line 4 is its second pair part, and the following turn initiates a new adjacency pair. And in Extract (3.02), Tony's "How are you" initiates a sequence with a first pair part at line 5, Marsha responds with a second pair part at line 6, and a new adjacency pair begins at line 8.

In closing sections of interactional occasions, as well, various component sequences may be formed up as two-turn sequences, composed only of the first and second pair parts of an adjacency pair. Extract (3.03) is the closing of a telephone conversation in which Charlie has called Ilene to tell her that a car trip on which she had planned to get a ride has had to be canceled.

```
(3.03) Trip to Syracuse, 2
1   Ile:           =Thanks inneh- e- than:ks: anyway Charlie,
2   Cha:           Ri:ght.
3   Ile:           Oka:y?
4   Cha:           Oka[y,
5   Ile: F →          [Ta:ke keyuh
6   Cha: S →       Speak tih you [(    )
7   Ile: F →                      [Bye: bye
8   Cha: S →       Bye,
```

Here the terminal exchange at lines 7–8 is accomplished in a minimal adjacency pair-based sequence, as is the pre-terminal exchange at lines 5–6 by which the parties mutually converge on closing.[3] These sequence types are generally accomplished through two turns. The exchange of "okay"s at lines 3–4 (which commonly form the pre-terminal exchange) here may represent the tail end of the preceding, extended "business" sequence of the conversation, and would then not exemplify the free-standing, maximally pared-down form of sequence which we are examining.

It is not only telephone conversations whose closings may be worked through with such minimal sequences. In Extract (3.04), Carol is leaving after a brief drop-in to an ongoing interaction in a college dormitory.

```
(3.04) SN-4, 5:32—6:04
1   Car:           I don't want them tih see me when I l(h)ook
2                  t(h)his good.
3                  (0.2)
4   Ru?:           ((cough))(H)(H)UH    ˙hhhh=
5   Car:           =N(h)o one des(h)erves it. ((hoarse voice))
6                  (0.2)
```

---

[3] If the phrase "take keyuh" appears strange, it is because the transcript is designed to convey how the utterance was actually delivered, rather than how it is properly spelled. Ilene speaks with a marked New York City accent, and so her "take care" comes out as "take keyuh." Readers who find some utterance in a transcript initially inaccessible might try saying it as printed to see if that helps grasp what was being said by its speaker.

```
 7   (?):          Tch ˙hh=)
 8   Car: F →      I'll see you all later,
 9   Rut: S →      Awri:ght,
10                 (1.4)          ((door opening, Carol leaves))
11   Mar: F →      Where were we.
12                 (0.5)
13   She: S →      I dunno.='ve you been studying lately¿
14   Mar:          No, °not et aw-° not et a:ll:. I hafta study
15                 this whole week.
```

Here Carol is finishing an account for not having brought an ice-cream sandwich which the others had expected, and then leaves with the start of a closing exchange (line 8) initiated with a common formula in closings, an invocation of future interaction (see line 6 in Extract [3.03] above), whose answering second pair part (at line 9) ends the sequence and the interaction (with Carol).

But Extract (3.04) also offers a display of a minimal two-turn adjacency pair which is *not* being used as part of the opening or closing (and is therefore not simply "ritual," as might otherwise be suspected). Carol's arrival had prompted a cessation of the interaction then in progress, and, following her departure, one tack (out of several alternatives) which the remaining parties can take is to return to what had been in progress, but was interrupted. This Mark seeks to do at line 11 (not surprisingly, perhaps, for it was he who was in the process of telling about a supposed "orgy"), but seeks to do with what might be called a "resumption search," a common occurrence after interruptions have run their course. Sherry at least prefers to steer the talk in a different direction, and, at line 13, first responds to Mark's resumption search, and then launches a new sequence of her own with a question (a new first pair part). The resumption search sequence ends up being a minimal two-turn sequence.

Even more remote from openings and closing are the final two instances to be offered here of two-turn sequences.

```
(3.05) Chicken Dinner, 3
 1   Sha:          eh hu[h   huh   hih   hih   hih-]hee-yee hee-ee  ]    [aah=
 2   Nan:               [eh-heh-hih-hih-hnh-hnh ]h n h-h_n_h hnh]-hn[h
 3   Sha:          =aah aah
 4                 (0.5)
 5   Sh?:          °˙hhh°
 6                 (.)
 7   Sha:          (Hih      ).
 8   Mic:          ha-ha.
 9   Sha:          (Hih      ).
10                 (2.3)
11   Mic: F →      Nance kin you- kin you cut my chicken.
12                 (0.3)
```

```
13  Nan: S →  Do yer own c[ut(h)'n(h)n(h)n]
14  Sha:                   [Are those peas ]any good?
15            (0.7)
16  Nan:      [Ther good ^for you,]
17  Mic:      [I don' know I I 'av]en' looked at['e m .] I ]haven'
18  Sha:                                     [Theh g]ood]faw you?
19            Who knowss:. Wuh wuh u-who aa-oodih you en authority?
```

```
(3.06) SN-4, 13:28—14:02
 1  Mar:      Hev en English takehome I 'aftuh do over the weekend,'n-
 2            (0.7)
 3  Mar:      study on Sunday 'n Monday,
 4            (˙)
 5  Rut:      (°Oh: I'm s:[:-      (0.2)     ((sn]eeze)))
 6  Mar:                  ['r that e:con test.]
 7            (2.0)
 8  She: F →  Howijuh like t'do our dishes.
 9            (0.6)
10  Rut:      eh huh-huh
11  Mar: S →  Can't wai:t.
12  Ma?:      ˙hhh hhhh ˙hh
13            (2.2)
14  Kar:      One a'these nights we gotta go swim la:ps.
15  Mar:      (°Too narrow.)/(°Dinero.)
```

Each of the exchanges marked by the arrows involves a sort of request, but in both instances these appear to be done and understood as mock requests. In Extract (3.05), two couples are having dinner at the apartment of one of them, seated somewhat awkwardly on the floor around a coffee table, and one of the guests asks his companion to cut up the portion of chicken on his plate. Her rejection of his request is gradually infiltrated by laughter, progressively displaying an understanding that the request was not serious, or could be treated as non-serious. Still, serious or not, the request sequence runs off in two turns.

In Extract (3.06), a hiatus has momentarily settled over this interaction in a dormitory suite, whose occupants Sherry, Ruth, and Karen have been dropped in on by Mark. The silence is broken by Sherry's request (or "invitation") to Mark that he wash their dishes. The laughter of Ruth registers the non-seriousness of this proposal, which is very likely to be understood as on her behalf as well, for the request comes from the residents as a "party"; this laughter colors the turn to which it is affiliated (rather than responding to it), much as the laughter in Nancy's turn in Extract (3.05) colors her turn, and displays an understanding of, and a stance toward, the talk which it targets. It is, then, not a separate "part" or position in the sequence. The sequence closes with Mark's rejection of the proposal at line 11, which returns the state of talk to the hiatus from which Sherry had with this sequence undertaken to extract it. Here again, then, a minimal two-turn sequence.[4]

It is clear that conversation does not lack for sequences fully composed by the minimal two-turn form of the adjacency pair, sequences which give no evidence in their execution or in the context surrounding them of being reduced, or elided, or missing some part. Indeed, unsystematic observation of interaction in real time (that is, not recorded data available for repeated examination) suggests that interactional settings which are badly under-represented in the data bases gathered until now may be even more common environments for two-turn sequences. I have in mind those interactions elsewhere called "continuing states of incipient talk" (Schegloff and Sacks, 1973:325), in which the participants are committed to co-presence by an event structure not shaped by the interaction itself. Sometimes this involves familiars, and even intimates, as with families in their home environment, co-workers in their work environment, etc., but it can include strangers as well, whose juxtaposition is wholly incidental, as with seat-mates on an airplane. In such settings, talk may proceed sporadically, in fits and starts, separated by long silences. Although there is at present no hard evidence, casual observation suggests that many such fits and starts may be realized in two-turn sequences.

Once having registered the robust presence in talk-in-interaction of sequences fully constituted by a single, basic, minimal adjacency pair, we need next to go on to note that a great many sequences involve expansion of this basic unit. Such expansions involve additional participation by the parties through additional turns (in contrast with expansion of the turns themselves), over and above the two which compose the minimal version of the sequence. These expansions occur in the three possible places which a two-turn unit permits: before the first pair part, in what we will call pre-expansions; between the first and the projected second pair part, in what we will call insert expansions; and after the second pair part, in what we will call post-expansions.

$$\leftarrow \text{Pre-expansion}$$

A   First pair part

$$\leftarrow \text{Insert expansion}$$

B   Second pair part

$$\leftarrow \text{Post-expansion}$$

As we will see, various forms of expansion can occur in each of these sequential positions, by which the parties accomplish (or seek to accomplish) a variety of interactional outcomes. Expansion in each of these positions can

---

[4] As will become clear later (in the discussion of "post-expansion"), these two-turn sequences are especially striking because of the rejections in them, a type of response which ordinarily leads to sequence expansion.

be substantial, and (with a few exceptions) expansion can occur in all of them for any given sequence. As a result, then, very long stretches of talk can be understood as elaborate structures built around a single underlying adjacency pair. In the chapters which follow, we will refer to this underlying adjacency pair as "the base pair," in contrast with its expansions.[5]

Indeed, the view underlying the orientation of this volume is not that they "*can* be understood" in this way, but that they *should* be understood this way, or even *must* be; and that many long stretches of talk cannot otherwise be understood for the coherent events which they were for their participants. If we take a unit like the adjacency pair to be the basic unit for sequence construction, then it is the *participants* whose unit it is, for it is *they* who do the constructing. And if talk is built around and between the parts of the basic adjacency pair in expanding it, it is the *parties* who do that talk, and design it for those places, as expansions and elaborations of that basic adjacency pair structure. If that is how the parties go about producing and understanding the talk and building sequences of talk-implemented courses of action, then that is what we must describe in understanding that construction of the interactional world, and giving a proper account of it. It is not, then, a metaphor only to say that very long stretches of talk may be supported by the armature of a single adjacency pair; it is a claim about how such stretches of talk were produced and understood by the participants, in their course, in real and experiential time.

---

[5] And in the annotation of the data extracts, the base pair will be marked by the subscript "b" (F_b and S_b), and pre-expansions, insert expansions, and post-expansions will be marked by the subscripts "pre," "ins," and "post" respectively. The reader has already encountered this usage in the data included in the discussion of counters in the preceding pages.

4 Pre-expansion

The first place at which a two-part unit can be expanded is before its first part – hence the term "pre-expansion." But that immediately confronts us with a question. How can we analyze and understand something like an utterance by reference to something else which has not yet occurred (and, indeed, which may end up *never* occurring, as we shall shortly see)? What justification might there be for such a procedure if we mean our analysis to be empirically grounded? The answer is that we proceed in that way because that is how the parties to conversation seem to use these exchanges in producing them and in understanding them. The parties to pre-expansion exchanges display an orientation in them to a base adjacency pair which may subsequently develop.

Note that we have already referred to "exchanges" in referring to pre-expansion. Virtually all pre-expansions are themselves constructed of adjacency pairs, and we will therefore regularly refer to them as "pre-sequences" (Sacks, 1992a:685–92 et passim). Both senses of this ambiguous term are relevant and important. They are themselves *sequences*, and they come *before* sequences – they are recognizably "*pre-*," that is, preliminary to something else. Often the "something else" they are preliminary to is quite specific: it is a first pair part of a particular pair type – an invitation, an offer, a request, an announcement.[1] Preliminaries that

---

[1] Although the text here is setting up the contrast between type-specific pre-sequences and the later-discussed generic pre-sequence, a more general point needs to be made as well. And that is that "pre-ness" is a property of utterances which speakers and recipients can orient to in sequential contexts other than first parts of adjacency pairs, let alone base adjacency pairs. There will be later occasion to discuss pre's which are positioned relative to second pair parts (such as "pre-rejection" or "pre-disagreement"), but "pre-ness" as a property may need to be treated as a property more general than that, and as not restricted in its positioning to adjacency pair organization, however much it is specially exploited in the organizational design of adjacency pair-based sequences. In this respect it would be like another sequential or relational property – adjacency – which has wide-ranging import for the relationship of units (turns, turn-constructional units, sequences, topics, etc.) in talk-in-interaction, but has a specially concentrated organizational application in the organization of adjacency pairs with respect to the relationship between first and second pair parts. The free-floating relevance of the feature "pre-ness" to the construction and understanding of utterances can be understood because of its import for an omnipresent concern for parties to talk-in-interaction about anything recognizable as a contribution to it or move in it – namely, "why that now." With respect to this omni-relevant concern, "pre-ness" is a widely possible analysis: something was done not as an action/move in its own right and analyzable in its own terms alone, but for its relevance to and bearing on some action/utterance projected to occur. And this issue and possible solution is relevant more generally than adjacency pair organization. See also the discussion below at pp. 244–46.

project such specific imminent FPPs we will call *type-specific pre-sequences* – for example, pre-invitations, pre-offers, pre-requests, pre-announcements. These then are *pre-sequences*, and what they commonly project, what they are regularly preliminary to, what they are pre-expansions of, is the specified *base sequence* – the base adjacency pair, with its base FPP and base SPP.

These two aspects of the pre-sequence combine to give pre-sequences their distinctive interactional import. The initial turn of a pre-sequence (like a pre-invitation) does two things: it projects the contingent possibility that a base FPP (e.g., an invitation) will be produced; and it makes relevant next the production of a second pair part, namely a response to the pre-invitation. And it is on this response that the projected occurrence of the base first pair part (e.g., the invitation) is made contingent. Some responses to the pre-sequence FPP (e.g., the pre-invitation) lead to the production of a base FPP (e.g., an invitation) and some do not. We turn to an examination of several type-specific pre-sequences.

Pre-invitation

The pre-invitation may be among the most readily recognizable pre-sequences in sheerly common-sense terms, so we will begin with an account couched in common-sense terms. When a caller follows the opening of a telephone call with the query "Are you doing anything?" or "What are you doing?", the recipient does not ordinarily understand that as asking for a factual description.[2] Rather it is ordinarily understood as a preliminary, and very commonly as a preliminary to a possible invitation (though it may sometimes not be discernible *what* sort of action is being led up to). What is wanted in response is, then, not a truthful, descriptively accurate response, and responses of that sort are treated as teasing, and as reflecting an intentional misunderstanding (as in "What are you doing?", "Talking to you", or "Breathing", etc.). Rather the response to such a question is meant to display the stance the responder is taking up toward the action to which the question was preliminary. If the invitation will be welcomed, then the answers should be "no" (to "Are you doing anything?") or "nothing" (to "What are you doing?"), or the like. If the prospective invitation is to be discouraged, if (for example) it is likely to be declined, then the answer to the preliminary – to the pre-sequence – should

---

[2] Although placement in the overall structure of the conversation can be important in constituting such a question as a recognizable pre-invitation, just-post-opening is not the only relevant position in this regard. A place otherwise suitable for launching a closing section may also enhance the potential recognizability of pre-invitations (Extract [4.03] below is a case in point, being initiated some ten to twelve minutes into the conversation), in large measure because closing is a relevant environment for arrangement-making, and invitations are a sequence type which can figure in arrangement-making.

be selected accordingly; for example, "yes, I have a term paper to finish." Perhaps the most telling evidence of the true status of the pre-invitation question can be seen when the response to the question is made contingent on what invitation in particular the caller has in mind; thus, "Are you doing anything?", "Why?" Of course, the answer to the question taken as a factual inquiry is unrelated to the reason for asking it; the "why?" response displays the understanding that the question is preliminary to something, and makes the answer contingent on what that "something" is.

We can characterize these different response types – these different types of second pair part to the pre-invitation – somewhat less informally along the following lines.

One class or type of response is the "go-ahead"; it promotes progress of the sequence by encouraging its recipient to go ahead with the base FPP which the "pre" was projecting. Extract (4.01) displays a case in point.

```
(4.01) JG 3:1 (Nelson is the caller; Clara is called to the phone)
1   Cla:              Hello
2   Nel:              Hi.
3   Cla:              Hi.
4   Nel: F_pre→        Whatcha doin'.
5   Cla: S_pre→        Not much.
6   Nel: F_b  →        Y'wanna drink?
7   Cla: S_b  →        Yeah.
8   Nel:              Okay.
```

Nelson's question at line 4 is one form which pre-invitations commonly take, and in this position – that is, after the (here minimal) opening section of the conversation. Clara's response exemplifies a go-ahead response to a pre-invitation, and Nelson does indeed go ahead (at line 6) to issue the invitation which his pre-sequence had foreshadowed, and Clara does the acceptance (line 7) which her response to the pre-invitation had foreshadowed.

A second class or type of response is the "blocking" response; that is, it raises the possibility that the invitation, if tendered, will be declined or rejected, and thereby discourages or blocks the invitation from being tendered at all. Extract (4.02) offers a case in point.

```
(4.02) SB,1 (Allen/Judy are married; John is Judy's fellow student)
1                 ring
2   All:          Hello?
3   Joh:          Yeah, is Judy there?
4   All:          Yeah, just a second.
5                 ((silence))
6   Jud:          Hello,
7   Joh:          Judy?
8   Jud:          Yeah,
9   Joh:          John Smith.
```

```
10   Jud:           Hi John.
11   Joh: Fpre→     Ha you doin-<say what 'r you doing.
12   Jud: Spre→     Well, we're going out.
```

Here, as in Extract (4.01), the caller asks just at the possible end of the opening (after the greeting exchange) what the recipient is doing, and this is a way of doing a pre-invitation, but in this case the response is different; it puts a blockage in the way of the issuing of the invitation.

Actually, it is not the *response* which first raises the possibility of trouble with the invitation. The pre-sequence FPP itself raises that possibility. One key thing which pre-sequences are designed to do is to help prospective speakers of base first pair parts avoid rejection, or, to put it more interactionally, to help the interaction avoid a sequence with a rejected base FPP. In effect, then, such pre-invitations provide an opportunity for the prospective invitation-recipient to indicate in advance whether there are obstacles to the invitation's acceptance. This allows the invitation to be issued if there are not, and to be withheld if there are, thus forestalling the need for, or possibility of, rejection.

A third sort of response can be termed "hedging," which can make a full response contingent on what the invitation is going to be. One form this can take is "why," either as the whole of the response, or in combination with another response type, for example, as a possible mitigation of a blocking response. Extract (4.02a) continues along these lines:

```
(4.02a)   SB,1  (continued)
1   Jud:          Hi John.
2   Joh: Fpre→    Ha you doin-<say what 'r you doing.
3   Jud: Spre→    Well, we're going out. Why.
4   Joh:      →   Oh, I was just gonna say come out and come over
5             →   here and talk this evening, [but if you're going=
6   Jud:                                      ["Talk," you mean get
7                    [drunk, don't you?]
8   Joh:          =[out you can't very] well do that.
```

Here we see that Judy, after having given grounds for not proceeding to the invitation, inquires after what it was *going to be*,[3] with a possible hint that the answer might contribute to some modification of her response. That prospect, which *is* sometimes realized, is that an otherwise non-viable possibility (a "foregone first pair part," as it were) can be revived once it

---

[3] It may be worth making explicit something that is hopefully already clear. Judy's "why" (line 3) is evidence that she has heard John's question as projecting a further contingent action; it is evidence (to her co-participant, and to us as well) that she recognizes his question as a pre. His answer confirms that she was correct in so understanding it; an answer is at hand for delivery. Quite often the response "why" is a "post-pre"; that is, it indicates that its speaker has understood something another has said as preliminary to something else. For an instance in which the status of the talk as a pre-sequence has been lost sight of, with a consequent loss of understanding, see Excerpt (4.27) below.

has been articulated. Here, however, John concludes his report of what the invitation was going to be with an assertion of its impossibility (although that is overlapped by Judy's somewhat facetious correction or reformulation of the problematic invitation).

Hedging responses to pre-invitations can take forms other than "why." In Extract (4.03), the hedge is first expressed in a "Uhm (0.3) possibly" (at line 2) and is then substantially elaborated, returning to a summary note of indeterminacy at its end (line 38).

```
(4.03) TG, 15:15-16:23
 1  Bee: F_pre→  °hmhhh ˙hh So yih gonna be arou:n this weeken'¿
 2  Ava: S_pre→  Uh::m. (0.3) Possibly.
 3  Bee:         Uh it's a four day weeken-I have so much work t'do it
 4                isn' ffunn[y.
 5  Ava: S_pre              [Well, tomorrow I haftuh go in.
 6                (0.2)
 7  Bee:         Y'have cla:ss [tomorrow?
 8  Ava:                       [hhhh
 9  Ava: S_pre   ((breathily)) One cla:ss I have.=
10  Bee:         =You mean:: Pace isn't clo:s[ed?
11  Ava:                                     [No we have off
12                Monday [°(b't not        ) ˙hhh
13  Bee:                [Mm I have off ts- Monday too. hmfff
14  Ava: S_pre   A:nd uh:m ˙hh I haftuh help- getting some schedules
15       S_pre   t'gether fuh- m-t! [my o:ld Mistuh Ba:rt.
16  Bee:                            [˙hhhh
17  Bee:         °Hmmm.
18  Ava: S_pre   A:nd I haftuh get the group tihgethuh fuh him.hh
19                (0.5)
20  Ava:         t! tch!
21  Bee:         BOY YUH BUSY KID! hh ˙hhh
22  Ava: S_pre   Yeh I know.He gay me [tickets t'the ballet in d-=
23  Bee:                             [hhh ˙hhh
24  Ava: S_pre   =exchange fuh that, so it['s not too] bad.
25  Bee:                                  [ O h  :  ] hh
26  Bee:         Busy busy [busy. ]
27  Ava:                   [°hhhhh]
28  Ava:         A::nd,
29  Ava:         hhh[hh
30  Bee:            [Oh I've been [getting,]
31  Ava: S_pre                   [S a t ]ihday I n- I've-g-I haftuh go-
32       S_pre   I think Sunday I'm going ice skating.
33                (1.2)
34  Ava: S_pre   I wz sposetuh go tuh A:lbany. But we'd haftuh leave
35       S_pre   t'morrow morning, so that wen ou:t. the window,
36  Bee:         °Mm,
37                (1.0)
```

```
38  Ava: S_pre→  En I don't know exagly what's going o:n.re[ally.
39  Bee: F_b?→                                          [Well if yer
40              arou:nd I'll probably see y(hh)ou hn[hh!  'hh
41  Ava:                                             [Why, whut's (Bob
42              doing)
43  Bee:        Uh-u-uh:: goin o:ff::
44  Ava:        Where's he goin.
45  Bee:        To Wa:shin'ton,
46  Ava:        Oh.
47              (0.7)
48  Bee:        He asn' been there sih-since Christmas [so:. HHe's going.
49  Ava:                                               [Mm.
50              (0.5)
51  Ava: S_b?→  Yeh w'l I'll give you a call then tomorrow.when I get in
52              'r sumn.
```

Here, after the long hedging response to the pre-sequence FPP, the problematic base FPP is articulated in something less than full "invitation" form
(lines 39–40), but in fact appears to be revived as a real possibility with the
response at lines 51–52.

We see from these instances that projected invitations which have been
rendered problematic by blocking or hedging responses to the pre-invitation
may be articulated nonetheless, sometimes in a diluted form linked more or
less overtly to the discouragement of the pre-sequence (note that the base
FPP in Extract [4.03] begins with "if yer around," which quite overtly links
back to the pre-invitation at line 1, "So yuh gonna be around this weekend?").
Once articulated, they are there for response, and may get a more "favorable" response than was adumbrated by the pre-sequence. Indeed, doing
the base FPP "nonetheless," after a blocking or hedging response to the
pre-sequence, may be understood as a bid to effect its action in the face of
hinted resistance, and the second part of John's response in Extract (4.02a)
(at lines 4–5) appears aimed to neutralize such an understanding.

But blocking and hedged responses to pre-sequences do not always elicit
versions of the discouraged or rebuffed base FPP. The response to the pre-
sequence may in fact block the initiator of the sequence from proceeding.
This is the case in Extract (4.04), which, however, turns out to be understood
(correctly) as having been not a pre-invitation but a pre-request.

```
(4.04) NB IV:9, 01:01-17
1  Mar:        . . .lo:, °hhuh°
2  Emm:        How'r you:.=
3  Mar: F_pre→ =Well wuhdiyuh doin. 'hh hnh
4              (0.5)
5  Emm:        .hhh (hhOh:) Margy?=
6  Mar:        =eeYeehuh.[a-
7  Emm: S_pre→           [Oh: I'm jis sittin here with Bill'n Gladys'n
```

```
 8            →    haa:eh fixin'm a drink they're goin out tih ↓dinner:.
 9                 (.)
10    Emm:        H[e's-
11    Mar:          [Oh::::. Oh.
12    Emm:    →    Why: whiddiyih waant.
13                 (1.0)
14    Mar: Fb  →   hhuhh Well?h I wunnid um come down en I wannidju
15                 tuh call some numbers back to me <b't it's
16                 no[t im[port'n
17    Emm:           [.hhh[Oh:::: honey I:'ll do it a:fterwards uh:::
18                 (.) Yeah ther- ther gonna(r)
```

After Emma's apparently blocking response (at lines 7–8) to Margie's pre-sequence (at line 3), Margie simply registers the information (line 11), but does not go on to say what prompted her inquiry. But Emma's ensuing utterance (line 12) shows that she understood Margie's line 3 not as a simple inquiry, but as preliminary to something which has been foregone, and she now goes in search of what that something is. In sequential contexts like this, "why" may be termed the prototype "post-pre"; that is, an utterance form employed to follow what is recognized to have been a pre-sequence, but a pre-sequence whose precise projected import remains unclear. Post-pre's may be deployed as responses to the FPP of a pre-sequence, but they may also follow responses to the pre-sequence FPP that are blocking or discouraging, as the potential recipient of the base FPP affirmatively seeks out what it would have been.

It is important to note that the result of a pre-invitation sequence can be that no base invitation sequence is done, whether or not there is a report of what it *would* have been. The fact that no invitation ends up being issued does *not* change the status of the pre-invitation as a pre-invitation. It was done as a pre-invitation, in order to accomplish that action; it was heard that way and responded to that way, as accomplishing that action. The prefix "pre-" is meant to capture the action being done, and not "occurrence prior to something else." Given the action that a pre-invitation is doing in circumventing rejection, the absence (i.e., the withholding or foregoing) of an invitation is one "natural product" of a pre-invitation pre-sequence, not something which qualifies or undercuts its standing as that type of conversational event.

Pre-offer

Although the forms of the utterances and the placement of the sequence type in its social occasion may differ, pre-offers work quite similarly to pre-invitations. Indeed, requests, offers, and invitations form a set of action types (with associated sequence types) which can be difficult to distinguish from one another. Invitations, in this regard, often appear to be a particular sub-class of offers, and their similarity in various respects is then not surprising.

Just as prospective inviters may seek evidence that their invitations will be accepted if tendered, so may those with something to offer try to assess whether their offer will be welcomed or not, and the actual offer may be made contingent on the outcome of that assessment. The instrument for the assessment is the pre-offer sequence.

In Extract (4.05), employees in a university bookstore are in a "continuing state of incipient talk" (see p. 26), talk which in this setting does not always pertain to their work. Here the matter at hand is the illness of Cathy's daughter.

```
(4.05) Bookstore, 2,1:107
1 Cat:                I'm gonna buy a thermometer though [because I=
2 Les:                                                   [But-
3 Cat:       =think she's [(got a temperature).
4 Gar:  F_pre →        [We have a thermometer.
5 Cat:  S_pre →  (Yih do?)
6 Gar:  F_b   →  Wanta use it?
7 Cat:  S_b   →  Yeah.
8                (3.0)
```

What is to be noted here is that Gary does *not* simply offer the thermometer after Cathy has articulated the need for one. The offer itself is preceded by a pre-offer, which here takes the form of a mention of its availability (line 4). Note that Gary's ownership of a thermometer is not itself grounds for mentioning it, or for mentioning it *here* in particular. The mentioning of it here, in this environment, after Cathy's declaration of intent to purchase one, invites understanding for what *other* action it might be implementing.[4] When Cathy registers this as news (line 5), she can be heard to be expressing interest in what might be being done through this telling (as compared to dismissing it as irrelevant, for example, which would be a blocking response to the same utterance understood as a pre-offer). In effect, this serves as a

---

[4] An important point deserves underscoring here. Whereas utterance forms such as "Are you doing anything?" have a surface character strongly indicative of their use as pre-invitation, and some utterance formats are virtually dedicated to such jobs (as with "guess what," to be discussed below as a virtually formulaic pre-announcement), some pre's do not appear on the scene virtually labeled as such. That "We have a thermometer" is a possible pre-offer must be analyzed out of an utterance which appears on the face of it to be a simple declaration of ownership. It is part of competent membership in the society/culture and being a competent interactant to analyze assertions of this sort for what (else) they may be doing at this moment, at this juncture of the interaction, in this specific sequential context. It follows that it is part of competent observational practice to achieve such analysis as well, however different the motivation for the analysis, and however different the consequences of its success or lack thereof.

go-ahead response to the pre-sequence, and when Gary then makes the offer (line 6), Cathy accepts it (line 7).

In Extract (4.06), the opposite outcome is arrived at. Peter and Marcus have been confirming arrangements about a meeting they are both to go to. The extract is taken from the closing of their conversation.

```
(4.06) JG
1    Pet:              I'll see ya Tuesday.
2    Mar:              Right.
3    Pet:              O[k a y Marcus  ]
4    Mar: F_pre→        [You- you're al]right [you can get there.
5    Pet:                                     [Ye-
6    Pet: S_pre→       Yeah
7    Mar:              Okay
8    Pet:              Okay
```

The issue appears to be whether Peter needs a ride or whether he already has a way of getting to this meeting. As in the previous extract, Marcus "leads" not with an offer, but with a pre-offer. When he establishes that Peter has resources for "getting there," he does not make the offer, an offer which would then have been at risk for rejection.

However, the transition from pre-sequence to base sequence is not always unproblematic. In Extract (4.07), Debbie has called to find out when her boyfriend is returning from out of town, and then undertakes to convey some possibly useful information to his roommate, Nick.

```
(4.07) Debbie and Nick, 1:34-2:59
 1    Deb:              ˙hhh Um:: u- guess what I've-(u-)wuz lookin' in
 2         F_pre→       the paper:.--have you got your waterbed yet?
 3    Nic: S_pre→       Uh huh, it's really nice °too, I set it up
 4    Deb:              Oh rea:lly? ^Already?
 5    Nic:              Mm hmm
 6                      (0.5)
 7    Deb:              Are you kidding?
 8    Nic:              No, well I ordered it last (week)/(spring)
 9                      (0.5)
10    Deb:              Oh- no but you h- you've got it already?
11    Nic:              Yeah h! hh=                   ((laughing))
12    Deb:              =hhh [hh ˙hh]                 ((laughing))
13    Nic:                   [I just] said that
14    Deb:              O::hh: hu[h, I couldn't be[lieve you c-
15    Nic:                       [Oh (°it's just)  [It'll sink in 'n two
16                      day[s fr'm now (then )((laugh))]
17    Deb: →            [       ((l a u g h))       ] Oh no cuz I just
18         →            got- I saw an ad in the paper for a real discount
19         →            waterbed s' I w'z gonna tell you 'bout it=
20    Nic:              =No this is really, you (haven't seen) mine, you'll
21                      really like it.
```

```
22  Deb:        Ya:h. It's on a frame and everythi[ng?
23  Nic:                                          [Yeah
24  Deb:        ˙hh Uh (is) a raised frame?
25  Nic:        °mm hmm
26  Deb:        How: ni::ce,
```

As we will see in the next section, the usage "guess what" is a common harbinger of some imminent telling of news, and Debbie's use of that form at the start of the turn at line 1 serves as such an advance notice. It is followed by an indication of the source of the information (the newspaper), but further progress of the telling is interrupted by Debbie's question to Nick, "Have you got your waterbed yet?"

As may be apparent to readers after examination of Extracts (4.05) and (4.06), this is not an idle question, but serves here as a pre-offer. What is on offer is information, but the information which Debbie has to pass on is relevant to someone still in the market for a waterbed, and so the offer of her information is made contingent on whether Nick would still be an interested party. Nick's response, repeated several times in the face of recurrent efforts by Debbie to effect its modification, is in effect a *blocking* response: he has his waterbed (and so is not an appropriate recipient of information on attractive ones to buy). Note that, although Debbie is poised to tell her information, in the absence of a go-ahead response to the pre-offer (or simply a post-pre, such as "why?") she cannot – or does not – do so. What she does do (at lines 17–19) is the stillborn version of the action – what it would have been had it come to pass, perhaps in the hope that its articulation would lead to its reanimation. But, as was pre-indicated in the aftermath of the pre-offer, this would-have-been offer is rejected as well.[5]

Although this sequence runs off much less compactly and smoothly (inter-actionally speaking) than the ones in Extracts (4.05) and (4.06), it displays the same sequence-organizational logic and dynamics.

Pre-announcement and other pre-telling

Announcement sequences are ones which tellers launch to con-vey "news" on their own initiative (that is, in contrast to tellings which are solicited by a question, for example). Commonly, two sorts of SPP are relevant response types for announcements, reflecting two sorts of interac-tional issue posed in announcement sequences: ones which register whether what has been told is in fact "news," i.e., was previously not known by the recipient; and ones which take up a *stance* toward the news, or assess it, whether in the terms in which it was presented (e.g., as good or bad news) or otherwise – see Terasaki (2004 [1976]) for early work in this area, and

---

[5] This episode is analyzed in greater detail in Schegloff (1995).

Maynard (2003) for recent work. Although both may be implicated, it is
to the former of these aspects of announcements that *pre*-announcements
appear most regularly to be directed.

One important constraint on "telling" – a constraint specific to each particular recipient of the telling and thus a feature of the "recipient design"
of the talk – is that, ordinarily, speakers should not tell recipients what
they suppose (or *ought* to suppose) the recipient already knows.[6] Although
they accomplish other outcomes as well, pre-announcements are aimed in
substantial measure to avoid rejection of what is to be told *as news*.

A great many pre-announcements are presented in one of a few recurrent turn formats. The basic elements of these formats can be represented
schematically as follows:

```
Guess                 what
                      who        ⎤
                                 ⎥  +    more or less detail
Y'know         +      when       ⎥
                      where      ⎦
Remember
```

A minimal, yet canonical, pre-announcement is formed from the virtually
dedicated phrase "guess what." But more extended pre-announcements get
fashioned as well, often deploying the common elements in variant forms,
as in Extract (4.08) below, in which "guess" is employed in a "puzzle" or
"challenge" version ("You'll never guess . . ."), or Extract (4.09), in which
"y'know" is cast into the form of an offer ("y'wanna know . . .").

```
(4.08) Schenkein II, 131
1  Ben: F_pre→   Hey you'll never guess whatcher Dad is lookih-
2                is lookin' at.
3                (1.5)
4  Eth:          He's coocoo.
5  Bil: S_pre→   Why what're you looking at.
6  Ben: F_b  →   A radar range.

(4.09) Terasaki, 2004:195
1  Jim: F_pre→   Y'wanna know who I got stoned with a few(hh) weeks
2                ago? hh!
3  Gin: S_pre→   Who.
4  Jim: F_b  →   Mary Carter 'n her boy(hh)frie(hh)nd. hh.
```

In these instances, and in others as well, aspects of the projected telling and
its topic are pre-mentioned and thereby previewed in the pre-expansion,

---

[6] "Ordinarily" because some activities are virtually defined by their being exceptions to this
constraint, such as reminiscing, which involves talking about precisely what one figures
the recipient to know as well. This kind of contingency might be provided for by the rather
awkward phrasing, "speakers should not tell recipients *as news* what they suppose (or *ought*
to suppose) the recipient already knows."

enhancing the resources from which to establish that the "news" is not pre-known. There are other recurrent formats for pre-announcements as well – for example, the form "I've/we've got + [characterization]," where the characterization is either of something that has been acquired (its acquisition being the news), as in Extract (4.10), or the characterization being of the sort of news about to be delivered, as in Extract (4.11):

```
(4.10)  Schenkein II, 38
1  Ben: F_pre→   Hey I got sump'n thet's wild
2  Bil: S_pre→   What.
3  Ben: F_b →    Y'know one a' these great big red fire alarm
4                boxes thet'r on the corner? I got one.
```

```
(4.11)  KC-4, 2:01-03
1  Rub: F_pre→   Hey we got good news
2  Kat: S_pre→   [ I  k n o w        ]
3  Dav: S_pre→   [Whats the good new]s?
```

Such pre-announcements may do one or more of the following: (a) they serve as an alert to recipients that what is to follow is built to be an informing or a telling of news; (b) they may offer a characterization or assessment of the news (good/bad news) or a pre-mention of the topic or topical domain of the news, thereby setting parameters for the recipient's parsing and recognition; (c) they may give evidence of the recency of what is to be reported, as evidence of its newsworthiness; (d) they make the actual telling a contingent next step, whether by formulating it as an offer or request to tell ("Y'wanna know who . . .") or by making the recipient-design constraint actionable (cf. Terasaki, 2004 [1976]).

Note that in virtually all circumstances, the "news" could in principle be told straight out, without any pre-sequence expansion, but each of the uses which pre-sequences have can be consequential if not addressed in a pre-sequence. Leaving aside the issue of "pre-knowness," there is the issue of the on-delivery recognizability of the news. Thus, the announcement at line 7 in Extract (4.12), analyzably touched off by the mention of "birthday cards" in line 3, is otherwise topically discontinuous with the preceding talk, in which a long sequence of arrangement-making is petering out in an unsuccessful conclusion.

```
(4.12)  TG, 18:34-19:08
1  Bee:          =I wanniduh look aroun fuh some cards,
2  Ava:          (Oh:.)/(Right.)
3  Bee:          Tch! I'll get some advance birthday cards, hhm hmh!
4                (0.6)
5  Bee:          ˙hhh A:n:d uh, (0.5) Me:h,
6                (0.2)
7  Bee: F_b →    Oh Sibbie's sistuh hadda ba:by bo:way.
8  Ava:          Who¿
```

```
 9  Bee:            Sibbie's sister.
10  Ava:            Oh really?
11  Bee:            Myeah,
12  Ava: Sb →       [° (That's nice.)/[° (Sibbie's sistuh.)
13  Bee:            [She had it yestihday. Ten:: pou:nds.
14  Ava:            ° Je:sus Christ.
```

The reference to "Sibbie's sister" marks the topic as someone whom Ava knows (cf. Sacks and Schegloff [1987]; Schegloff [1996c] on recognitional reference to persons), and Ava *is* eventually able to recognize who is being talked about with no further identifying information, just a repeat (lines 8–12). But such momentary failures to hear/understand are not unusual in otherwise unprepared announcements, and show by contrast the work that can be getting accomplished by pre-expansion (such as "guess what," or "guess who had a baby," etc.).

As with other pre-sequences discussed above, one central type of SPP is the go-ahead response. These response turns are, of course, fitted to the FPPs to which they are responsive. One particularly common exchange has the SPP repeat the question word which was used in the pre-announcement turn. Thus, we find exchanges such as "guess what," "what"; "guess who," "who," etc. Or, if the "y'know who/what, etc." format has been employed, a "no" may serve as (part of) a go-ahead response.[7]

(4.13) Terasaki, 2004:184
```
1  Del: Fpre→    Didju hear the terrible news?
2  Rec: Spre→    No. What.
```

(4.14) IPD, 16
```
1  Pol: Fpre→    D'you know what's happening at the Fairgrounds then?
2  Cal: Spre→    No
```

Two types of response to pre-announcements, however, provide for a different trajectory for the projected sequence. Both can short-circuit the path to a base first pair part, ordinarily by claiming or showing that the recipient-design constraint of "newsworthiness" is not met. In the "blocking" response the prospective recipient claims already to know the news, e.g., "I know," as in Extract (4.11) above (at line 2) or Extract (4.15):

(4.15) Schenkein II, 216
```
1  Fay: Fpre→    Didju hear about thee, pottery and lead poisoning
2                [(               )
3  Lor: Spre→    [Yeah Ethie wz just telling us [(           )
4  Fay:                                          [I read an article
5                en I ca- in a the- I 'nno whether it was Newsweek
6                'r Time 'r what . . .
```

---

[7] See note 9 below.

In the "pre-empting" response, the prospective recipient not only claims already to know, but displays this knowledge by pre-emptively undertaking the telling which the pre-announcement was taken to project.

```
(4.16) Schenkein II, 217
 1  Bil: Fpre→   Didju hear about that guy who got-tho-tho-that
 2                family in New Mex[ico (    )
 3  Eth: Spre→                    [.hhh Oh:::=
 4       Spre→   =[Oh::: that    [(mercury) poisoning?
 5  Lor:         =[That wz so    [(         )
 6  Bil:                         [(         [     )]
 7  Fay: Spre→                              [Oh thee] you
 8       Spre→   mean [in thee wheat? [in thee grain?
 9  Eth:          [((gasp))          [
10  Jac: Spre→                        [The mercury poison[ing?
```

The telling is thereby curtailed as "announcement," though it may continue under the guise of reminiscence, "discussion," etc. (as in Extract [4.15] at line 4).

Pre-announcements, then, like pre-invitations, pre-offers, and many other pre-sequences (but not all),[8] seem directed largely to pre-assessing the likely fate of a FPP of a particular type were it to be introduced by the speaker, and responses serve (and are designed to serve) either to encourage or to discourage the subsequent production of the base sequence. Note again that it is this interactional job and the parties' orientation to it which underwrites our characterization of these as *pre*-invitation, *pre*-offer, *pre*-announcement, etc. and not the placement of these exchanges before invitations, offers, or announcements. For, of course, these pre-sequences may turn out *not to occur before invitations, offers, announcements*, etc.; and far from this discrediting their status as pre's of those sorts, such outcomes can testify to their effectiveness at the job they were introduced to accomplish.

Announcement sequences are, of course, just one way of organizing the activity of "telling" in talk-in-interaction, and are employed to convey certain forms of telling in certain formats for telling. Among the other modes of telling, a particularly common one is story-telling, in which the "telling" part can have a distinctive character and shape. But the recipient-design constraint on telling to the already-knowing pertains to a broad range of forms of telling. The pre-expansion described above for announcement sequences under the rubric "pre-announcements" has a counterpart form of pre-sequence for story-telling; namely, the "story preface" (Sacks, 1974).

Not all story-tellings begin with story prefaces or story-preface sequences; some stories are told in response to (or *as* a response to) questions; some stories are presented as disjunctive tellings, interruptive

---

[8] See the later discussion of pre-sequences for dispreferred sequence types, such as pre-requests, in Chapter 5.

of the otherwise ongoing talk, and touched off by something just said, just noticed in the environment, just recalled, etc. (Jefferson, 1978a). But some story-tellings do begin with a pre-sequence, and such story prefaces are commonly designed to address a range of issues aside from "already-known-ness," issues to be taken up more extensively in a treatment of story-telling elsewhere.

In the present context, we need mainly to note that story-telling and other tellings such as announcements appear on the one hand to be treated as same sorts of activities, posing in common such issues as "already-known-ness" vs. "news-ness," as witnessed by the use of similar pre-expansions at the start of these activities. On the other hand, these are treated as different *kinds* of telling which are differently organized; witness the fact that there appear to be distinct forms of pre-sequence for different types of prospective telling – pre-announcement turns and story-preface turns are differently designed and differently used.

Still, different types of telling sequences can be closely linked and may blend virtually imperceptibly into one another. What we can call more generically "pre-telling sequences" may remain indeterminate in what sort of telling will follow, leaving that to be collaboratively crafted by the parties. The pre-telling may be followed by an initial pass at telling in canonical "announcement" format, i.e., a telling packaged in a single, grammatically simple, turn-constructional unit. Following uptake of that initial telling, the sequence may be quickly brought to closure as an announcement sequence, or may get further elaborated as a story-telling or by other forms of subsequent elaborated telling.

For example, in Extract (4.17), Marsha's telling about how son "Joey" is traveling back to his father's house is prompted by a question (line 9), but is format-organized as an independent, speaker-initiated telling.

```
(4.17) MDE-MTRAC 60-1/2, 1 Stolen, 1:01-34 (previously appeared as [2.04])
 1              ring
 2   Mar:      Hello:?
 3   Ton:      Hi: Marsha?
 4   Mar:      Ye:ah.
 5   Ton:      How are you.
 6   Mar:      Fi::ne.
 7              (0.2)
 8   Mar:      Did Joey get home yet?
 9   Ton:      Well I wz wondering when'e left.
10              (0.2)
11   Mar: →    ˙hhh Uh:(d) did Oh:.h Yer not in on what
12              ha:ppen'.(hh)(d)
13   Ton: →    No(h)o=
14   Mar: →    =He's flying.
15              (0.2)
16   Mar: →    En Ilene is going to meet im:.Becuz the to:p wz
```

```
17              ripped off'v iz car which is tih say someb'ddy
18              helped th'mselfs.
19   Ton:       Stolen.
20              (0.4)
21   Mar:       Stolen.=Right out in front of my house.
22   Ton:       Oh: f'r crying out loud,=en eez not g'nna eez not
23              g'nna bring it ba:ck?
24   Mar:       ˙hh No so it's parked in the g'rage cz it wz so damn
25              co:ld. An' ez a matter fact snowing on the Ridge Route.
26              (0.3)
27   Mar:       ˙hhh So I took him to the airport he couldn' buy a
28              ticket.
29              (˙)
30   Mar:       ˙hhhh Bee- he c'd only get on standby.
31              (0.3)
32   Ton:       Uh hu:[h,
33   Mar:             [En I left him there et abou:t noo:n.
34              (0.3)
35   Ton:       Ah ha:h.
36              (0.2)
37   Mar:       Ayund uh,h
38              (0.2)
```

Note here that the pre-telling (at lines 11–12) is overtly directed to the non-informedness of the prospective recipient, i.e., that the recipient-design constraint on telling warrants (perhaps even mandates) the telling being launched. The non-informedness is confirmed at line 13 – in effect, a go-ahead response to the pre-telling. The telling is then initially delivered as a single, compact assertion of news, "He's flying" (at line 14). When no receipt is forthcoming, addressing either the newsworthiness of what has been told or the recipient's stance toward it, the teller Marsha resumes the telling (line 16) and elaborates it on several fronts, some addressing the practical consequences of the news (line 16), some in story-telling form (lines 16–18, lines 24–33), some delivering additional "information."

"Telling," then, is a generic type of activity in talk-in-interaction, but it can take various organizational forms, both with respect to the turn-organization in which the telling is done and the sequence organization in which the telling is embedded. These distinct formats can be envisioned and projected at the outset, with the form of the launching of the telling – for example, the form of pre-sequence employed – beginning the constitution of a determinate shape to the telling. Or the telling can be built from the outset in a less determinate manner, with the turn-organizational and sequence-organizational format being constituted step-by-step as the telling develops. Or the telling can be projected to take a determinate trajectory, but undergo modification and re-organization in the course of its progressive realization. The forms are not locked in and frozen. Yet there *are* forms, forms oriented to as distinct formats for telling by the participants, and these affect the shape that the telling – and the being told – comes to have. And both the distinctive shapeliness and the flexibility are represented in the pre-expansions which telling can be given.

A different kind of type-specific pre-sequence: the pre-pre

There is a kind of pre-sequence which is distinctive in a number of respects. Although it is type-specific, the projected base sequence type for which it serves as a pre-expansion can vary. Pre-pre's take the form "Can I X?" or "Let me X", where "X" is the name of a projected future action (an "action projection"). Thus, "Can I ask you a question?", "Can I tell you something?", "Can I make a suggestion?", or "Can I ask a favor?" each project a different base FPP and the sequence which it would engender. These pre-expansions are thus type-specific. Indeed, it might well be thought that such utterances would exemplify, respectively, a pre-asking, a pre-telling, a pre-offer, and a pre-request.

However, examination of sequences in which such utterances figure shows that they are not used as pre-sequences of this sort, and are not understood this way (Schegloff, 1980). They do not appear designed to anticipate and avoid rejection, declining, already-known-ness, etc., and rarely get blocking SPPs in response (except as transient teases or jokes, as in the common retort to "Can I ask you a question?": "You already did"). And, although they are regularly followed by "go-ahead" SPPs, those are not themselves followed by the base FPP which was projected in the initial turn. That is, "Can I ask you a question?", "Sure" is not ordinarily followed by a question, which suggests that the work it was doing was not "pre-questioning" along the lines we have so far been discussing.

Rather, these utterances with action projections serve to allow some preliminaries germane to the projected sequence to get accomplished or established before the base sequence itself has its FPP articulated. The action-projection utterance is then preliminary *not* in the first instance to the action which it names, but to a preliminary or some preliminaries to that action. Hence the term we use to refer to them – "preliminaries to preliminaries," or "pre-pre's." Pre-pre's seem to exempt what directly follows them from being understood as the base FPP, and allows them to be attended to as preliminaries to the base FPP, while providing recognition criteria for the base FPP when it "arrives" – i.e., it will be a question/telling/offer/request, etc.[9]

---

[9] Having noted earlier that "pre-ness" can be a readily recognizable feature of some turns-in-position, and that recipients may have, as an interpretive resource for the question "why that now?", that an utterance is to be understood for its service as preface to something else, we note here that speakers may not rely on these resources and may take measures to pre-mark some immediately ensuing talk as intentionally preliminary.

There are two main sorts of preliminaries which are pursued or secured in the space opened up by pre-pre's: pre-mentions and pre-conditions.

The prospective doer of an FPP may face the contingency that it will involve a reference or mention which its recipient cannot be presumed to know or be able to recognize, and therefore some preliminary work is in order, either to establish that the mention/reference will be recognizable or to do the work that will make it so. Once that preliminary is accomplished, the sequence can proceed to the base FPP. For example, in Extract (4.18), Laurie has called Fred to inquire about the well-being of a mutual friend who has just given birth.

```
(4.18) ST (Schegloff, 1980:112)
1    Fre: Fpre→ Oh by the way((sniff))I have a bi:g favor to ask ya.
2    Lau: Spre→ Sure, go'head.
3    Fre: Fpre→ 'Member the blouse you made a couple weeks ago?
4    Lau: Spre→ Ya.
5    Fre: Fb  → Well I want to wear it this weekend to Vegas but my mom's
6                buttonholer is broken.
7    Lau: Sb  → Fred I told ya when I made the blouse I'd do the buttonholes.
8    Fre:        ((sniff)) but I hate ta impose.
9    Lau:        No problem. We can do them on Monday after work.
```

Upon completion of that sequence, Fred's utterance at line 1 does project a request, but is not properly analyzed as a pre-request. In the space – the turn and sequence space – which the pre-pre engenders, Fred establishes the recognizability of the object to which his request pertains (lines 3–4), and only then (line 5) conveys the request which had been projected in the action projection.

And, in the following extract, a caller to a radio talk show conveys to the host the background to which her question will unavoidably make reference, thereby arming him to understand it and respond.

```
(4.19) BC, Red Book:190 (Schegloff, 1980:107)
1    Cal:        I've listen' to all the things that ch'uve said, an' I
2                agree with you so much.
3         Fpre→ Now, I wanna ask you something,
4         Fpre→ I wrote a letter.
5                (0.3)
6    Bra:        Mh hm,
7    Cal: Fpre→ T'the governor.
8    Bra:        Mh hm::,
9    Cal: Fpre→ telling 'im what I thought about i(hh)m!
10   Bra: Spre→ (Sh:::!)
11   Cal: Fb  → Will I get an answer d'you think,
12   Bra: Sb  → Ye:s¿ . . .
```

The space to introduce the "background" is reserved by the pre-pre at line 3, the background is provided at lines 4, 7, and 9, and this background supports the formulation of the question (at line 11) as an inquiry about "getting an answer," understandable only by reference to the preliminary with which it is symbiotic.

It is worth noting that "backgrounds" and "preliminaries" need to be fashioned as such; specific practices of talking may be involved in rendering some spate of talk as "preliminary." Until the "foreground" move or action is produced, the same talk can be understood – as it is being articulated in its course – as what the speaker means to be saying/doing in its own right, often with untoward results.[10] What is conveyed in the talk is not "naturally" foreground or background, preliminary, or the "main event." It needs to be worked up to be the activity the speaker is constructing, and pre-pre's are a resource in crafting a spate of talk as auxiliary to some other, yet-to-be-delivered talk.

For other prospective base FPPs the contingency needing to be addressed first, before the base FPP, involves not something to be mentioned or referred to but some pre-condition on which the viability or propriety of the projected sequence is contingent, and establishing or securing this is a second matter addressed in the space set aside by pre-pre's. In Extract (4.20), such a use of a pre-pre figures in the story which Jack is telling Mark, turning on his status as a "born again Christian."[11]

```
(4.20) Sugihara, 1977:32-36 (Schegloff, 1980:121)
 1  Jac:          I was readin: the word one time an' this guy sittin'
 2       Fpre →   next tuh me I y'know (       ) an' he said "Hey Can
 3       Fpre →   I ask you something? 're you a Christian?" I said
 4       Fb   →   "Oh yeah," "Why don't we:: (0.5)
 5                [ (                )
 6  Mar:          [He was readin' the work next to [you?
 7  Jac:                                          [No I was readin'
 8                the word, and 'asked me if I wuz a Christian y'know
 9  Mar:          Uh huh=
10  Jac:          =I said "oh yeah" an' we started sha:ring and . . .
```

In recounting his story, Jack incorporates in the approach by the stranger which he is reporting his pre-pre, "Can I ask you something." Of course, the following question, "Are you a Christian?" has thus been marked as *not*

---

[10] As in Extract (4.28), below, where what is presented as a good deed entitled to appreciation (at lines 46–47) is misunderstood as an apology to be accepted (at lines 49–52); when examined closely, it turns out that the report of the good deed was not marked as a preliminary. When it is subsequently so marked at lines 53–54, the sequence runs off quite differently.

[11] In this extract, "the word" (at lines 1 and 8) refers to the Bible.

the question he has projected, but as a preliminary to it.[12] And what that preliminary is doing is establishing that the pre-conditions for the projected action are met, i.e., the pre-condition for inviting him to "share" – namely that he is born again. And (he reports) when that preliminary had been satisfactorily addressed, he directly proceeded to the base FPP (at line 4), "Why don't we . . .".

Although most preliminaries pursued after a pre-pre involve pre-mentions or pre-conditions, there can be other sorts as well. For example, in Extract (4.21), Bonnie has called Jim (they are about 14 or 15 years old, intermittent boyfriend/girlfriend), and after talk about attendance at a scheduled meeting of a youth group to which both belong Bonnie launches a new sequence:

```
(4.21)BB Gun, 2:04—12
 1  Bon: Fpre→   But- (1.0) Wouldju do me a favor? heheh
 2  Jim: Spre→   e(hh) depends on the favor::, go ahead,
 3  Bon:         Didjer mom tell you I called the other day?
 4  Jim:         No she didn't.
 5              (0.5)
 6  Bon:         Well I called. (.) [hhh ]
 7  Jim:                            [Uhuh]
 8              (0.5)
 9  Bon: Fb →    .hhh 'n I was wondering if you'd let me borrow
10              your gun.
```

Here Bonnie's utterance at line 1 may initially appear to be a pre-request, but what follows is not the request. As with a similar earlier exemplar, this appears to be a pre-pre, and what Bonnie introduces into the preliminary space is evidence of the seriousness of her request; namely, that this is not the first time she has tried to make it. This preliminary is, then, neither pre-mention nor pre-condition. The full range of preliminaries which prospective FPP speakers may seek to make room for remains to be determined.[13]

---

[12] Indeed, in view of the narrative practice here of not assigning the successive utterances to their speaker by name, the teller relies on his interlocutor to use an analysis of pre-pre's and how they work in order to parse the narrated events properly in the first instance. For example, in reporting two-person conversations, it is not uncommon to use a rule of alternation, in which each next turn-constructional unit is assigned to the "other speaker." Here, that would result in assigning "Hey can I ask you a question?" and "Are you a Christian?" to different speakers, as if permission to ask a question were contingent on being a Christian. Of course, this is incorrect, but that turns on being able to hear that "Can I ask you . . ." is a pre-pre, "Are you . . ." is a preliminary, "Oh yeah" is a response to the preliminary, and "Why don't we . . ." is the contingently projected base FPP, with speakership assigned by tracking the parts of the sequence as they play out. The import of this is that the practices and structures which we are describing inform not only the co-construction of the talk in its course, but also the construction and interpretive uptake of narrative accounts of such exchanges in subsequent interaction.

[13] As it happens, not all action projections are doing the work of "pre-pre"s. They also are used as "pre-delicates"; that is, they alert the recipient that what their speaker is going to do in the base first pair part is delicate or problematic. In some cases, such as the one

Generic pre-sequence: the summons–answer sequence

The pre-expansions discussed to this point have all been type-specific – that is, in some fashion designed to be suited to, and specific to, some particular type of base sequence which they therefore contingently project. But there is one type of pre-sequence which is not directed to any sequence type in particular, but rather is aimed at a feature generically relevant to the efficacy of talk-in-interaction – the attention, or mobilized recipiency, of an interlocutor. The default modality for displaying such attention in co-present interaction is gaze direction, and recipients (in the absence of accountable grounds for doing otherwise, such as engagement in other simultaneous activities) properly direct their gaze to speakers (Goodwin, 1981). But speakers, or incipient speakers, unassured of the attention of prospective addressees or of their availability to interact (or given affirmative reasons for questioning such availability or attention, such as observable

presented below, this is displayed in other ways as well. Here Pam had called Vicky earlier, and Vicky is now returning the call. Pam has been called to the phone:

```
(4.22) Erhardt, 8:1 (in Schegloff, 1980:131-32)
 1   Pam:           H'llo::,
 2   Vic:           Hi:. Vicky.
 3                  (0.4)
 4   Vic:           You ra:ng?
 5   Pam:           Oh hello there yes I di::d.
 6           →      .hh um I nee:d tuh ask you a questio:n?
 7                  (0.4)
 8   Pam:    →      en you musn't (0.7) uh take it personally
 9           →      or kill me.
10                  (0.7)
11   Pam:    →      I wan to kno:w, (0.7) whether you: will(b)
12           →      would be free:, (.) to work o:n um tomorrow night.
13                  (0.4)
```

Clearly Pam's request is being treated as problematic, and the action projection at line 6 is hardly the only indication of that. But in other cases, it is not otherwise apparent that the matter being broached is delicate, and the recipient might otherwise take the question as a simple request for information. In Extract (4.23), for example, 19-year-old Joey has called his mother, Marsha, long distance, and is asking about an investment which she either advised him to make, or made on his behalf, and which has declined substantially in value. After an upbeat and joking opening, Joey comes to the reason for his call:

```
(4.23) MDE, Stock (in Schegloff, 1980:133)
 1   Joe:    →      Uhm (0.3) Can I ask you something?
 2   Mar:           Yeah.
 3   Joe:           What has happened to Standard Prudential.
```

Here it is the action projection at line 1 that marks the question which it projects as not the simple request for information that it might ordinarily be heard as. He is "rubbing it in" that his interests were not well served by his mother's conduct of his affairs. For a fuller account of how these two uses of action projection are distinguished by parties to ordinary conversation, see Schegloff (1980). For a discussion of why pre-pre's are not needed when interviewers "lead up to a question" in broadcast news interviews, see Schegloff (1988/89, 1992b).

involvement in another activity or non-response to already produced talk or other action), may undertake to secure the attention of their co-participant. In particular, they may seek to secure that attention *before* the beginning of their talk-in-the-base-sequence lays claim to the attention of the recipient, which leaves the beginning itself vulnerable to impaired uptake, hearing, or understanding. The generic sequence-embodied practice for doing so is the summons–answer sequence.

Some structurally specifiable locations in talk-in-interaction are specially common environments for the use of this sequence, the most obvious being openings. Not uncommonly, the summons–answer sequence is the first sequence in an episode of interaction, preceding even greetings, for it is by way of the summons–answer sequence that an interlocutor is recruited for participation in the interaction (including its greetings), the instrument of recruitment turning on securing the attention of the prospective participant (Schegloff, 1968, 2002a [1970]).

But even within already ongoing interactions, the issue of the availability and attention of an intended recipient may be (claimably) at issue, whatever base sequence may be awaiting launching. Then the generic pre-sequence may be invoked to mobilize that attention which is taken to be prerequisite to the efficacy of any interaction, and be understood as preparatory to some incipient, but as-yet-unspecified, project. When employed, the summons–answer sequence is understood to be invoked "for cause" – that is, it embodies the claim that the recipiency of its target for what is to come is in some respect problematic (Schegloff, 2002 [1970]).

Various forms are used to implement the summons – most commonly the name (or title) of its target, a courtesy term (such as "excuse me"), or physical contact. As with other pre-sequences, there are both go-ahead and blocking second pair parts. The go-ahead response is generally articulated with "yeah" or "what," but may also be displayed by redirection of gaze to, or re-orientation of posture at, the summoner, or some other indication that the summoned is aligning as recipient to the summoner.[14] In Extract (4.24), Don is examining a video camera which has been set up in the dining room of John and Beth's apartment to record the dinner which is about to begin.

---

[14] The fact that responses to a summons like "yeah" or a re-orientation of eyes or body towards the summoner are taken as "go-ahead" responses and are followed by talk by the summoner that gets understood as "what the summoner was summoning them for" shows that when the response to the summons is "what" (as it often is), the ensuing talk by the summoner is not to be understood as "answering the question articulated by 'what'," but rather as following a response to the pre-expansion FPP that is a go-ahead response. The same is true of other pre-expansions which can take "what" or some other "question word" as their SPP – most notably pre-announcements such as "guess what I did," "what," "guess who," "who," etc. The ensuing talk is the base FPP of the sequence which was projected by the pre-sequence, and not the SPP response to the question word that served as the go-ahead response in the pre-sequence.

```
(4.24) Chinese Dinner, 2:10-28
 1  Don:              Izzit ai:med right¿
 2                    (0.7)
 3  Bet:              Ah, John wz determining tha:t a minute ago.=
 4  Bet:              =[I'm not sure,
 5  Ter:              =[Mm lemme pour[it!)
 6  Don: Fpre  →      ((Calling))        [(Say)John
 7  ???:              (                  [            ), ]
 8  Joh:        →     ((Calling from kitchen))[J's[leave it o:n!]
 9  Ter:                                      [(Lemme- le::h-)
10  Don: Fb    →      I:s this ai:med accurate enou:gh?
11                    (0.5)
12  Joh: Sb    →      Yes it's aimed et the table.
13  Don:              Grea:t.
14                    (1.0)
```

When Beth in effect redirects the inquiry to John, who is in the other room
(lines 3–4), Don employs a summons (line 6) to mobilize John's attention
and participation, and, upon receiving evidence that John is attending (line
8), re-asks his question to John (line 10).

Later, at the table, before launching a request sequence to have something
passed to him, Don uses a summons (line 5) to secure the attention of a young
child, and, when in response Jerry looks to him, he proceeds with the request
(line 8).

```
(4.25) Chinese Dinner, 25:20-27 (simplified)
 1  Bet:             =(um)in[i z      life [y'know,
 2  Ann:                    [Mm-hm?        [
 3  Joh:                                   [((cough))
 4  Ann:                    [Mm-hm?
 5  Don: Fpre→       Hey Jerry?
 6  Jer:             [((looks to Don))
 7  Bet:             [ An' it-[ he- he- i t- ]
 8  Don: Fb  →                [Will you pass ] that uh,
 9  Jer:             Uh this?
10  Don:             This one here,
11                   (0.5)
```

A few minutes later Don has gone to the kitchen to get some supplementary
cutlery, and is distributing them at the table, and only his wife has yet to get
a knife.

```
(4.26) Chinese Dinner, 29:11-18
 1  Don:             Mm. Here'r the knives,
 2  Bet:             °Okay gimme two[maybe three[(        ).
 3  Ann:                           [Mm hm      [(            ).
```

```
 4   Jer:                Guess what I have a[loo:se tooth.
 5   Don: Fpre→                           [Hey Ann?
 6   Ann:                ((looks to Don))
 7   Don: Fb  →          Dju wa[nt a knife?
 8   Bet:                      [Oh yea:h.=
 9   Ann: Sb  →          =[Nyeh,
```

Before initiating an offer (or pre-offer) sequence to his wife (line 7), he
"prepares the field" with a summons–answer sequence (line 5), the "answer"
again being furnished by gaze direction.

Blocking responses can be effected by a withholding of any such go-
ahead response, though such an effect may be achieved without design.
That is, as the doing of the summons is warranted in the first instance by
the possible non-attention of the target, failure of the summons to attract
target's attention is more a default than an action of the target's – though it
can be that as well, when the target has observably registered the summons
and is analyzably withholding a response.

As with other pre-sequences, there is an intermediate or mixed type of
response as well, here involving registering of the summons but with a
response aiming to block or forestall progression to the further talk which
the summons projects, either temporarily or substantially – responses such
as "I'm busy," "Just a moment," "Be right there," "I'm in the bathroom,"
or "Leave me alone!"

In Extract (4.27), Vic is a janitor/custodian, socializing with his buddies
in a local used-furniture store. His wife Carol comes to the door and "calls
him," i.e., summons him (lines 4–5).

```
(4.27) US, 3:10-6:07 (lines 1-14 appeared previously as Extract [1.06])
 1   Mik:            Jim wasn' home, [°(when y'wen over there)]
 2   Vic:                            [ I  didn'  go  by  theh.]=
 3   Vic:            =I [left my garbage pail in iz [hallway.=
 4   Car: Fpre→         [Vi:c,                      [
 5   Car: Fpre→                                     [Vic(tuh),
 6   Vic: Spre→        =Yeh?
 7   Car: Fb  →        C'mmere fer a minnit.
 8                     (0.7)
 9   Vic:             Y'come[he:re.
10   Car:                   [You c'co[me ba:ck,
11   Vic:                            [please?
12   Vic:             I haftuh go t'the bathroom.=
13   Car:             =Oh.
14                    (3.5)
15   Vic:             ((((From a distance))I cleaned'n=I left
16                    my garbage pail in the ha:llway yihknow'm I nope-I
17                    hope he don't c(h)laim it yuh kno(h)w,
18
```

```
19                  .
20                  . ((70 lines of transcript omitted; about 3 minutes))
21                  .
22   Ric:           That's I betcha it's the same ((ULULATING HORN)) kid
23                  who set fire to the, couch outside of the=
24   Vic:           =The blond headed kidjeh ((END HORN))   d'same kid.
25                  Becawss I caught him light'n on dih couch. Yeh. Dih kah-
26                  the same- the, duh, couch. Fronna dih stow. Yes. Sa:me
27                  kid.
28                  (0.7)
29   Mik:           He a firebug?
30   Vic:           Yes. He['s intuh dat.
31   Mik:                  [Mfhhh!
32                  (1.0)
33   Vic:           But now he's slowed down a li'l bit becawss he n- he
34                  kno:ws thet, other people know.
35                  (1.0)
36   Vic:           Bud if he gets intuh dat he can't, eh- h-help what 'e
37                  feels he still does it.
38   ???:           ((in background))(Sta:nding, y'know, went tuh see,)
39                  (3.0)
40   Vic: S_pre  →  °Yeh honey?
41   Car:       →   What,
42   Vic:           You said fer me tih come tih you?=Wu:djuh want ho[ney?
43   Car:                                                           [Yeuh.
44                  (0.5)
45   Vic:           Wha[t.
46   Car:              [I ash you t'take a walk across th'street with me
47                  fer a minnit=
48   Vic:           =Okay (honey. Okay.)/(I'll be back.)
49                  (1.0)
50   Vic:           I'll be (right witchu.)/(back inna minnit.)
51                  (1.5)
52   Vi?:           (                        ).
53   Jo?:           (Yeh have fun.)
54                  (3.5)
```

Note, then, that when Vic does not respond promptly to Carol's summons
(line 4) she repeats the summons (in "upgraded" form, here by full rather
than shortened first name, at line 5) and this gets a go-ahead response.

The base sequence which Carol then initiates is almost certainly not
the one on whose behalf the summoning was done. Vic's response across a
considerable distance projects on his part an orientation to a brief exchange,
and one which can be conducted "publicly." Carol's request for his approach
appears designed to allow a longer and more private exchange. That this
is the understanding of the parties can be seen in Carol's understanding of

Vic's resistance (his counter at line 9) as grounded in his suspicion that she is trying to extract him from his current interaction altogether, and her reassurance (line 10) that this is not the case. In effect, this request sequence is a magnified recapitulation of the summons–answer sequence, and to this Vic responds with something less than an accession, the cognate of a go-ahead to this larger-scale bid for his interactional availability (line 12).

Several minutes later, Vic in effect redoes the second pair part to this magnified summons (line 40), but, now that it is no longer adjacent to the FPP to which it is meant to be a response, it escapes recognition for what it is – witness Carol's puzzled response at line 41. Eventually Carol extracts Vic from his setting (although, true to her word, he returns shortly). It later appears that what is involved here is a complaint sequence which Carol voices to Vic about some objects which he has given away to the others in the shop without consulting her. The summons–answer sequence and the request which is its follow-up are, then, serving here as generic pre-sequences to establish the conditions for efficacious pursuit of the base sequence which Carol means to initiate, a sequence whose character is not overtly pre-indicated in the pre-expansion.

Multiple pre-expansions

We have briefly discussed several varieties of pre-expansion: type-specific pre-sequences of various sorts, pre-pre's, and a generic pre-sequence. There are no restrictions, however, on pre-sequences (although there are positional affinities; for example, summons–answer sequences are more likely to come first). Several pre-expansions may be introduced before the FPP of the base adjacency pair (although, of course, one consequence of the pre-sequences may be that the base adjacency pair is derailed). Here we can examine only briefly one instance of such a multiple pre-expansion to convey some sense (however conservative) of the extensiveness of the stretch of talk that can precede the base FPP.

In the case of Extract (4.28) below, the base FPP does occur; it is Vic's request at lines 76–79. One of Vic's colleagues in the used-furniture store group is James, a janitor/custodian in a neighboring building. Earlier in the day, someone had broken a window in James's building in his absence, and Vic had "cleaned up the mess" on his behalf. Upon James's arrival at the store which is their hangout, Vic goes on at some length about the favor he has done James, while James goes on at some length in anger about the breaking of the window and his determination to find out who did it. Before James's arrival Vic had speculated with the others whether he would be able to retrieve from James the barrel in which he had put the broken glass, and in the episode reported in Extract (4.28) Vic is launching a sequence designed

to request return of his barrel (also referred to in the extract as a "pail" or
"can"). That is the FPP at lines 76–79 at which he eventually arrives.

```
(4.28) US, 52:09-54:05
 1  Jam:        I'm-I'm reti:rin anyway an' uh somebody ehss kin have
 2              that damn fuckin job.
 3  ???:        hhh[hh!
 4  Jam:           [They c'n take it en stick it up theh damn ass.
 5              (0.5)
 6  Jam:        E(hh)h! Yeh that's [right I'm-=
 7  Vic:                           [I unduh[stand.
 8  Jam:                                   =[I'm worreh [but-but-but I=
 9  Vic: a→                                             [Ja:mes
10  Jam:        =[must say dat.[Yihknow what I mean,
11  Vic: a→      [Ja:mes.      [
12  Vic: a→                    [Ja:mes.
13  Vic: a→      Ja[mes.
14  Jam: b→        [Yeh right.=
15  Vic:        =[I left it theh-]
16  Jam:        =[I'm gettin sick] a' dis shi[t.
17  Vic:                                     [Have a beeuh,
18  Jam:        [Yeh.
19  Vic:        [Have a beeuh.
20  Vic:        I left [it-
21  Jam:               [e(hh)h!
22  Vic:        I left- Have a beeuh.
23  Jam:        Eh-hey let's gi(h)tta- let's ge(h)tta bo(h)ttle
24              wai(h)ta sekkin=
25  Mik:        =E wantsa boddle. [uh huh-huh-huh!
26  Jam:                          [(Down with beer!)/(Damn the beer!)
27              Agghh! [Shit
28  Mik:               [(Yeh [get           )
29  Ric:                     [ha hah hah hah [hah
30  Vic:                     [I'm not intuh  [the boddle.
31  Jam:                                     [Hu:h?
32  Jam:        Huh?
33  Vic:        I'm not intuh [liquor.
34  Mik:                      [(Look)-/(Ehyeh?)
35  Jam:        [(Looka dis.)
36  Mik:        [Soon ez Sonny gets back frm the stoh.=Sonny's up et
37              the stoh.
38  Jam:        [  Uh   h u [h?
39  Mik:        [Wait'll he [gets back.=
40  Vic: c→                 [Ja:mes,
41  Jam: d→     =Uh right.=
42  Jam: d→     =[(Uh hah?)
43  Vic:        =[The pail is in yuh hallway,
```

```
44  Vic:           [(Uh,)
45  Jam:           [I know it hu(hh)[h!
46  Vic: e→                        [The-the- I didn' have a broom wit'
47       e→        me, if I adduh hadda [broom I'd uh swept [up.
48  Jam:                              [e(hh)h!              [
49  Jam: f→                                                  [That's
50                 alright.
51  Vic:           So [(dat's, right on.)
52  Jam: f→           [That's a'ri'- somebody- [got it up, I don'know who.
53  Vic: g→                                    [(Look). But do me a favr-
54  Vic: g→        Do, me, one fa:vuh, I [cleaned it up!
55  Jam:                                 [Yeh hh
56  Jam:           Yeh right. Ih-deh ca:n, (I- brought de) can
57                 (I'll) set it dehr own the sidewalk.
58  Vic:           [No.
59  Jam:           [Izzat ehkay=
60  Jam:           =[No.
61  Vic:           =[Didjeh [sweep up duh rest a' duh me[ss.
62  Mi?:                    [(            )                [
63  Jam:                                              [NO I didn' sweep
64                 up nothin!
65  Vic:           Well o[kay well that's why I left the can=
66  Jam:                 [Leave ih deh.
67  Vic:           =[innuh hallwa:y
68  Jam:            [I'll do it (early) [in nuh maw:ning.
69  Vic:                               [so if you hadda br[oo:m then you=
70  Jam:                                                  [Yeh right.
71  Vic:           =c'd sweep up duh dust=
72  Vic:           =[(                )-
73  Jam:            [Very, uh- very good I [appreesh-`hhh
74  Vic:                                   [the glass,
75  Jam:           I apprecia[te that Victuh,
76  Vic: h→                  [Tomorruh I-
77  Vic:           No.=
78  Jam:           =[E(hh)h yeh.
79  Vic: h→        =[Tomorruh I want my pail back. Dass a[ll.
80  Jam:                                                 [Ye(hh)h!
81  Jam: i→        I don''now I may keep [dat pail.
```

The sequence is too long and complicated to explicate here in any detail.
For present purposes we need mainly to note that the base sequence appears
at lines 79 and 81 at arrows "h" and "i": a request and its (almost certainly
mock-) rejection. But the pre-expansions begin at line 9 with the summonses
at the "a" arrows and the eventual go-ahead response at arrow "b", line 14.

Note that what Vic begins saying thereafter (at line 15), "I left it
theh-," is the theme present at the end, lines 65–67, "that's why I left the can
innuh hallwa:y," suggesting that it was on behalf of this sequence that the

summoning at lines 9–13 was initiated. That summons–answer sequence, then, was a pre-expansion of the eventually realized request sequence at line 81, all the intervening talk – and apparently unrelated sequences – notwithstanding.

Note further that after the "side sequence" (Jefferson, 1972) concerning beer/liquor, Vic begins again, again with a summons–answer sequence (lines 40–42). What he produces thereafter is meant to be preliminary, but is not marked as such – there is no pre-pre, for example, and it is quickly clear that James does not understand it as preliminary. For example, he treats the statement about the pail being left in the hallway as misplaced telling of something already known (lines 43–45), as if it were meant as an informing. And, even more problematically, he treats the comment about Vic not having swept up as an apology to be accepted, rather than as an account for the pail still needing to be returned (lines 46–52). Vic then does a pre-pre (lines 53–54), and although James continues to try to anticipate and pre-empt the projected action (a request) at lines 56–57 and 73–75, the status of Vic's talk as preliminary is now secure.[15] James's efforts at pre-emption are rejected (at lines 58 and 77, respectively), and Vic eventually articulates the base FPP at line 79.

The point here is the substantial spate of talk which is properly understood by reference to what is being worked up to – by reference, that is, to its status as pre-expansion. In this instance, as it happens, not all of it is smoothly understood, but this is not intrinsic. Substantial pre-expansions can run off unproblematically, with summons–answer sequences followed by type-specific pre-sequences or pre-pre's, and the pre-pre's being themselves substantially expanded. Pre-expansion is one ample locus for substantial sequence expansion.[16]

[15] It may be mentioned that James's efforts to pre-empt are sequentially appropriate. We will discuss later on (in Chapter 5) relatively dispreferred FPPs like requests, and what is commonly treated as the appropriate response to their pre-expansions, namely, preemption.

[16] It is worth mentioning that some utterance forms which serve as common pre-expansion first pair parts can also be deployed instead as initial parts of the first pair part turn of a base adjacency pair. For example, the name of the targeted recipient may be said and no opening left for a response, as in "Alvin,=can you come a bit closer to the ta:ble maybe even there?"; in this case, Alvin looks to the speaker directly after his name has been said, but the name has been deployed here as a turn-initial address term, not as the first pair part of a summons–answer sequence, as is the case in Extracts (4.25) and (4.26) (discussed at greater length in Schegloff [2003]). Other possible pre-sequence first pair parts which may instead be deployed as turn-initial "action-type markers" are pre-announcements ("guess what + [telling]"), story prefaces ("The funniest thing + [telling]"), and probably others. Line 1 in Extract (4.07) above displays such a use of "Guess what."

An important issue is involved here, which can only be mentioned in this context, and that is the possible trade-offs between turn organization and sequence organization in getting various interactional jobs done. In this note we have mentioned that some jobs can either have a sequence dedicated to them or can be done as part of a turn's construction. Elsewhere we will see that some activities get done alternatively by expanding a turn or by expanding a sequence. There are varied resources not only *within* a domain of sequential organization but *between* domains of sequential organization which parties can mobilize for the implementation of their interactional projects.

One recurrent theme in many of the pre-expansions discussed here (and in others not discussed here) is their orientation to avoidance of problematic responses to a base FPP – most notably rejection (as with invitations, offers, requests, tellings-as-news, etc.), but also non-uptakes (as in troubled hearing or understanding). The mobilization of such sequence-structural resources leads us to focus more closely than we have so far on the relationship between alternative second pair parts of adjacency pairs.

At the outset of our discussion of adjacency pairs, we noted that, with very few exceptions, there are alternative SPPs which will satisfy the constraints of adjacency pair organization and its relevance rules – in particular, the conditional relevance of a second pair part on a first. However, the set of alternative possible SPPs for a given sequence type is itself structured; the alternatives are not homogeneous or symmetrical, as the orientation of much pre-expansion to the avoidance of certain types indicates. Because the import of these asymmetries extends well beyond expansion, we will temporarily set aside our discussion of other sequence expansions, and turn to a discussion of the differential treatment of SPP alternatives under the rubric of "the organization of preference/dispreference."

5 The organization of preference/dispreference

We ended our initial discussion of pre-sequences with the observation that they seem largely designed to avoid various kinds of trouble in the sequence which a prospective first pair part would start. For one, the generic pre-sequence – the summons–answer sequence – is designed to avoid trouble due to non-uptake of the whole of the utterance; that is, trouble (on the addressee's part) in registering that one is being addressed, and with what. The summons–answer sequence is built and deployed to establish the availability and the alignment of the addressee as recipient for the talk about to be done – *if* the addressee is available for interaction or for its next increment by this speaker (and to *secure* that availability and recipiency, if it is problematic). Again, one main use of "pre-pre's" is to establish in advance that the addressee knows the things, persons, etc. that an imminent first pair part will make reference to, thereby contributing to the avoidance of its "failure" because of trouble in its "infrastructure" of understandability.

But the most common potential trouble of a projected adjacency pair-based sequence which pre-sequences seem built to anticipate and to circumvent is rejection or disagreement, or, to use the more general term, "dispreferred responses." It may be useful at the outset to try to sort out these terms and what we will – and will *not* – mean by them.

Preferred and dispreferred responses: the terms

We noted earlier that there are some sequence types in which there is one central type of second pair part. In greetings and farewell exchanges, for example, although there are various forms used to do a response – for example, such various return greetings to "Hi" as "Howarya," "Howyadoin," "Hi," etc. – there is really only one *type* of second pair part, the return greeting.

But such sequence types are the exception. In the vast majority of sequence types, there are not only alternative responses which a first pair part makes relevant and a recipient of a first pair part may employ; there are alternative *types* of response, and these embody different alignments toward the project undertaken in the first pair part. A recipient of an offer or an invitation may accept it or decline it. Requests can be granted or rejected. Obviously there are different particular forms which can be used to do either of these, but accepting and declining, granting and rejecting, are fundamentally different *types* of responses and alignments to the offer or invitation. We already have had some exposure to these different *types* of second pair part in discussing such responses to pre-sequences as go-ahead responses, blocking responses, and hedging responses. And perhaps we can use one of those discussions as a point of departure for the next important observation.

That observation is that the alternative types of second pair part which a first pair part makes relevant are not equivalent, or equally valued. They are not "symmetrical alternatives" (Schegloff and Sacks, 1973:314). Sequences are the vehicle for getting some activity accomplished, and that response to the first pair part which embodies or favors furthering or the accomplishment of the activity is the favored – or, as we shall term it, the preferred – second pair part.

For example, the summons–answer sequence is a sequence designed to mobilize, secure, or establish the availability, attention, and aligned recipiency of its addressed target. The two main types of response are the go-ahead and blocking responses. The former embodies what the sequence is designed to do – it displays (or at least claims) the attentiveness of its speaker; the latter embodies a problem in its realization (Schegloff, 2002a [1970]). The former is preferred, the latter dispreferred. And these different "values" are embodied, as we shall see, in the different practices by which preferred and dispreferred responses are respectively formed up.

The key issues in the organization around "preference" and "dispreference" concern the alignment in which a second action stands to a first, and the alignment which recipients take up toward a first pair part by the second pair part which implements their response (Pomerantz, 1984:63–64). Roughly speaking, such alignments are of two types, which we can call "plus" (+) and "minus" (−).

For some types of first pair part – such as assessments (Pomerantz, 1978, 1984) or questions of the so-called "yes/no" type (Sacks, 1987 [1973]) – +responses (read this as "plus responses") readily lend themselves to formulation as "agreements," and −responses (read this as "minus responses") as "disagreements." For other types of first pair part – such as requests, offers, invitations, announcements, etc. – the terminology of "agreement" and "disagreement" seems less felicitous. For requests, the +response invites formulation as "granting" or "acceding" and the −response as "rejecting" or "denying." For offers and invitations, "accept" seems more apt for the +response, and "decline" joins "reject" as an apt term for the −response.

The +response, then, embodies an alignment with the first pair part, and the −response a distancing from it. As we will see, this is not necessarily an alignment with, or distancing from, the *speaker* of the first pair part (although

it *may* be that as well), but the *project* of the first pair part, and the course
of action it is designed to implement. Generally speaking, interactional
projects and courses of action are implemented in sequence organization
in such a way that +responses (acceptances, grantings, agreeements, etc.)
are *preferred* and −responses (rejections, declinings, disagreements) are
dispreferred. But there are exceptions and complications to this general
preference structure, which we can do little more than register here. For
example, agreement is not always the preferred response to an assessment:
after a self-deprecation ("I'm so dumb I don't even know it!"), agreement
may be *dis*preferred and disagreement preferred (Pomerantz, 1984:83–90);
indeed, disagreeing with the negative self-assessment is a way of aligning
with its speaker, not disaligning! Another example: although generally it
appears that accepting is the preferred response to offers (or, as we will
sometimes put it, "offers prefer acceptances"), this may be contingent on
the item being offered and the context. Some offers ("Would you like the last
piece of pie?") may more cogently be understood as preferring rejections
(and may be termed "pro forma" accordingly).[1]

Another complication is that the range of response types (or SPPs) to
some first pair parts do not at first readily seem to lend themselves even
to the general terminology of plus/minus. For example, "agreeing" or "disagreeing" with an announcement (as well as "accepting" or "rejecting" it)
suggest a stance toward the factual accuracy of what has been told, and
these may of course be involved. But the generic issues for announcement sequences concern the recipient's alignment toward the first pair part
as news (as compared to "already known") and toward the assessment
of the news (e.g., as "good" or "bad") which informs its delivery. Once
made explicit in these terms, it seems apt to understand alignment with
the designed presentation of the news by the recipient of an announcement
(i.e., that it *is* news and of the sort presented by the teller) as, in effect,

---

[1] For example, in the following exchange, two sisters in their late middle years have just
agreed to go to the shopping mall together. Their homes are not far apart. Emma – the
one who has been approached for the expedition and who is recently recovered from light
surgery on her toe, follows up on the decision to go (line 5):

```
(5.01) NB IV:10, 41:32-41
1 Lot:      ↑W'l I jus thought mayb we g'd gover duh Richard's fer lunch
2           then after uh get muh hair ↓fixed.
3 Emm:      Awri:ght.
4 Lot:      Oka:y,
5 Emm:  →   .hh I: C'D WA:LK DOW:N MEETchu:,
6           (0.7)
7 Emm:  →   Why don't I DO th*at. .
8 Lot:      If you wa:n' to in if you feel like you don'wan' to theh-
9 Emm:      A A'R I :GHT.,
```

It appears as if the offer to walk over might have been designed for rejection or a counter-
offer, and when none is forthcoming Emma undertakes "seriously" to do what she had
apparently just "offered" to do.

preferred "agreement," and *non*-alignment – in either respect – as dispreferred "rejection."[2]

Perhaps more complicated are complaint sequences, in which a range of possible responses can be relevant next in general (i.e., across an aggregate of particular complaints), but not all of which may be relevant on any particular occasion, for some particular complaint sequence with some particular complainant/recipient combination. Nor is it always clear what second pair part to complaints is preferred or dispreferred (and more or less) among such response types as agreeing, co-complaining (or joining the complaint), doing a remedy, offering a remedy, disagreeing/ rejecting, counter-complaining, and others.

It is important throughout this discussion of preference and dispreference to keep clearly in focus that this is a social/interactional feature of sequences and of orientations to them, *not a psychological one*. It is not a matter of the motives or desires or likings (in that sense of "preferences") of the participants – whether speaker or recipient, of first or second pair part (although in any given case the sequential preference and individual leaning may coincide, perhaps even in most cases). "Preferred" and "dispreferred" rather refer to a structural relationship of sequence parts.

For example, the fact that I may prefer that you not be there when I do a summons by calling out to you, or knocking on your door, or calling you on the telephone, does not change the differing "weights" or "valences" that go-ahead and blocking responses have in the summons–answer sequence. Similarly, many have had the experience of inviting to a social or family affair someone who "must be invited," but whom nobody wants to come. And the person receiving the invitation may quite dislike the people who will be at the affair and much "prefer" to miss it. And yet, come the event, they are together. The invitation, once issued, has a dynamic of its own.

---

[2] As in the following exchange, in which Kathy does not align in either respect (see lines 2 and 12–13):

```
(5.02) KC-4, 2:1-17
 1 Rub:        Hey we got good news
 2 Kat:  ->    [  I  k n o w   ]
 3 Dav:        [Whats the good new]s?
 4 Fri:        [Ya heard it?]
 5 Rub:        [ Oh   ya do? ]
 6             (0.5)
 7 Dav:        (What's-)
 8 Rub:        °Oh good
 9             (0.8)
10 Dav:        Oh yeah, mmhmm
11             (1.0)
12 Kat:  ->    except I don know what a (0.2) giant fullucular::
13       ->    lympho: blastoma is
14 Rub:        Who the hell does, exc[ept a] doctor
15 Kat:                             [ Well]
16 Dav:        Mm
17 Kat:        (I d'nno-)=
```

Invitation sequences "prefer" acceptances and disprefer declines, and this is so whatever the personal predilections of the participants for the particular event at issue.

And an office mate looking for a ride in a colleague's car may formulate a pre-request as "You're not going downtown, are you?" – a turn format grammatically apparently aligned to a "no" answer, although its speaker may transparently "want" a "yes" (if the utterance is in context a *recognizable* pre-request). While in such an exchange the speaker has apparently designed the turn to display an orientation to a "no" answer, the action which a first pair part enacts (such as "pre-request") can embody or carry a preference quite apart from the turn format through which the speaker implements it, with both of these analytically to be distinguished from the personal desires or tastes of the speaker.

There can be, then, alternative groundings of preference (Schegloff 1988b:453–55). Some preferences are grounded in the character of the course of action, and the directionality of its trajectory toward realization or "success"; we may think of these as preferences based in sequence structure – the structure of the course of action in progress. So, for example, summons–answer sequences are designed to mobilize the attention of one or more recipients for some further talk or action whose occurrence is contingent on the success of the sequence in attracting the attention of a recipient. A "go-ahead" response is preferred, as it provides for the further advance of the trajectory of the sequence on its course of action.

On the other hand, some preferences are grounded in the design of the turn embodying the first pair part, often through resources such as grammatical format (question formats can apparently be specially adaptable in this regard), prosody, diction (e.g., word selection), and other features of turn design; we may think of these as preferences based in speaker practices. For example, linguistics use the term "negative polarity marker" for elements in a grammatical construction (most often in a question) that have it "tilted" (so to speak) toward a negative reply (for conversation-analytic work that displays the relevance of negative polarity and provides citations to the relevant literature, see Heritage [2002] and Koshik [2002]). In Extract (5.03), Bee, who used to attend the same college as Ava but has transferred, is getting updated on recent events:

```
(5.03)  TG, 4:35-5:01
1 Bee:        Eh-yih have anybuddy: thet uh:? (1.2) I would know
2             from the English depar'mint there?
3 Ava:        Mm-mh. Tch! I don't think so.
4 Bee: F->    °Oh,=<Did they geh ridda Kuhleznik yet hhh
5 Ava: S->    No in fact I know somebuddy who ha:s huh [now.
```

It is the "yet" in the question at line 4 that is the negative polarity item and exhibits the orientation of the question to a "no" answer. Not only is the answer at line 5 a negative answer, it begins with a "no," and with no delay at all in its delivery – features which will be discussed below as characteristics of the delivery of a preferred SPP. (Note that there does not appear to be any sequence-intrinsic SPP that would either advance or obstruct the further trajectory of the sequence; the turn-design feature is here what shapes the asymmetry between preferred and dispreferred SPPs.)

Although it is often the case that what is projected by the design of the turn, on the one hand, and the type of response which forwards the project of the sequence, on the other hand, are congruent, sometimes sorting out their mutual bearing can be complicated. In referring to preferences for agreement, acceptance, alignment, etc. in this discussion, it is both such normative features of action-types-in-their-sequence and such features of turn design that are involved that we have in mind, but *not* the "desires" or "attitudes" of the participants of the moment as separately entertained features. Of course, to the degree that the design of the turn or the structure of the sequence appear to reflect what are vernacularly understood as "desires" or "attitudes," they figure in our understanding, but this is by virtue of their interactional expression, not their status as "private" motivational states.

If "preferred"/"dispreferred" refer not to tastes/desires of the participants but to the sequential practices and structurings of an interactional project – that is, the activity and the sequence through which it is prosecuted – what observable events in talk-in-interaction is our attention being directed to by these terms? What practices of turn and sequence construction are involved?

And how do these different practices for preferred and dispreferred responses help us understand an important aggregate or distributional fact – namely, that with considerable regularity (although clearly not invariably) responses to first pair parts deliver the preferred type of second pair part?

As elsewhere in understanding talk-in-interaction, we need to understand the practices bearing on the construction of single episodes in their course in order to understand such aggregate, distributional outcomes. Our discussions of the two issues will proceed hand in hand. But we begin with the features that differentiate preferred from dispreferred responses, and the practices by which these differential features are produced.

Preferred and dispreferred responses: the practices and features

Turns which embody and implement preferred and dispreferred responses are commonly characterized by contrasting configurations of features. Not all the features occur on each occasion, and it can happen that a preferred SPP is delivered with some feature characteristic of dispreferred turn types and vice versa (for one example, see Extract [5.13] in footnote 5 below). Nonetheless, a cluster of features regularly produced together come to constitute a turn as one or the other; see, for example, Pomerantz

1984; Sacks, 1987 [1973]; Schegloff, 1988b. Among the most recurrent and central features is compromising the adjacency of the first and second pair parts, and, when they are in adjacent turns, compromising the contiguity of the two by having other elements intervene between them.

Mitigation

Dispreferred responses may be mitigated or attenuated, as in the following two instances.

```
(5.04) Sacks, 1987 [1973]:60
1  A: F -> Is it near Edinburgh?
2  B: S -> Edinburgh? It's not too far.

(5.05) NB III: 3 (Sacks, 1987 [1973]:58)
1  A: F -> Yuh comin down early?
2  B: S -> Well, I got a lot of things to do before gettin
3        -> cleared up tomorrow. I don't know. I w- probably
4        -> won't be too early.
```

In Extract (5.04), the place that has been asked about is, in the answerer's view, *not* near Edinburgh. But the turn is designed to mitigate and attenuate the distance, and avoid too overt a disalignment. And Extract (5.05) ends not only with "[not] too early" as an attenuation of "no," but is interrupted to insert a mitigation of the assuredness with which even this is put forward ("I w- probably won't . . .").

Indeed, a dispreferred response may be mitigated even to the vanishing point, i.e., where the dispreferred response is not in fact articulated at all.

```
(5.06) MDE: Stalled, 1:7-23
 1 Don: Fpre -> Guess what.hh
 2 Mar: Spre -> What.
 3 Don: Fb   -> ˙hh My ca:r is sta::lled.
 4             (0.2)
 5 Don: Fb    ('n) I'm up here in the Glen?
 6 Mar:        Oh::.
 7            {(0.4)}
 8 Don:       {˙hhh }
 9 Don: Fb    A:nd.hh
10             (0.2)
11 Don: Fb    I don' know if it's po:ssible, but {(˙hhh)/(0.2)} see
12             I haveta open up the ba:nk.hh
13             (0.3)
14 Don: Fb    a:t uh: (·) in Brentwood?hh=
15 Mar: Sb->  =Yeah:- en I know you want- (·) en I whoa- (·) en I
16       ->    would, but- except I've gotta leave in aybout five
17       ->    min(h)utes.[(hheh)
```

By the time Marcia responds at lines 15–17, it has become clear that Donny is soliciting her help (*how* this becomes clear will become clear as we return to this episode in various connections in various chapters of this book.) Note that Marcia's rejection of this request, a dispreferred response, is never actually articulated; it is attenuated to the vanishing point, expressed in the end by her account for the rejection.

Elaboration

Preferred responses are likely to be short and to the point, while dispreferred ones are more elaborated. Specifically, dispreferred responses are commonly accompanied by (among others) accounts (as in Extract [5.05], line 2, "I got a lot of things to do"), excuses (as in [5.06], lines 16–17, "I've gotta leave in about five minutes"), disclaimers (as in [5.05], line 3, "I don't know"), and hedges (as in Extract [5.07]).

```
(5.07) TG, 18:12-16
1 Ava: F ->    [Maybe if yih come down I'll take the car (down).
2 Bee: S ->    t! We:ll, uhd-yihknow I-I don' wanna make any- thing
3        ->    definite because I-yihknow I jis:: I jis::t thinkin:g
4        ->    tihday all day riding on th'trains hhuh-uh ˙hh[h!
```

Here, Ava is making the nth of many efforts to induce Bee to accept her invitation to come to school with her the next day, to be met again by resistance, here in the form of a hedge ("I don't wanna make anything definite.").[3]

---

[3] Other types of such elaborations include apologies and appreciations, as in Extracts (5.08) and (5.09) below.

```
(5.08) SBL T1/S1/C10, simplified
 1 B:      And uh the- Uh if you'd care to come over and visit a little
 2         while this morning, I'll give you a cup of coffee.
 3 A:->    hehh! Well that's awfully sweet of you, I don't think I can
 4         make it this morning, hh uhm I'm running an ad in the paper
 5         and-and uh I have to stay near the phone.
(5.09) NB II:2:17-18
 1 Emm:    [Wanna c'm] do:wn 'av [a bah:ta] lu:nch w]ith me?=
 2 Nan:                          [°It's js] (      )°]
 3 Emm:    =Ah gut s'm beer'n stu:ff,
 4         (0.3)
 5 Nan: ->  ↑Wul yer ril sweet hon: uh:m
 6         (.)
 7 Emm:    [Or d'y]ou'av] sup'n [else °(      )°
 8 Nan:    [L e t-] I : ] hu.   [n:No: I haf to: uh call
 9         Roul's mother, I told'er I:'d call'er this morning
10         I [gotta letter]'from'er en .hhhhhh A:nd uhm
11 Emm:       [°(Uh huh.)° ]
12         (1.0)
```

In these exchanges, invitations are declined, but in each case an early component of the turn is an appreciation of the invitation about to be declined. That such appreciations are hearable for the dispreferred response they pre-monitor can be seen in Extract (5.09) at line 7,

Preferred responses not only are designed to be short and unequivocal; they are not ordinarily treated as "accountable."[4]

Default

Preferred responses may be treated as the default or "response of reference." What amount in the end to dispreferred responses may be shaped in their production as preferred ones, as in the following instances offered as exemplars by Sacks.

```
(5.10) Sacks, 1987 [1973]:62
1  A: F -> That where you live? Florida?
2  B: S -> That's where I was born.
```

```
(5.11) Sacks, 1987 [1973]: 62
1  A: F -> How about friends. Have you friends?
2  B: S -> I have friends. So-called friends. I had friends.
3         -> Let me put it that way.
```

In the first of these, it is clear that 'B' does *not* live in Florida, but the response does not *say* that, but is shaped to provide something which *is* Florida-related instead. In the second, the upshot of "I had friends" is that the speaker no longer has them, but the response initially is couched as an agreement, then makes the friends merely apparent or conventional ("so-called") so as to still have them, then makes them past, so as still to take an affirmative stance toward the question. (This feature of answering is distinct from that taken up in Raymond [2003], to be discussed below, which, however, is also in play here.)

The opposite shaping – of what are basically preferred responses in the direction of appearing to be dispreferred ones – is uncommon.

Relatedly, speakers on occasion give a quick response to a first pair part which turns out to require revision – indeed, reversal – even before its articulation has been completed. Regularly, it is a preferred response which has been launched as a default and is reversed in its course into a dispreferred response type, as in the following extract:

```
(5.12) TG, 4:12-16
1 Ava:      [Oh I ha]ve thee- I have one class in the e:vening.
2 Bee: F -> On Mondays?
3 Ava: S -> Y-uh::: Wednesdays.=
4 Bee:      =Uh-Wednesday,=
```

where the inviter intervenes to ask whether the invitee has an alternative commitment. For a detailed examination of these practices, see Drew (1984).

[4] As with a lot else in this discussion, much more could be written about the construction and practices of providing accounts than can be accommodated here. See, for example, the discussion in Heritage (1988) on the special status of accounts grounded in "inability" as compared to other types of account; see also Drew (1984).

Although the class in question is Ava's course and she knows it meets Wednesdays rather than Mondays, her default response is to accept Bee's guess ("Y-" is most likely the start of some version of "yes"), and she must undertake in the course of its production to override this incipient response in favor of a correction of Bee's guess. It is exceedingly rare for initial, "default" responses to be *dis*preferred, and to require mid-course correction to a preferred response.

Positioning

Preferred responses generally are delivered in a turn which begins after the single beat of silence that composes what is treated by participants as a "normal" transition space; that is, one which carries no import other than the straightforward passing of the turn from prior speaker to next speaker (or even a shorter-than-normal transition space), and they come early in the next turn, with no turn-internal initial delays. They are placed "contiguously" (Sacks, 1987 [1973]) with their respective first pair parts. The positioning of dispreferred second pair parts, on the other hand, is done differently.[5] Most important here is that they are ordinarily *not* done contiguously. Various practices are employed to break the contiguity of first and second pair part; here we touch on several of them.

1. *Inter-turn gap.* The transition space between the first pair part turn and a dispreferred second pair part turn is commonly overlong, i.e., a gap. That is to say, the recipient of the first pair part does not start a responsive turn "on time," and the silence breaks the contiguity of first and second pair part, as

---

[5] This differential positioning is both empirical and normative – that is, most preferred and dispreferred second pair parts are done these ways, and that is the empirical aspect of the observation. Those that are not may get a special import or understanding by reference to the variation, i.e., from being delayed although preferred, or contiguous although dispreferred, and this is the normative aspect of the observation. Thus, in the following episode Ava's negative and dispreferred response (at line 3) to Bee's offering of a topic of possible mutual interest is done with "unseemly" haste, especially when it turns out that a positive response was available (discussed in Schegloff [1988b:454]):

```
(5.13) TG 04:37-5:03
1 Bee:    Eh-yih have anybuddy: thet uh:? (1.2) I would know from the
2         English depar'mint there?
3 Ava: -> Mm-mh. Tch! I don't think so.
4 Bee:    °Oh,=<Did they geh ridda Kuhleznik yet hhh
5 Ava:    No in fact I know somebuddy who ha:s huh [now.
6 Bee:                                              [Oh my got hh[hhh
7 Ava:                                                           [Yeh
```

Conversely, one may wonder whether the practice of many parents and caregivers of acceding to children's requests only after a "thoughtful" delay may not be a device for generating an image of beneficence, for the delay projects an incipient rejection, after which a granting of the request may appear markedly generous.

It is perhaps worth making explicit that sequential organization can engender and support such vernacular characterological and affective readings, but that character traits and emotional states do not serve to exhaust or to "explain" features of sequential organization and practice such as the delay of dispreferred responses.

in the following extracts, featuring respectively an offer and an alternative invitation (in Extract [5.15], after Karen has declined Vicky's invitation to come and watch a television program at her place).

```
(5.14) NB IV:10, 41:17-21
1 Lot: F -> ↑Don't chu want me tih come dow:n getchu
2              dihmorr'en take yih dow:n dih the beauty parlor?
3          -> (0.3)
4 Emm: S -> What fo:r I ↑jis did my hair it looks like pruh-
5              a perfess↓ional.
```

```
(5.15) Erhardt, 1:26-28
1 Kar: F -> °Gee I feel like a real nerd°<you c'n ahl come up here,
2          -> (0.3)
3 Vic: S -> Nah, that's alright wil stay down he⌈re,
```

In each extract, the dispreferred response follows a noticeable gap after the first pair part.

2. *Turn-initial delay.* Once the response turn begins, the turn-initial position is occupied with other than the second pair part itself. Sometimes this position accommodates delays and their predecessors ("pre-pausals" such as "uh"), delaying the second pair part within the turn after the turn's beginning, in addition to – or instead of – delaying the beginning of the turn itself.

```
(5.16) TG, 15:15-16
1 Bee: F -> °hmhhh ˙hh So yih gonna be arou:n this weeken'¿
2 Ava: S -> Uh::m. (0.3) Possibly.
```

Or the turn's beginning may be constituted by hedges (e.g., "I dunno") or other discourse markers (e.g., "Well"), with or without ensuing (further) silence.

```
(5.17) TG, 19:30-32
1 Ava: F ->    [Well if you wan' me (to) give you a ring tomorrow
2              morning.
3 Bee: S -> Tch! ˙hhh We:ll y-you know, let's, eh- I don'know,
4              I'll see (h)may⌈be I won' even be in,⌉
```

However slight the interpolation may appear to be, its effect in displacing and deferring the second pair part, and thereby undermining a contiguous relationship to the first pair part, can serve to anticipate a dispreferred response, an anticipation which is is regularly realized in the more or less immediate aftermath.

3. *Anticipatory accounts, etc.* As noted earlier, dispreferred responses are commonly accompanied not only by such hedges as appear in Extract (5.17), but also by accounts, excuses, appreciations, etc. and such components regularly are positioned early in the turn, where they serve as well to delay

the second pair part itself and thereby (further) to break contiguity with the first pair part. In the earlier-examined Extract (5.05), reproduced below, A is asking her husband whether he will be coming to their "vacation home" at the beach for the weekend early:

```
(5.18) NB III:3 (Sacks 1987 [1973]:58) (previously [5.05])
1 A:   F -> Yuh comin down early?
2 B:   S -> Well, I got a lot of things to do before gettin
3            cleared up tomorrow. I don't know. I w- probably
4            won't be too early.
```

This dispreferred response is deferred to the end of the turn by a turn-initial marker ("well"), a hedge ("I don't know"), and an account ("I got a lot of things . . .").

Similarly, expressions of appreciation and regard for the first pair part about to be rejected, or its speaker, commonly precede, and thereby defer, the second pair part within its turn, breaking contiguity by coming between the first pair part and its second pair part.

```
(5.19) NB II:2, 12:18-29 (previously [5.09] in note 3)
 1 Emm: F ->     [Wanna c'm] do:wn 'av [a bah:ta] lu:nch w]ith me?=
 2 Nan:                             [°It's js] (       )°]
 3 Emm:          =Ah gut s'm beer'n stu:ff,
 4               (0.3)
 5 Nan: pre-S-> ↑Wul yer ril sweet hon: uh:m
 6               (.)
 7 Emm:          [Or d'y]ou'av] sup'n [else °(       )°
 8 Nan: S ->     [L e t-] I : ] hu.    [n:No: I haf to: uh call
 9         ->     Roul's mother, I told'er I:'d call'er this morning
10                I [gotta letter] from'er en.hhhhhh A:nd uhm
11 Emm:             [°(Uh huh.)°  ]
12                (1.0)
```

Here, the appreciation at line 5 not only defers the second pair part itself, but does so with a topically appropriate assessment term.

All of these practices singly and cumulatively can have the consequence of providing something other than the second pair part directly following the first pair part, where otherwise a preferred second pair part would have been produced or at least begun. Accordingly, such silences and non-second pair part turn-initial turn components (as well as other disruptions of contiguity not discussed here) can serve for co-participants as signals of upcoming dispreferred second pair parts. They get their sense as "pre-disagreements" – as projections of "–responses" – just by virtue of their use to disrupt contiguity.

4. *"Pro forma" agreements.* There is a potential complementarity between the early and contiguous placement of preferred responses and the delayed positioning of dispreferred responses which allows them to be

combined in a not-uncommon package of "agreement + disagreement."
Such turn formats constitute another contiguity-breaking practice.

In this practice it is an agreeing response which serves to delay the dispreferred one. The most common exemplar of this combination is the familiar
"yes, but . . ." In a format of this sort, the "real" (i.e., interactionally consequential) – dispreferred – second pair part gets done as an exception
or modification of an initial, apparently preferred, response – even such
emphatically preferred, agreeing responses as in the following extract, in
which A is asking B whether anything has been heard from the husband
who has deserted her:

```
(5.20) NB II 2 (Sacks 1987 [1973]: 63)
1 A: F -> 'N they haven't heard a word huh?
2 B: S -> Not a word, uh-uh. Not- not a word. Not at all.
3       -> Except- Neville's mother got a call . . .
```

Agreements – no matter how forceful – can thus be rendered equivocal
objects, serving not only as preferred responses but also as mere turn-initial
components which can intervene between first pair parts and dispreferred
second pair parts to get the latter positioned non-contiguously.

5. *Pre-emptive reformulation with preference reversal.* An additional feature of the organization of preferred and dispreferred responses relative to
first pair parts implicates practices employed by the *first* pair part speaker,
not the (potential) second pair part speaker. These practices contribute substantially to the interactional "density" of this sequential arena – after a first
pair part and before its second pair part.

The normative weight of the asymmetry of preferred and dispreferred
responses is properly borne by both (or all) of the participants, and not just
the recipient of the first pair part. It is misleading to understand a sequence's
development as the production by one speaker of a first pair part, and the
obligation of its recipient to produce a preferred response if possible, and
an account for a dispreferred response if it is not possible. Rather, it should
be understood as a joint project of both parties to arrive at a sequence –
an adjacency pair – whose parts are contiguous and in agreement, or in a
preferred relationship. Trouble in achieving this outcome can be addressed
by either (or any) party.

When trouble is evidenced by some form of pre-disagreement after a first
pair part – an overlong transition space, a turn-initial delay or account, etc. –
the harbinger of a problematic response can afford the first pair part speaker
an opportunity to change the first pair part to a form which will allow the
response which is apparently "in the works" to be delivered as a preferred
response, rather than a dispreferred one.

Consider, for example, the following exchange, in which A is asking B
about the quality of the food in a cooperative housing arrangement.

```
(5.21) Sacks 1987 [1973]:64
1 A: F ->      Good cook there
2              (0.?)
3 A: F_rev->   Nothin special
4 B: S_agree-> No, everybody takes their turn
```

At line 1, A offers a candidate assessment of the food, a first pair part which makes agreement or disagreement relevant next (cf. Pomerantz [1984], who, however, does not couch her discussion in adjacency pair terms). The developing silence at line 2, coming as it does where a preferred, agreeing response should already have begun, serves as a harbinger of a disagreement "in the works." One possible sequel, of course, is for the silence to develop up to a point, with the subsequent production by B of a dispreferred response, very likely with some account.

But what happens, in fact, is different. The first pair part speaker talks again, and in effect re-asks the question in reversed form. The negative answer, which would have been a disagreement with the first formulation of the assessment and was accordingly being delayed, can now be produced as an *agreement* with the revised formulation of the assessment. And, in fact, B responds to the revised first pair part with no delay, but after a normal transition space, and with the second pair part in turn-initial position, i.e., as a preferred response.

Yet another way in which the parties may tacitly collaborate in avoiding a sequence with a dispreferred response should alert us to the fact that not everything in interaction is done vocally (in which I include withholding vocalization, as in Extract [5.21]). In the following extract, Curt and Mike are at a summer picnic at Curt's house; they are discussing the automobile races that Mike had gone to the night before, and, at this point, the fellow who won the feature race – a fellow named "Al."

```
(5.22) Auto Discussion, 5:35-6:68
1 Cur:     [He- he's about the only regular <he's about the
2     ->   only good regular out there,'z Keegan still go out?
3 Mik:     Keegan's, (0.2) out there(,) (he's,) he run, (0.5)
4          e:r he's uh:: (0.3) doin real good this year'n
5          M'Gilton's doin real good this year, . . .
```

Although it is easy to overlook in the transcript, something very much like the story of the exchange we just examined is going on here, but it is signaled not by silent delay, but by a rush to talk further. At line 2 we can see that Curt has no sooner come to the possible end of his turn with the phrase "out there" than he rushes ahead to start a next unit of the turn – "[doe]'z Keegan still go out." And what he has maneuvered to be able to say is something contradictory to what he has just said – another good regular racer who is racing, in addition to Al. What is going on? As Curt was finishing that first unit in his turn with "out there," he sees Mike starting to shake his head laterally – a conventional head gesture for signifying disagreement. So here is another form of pre-disagreement, and we can see its effect – Curt tries to anticipate what Mike's disagreement is so as to avoid it – the preference for agreement. And, at least in the short run, he succeeds: Mike cuts short his disagreeing head shake and converts it into nodding, as he ratifies Curt's guess about another good regular, and the sequence ends up with a preferred second pair part. (For a full examination of this exchange, see Schegloff [1987].

So, not only can the prospect of a dispreferred response get addressed in pre-expansions before the first pair part is articulated at all, allowing that first pair part to be avoided or recast; the practices for building adjacency pair-based sequences provide the first pair part speaker other "escapes" from dispreferred trajectories, even after the first pair part has been produced. In a sense, then, both first pair part speaker and second pair part speaker have a role in the production of both the first pair part and the second pair part.

The bearing of these positioning practices for second pair parts, and of the delay of dispreferred second pair parts in particular, on *the greater aggregate frequency* of preferred second pair parts adds to a number of other factors contributing to this asymmetry.

(1) First, some first pair parts which might have elicited dispreferred responses will have not been delivered because a pre-expansion established the possibility that a preferred response might not be forthcoming.
(2) Second, as noted above, some responses get "shaped" in the direction of preferred second pair parts, in partial independence of the "facts," or other extra-sequence considerations, and may successfully be brought off as preferred, not dispreferred, second pair parts.
(3) Then, third, the practices for producing dispreferred second pair parts can provide multiple opportunities for derailing and pre-empting such responses, for either party to revise the sequence in ways that permit preferred responses to be given, even if they are given to rather different preceding talk than was in the first instance being responded to.

With all that, of course, there is no shortage of dispreferred responses in talk-in-interaction. Every social setting is a world full of diverse interests and positions and turf and stances, all being managed (among other ways) in talk-in-interaction, and these are not suppressed or dominated by the organization of preference/dispreference.

And yet such a preference organization *is* clearly operative. It *is* clearly oriented to by the parties in forming up their conduct both separately and interactively. It clearly serves as a vehicle through which initially ill-fitted positions, interests, etc. get mutually adjusted and even, on occasion, reconciled. And it clearly channels the forms which disagreement and mis-alignment take, even when they *cannot* be reconciled, and serves as a kind of metric for the seriousness which the parties wish to accord their misalignment.[6]

Multiple preferences

There is a further complication which requires introduction here if we are to be in a position to address the preference structure of most adjacency pair-based sequences. We have so far proceeded as if first pair part turns enacted only a single first pair part, but this is often not the case. What is at issue here is not turns with multiple turn-constructional units, each embodying a different first pair part (although that can also happen). The issue here is a different one.

Some types of first pair part can function doubly, both as actions in their own right and as vehicles or formats for other actions. For example, assessments are a type of turn which can constitute a first pair part, making agreement or disagreement relevant next, as in Extract (5.23) with agreement and Extract (5.24) with disagreement, respectively.

```
(5.23) JS II:28 (from Pomerantz, 1984:65)
1 Jim: ->    T's- tsuh beautiful day out isn't it?
2 Len: ->    Yeh it's jus' gorgeous . . .

(5.24) NB IV:11:1 (from Pomerantz, 1984:70)
1 Ali: ->    God izn it dreary
2            (0.6)
3 Ali:       [Y'know I don't think-
4 Bet: ->    [.hh It's warm though,
```

But assessments can also be the vehicle or format for such other actions as self-deprecations, as in Extract (5.25) (Pomerantz, 1984), or compliments, as in Extracts (5.26) and (5.27) (Pomerantz, 1978):

[6] For example, there can be a point in the development of a disagreement or conflict at which the practices described here as characteristic of doing dispreferred responses are abandoned, and parties begin to formulate their positions and stances in unmitigated and full-blooded forms, not delayed but prompt and even overlapping their interlocutor's talk. We can see in this a "graduation" from disagreement/conflict being reined in into full-fledged "arguing" or "fighting." And the activity of "arguing" or "fighting," as an activity in its own right, may have its own preferences and dispreferences. Yelling, interrupting, not modulating one's position, etc., can thus serve as an indication of the vehicle within which differences are to be worked through, and thereby potentially serve as an indicator of severity. We have, however, virtually no naturalistically grounded analyses of actual arguing of this sort, and the account in this note must be regarded as impressionistic and casual at best, and wrong at worst.

```
(5.25)    SBL-2-2-2-3R, 51 (from Pomerantz, 1984:85, retranscribed)
1 Chl: ->   En I n:ever was a gr(h)ea(h)t br(h)idge [play(h)er]=
2 Cla:                                              [ Y e :: h]
3 Chl:      =Cl(h)a [ heh? ]
4 Cla: ->   =,hhh   [Well I] think you've always been real good . . .

(5.26)    NB:5 (from Pomerantz, 1978:98)
1 Ann: ->   ...you've lost suh much weight
2 Pat: ->   Uhh hmhh uhh hmhh [well, not that much
3 Ann:                        [Aaghh Haghh haghh

(5.27)    WS:YMC, 4 (from Pomerantz, 1978:102)
1 Roz: ->      You're a good rower, Honey.
2 Joe: ->      These are very easy to row. Very light.
```

Each of these actions – whether self-deprecation or compliment – constitutes a distinct action aside from the assessment being done through the turn; each is in that respect a distinct first pair part, making its own set of second pair parts relevant next, with a set of issues not invoked by assessments per se.

Announcements, noticings, or, more generally, tellings can be first pair parts in their own right, making relevant a sharing of the noticing (as in Extract [5.28]), assessments of what has been told, and/or responses to its status as "tellable."

```
(5.28)    [C-J:12-13] (Chris and Jean are driving on the Freeway)
 1              (18.0)
 2 Jea: ->     There's MahCo:(hh)
 3              (1.3)
 4 Chr:        Where,
 5              (0.8)
 6 Jea:        There,
 7              (1.2)
 8 Chr:        Huh?      ((Said through a yawn))
 9              (0.2)
10 Jea:        Mah:ko: MayCo
11              (1.0)
12 Chr:        May Company?
13 Jea:        (yeah)
14 Chr: ->     Oh
15              (8.0)
```

But some tellings are the vehicle for other actions; "You're standing on my foot" is not meant only as a telling, it is a complaint; it wants more response than the news value and a sympathetic receipt; it wants a remedy.[7] Here is the beginning of an interaction mentioned earlier, at Extract (3.04), and taken up in greater detail, as Extract (7.45) at pp. 159–61 below.

```
(5.30)    SN-4, 5:01-15
 1                     ((door squeaks))
 2  She:         Hi Carol.=
 3  Car:         =H[i : .]
 4  Rut:           [CA:RO]L, HI::
 5  She:    Fb->  You didn' get en icecream sanwich,
 6  Car:    Sb1-> I kno:w, hh I decided that my body didn't need it,
 7  She:    ->    Yes but ours di:d=
 8  She:          =hh heh-heh-heh [heh-heh-heh [`hhih
 9  ???:                          [ehh heh heh [
10  (???):                                     [(        )
11  Car:    Sb2-> hh Awright gimme some money en you c'n treat me to
12                one an I'll buy you a:ll some [too.]
13  She:    ->                                 [I'm ] kidding, I don't
14                need it.
15                (0.3)
```

Although "You didn't get an ice cream sandwich" is surely doing a noticing, it is equally surely not doing a noticing alone. It is doing a complaint as well, and Carol, at lines 11–12 and in later parts of the sequence not shown here, has to deal with it as a complaint, and not only as a noticing, which is her initial response at line 6.

And questions may simply request information, but they may serve as the format for doing other actions as well. "Would you like a cup of coffee?" does not merely ask; it offers. And a response such as "Yes, thank you" addresses both the action and the format through which it was implemented.

---

[7] And different recipients may understand a first pair part differently and respond differently. In the following exchange, a British health visitor, charged with the supervision of first-time mothers and families, comments to the parents on the new infant's sucking on something:

```
(5.29) Drew and Heritage 1992b:33
1 HV: He's enjoying that [isn't he.
2 F:                     [°Yes, he certainly is=°
3 M:  =He's not hungry 'cuz (h)he's ju(h)st (h)had 'iz bo:ttle.hhh
4     (0.5)
5 HV: You're feeding him on (.) Cow and Gate Premium.=
```

The health visitor's (HV) utterance at line 1 can be taken as a simple "noticing," for which the father's (F) somewhat upgraded agreement is an appropriate, preferred response. The mother's (M) response, however, displays that she hears something else. As Drew and Heritage remark, "In replying that way, she treats the health visitor's remark as implying that the baby is 'enjoying' whatever he's sucking or chewing because he might be hungry – an implication which she rebuts with the account that the baby has just been fed. The mother's response is, then, a *defence* against something which she treats as implied in the health visitor's remark" (1992b: 33). She hears the noticing to be a vehicle for a possible critique, which makes relevant quite a different set of responses than a noticing per se does.

The "yes" answers the question; the "thank you" responds to the offer. And such "double-barreled" first pair part utterances commonly have both their "barrels" responded to, and regularly in that order: first the format or vehicle, then the action implemented through it. Consider, for example, the following offer sequence:

```
(5.31)   Davidson, 1984:127
1  Ali:  You wan' me bring you anything?
2        (0.4)
3  Bet:  No: no: nothing.
4  Ali:  AW:kay.
```

Alice's turn at line 1 is a question of the type that makes a "yes" or "no" answer relevant next, but it also serves to implement an offer, which makes "acceptance" or "rejection" relevant next; furthermore, in the construction of the question, it has been designed for a "yes" answer (as compared to the possible alternative design, "you don't want me to bring you anything, do you?"). So both in terms of the design of the turn, and in terms of what will forward the course of action which the turn initiates, an accepting response is preferred. Note, then, that the SPP turn at line 3 has an answer to the question first ("no"), followed by a response to the offer ("nothing"), both of them delivered after a delay of 0.4 second, as befits the production of a dispreferred SPP.

Once we appreciate that more than one adjacency pair may be set in progress at the same time by the same turn-constructional unit,[8] we are alerted to the fact that more than one preference structure may be involved – one activated by the formatting first pair part, and one by some other action which it is carrying. And these two preference structures may be congruent or cross-cutting.

In congruent preference structures, the same response which is preferred in one is preferred in the other, as with "yes, thank you" in response to "Would you like a cup of coffee," or the "No no nothing" in Extract (5.31). They are an agreement with the "yes/no" question and an acceptance of the offer (or invitation), or a disagreement and rejection to both. When the preference structures are congruent, delivering the second pair part is (in this regard, at least) uncomplicated. If the second pair part to be delivered is preferred, it should be done contiguously, simply, etc.; if dispreferred, then delayed, with an account, etc.

But what if there are cross-cutting preferences? What if the response which is the preferred second pair part for one aspect of the first pair part

---

[8] It may turn out that many more action types can serve as the vehicle for other actions done through them, and not just the assessments, tellings, and questions discussed here, but it will take further investigation to determine this.

turn is dispreferred for the other?[9] Which practice or set of practices for responding should – or does – the responder employ? Consider the following episode, in which two older women who are sisters are talking. B has recently had an operation on her toe, and A is inviting her to join in an expedition to the local shopping mall and the hairdresser.

```
(5.32)      Sacks 1987 [1973]:64
1 A:    F ->     Can you walk?
2                (0.4)
3 A:    Frev->   W'd be too hard for yuh?
4 B:    Sagree-> Oh darling, I don't know. Uh it's bleeding a little,
5                'e j's took the bandage off yes'day.
```

An invitation to, or offer of, an outing is in prospect here, and the question at line 1 is its pre-invitation or pre-offer. The preference structures activated by the utterance at line 1 appear congruent: an affirmative reply would constitute both an agreeing answer to the "yes/no" question and a go-ahead response to the pre-invitation. The silence which follows at line 2 gives evidence that an affirmative response is not forthcoming. A here reacts as did A in Extract (5.21): she revises the first pair part with reversed preference structure, but the result is complex. The new version of the utterance at line 3 presents two first pair parts with cross-cutting preferences. It is the question which has had the preferences reversed. The delay in responding to "Can you walk?" adumbrates a negative response; "W'd be too hard for you?" allows that response to be done as an agreement. However, that agreement with "be too hard" would also constitute a dispreferred response to the pre-invitation – a blocking response to actually issuing it, adumbrating a rejection of it were it actually tendered.

Note, then, how the response is constructed. The actual response to the revised question is attenuated to the point of invisibility; B never actually says it would be too hard. Instead, she hedges, and gives accounts for not going. She does all of this directly on completion of the first pair part's revision with no further delay in the onset of a responding turn, but what is in the turn is thoroughly characteristic of a dispreferred response. It is, then, the preference structure of *the action being implemented* which dominates

---

[9] A transparent exemplar from the mass media involves a quiz show contestant in the following exchange with the host: (17 December 1994):

```
C:   Do you mind if I ask a question.
H:   Yes.
C:   Oh you do mind.
     ((Laughter))
```

Here the question as question and the question as request for permission and as pre-request have cross-cutting preferences. The "yes" is meant to be a go-ahead to the pre-request – it is "positive." But, taken as an answer to the question, it amounts to a blocking response. Making explicit that – clearly unintended – analysis is the intentional misunderstanding which constitutes "a joke," and which draws the laugh.

here and shapes the construction of the second pair part turn, not that of the action's vehicle, which at most is expressed in the contiguous startup of the responding turn (cf. Pomerantz [1978] for a related line of analysis).[10]

Type conformity

As it happens, Extracts (5.31) and (5.32) allow us to introduce yet another set of contingencies and constraints, in addition to those already mentioned – promoting the course of action and the design features of the FPP. This additional consideration has to do specifically with FPPs that are formatted as questions, and, even more specifically, ones which are formatted as so-called "yes/no" questions. Because what is at issue here turns on the grammatical character of such turns, we will adopt the more grammatical name for them – "yes/no interrogatives" (in keeping with the usage of Raymond [2000, 2003], on whose work this account is based). Questions (or interrogatives) as first pair parts make "answers" the relevant second pair part. Some types of question further specify what should occur in answering second pair part; these are the "wh-interrogatives," so called for the words that ordinarily begin them – "who," where," etc. Questions that begin with (or include) "who" make a person reference relevant as the answer; "where"-interrogatives make a place reference relevant in their answer; "when"-interrogatives make a time reference relevant; "how long"-interrogatives make a duration answer relevant, and so on. These are type-specifying questions; they make relevant not any form of answer, but specific *types* of answer. When a response delivers the type of answer the question made relevant, it is "type-conforming"; if the response is an answer, but the answer is not fitted to the type made relevant by the question, it is "non-conforming" (Raymond, 2003:946).

"Yes/no interrogatives" are even more constraining; they specify that the answer they make relevant be expressed in either of two words: "yes" or "no" (or equivalent tokens such as "yeah," "uh huh,"etc. on the one hand

---

[10] Some readers will recognize in this discussion of action and format or vehicle a different take on so-called "direct and indirect speech acts" as treated in linguistic and philosophical pragmatics (e.g., Searle, 1969, 1975). For those unfamiliar with this literature, it is concerned with understanding how utterances such as "Do you know who's going to that meeting?" (Schegloff, 1988c:55–60) or "Can you reach that book?" (Levinson, 1983:357ff.) can come to be understood as requests for information or services respectively, when they literally appear to request information concerning states of knowledge or physical capacity. Levinson (1980, 1981, 1983:226–83) offers a cogent critique of "speech act theory" within the terms of a general pragmatics, and one form of an alternative to it prompted by his account of conversation analysis (1983:356–64), albeit one focused on indirect requests. For other critiques grounded in conversation analysis, see Schegloff (1988c, 1992a:xxiv–xxvii, 1992c). The line sketched in the present text suggests a different kind of resource, which provides for a variety of combinations of actions and the formats through which they are realized, with some evidence that these discriminatable facets of an utterance-in-its-sequence are oriented to as such by the participants.

or "nuh-uh," "nope," etc. on the other), and it is this type of FPP that is the focus of the following paragraphs. It turns out that both preferred and dispreferred second pair parts can be delivered either in a type-conforming format (that is, one which has a "yes" or a "no" or some variant of these in it) or in a non-conforming format (that is, one which does not include a "yes" or "no" or variant, even though it is aligning or disaligning relative to the first pair part). In other words, this is a feature of responses to "yes/no" interrogatives (and whatever other action may be implemented through them) that is independent of whether the response is preferred or dispreferred in the terms we have previously examined. But does this matter or is it an artifact of random distribution? Is it attended to by the participants? Is a speaker of a second pair part doing something distinctive by designing the second pair part in a type-conforming or non-conforming way? And does the recipient understand these differently? Can it really be a matter of using or not using these particular words? Yes it can.

Raymond (2003) shows that the same considerations that underwrite our understanding of preferred and dispreferred second pair parts as presented elsewhere in these pages will underwrite the same understanding of type-conformity, namely: there is a preference for type-conforming over non-conforming answers to "yes/no" interrogatives, and it is evidenced by: the substantially greater commonality of type-conforming responses; the default form of type-conforming answers as compared to non-conforming ones[11]; and the different consequences of the two forms. As the evidence summarized by these points cannot be presented here (see Raymond, 2003), our discussion will be limited to a brief display of how the difference between type-conforming and non-conforming answers to "yes/no" interrogatives shows itself.

In Extract (5.33), Gerri is asking Shirley about a woman dying of cancer.

```
(5.33)  Gerri and Shirley (from Raymond, 2003:946)
1   Shi:      ...she fee:ls ez though,.hh yihkno:w her mother is in:
2             such agony now that w'd only make it worse.=
3   Ger: ->   =.hh Wul will the remaining three yea:rs uhm see her in
4             pai:n
5   Shi: ->   .hhh She already is in a great deal of pain.
6             (0.7)
7   Shi:      C 'she has the chemotherapy the radiation.
```

The action at lines 3–4 is a request for information; the question is in a format that takes a "yes" or "no," and, in keeping with the general preference for

---

[11] Raymond writes (2003:949), "in type-conforming responses, a speaker's stance toward the course of action initiated by a FPP is stated simply and straightforwardly (e.g., through a 'yes' or 'no,' which may be subsequently elaborated), while nonconforming responses specifically depart from the constraints embodied in the grammatical form of the FPP to produce an action not contemplated by it."

agreement, prefers a "yes." And Shirley does, in fact, confirm the possibility raised by Gerri's question, but she does not do so in a type-conforming way; there is no "yes," even if she is doing a confirmation. In effect, Shirley declines to buy into the possible presupposition that pain is a matter for the future, which a simple "yes" might be taken to subscribe to. Instead, she contests that possible understanding while nonetheless affirming the overt issue posed by the question.

In Extract (5.34), we can see more overtly displayed how type-conforming and non-conforming are engaged with such possibilities.

```
(5.34)    SF 2 (from Raymond, 2003:949)
 1 Mar:     .hhhh Oh::. ((Vl))hhhhmhhhh Wudje talk about.hh
 2 Bob:    Oh I don't remember no[:w,
 3 Mar:                          [.hhhhhhh=
 4 Bob:    =.hh hhheh=heh=[heh
 5 Mar: ->               [W'l dih you talk aboutcher future?hh
 6         (0.2)
 7 Bob: -> No:. [Nothing so intricate.h
 8 Mar:        [Oh
 9 ???:     .Hhhhhhh
10 Mar:    Oh [(it-)
11 Bob: ->    [En what future.
12 Mar:    Jis surface.
```

In this conversation between two young men, the talk has turned to a lengthy conversation Bob had with a mutual friend, Joan, and Mark is exploring the possibility of a budding romantic relationship. This is what clearly underlies his question at line 5, to which Bob replies with a type-conforming SPP. In other words, he is doing here just what Shirley declined to do in the exchange in Extract (5.33). And here we can see the consequences. If Shirley's non-conforming answer resisted buying into the premises of the question to which she was replying, then Bob's type-conforming answer does just that – to his almost immediate regret, for he finds himself having attested to there being a "future" for them, an attestation which he tries to retract at line 11, but surely to mixed success at best.

The upshot of the discussion so far in this section is that sequences whose FPP is in a turn formatted by a "yes/no" interrogative are informed by another order of organization in addition to those we have explicated for adjacency pairs more generally. This additional organization also has a preference structure – one which prefers type-conforming answers to non-conforming ones, with non-conforming ones commonly engendering sequential consequences, even if the action performed by the second pair part is a preferred one which would otherwise not engender such consequences. This is a contingency which the parties must address in real time;

for analysts it presents another order of possibilities which require attention in examining a stretch of talk.

Summary remarks on preferred and dispreferred second pair parts

There is, then, a pervasive orientation by participants to the asymmetry of types of response to a first pair part, an orientation with implications for the conduct of *both speakers and recipients* of first pair parts, as we have seen.

In that light, we should appreciate that pre-sequences or pre-expansions are measures undertaken by the *speaker* – or the *prospective* speaker – of a base first pair part to maximize the occurrence of a sequence with a preferred second pair part.

In a similar vein, we can approach insert expansions or insert sequences as measures initiated by the *recipient* of a first pair part – i.e., by the *prospective second pair part speaker* – to get a sequence whose parts are in a preferred relationship. As we will see, insert sequences are not exclusively directed at preference issues (just as *pre*-sequences are not), but such issues are commonly involved.

Before turning to examine insert expansion, however, there is another aspect of preference organization that requires some discussion, and which also implicates in the first instance the (prospective) speaker of a first pair part.

Preferred and dispreferred first pair parts

Early in this discussion of preference and dispreference, we were at pains to distinguish the personal "preferences" or wishes of the participants on some particular occasion from the usage of the term "preference" which invokes interaction-structural features of the organization of the sequence and practices for its implementation. On the one hand there are recurrent compositional features (what sorts of parts compose the responses) and positional practices (that is, where the responses and their parts are placed) of the way responses are implemented that differ systematically and are formulated by the terms "preferred" and "dispreferred." On the other hand, these different types stand differently to the "project" or "activity" which the sequence appears designed to implement.

These two sorts of features – relationship to an underlying project or activity and the positioning and composition of the talk – also appear to organize some alternative sets of *first pair parts*. In doing so, they structure asymmetrically alternative sequence types as ways of achieving some interactional project or outcome.

We will briefly examine three such pairs of sequence types. In accomplishing the transfer of something of value – whether object, service, or information – from one person to another, there appears to be a preference for offer sequences over request sequences. In achieving the official and explicit registering of some feature of the environment of the interaction affiliated to or identified with one of the participants – and "positively valued" features in particular – there appears to be a preference for noticing-by-others over announcement-by-"self" (where "self" is the one characterized by the feature). At the opening (potential or in process) of an interaction, there appears to be a preference for a party to be recognized (if possible or relevant) over self-identification.[12] In the case of each pair, there are different routes to a common outcome – the transfer of a value from one person to another, the incorporation of an explicit registering of something affiliated to or identified with one of the participants in interaction, the achieved identification of a party – or incipient party – to the interaction. Our discussion will be limited to several points.

First, the alternative sequence types are properly initiated by – and their respective first pair parts are properly done by – different parties. Unlike alternative second pair parts which, however collaboratively arrived at, finally are selected between for articulation by a single person/party – the recipient of the first pair part – the alternatives in these contrasting pair types involve action by different persons: offering by one who has the valued transferable rather than requesting by its potential recipient; noticing by a co-participant rather than announcing by the one whose feature is at issue; registering that someone has been recognized rather than that person – on their own initiative – identifying themselves.

Second, the preference structure requires action by one who may not be aware that such a project is even relevant. There are differences of awareness and of relevant participation capacity here that are quite unlike – in some respects – those which characterize asymmetrical *second* pair parts.

Third, like alternative second pair parts, one way in which dispreference is realized is through delay and other constraints on enactment. This point is, in the nature of the case, difficult to demonstrate, for if a dispreferred first pair part is delayed in potential favor of the preferred alternative, it may turn out to have been withheld altogether, if the preferred sequence type is not initiated by the other (or another) participant.[13] In the case of being recognized

---

[12] The last of these could be treated as a kind of special case of the preference for noticing-by-other over announcement-by-self.

[13] It may be difficult but it is not impossible. A look back at Extract (5.06) on p. 64 may remind the reader of the SPP that was mitigated to the point of invisibility. But notice now that the FPP – at least the request that is being brought off in it – is also mitigated

and self-identification, the whole interaction may not materialize, as one prospective participant awaits being recognized by another, and withholds interactional participation until it is forthcoming, which it may never be.

Still, there is potential distributional evidence that such first pair part preference structures issue in (at least temporary) withholdings of the dispreferred first pair parts. For example,

- Requests appear disproportionately to occur late in conversations, as late topics or even as ostensible afterthoughts, i.e., done after the initiation of the conversation's closing, and seem especially problematic and unlikely to occur in first topic position. For example, some phone calls which appear (in retrospect upon their completion) to have been made specifically to do a request may have several topics raised, and other sequences worked through, before the request is articulated.

- Requests are regularly accompanied by accounts, mitigations, candidate "excuses" for the recipient, etc. which are done in advance of the request itself, i.e., which defer requests within their turns, and may expand to defer the turn in which the request is made, if it is made at all.[14] These are all familiar trappings of dispreferred *second* pair parts. As with dispreferred second pair parts, they may be attenuated to the point of actual non-articulation, as in Extract (4.18) above (at lines 5–6), or Extract (5.06), where the first pair part speaker never actually articulates what he is after.

- As with other "sensitive" or "delicate" conversational practices or actions, the occurrence of one may "license" the occurrence of others. And so one may find requests occurring as actual or virtual reciprocals (see Chapter 10, on Sequences of sequences); that is, after one has been

and circumlocuted to the point of invisibility. So here is a conversation constituted almost entirely by a dispreferred request FPP and a dispreferred rejection SPP, each mitigated to virtually virtual status. This sequence is taken up in detail in Schegloff (1995, 1996b).

[14] For example, in the following exchange such an account accompanies a request by one family member to another for what Goffman (1963) called a "free good," the sort of request object (like directions or the time of day) which strangers are entitled to make of strangers without account.

```
(5.35) Post-Party, 2:27-29
1 Ann:   Marty she took my ma:tches [ k  i   n   I ] have a match,
2 Fre:                              [(door locked)?]
3 Mar:   Su:re, hmhh
```

The request here comes packaged with an account (and one which deflects responsibility for the "need" onto another) which precedes the request itself. Of course, not all requests are accompanied by accounts, and not all actions which are on occasion accompanied by accounts are thereby shown to be structurally dispreferred. Here the recurrent provision of accounts with requests is one of a constellation of features pointing to its relatively dispreferred status.

done by A to B (and is complied with), another is done by B to A[15] –
and a request often appears to have been recognizably withheld until it
could be done in such an "accommodating" or "exchange" position.

- One evidence of the treatment of requests as dispreferred is the
  masking of them as other actions – often as ostensible offers, as in
  Extract (5.38).

```
(5.38)    SBL 1,1,1
 1 Bet:        And uh because I'm s'pposed to be hostess Sunday,
 2 Ali: Fpre->  Oh uh didju want relief on that.
 3 Bet: Spre->  Well I don't know, there's nobody else down with me,
 4             I spoke to uhm
 5 Ali: Fb ->   Well, I'll- I can help you,
 6 Bet: preSb-> Uh well, I probably it's only between twelve and twelve
 7             thir[ty,
 8 Ali: Fb->        [Yes, so that's r- I can help at that time,
 9 Bet: preSb-> Uh because uhm I think what's her name? uhm (0.4)
10 Ali:        Oh
```

[15] For example, the following exchange occurs as two roommates are moving to settle down
for a spell in the living room:

```
(5.36) N & J, 1
 1 Jul: ->  Shut the drapes, will ya Nan?
 2 Nan: ->  'Nkay. Willya get the iced tea ('n pass it to me¿).
 3          (1.0)
 4 Jul:     Where is it?
 5          (0.5)
 6 Nan:     On the floor.
 7          (0.8)
 8 Jul:     Oh:
```

And in the following exchange, Dad is just asking nine-year-old daughter Cindy about her
day as they begin to have dinner.

```
(5.37) Stew Dinner, 3:11-30
 1 Dad:     So Ci:n (0.2) tell me about your day.
 2          (0.5)
 3 Cin:     Uh::_ .h
 4 Dad:     Wha'd=ju (d) learn.
 5          (1.0)
 6 Dad:     [O:^::H yeah (we) went to thuh- we went to uh: (.)
 7 Cin:     [Uh:m-
 8 Cin:     Claim Jumper.
 9 Dad:     Claim Jum[per today.
10 Mom:              [(>uh huh<)
11 Mom: ->  May I have a roll [please,
12 Cin:                       [For a field trip.=
13 Dad: ->  =Sure.
14 Dad: ->  An' may I have thuh -butter please.
15 Mom: ->  Yes.=hh
16          (0.5)
17 Cin:     Went to Claim Jumper for (our)/(uh) fie:ld trip.
18 Dad:     Yiea:h, an'- an'- tell me about it.
19          (0.5)
```

```
11                    (0.2)
12 Bet:               that's on in the morning?
13                    (0.2)
14 Ali:               Sue?
15 Bet:               Uh Sue Brown, I-she usually stays till eleven.
16 Ali:               Yeah, mm hm,
17 Bet: Sb->          Uh and uh so uhm but I think uh that it will work out
18                    alright, uh well, I don't know, I (thought) I would
19                    call Maryanne, I thought I'd let her call me, because
20                    (she hadda) day yesterday. [And-
21 Ali: Fb->                                     [Well if you- If you want
22                    help Sunday, I'll do it.
```

Betsy and Alice are talking about a "staffing problem" for an activity organized by a group of which they are both members. Alice's pre-offer (at line
2) appears to get some encouragement from Betsy's response (at lines 3–4),
with its possible complaint about the lack of support and incipient report
of seeking out such support. Alice's "offer" (at line 5), however, is met
with by-now-familiar evidences of a dispreferred response in the works,
in its turn-initial delays, in an account which mitigates the need for what
is being offered and puts strict constraints on the qualifications for such
help. In the face of all this, Alice reaffirms the offer (line 8). Again, the
response is packed full of pre-disagreements, including substantial defer-
rals of response, a virtual claim of no need (lines 17–18, "will work out
alright"), and even direct nomination of alternative sources of help (lines
18–20). When, in the face of all this, Alice once again renews her "offer,"
the possibility is raised that there is a request to be allowed to help at work
here, a request masquerading as an offer.

Sometimes such a masquerade is penetrated and the apparent offer is
overtly exposed as a request after all.

```
(5.39)  NB IV:10, 41:17-35 (previously [5.14])
 1 Lot: Foff1->  ↑Don't chu want me tih come dow:n getchu
 2               dihmorr'en take yih dow:n dih the beauty parlor?
 3               (0.3)
 4 Emm: Srej1->  What fo:r I ↑jis did my hair it looks like pruh-
 5               a perfess↓ional.
 6               (0.3)
 7 Lot: Foff2->  ↑I mean uh: you wanna go 'd the store er anything over
 8               et the Market[Ba:sket]er an]ything?]
 9 Emm:                       [.hmhhh ].thhh].hhh .h]h=
10      prerej-> =W'l ↑HO[NEY]AH]
11 Lot: Foff3->         [or ]Ri]chard's?
12               (0.2)
13 Emm: Srej ->  I've bou↑:ghtEVrythai:ng?
14               (0.9)
```

```
15 Emm: F_off -> If[you wa]nt ↑ME TIH go 't the beaudy pahler ah wi:ll,
16 Lot:        [°Oh:.°]
17             (.)
18 Lot: S_acc -> ↑W'l I jus thought mayb we g'd gover duh Richard's
19             fer lunch then after uh get muh hair ↓fixed.
20 Emm:        Awri:ght.
21 Lot:        Oka:y,
```

Here two late middle-aged sisters are talking, and "offers" at lines 1–2 and 7–8 are rejected at lines 4–5 and 9–10 and 13 respectively, with the incipient rejection at lines 9–10 prompting yet a further pursuit of the "offer" at line 11. Finally, Emma unmasks the offers (couched as "you wanna"s) by offering in turn, "If you want me to go to the beauty parlor I will" (line 15), revealing an understanding of the putative offers as masking requests.

There are, then, various clues to suggest that requests are dispreferred practices as compared to offers.[16] We will focus here, however, on another, already familiar characteristic of dispreferred options – the provision of enhanced opportunities to maximize the achievement of preferred alternatives.

The most overt such occurrences (of which, as it happens, no taped instances are at hand) may be familiar from occasions on which someone has a new article of clothing, a new hairstyle, a new object in, or arrangement of, living quarters, etc., which is not registered by an interactional co-participant. The bearer/owner of "the noticeable" may register the failure to notice quite early in the interaction, for ordinarily such a noticing should be done at first opportunity, which generally means after initial perceptual exposure (more on this in the volume on the overall structural

---

[16] Not infrequently these may be exploited together. See, for example, Extract (4.18), reproduced below.

```
(5.40) ST (Schegloff, 1980:112)
1 Fre:  Oh by the way ((sniff)) I have a bi:g favor to ask ya.
2 Lau:  Sure, go'head.
3 Fre:  'Member the blouse you made a couple weeks ago?
4 Lau:  Ya.
5 Fre:  Well I want to wear it this weekend to Vegas but my mom's
6       buttonholer is broken.
7 Lau:  Fred I told ya when I made the blouse I'd do the buttonholes.
8 Fre:  Ya ((sniff)) but I hate ta impose.
9 Lau:  No problem. We can do them on Monday after work.
```

In deferring the request itself with a pre-pre and its preliminaries, an orientation is displayed to its dispreferred status. Note as well that this request is "snuck in" to a conversation initiated by the requestee, in which the requestee had made a request for information. The characterization "snuck in" is warranted by the request being introduced with "by the way," a "misplacement marker" (Schegloff and Sacks, 1973) – that is, marked as occurring out of place – in a fashion which exploits the possibility of placing the request after its addressee has made a request. Note finally that this "request" is attenuated to the point of disappearance; although his need and the impossibility of doing the job himself are articulated, the requester never actually says what he is after and that he is requesting it.

organization of single conversations). In the absence of a noticing, and as a pre-alternative to announcing or pointing out the noticeable, the bearer may ask, "Do you see anything different?" Such a tack yet again embodies the preference for noticing over telling by using the turn in which telling ("calling attention to") might have been done instead to overtly solicit noticing by making it relevant with a riddle. In a fashion, such a move addresses the earlier-noted problem that the first pair part preference structure requires action by one who may not be aware that such a project is even relevant. The "riddle" question makes it relevant, while still allowing at least elements of the preference for noticing – "prompted noticing," as it were.[17]

[17] Many of the observations and findings touched on in this section (as in this chapter and in this book as a whole) have reverberating consequences – some of them quite substantial – for much else in interaction and in the social fabric woven from it. Most of these consequences cannot be taken up in this book, which is designed to offer an "internalist" account; that is, one concerned to explicate the internal organization of the practices of talk-in-interaction. That task itself strains the binding of this volume. But it is worth briefly exploring occasional "reverberations," if only to recall recurrently that talk-in-interaction is the hub of a wheel of social practices which radiate out from it and are interrelated. Consider, then, some possible consequences of an orientation to the preference for noticing over announcing.

We need first of all to distinguish explicitly between that usage of "noticing" which is taken to refer a perceptual/cognitive event, and noticing which intends an interactional event. And within the latter category we need to distinguish between a noticing implemented by an utterance (the usage tacitly employed in this text until now) and one implemented body-behaviorally – by staring, doing a "take," averting one's eyes, smiling, sharing a mutual glance with a companion, etc.

These usages invoke partially independent types of occurrences. The initial common understanding might be that an interactional noticing can only follow a perceptual/cognitive one, but, of course, one can say, "Isn't that a new X?" when one "knows" it is not; an interactional noticing need not be engendered by a perceptual/cognitive one. And many (perhaps most) perceptual/cognitive noticings do not get articulated interactionally at all. But one key normative trajectory is an interactional noticing presented as occasioned by a perceptual/cognitive one.

If parties to interaction orient to the preference for noticing – or, rather, getting something noticed – over announcing it, then they may compose themselves and/or their environment to enhance the possibility of "noticing" by others. That is, they may organize their conduct to introduce into "situations" (Goffman, 1964) materials which can be treated as "noticeables."

Registering that possibility can lead us to make explicit that there are vernacular cultural canons for "noticeability" and practices for "registering noticeables" – canons and practices for both perceptual and interactional noticing. Further, that the canons and practices of interactional noticing ought to be (and can be held responsible for being) recipient-designed, and, if they fail in this regard, can have the noticing be found "picky," or "cheeky," or "unwarranted," or "bizarre," etc.

The upshot is that when one party to an interaction "notices" something – that is, articulates a noticing (e.g., "y'sound happy," "hey, the place looks different," "you're back," etc.) – something more may be involved than a docile, dormant world which "just happened to be there like that" and was noticed. Effort is likely to have been invested in having it "naturally" be like that, effort designed by reference to canons and practices for noticing (and for getting things into the world by having them noticed rather than by announcing them), as anyone who has (been) courted, or sought a job, or hosted a guest (or been one) at home, or gotten dressed in the morning – or in the evening – may very well know. Intonation contours may be used to convey – to embody – well-being or excitement or despair rather than utterances being used to announce "I'm great" or "I'm awful," at least

The preference for recognition over self-identification can be exemplified in the opening of telephone conversations.[18] On the one hand, callers may embody and impose a requirement of recognition on answerers by providing in their first turn a minimal voice sample articulating a greeting, the return to which is taken to convey – and thereby claim – reciprocal recognition, as in exchanges like the following:

```
(5.41)   TG, 1:01-04
1 Ava:       H'llo:?
2 Bee: F ->  hHi:,
3 Ava: S ->  Hi:?
4 Bee:       hHowuh you:?
```

A number of other types of first turn by caller accomplish closely related outcomes, but this is the clearest and "purest," i.e., doing little else. On the other hand, callers may, in their first turn, also identify themselves:[19]

```
(5.43)   Schegloff, 1979:31
1 Ric:        Hello,
2 Mar: ->     Hey:: R:i:ck, thisiz Mark,=is Bill in?
```

```
(5.44) MDE: Stalled, 1:2-06 (previously part of [5.06])
1 Mar:   Hello?
2 Don: ->   'lo Marcia,=[('t's) D]onny.
3 Mar:               [Y e a: h]
4 Mar:   Hi Donny.
5 Don:   Guess what.hh
6 Mar:   What.
7 Don:   'hh My ca:r is sta::lled.
```

in part by reference to the preference for noticing over announcement (for an empirical exemplar, see the discussion of Extract (7.39) at pp. 152–53 and footnote 18 of Chapter 7). And so also with a vast range of deployments of demeanor, of dress, of possessions and surroundings, of comings and goings, of presence and absence, etc.

Here I have been able only to hint at such ranges of conduct which appear at least partially sensitive to, and oriented to, conversational practices. I have invoked the reader's experience in the most vernacular terms. This is no proof, nor even evidence. It is meant only to stimulate reflection on, and perhaps even inquiry into, the range of other aspects of the organization of conduct whose understanding may be deepened by seeing their connection to practices of talk-in-interaction.

[18] I am dealing with telephone conversations in the United States. There is some disagreement about the extent to which many of the same processes hold for other cultural settings, even ones which apparently differ (as in cultures where even "private" phones are answered with self-identification); see Schegloff (1968, 1979, 1986, 2002a [1970], 2002b, 2004a [1970]), Hopper and Koleilat-Doany (1989), Hopper *et al.*, (1990/91), Houtkoop-Steenstra (1991), Lindström (1994) and Park (2002).

[19] By this I mean "serious" self-identification, which adds identificatory resources to those presumably available from the voice alone, rather than such playful gambits as the following:

```
(5.42) Schegloff, 1979:31
1 Mar:    Hello?=
2 Gin: ->  =Hello it's me.
```

Unlike the solicitation of recognition, self-identification (by a caller who is recognizable to the answerer of the phone) is uncommon, and rarely comprises all of the caller's first turn. With great frequency it occurs when the answerer is not the targeted recipient of the call, and is about to be confronted with a "switchboard request," as in Extract (5.43), or as a "compression device" – that is, a display of compressing into one turn what might otherwise occupy two; an indication that matters of some urgency are to be taken up, as in Extract (5.44). In these cases, the issue of recognition/self-identification as a matter of moment in its own right is foreclosed, and the opportunity for "being recognized" is pre-empted.

However, when the entitled claims of recognizability by caller are not sufficiently strong to permit a simple greeting, and are not to be foreclosed altogether, the preference for recognition over self-identification is embodied in a somewhat expanded sequence, in which the caller first displays recognition of the answerer by articulating their name, with or without a greeting, in intonation contours ranging from declarative downward to "questioning" upward. If the answerer does no more than confirm that they are the person named, then the caller may proceed to self-identification, as in the following:

```
(5.45) Schegloff, 1979:54
1 Cat:        Hello?
2 Sta:   ->  Hi. Cathy?
3 Cat:   ->  Yeah?
4 Sta:   ->  Stanley.
5 Cat:        Hi Stan

(5.46) Schegloff, 1979:54
1 Lau:        H'llo:
2 Pam:   ->  Laura?
3 Lau:   ->  Yeah,
4 Pam:   ->  This is Pam.
5 Lau:        Hi.

(5.47) Schegloff, 1979:54
1 Mar:        Hello.
2 Ber:   ->  Hello, Mary?
3 Mar:   ->  Yes?
4 Ber:   ->  Hi. This is Bernie Hunter.
5 Mar:        Oh hello:. How are you.
```

However, the pre-expansion of this self-identification provides an opportunity for the realization of the preference for recognition over self-identification, as in the following instances:

```
(5.48) Schegloff, 1979:51
1 Con:        Hello.
2 Joa: ->    Connie?
3 Con: ->    Yeah Joanie
```

```
(5.49) Schegloff, 1979:52
1 Ils:        Hello:.
2 Bet: ->     H'llo Ilse?
3 Ils: ->     Yes. Be:tty.

(5.50) Schegloff, 1979:52
1 Don:        [Hello?]
2 Jim:        [Hello,]
3 Jim: ->     H'llo, Donna?
4 Don: ->     Oh, yeah. Hi Jim,
```

The overwhelmingly greater deployment of this resource as compared to straightforward self-identification (which is less "chancy" in not allowing an opportunity for *failure*-to-recognize, and whose greater "sequential efficiency" is exemplified by its adoption to show urgency) displays an orientation to the preference for being recognized over self-identification and provides the sequential resource for its achievement-if-possible. (A fuller discussion, with a range of variation in how such sequences run off, may be found in Schegloff [1979].)

There is a respect in which pre-expansions for dispreferred (or *less* preferred) sequence types differ from those discussed earlier. In the pre-sequences discussed earlier, the preferred response to the pre-sequence first pair part – pre-invitation, pre-offer, pre-announcement – was the go-ahead. Where it was relevant or possible, as in pre-announcement sequences, the pre-emptive response was *dispreferred*; it subverted achievement of the project of telling news.

In pre-expansions of dispreferred sequences (i.e., sequences with dispreferred first pair parts), however, pre-emptive responses are the *preferred* ones. It is the *pre-emption* of the need to self-identify which is the pay-off of the pre-expansion; for the answerer to merely confirm their identity and forward the sequence to its base first pair part of self-identification would not be optimally responsive to the preference structure involved. This can be seen even more clearly with the way pre-requests appear to figure in working out the request/offer configuration.

The preferred response to a pre-request is *not* a go-ahead response; this simply forwards the sequence to a first pair part – a request – which is the less preferred way of implementing the project at hand. Of course, this is less dispreferred than a blocking response, which moves to frustrate the project or activity altogether. Still, the preferred response to the pre-request is to pre-empt the need for a request altogether by offering that which is to be requested. To be sure, it is not always possible for the projected request recipient to anticipate what the request target is to be, and it is not always projectable that it is a request which is in the offing. And projected request recipients thus may have as a possible claim that they had not discerned the imminence of the request or its object. But, when possible, the preferred response to the pre-request is a pre-emptive offer, as in the following two episodes.

```
(5.51) SBL 2,2,4
 1 Bet: ->      And uhm I have her book
 2              (1.0)
 3 Bet: ->      Have you read it?
 4 Abb:         I think I have seen her book, I don't know
 5              whether I've read it all or not.
 6 Beth         I Believe in Miracles.
 7 Abb:         Yes,
 8 Bet:         And uh [I (have)-
 9 Abb: Fpre->         [You have it you say?
10 Bet:         Uh I Believe in Miracles
11 Abb: Fpre->  I say do you have it?
12 Bet: Spre->  Yes.
13 Abb: no F->  Uh huh,
14 Bet: Fb ->   And I'll be glad to (.) let you have it (a week'r two).
15 Abb: Sb->    Yes I'd like to.
```

Although it seems likely that Beth is airing a pre-offer at lines 1–3, the response by Abby is sufficiently restrained as to not promote an overt offer. Her retrievals (at lines 9 and 11) of Beth's mention of having the book at issue serve here as pre-requests. Note that, when Beth vigorously confirms her possession of the book, her "agreeing" response with the pre-request does not itself prompt proceeding to the request. Rather, Abby registers the agreement (line 13), and does so with a token otherwise used to indicate the continuing relevance of a larger unit of talk not yet possibly complete. The floor is thereby returned to Beth, who now allows the transaction to proceed by the preferred sequential path; her offer (at line 14) pre-empts the need for Abby to do a request; and, not surprisingly, the offer is accepted.

A different outcome occurs in the following episode, which nonetheless also evidences the orientation of interactants to a preference for offers over requests. This episode should already be familiar from the discussion near the end of the earlier section on pre-expansion (see the discussion of Extract [4.28] at pp. 54–56; lines 1–26 below correspond to lines 54–80 in Extract [4.28]). In it, one custodian – Vic – is retelling the job he did for the custodian of a nearby building – James – *to* that colleague, as a lead-in to requesting the return of his garbage can. Recall that the base adjacency pair's first pair part here is the request (at line 25 in this more-narrowly drawn excerpt).

```
(5.52) US, 53:20-54:05
 1 Vic: Fpre->  Do, me, one fa:vuh, I [cleaned it up!
 2 Jam:                               [Yeh hh
 3 Jam: Fb->    Yeh right. Ih-deh ca:n, (I- brought de) can
 4              (I'll) set it dehr own the sidewalk.
 5 Vic: Sb->    [No.
```

```
 6 Jam:         [Izzat ehkay=
 7 Jam:         =[No.
 8 Vic:         =[Didjeh sweep up duh rest a' duh me[ss.
 9 Jam:                                            [NO I didn' sweep]
10              up nothin!
11 Vic:         Well o[kay well that's why I left the can=
12 Jam:               [Leave ih deh.
13 Vic:         =[innuh hallwa:y
14 Jam:          [I'll do it (early) [in nuh maw:ning.
15 Vic:                             [so if you hadda br[oo:m then you=
16 Jam:                                                [Yeh right.
17 Vic:         =c'd sweep up duh dust=
18 Vic:         =[(            )-
19 Jam:          [Very, uh- very good I [appreesh-˙hhh
20 Vic:                                 [the glass,
21 Jam:         I apprecia[te that Victuh,
22 Vic:                   [Tomorruh I-
23 Vic:         No.=
24 Jam:         =[E(hh)h yeh.
25 Vic: Fb->    =[Tomorruh I want my pail back. Dass a[ll.
26 Jam: Sb->                                          [Ye(hh)h!
```

There is a rather elaborate pre-expansion of this base sequence, including a
pre-pre which makes clear that it is a request which is in the offing.[20] Then
note that, directly after this is made clear (line 1, "Do me one favor"), James
responds with an *offer*, to put the can on the sidewalk (lines 3–4, "Yeh right.
Ih-deh ca:n, (I- brought de) can (I'll) set it dehr own the sidewalk"). As it
happens, Vic has other business to get done in this sequence, and so rejects
the offer here, even though it appears to be substantially what he goes on
to request. There may be various grounds for rejections of the offers put
forward by projected request recipients as pre-emptive responses – most
commonly that the offers err in anticipating what was to be requested. Still,
it is clear from the close juxtaposition of this offer to the projection of a
request-in-the-works that this is the preferred response to a pre-request,
where possible.

   If a pre-emptive offer is not possible, or is withheld, then the familiar go-
ahead response – while not optimal – is next-preferred, as in the following:

```
(5.53) SBL 1,1,12
 1 Abb: Fpre->   And uhm (0.8) I want(ed) to ask too, do you still
 2                have a copy of The Cro- ih Cross and the Switchblade?
 3 Bet: Spre->   Yeah.
 4 Abb: Fb ->    May I read it again?
 5 Bet: Sb ->    Yes, you sure may, I've got it on my bedside and
```

---

[20] As previously noted, many pre-pre's occur in the pre-environment of requests.

```
 6              I intend to read it again myself, and I started it,
 7 Abb:        Uh huh,
 8 Bet:        But then in the meantime, you know, it's kind of a
 9             book you have to kind of feel in the mood to read.
10 Abb:        Yeh- well, I've just had kind of: an urge to read
11             [it again,=
12 Bet:        [Yeah.
13 Abb:        =so I thought if you still have it, [why uh
14 Bet:                                            [Well,-
15 Bet:        Yeah, I have it, [and I'll bring it-
16 Abb:                         [and will loan it to me,-
17 Bet:        Uh huh, and I'll bring it over and letchu read it.
18 Abb:        Okay::y,
```

Here the pre-request (at lines 1–2) seems to provide ample resources for a pre-emptive offer, and so the simple go-ahead response (at line 3) might well be taken as intimating a somewhat less than enthusiastic orientation to what is in progress. And, to be sure, it turns out that the requestee herself still has designs on the requested object (lines 5–9), which she articulates in response to the overt (although modulated) request (at line 4).[21] By the time the request is reprised (at lines 10–11, 13, and 15), the request has been upgraded to an explicit "loan," and no longer waits for an offer, while the requestee hastens to make the offer before receiving the request (line 14), and makes the offer more forthcoming, i.e., undertaking actual delivery (lines 15 and 17).

There is, of course, a relationship between the preference structure obtaining between alternative second pair parts and that obtaining between alternative first pair parts. If a prospective requester can be offered what is wanted, the request does not risk rejection (and neither does the offer). If a self-presenter can get recognized in advance, then the awkward possibility of identifying oneself to no recognition is obviated. That is not all that is involved in preferences between alternative sequence types, but it is one element.[22]

[21] Note that she does not request to "borrow" the book, but to read it – perhaps induced by the withholding of an offer in response to the pre-request.

It is also in point to note that this sequence is initiated just after Abby has reported that she has a book for Beth in her car. Lest it be thought that this is a incidental placement, the exchange leading to Extract (5.53) starts with an utterance that shows their intimate connection. Abby says, "Oh another thing I wanted to ask- or *tell* you, Uh I have that <u>book</u> in my <u>car</u>, I meant to get by and give it to you, you know that Slaughter book?" The placement of a request after one made by its recipient – and, even better, after that one has been satisfied – is here displayed not only in the fact of its placement, but in the conjunction displayed by the speaker's replacement of "I wanted to ask" by "I wanted to tell."

[22] Although it is not possible here to spell out the details, there may be for some readers an apparent affinity here with the literature on "face" whose origin in recent social science may be traced to Goffman (1955, inter alia), and whose development for application

Another possible connection between the preference structure of FPPs and that of SPPs is suggested by an observation made by Lindström (1997). Working with Swedish materials, she noticed a difference in the form taken by preferred responses to "immediate" requests and preferred responses to "deferred" requests. "Immediate" requests refers to requests whose satisfaction can be achieved in the immediate aftermath of the request; "deferred" requests are ones whose satisfaction will not occur in the immediate context of the request sequence. Lindström noticed that, in responding favorably to a deferred request, a simple agreement token was not taken as a firm granting of the request; more was required.[23]

Almost certainly Lindström's observation is not limited in scope to Swedish conversation. Here are two extracts that provide an initial basis for further exploring this issue. The first shows minimal agreement tokens, or compliance markers, as SPPs to requests at the dinner table (as did Extract [1.03] at the very beginning of this work).

```
(5.54) Stew Dinner, 3:11-30 (previously [5.37] in note 15)
 1 Dad:        So Ci:n (0.2) tell me about your day.
 2             (0.5)
 3 Cin:        Uh::_ .h
 4 Dad:        Wha'd=ju (d) learn.
 5             (1.0)
 6 Dad:        [O:^::H yeah (we) went to thuh- we went to uh: (.)
 7 Cin:        [Uh:m-
 8 Cin:        Claim Jumper.
 9 Dad:        Claim Jum[per today.
10 Mom:                 [(>uh huh<)
11 Mom: F->    May I have a roll [please,
12 Cin:                          [For a field trip.=
13 Dad: S->    =Sure.
14 Dad: F->    An' may I have thuh -butter please.
```

to language usage is most fully and accessibly realized in Brown and Levinson's work on "politeness" (1978, 1987). To such readers many of the points made about preference organization, and especially about dispreference, will seem to converge with discussions of negative and positive face. However, different goals of inquiry, strategies of theorizing, and analytic procedures underlie the two lines of work, and render such apparent convergences problematic. The very concept of "face" is a conceptual stipulation as a point of departure for the theorist's theorizing in one line of work, not grounded empirically in the practices of interactional participants as is required by the other line of work, but used rather as an interpretive analytic resource of academic inquiry. The two lines of work may be taken by some to be "logically compatible," but, as Ernest Nagel showed some years ago (1961) with respect to "constructionist" and "correspondence" theories of science, logically compatible (even logically equivalent) stances can be immensely divergent in their psychologies and strategies of inquiry and in the import their results are found to have. For a discussion of the relationship between conversation analysis and the "face-based" account of interaction developed by Goffman, see Schegloff (1988a:93–100).

[23] There is an echo here of Pomerantz's (1984) observation that agreeing with an assessment was not effectively done by producing another assessment of the same valence as the initial assessment; an upgraded assessment term was required to do a full-fledged agreement.

```
15 Mom: S->    Yes.=hh
16             (0.5)
17 Cin:        Went to Claim Jumper for (our)/(uh) fie:ld trip.
18 Dad:        Yiea:h, an'- an'- tell me about it.
19             (0.5)
```

Here, the two SPPs are minimal, are followed by delivery of the item requested, and the whole exchange runs off without a hitch. Compare with that Extract (5.55). A few days before the Thanksgiving holiday, Emma has called her adult daughter to report that her (Emma's) husband has left her. Among the more immediate practical consequences is the fate of the large family gathering which was to have celebrated the holiday. The following extracts come several minutes into the conversation.

```
(5.55) NB IV, 7, 3:10-20, 18:40
 1 Emm:        .hhh[hh
 2 Bar:            [Is this been goin on lo:ng er wha:t.
 3 Emm:        OH:::: I DON'T KNOW I JIS CA:N'T SEEM TUH
 4             SAY BLUE IS BLUE HE AR:GUES e-WITH ME ER::
 5             *u- (.) u-SOMETHING EN: AH: DON'T DO THIS
 6             RI:GHT'n THAT RI:GHT. .hhhhh I NEED hhHE:L:P.hh
 7             (.)
 8 Emm: F      EN BARBRA wouldju CA:LL im dihni:ght for me,h
 9             (.)
10 Bar: S      Ye:ah,
11 Emm: ->     .h HU:H?h
12 Bar:        Well if ↑he dezn't co:me I won't uh:: (0.2)
13             t-dra:g (.) Hugh en ↓evrybuddy do:wn↓
14             .
15             . ((eleven lines deleted))
16             .
17 Bar:        =[°(          )°
18 Emm: F      =[Uh will YOU CALL IM DIHNI:GHT [for me,=
19 Bar: S                                     [°Yeah°
20 Bar: S      =Ye:ah,
21 Emm: ->     ↑PLEA-:SE,=
22 Bar: S      =Ye:a[h.
23 Emm: ->          [An' reverse th'↓cha::rge, °.hhh°
24 Bar:        ↑↑Oh: don't be sill↓y.
25 Emm:        .t.h[hhh.h]hh
26 Bar :           [No:. ]
```

At line 8, Emma asks her daughter to call the estranged husband/father for her, a request which is followed my a micro-gap of silence and a simple agreement token, "yeah." This is immediately treated as a trouble source by Emma (line 11), and the response to it indicates that Barbara is preoccupied with the immediate consequences for her family, not calling on her mother's behalf. A bit later on, Emma asks again, showing that she did not figure she had received a reliable favorable response before. This time there is no intervening rejection-prefiguring silence, but an early agreement token, and then another latched to the end of Emma's request – both of them simple "yeah"s. Again Emma shows that she does not hear in them reliable accessions to her request, and she upgrades the request to an entreaty (line 21). Once again she gets a simple "yeah," and proposes a way that Barbara can avoid the charges and make her estranged husband pay, but this is rejected by Barbara. Here, then, we see that the same simple "yeah" which suffices to register an accession to an immediate request is deeply and repeatedly insufficient to register accession to a deferred request. Doing a request being dispreferred to begin with, and the deferred request imposing the further burden of remembering to execute at a remote time, and here further encumbered by the intra-familial tension, all conspire to raise the bar of a convincing accession to the request. There surely appears here to be a linkage between the dispreferredness of the first pair part and what it takes to convey a credible acceptance/granting of it with a preferred second pair part.

The discussion so far has featured measures which the (prospective) *first* pair part speaker may take in negotiating the shoals of preference/dispreference, acceptance, and rejection. But attention must also be paid to measures available for deployment in the first instance by the *recipient* of the first pair part, and for those we turn to an examination of insert expansion.

6 Insert expansion

One upshot of our discussion of the organization of preference and dispreference was that the production of a sequence whose first and second pair parts are in a preferred relationship to each other is something which both parties – an F speaker and an S speaker – can be oriented to and can take measures to achieve (although they do not always achieve it). We noted, for example, that first pair part speakers can re-do a question to reverse its displayed preference so that the response which seems to be "in the cards" can be done by its speaker as an agreeing or preferred response rather than a dispreferred one, and that the practice of deferring dispreferred responses can provide the opportunity for just such a redesign of the first pair part. In this light, we could understand pre-expansions as resources which a prospective F-speaker can initiate to implement an orientation to the possibility of a dispreferred response, and whose outcome can ground moves to proceed to the first pair part or not, and what type of first pair part and how constructed. Like pre-expansions, many insert expansions are oriented to issues of preference and dispreference, but that is not their universal preoccupation.

With insert expansions, we come to a type of expansion which prospective *S-speakers* can initiate. Insert expansions, like pre-expansions, are themselves constructed out of adjacency pairs and take the form of insert *sequences*. As the "pre-" in "pre-sequences" registers their placement before a first pair part, so does the "insert" in "insert sequences" register their positioning between the parts of the base adjacency pair – after the base first pair part and before the base second pair part, as in Extract (6.01).

```
(6.01) SBL 2,1,8 (Schegloff et al., 1977:368)
1 Bet:  F_b   ->   Was last night the first time you met Missiz Kelly?
2                  (1.0)
3 Mar:  F_ins ->   Met whom?
4 Bet:  S_ins ->   Missiz Kelly.
5 Mar:  S_b   ->   Yes.
```

Both elements are indispensable to what is meant by insert expansion: a) position between a first pair part and a projected second pair part, and b) that the insert expansion is initiated by the *recipient* of the preceding first pair part. The following extracts may initially appear to exemplify insert

expansions but do not, because the talk that follows the first pair part is by
the same speaker and not by the recipient. Although such occurrences are
fully worthy of study and description in their own right, they exemplify a
practice different from insert expansions.

```
(6.02) SN-4, 3:23-28
1 Mar: Fb-> Have you heard about the orgy we had the >other night?=
2      F -> That's how I got (th')< black eye:.=Y'like the black
3          eye:?
4 Rut: S-> Oh it's lovely.=
5 Mar:     =Great.
6 Mar: ->  ˙hhhh Ennyway-, ˙hh u:m(-) we were havin' this orgy . . .
```

This might be taken as a story preface or pre-telling first pair part followed
by a solicit of confirmation for an assessment – a first pair part followed
by a first pair part apparently characteristic of insert expansion – but here
the progress of the sequence is halted to introduce a parenthetical side
comment, one not apparently in the service of the sequence of the first pair
part which has just preceded (as is marked by the "Anyway" on line 6, a
usage regularly employed as a "right hand parenthesis marker" showing
that what is to follow will be disjunctive with what has just occurred, and
resumes something which preceded it). The same is the case in the following
exchange:

```
(6.03) Stalled, 1:7-23 (previously [5.06])
 1 Don: Fpre-> Guess what.hh
 2 Mar: Spre-> What.
 3 Don: Fb  -> ˙hh My ca:r is sta::lled.
 4              (0.2)
 5 Don: F   -> ('n) I'm up here in the Glen?
 6 Mar: S   -> Oh::.
 7              {(0.4)}
 8 Don:        {˙hhh }
 9 Don:        A:nd.hh
10              (0.2)
11 Don:        I don' know if it's po:ssible, but {˙hhh}/(0.2)} see
12             I haveta open up the ba:nk.hh
13             (0.3)
14 Don:        a:t uh: (˙) in Brentwood?hh=
15 Mar: Sb  -> =Yeah:- en I know you want- (˙) en I whoa- (˙) en I
16          -> would, but- except I've gotta leave in aybout five
17          -> min(h)utes.((hheh)
```

The announcement/complaint (cf. Schegloff, 1995) at line 3 is added to a
number of times in an elaborate turn expansion before a second pair part
is produced at lines 15–17, but the exchange at lines 5–6, although it is an
adjacency pair occurring between a base first pair part and a projected base
second pair part, does not have the other common characteristics of insert

expansions. Like the preceding extract, it is rather a kind of parenthetical insert added to the preceding first pair part, with a responsive uptake by the recipient (see the discussion of Extracts [13.08] and [13.09] at pp. 241–42 below, in the discussion of incidental sequences).[1]

Of course, the characterization of insert expansions as "before the base second pair part" is promissory; although available to a post hoc examiner of a transcript and tape, for the participants it has not yet happened; there is no second pair part for the insert sequence to come before. But this promissory character of insert sequences is an indigenous property – a feature oriented to by the participants. It must be recalled that the first part of such an insert expansion – the first pair part of the insert sequence – comes in a turn (after the base first pair part) at which the speaker is otherwise obligated to produce a response to the base first pair part. The initiation of the insert sequence displaces the base second pair part. But the term "displaces" is meant to register the status which such insert first pair parts have for the parties. Unlike "counters," which cancel and redirect the sequential force of the base first pair part and redistribute the responsibility for producing a base second pair part, the initiation of an insert sequence is understood to *defer* the base second pair part. The insert sequence is understood to have been launched to address matters which need to be dealt with in order to enable the doing of the base second pair part. They project the doing of that second pair part upon completion of the preliminary work. Rather than neutralizing or redirecting the conditional relevance of the base second pair part, insert sequences carry it forward and renew it. When an insert sequence

---

[1] Even some sequences initiated by recipient of a base FPP in the following turn may not end up constituting recognizable insert expansions, characteristically if they are designed to show themselves addressed not to the FPP which they follow but to other sources in the preceding talk. In Extract (6.04), for example, Rita has called her brother and sister-in-law, and after a brief conversation with her brother, her sister-in-law Evelyn is called to the phone. The extract begins shortly thereafter.

```
(6.04) Berkeley, 3:29-36
1 Eve:     [H ]i Rita.
2 Rit:     [w-]
3 Rit:     Hi Evelyn. how ar[e you.
4 Eve:->                    [I hadda come in anothuh room.
5          (.)
6 Rit:->   oh:.uh huh.
7 Eve:     I fee:l a bissel farshickert.
8          (0.2)
```

Here, although it is the recipient of the base first pair part ("how are you") who follows in the next turn with what amounts to a separate first pair part (a non-responsive "telling"), what transpires between the base first pair part and second pair part ("I feel a bissel farshickert," – the Yiddish expression meaning "a little tipsy") is designed not to be an insert expansion, but a delayed account for her slowness in picking up the phone. The "design" can be seen not only in the overt disjunctiveness of what is addressed by Evelyn's turn with what had been addressed by Rita's, but in the interruptive entry by Evelyn before Rita's question could be brought to possible completion, allowing as a fictive premise that its relevance had not yet become sequentially constraining ("fictive" in that, as soon as Rita registers Evelyn's account, Evelyn goes on to answer the question which she had "interrupted").

is completed, the base second pair part is once again relevant next. Of course, the most salient feature of insert expansions is that they intervene between first and second pair parts, and by compromising the progressivity of the base sequence, they project the possibility of a dispreferred response

Our discussion of insert expansions will discriminate two types by reference to the problems they show themselves addressed to. Some insert sequences can be termed "post-firsts" and others "pre-seconds." That is, the interval between the base first pair part and second pair part seems differentiated between opportunities to address issues raised by what has just preceded and ones which address contingencies of what is to be done next. Not surprisingly, when both are done in an insert expansion, post-firsts precede pre-seconds, and we will take them up in that order.

Post-first insert expansion

Although there are various types of pre-second insert sequences specified to the type of base sequence in which they occur, there appears to be only one type of "post-first" insert sequence. (It may be recalled that, among pre-expansions as well, there were "type-specific" pre-sequences and a "generic" pre-sequence.)

Post-first insert sequences are "repair" sequences – sequences addressed to problems in hearing or understanding the preceding talk (Schegloff et al., 1977). Now "repair" is a whole other order of organization in talk-in-interaction, and it is the topic of a whole separate domain in conversation analysis. But we need to have a grasp of it for our understanding of sequence organization, and so we will begin with a brief overview of the domain of repair organization – just enough to put us in a position to deal with its involvement in sequence expansion.

Capsule review 3: repair

Parties to talk-in-interaction recurrently find themselves confronting troubles or problems in speaking, hearing, or understanding, the talk. These are not necessarily "objective" problems; speakers do make "errors" of grammar, word meaning, pronunciation, etc. – as measured by "official" normative standards, or local informal ones – without addressing them, and may set out to "correct" talk which was apparently unblemished. Recipients may apparently fail to hear, or mishear, utterances which are crystal-clear to others, and apparently have no problem with talk blotted out by a hovering helicopter. Not only are "obvious" troubles unaddressed; anything in the talk may be treated as in need of repair. Everything is, in that sense, a possible repairable or a possible trouble-source. It is overt efforts to deal with trouble-sources or repairables – marked off as distinct within the ongoing talk – that we are terming "repair."

Such efforts to deal with "trouble" in speaking, hearing, or understanding, the talk are usefully analyzable into phases. Most important for our purposes is a distinction between *initiating* a repair undertaking and "*solving it*," or carrying it through to completion. This is an important distinction because the phases may be carried through by different parties. Sometimes the same speaker initiates a repair and completes it; sometimes one party initiates the repair but another completes it. In describing such divisions of labor, the key way of "casting" or describing the participants is to contrast the person who was the speaker of the talk being repaired (the speaker of the trouble-source) with everybody else in the interaction. We can then speak of someone repairing a trouble in their own talk as engaged in "self-repair," and the launching of such an undertaking as "self-initiation of repair." If someone other than the speaker of the trouble-source launches an effort to address a problem in it, we can speak of "other-initiation of repair," and if they carry it through to conclusion we can speak of "other-repair."

It is quite common for a speaker to address some problem in their own talk – past or upcoming – and carry through the repair to completion: self-initiation of repair leading to self-repair. It is much less common (for reasons that do not matter here) to find other-initiated repair leading to other-repair; correcting a prior speaker is the main instance, and it is relatively rare. What is much more common is for other-initiation of repair to lead to self-repair. That is, if a recipient of some talk has a problem in hearing or understanding it, they initiate repair with talk which undertakes to locate the trouble, but they leave it to the speaker of the trouble-source to accomplish the actual repair.

Such other-initiated repairs are initiated with forms of utterance which locate with varying degrees of specificity what the source and/or the type of the problem is. The least specific take the form of queries such as "Huh?" or "What?" or "Pardon me"; they increase in specificity (or power to locate the trouble) when made category-specific ("Who?", "Where?", etc.), or by repeating the target repairable, and most specific of all when offering for confirmation some formulation of the hearing or understanding which the trouble-source produced. These forms for the other-initiation of repair are largely questions, and, in any case, they are first pair parts.[2] They select the speaker of the trouble-source which they have located as next speaker, and make the relevant second pair part to be supplying a repair for the trouble which that speaker can see to be involved. The "other-initiated repair sequences" are, then, themselves organized by adjacency pairs, and are themselves sequences. So much, then, for the "capsule review" on repair; with that overview in hand, we return to our larger project.

[2] By "question" here I mean "interrogative," formed with a so-called question word and/or an upward intonation. But even ones which have neither – for example, partial repeats of the prior turn with "comma" or "period" intonation – may constitute first pair parts.

Other-initiation of repair is highly concentrated in its placement. Overwhelmingly, repair of problems in hearing or understanding some talk is initiated in the turn following the one in which the trouble-source occurred. Other-initiations of repair can occur in the next turn after *any* turn-at-talk. Accordingly, they may also occur after a turn containing a base first pair part, and, when they do, they displace the second pair part that was otherwise relevant there, and do so with another first pair part – the first pair part of an insert sequence. It should now be clear why such other-initiated repair sequences can be properly understood as "post-first"; they are "follow-ups" to the base first pair part which they follow, addressed to clearing up problems in its hearing or understanding which may interfere with the production of an appropriate response to it, or even grasping what an appropriate type of response would be.

In observing in the preceding paragraph that other-initiation of repair displaces the base second pair part and ensures a further displacement by making relevant next a repair-relevant second pair part, we have been in effect noting as well that such repair sequences break contiguity between the first pair part and second pair part of the base adjacency pair. Like gaps, turn-initial markers, hedges, accounts, etc., then, other-initiated repair sequences can operate as *pre-rejections* and *pre-disagreements* – as harbingers of dispreferred base second pair parts. Consider such exchanges as the following:

```
(6.05) TG, 1:16-21
1 Bee:  F_b   -> =[W h y]whhat'sa mattuh with y-Yih sou[nd HA:PPY,] hh
2 Ava:                                                [  Nothing.]
3 Ava:  F_ins -> u- I sound ha:p[py?]
4 Bee:  S_ins ->                [Yee]uh.
5                 (0.3)
6 Ava:  S_b   -> No:,


(6.06) Schegloff et al., 1977:367
1 A:           Were you uh you were in therapy with a private doctor?
2 B:           Yah.
3 A:  F_b   -> Have you ever tried a clinic?
4 B:  F_ins -> What?
5 A:  S_ins -> Have you ever tried a clinic?
6 B:  S_b   -> ((sigh)) No, I don't want to go to a clinic.


(6.07) Schegloff et al., 1977:368
1 Sta:         That's all. But you know what happened that night
2       F_b   -> we went to camp. Forget it. She wouldn't behave for
3             -> anything.
4 Ala:  F_ins -> W-when.
5 Sta:  S_ins -> When we went to camp.
6 Ala:  S_b   -> She behaved okay.
```

In each case, a base first pair part (marked with an F_b) is followed by an other-initiated repair (F_{ins}, for "insert first pair part), whose pre-indication of a dispreferred response is confirmed by the ensuing base second pair part (S_b) – a disconfirmation, a rejection of a pre-proposal, and a disagreeing assessment, respectively.

Note, however, that in each of the preceding extracts, the speaker of the repairable responds to the other-initiation of repair with a reaffirmation of the prior utterance. That is, in responding to possible evidence of upcoming disagreement or rejection, they make no adjustment in the prior turn which might avoid that dispreferred response.

But, like other pre-disagreements, other-initiated repair provides its recipient an opportunity to adjust the utterance faced with incipient disagreement or rejection, to back down, to formulate an alternative *to* it or an alternative formatting *of* it, etc. And, indeed, first pair part speakers may respond to other-initiated repair in a fashion like that described earlier in response to a gap which breaks contiguity – with an alteration of the utterance threatened with non-alignment, as in the following extracts:

```
(6.08) US, 27:30-28:02
 1 Mik:            You have a tank I like tuh tuh- I-I [like-
 2 Vic:                                                 [Yeh I gotta
 3                 fa:wty:: I hadda fawtuy? a fifty, enna
 4                 twu[nny:: en two ten::s,
 5 Mik:              [Wut- Wuddiyuh doing wit [dem.
 6 Ric: Fb   ->                               [But those were uh:::
 7      Fb   ->  [Alex's tanks.
 8 Vic:          [enna fi:ve.
 9 Vic: Fins1->  Hah?
10 Ric: Sins1->  Those'r Alex's tanks weren't they?
11 Vic: Fins2->  Podn' me?
12 Ric: Sins2->  Weren't- didn' they belong tuh Al[ex?
13 Vic: Sb   ->                                    [No: Alex ha(s)
14           ->  no tanks Alex is tryintuh buy my tank.
15              (1.2)

(6.09) IND PD:14
 1 Pol: Fb   ->  Is she pregnant?
 2 Cal: Fins ->  Huh?
 3 Pol: Sins ->  She's not pregnant is she,
 4 Cal: Sb   ->  I don't know.

(6.10) Virginia, 11:14-26
 1 Wes: Fb ->  =(Now) you taught 'er howda dance, didn' y(ou)?
 2             (1.0)
 3 Vir: Fins ->  Hu[h?
 4 Wes: Sins ->    [Weren'[t ya teachin her some new steps th' otha day?
 5 Vir:                   [Yeah
```

```
 6 Vir: Sb ->    Y:eah.
 7              (1.8)
 8 Vir:         Nobody'ull da[nce  with  her:.  ]
 9 Wes:                      [(Seems like she-)]
10              (0.2)
11 Wes:         They wouldn't- they won't- they don't like t'dance
12              with'ur?
13 Vir:         No they do
14              (1.8)
15 ???:         phhh!
16 Pru:         Wha(h)h hhuh huh ˙uh ˙uh (˙hh)
17              (.)
```

In the first of these episodes, Mike is expressing an interest in some
"fish tanks" (aquariums) of Vic's (he thinks), when Rich enters to challenge
Vic's claim to ownership with a strong, affirmative counter-assertion (lines
6–7). Note that, in response to Vic's first other-initiated repair (at line 8),
Rich's challenge is weakened by the addition of a tag question, and in
response to the second (at line 12), Rich's assertion has become a question
from its very start. However, these backdowns in Rich's responses to the
pre-rejection import of Vic's repair initiations are not sufficient to deflect
Vic's dispreferred response, which is delivered full-bore (at lines 13–14) in
answer to the most backed-down version of Rich's intervention.

In the second extract, someone has called the police for assistance with
a woman who is bleeding. In response to the inquiry about her possible
pregnancy, the caller initiates repair. Note that the response appears to adjust
to the disagreement-implication of this breaking of contiguity by reversing
the preference of the question. The response to the repair initiation is built
to prefer a "no" response. As it happens, the caller pleads ignorance.

In the third of these exchanges, family members at the dinner table are
engaged in a mix of bickering and teasing. The focal point is the 14-year-
old Virginia, who has asked her mother (in this single-parent household)
for an increase in her allowance, among other complaints. Some of these
(half-mock) complaints are targeted at her older sister, Beth, who is videotaping the scene for her college course, and is supposed to withhold participation in the event, a stricture which makes her an appealing – because
disabled – target for teasing. In the sequence in Extract (6.10) above, the
older brother Wesley has joined in the teasing. Note that, even though the
whole exchange is a joke, when Virginia responds to the question at line 1
with other-initiated repair, Wesley moderates the claim for which he is asking confirmation: not that Virginia taught Beth "how to dance," but that she
taught her "some new steps." (Wesley gets the confirmation he was seeking,
though the "agreement" at line 5 shows that this was not necessarily contingent on his modulation of the query; still, the point here is his backing
away from his initial position in his response to the repair initiation.)

Of course, not all repair sequences initiated after a first pair part signal disagreement or rejection. There may be a repairable in the turn requiring attention, and even if the turn contains a first pair part, the break in contiguity which ensues is merely incidental to the repair operation per se. For example, here again is Extract (6.01):

```
(6.01) SBL 2, 1, 8 (Schegloff et al., 1977:368)
1 Bet: Fb -> Was last night the first time you met Missiz Kelly?
2               (1.0)
3 Mar: Fi -> Met whom?
4 Bet: Si -> Missiz Kelly.
5 Mar: Sb -> Yes.
```

Here the delay (at line 2) and the repair initiator (at line 3) both violate contiguity, but turn out not to implicate preference issues. Indeed, it is plausible on the face of it that recipient might not recognize the reference to "Missiz Kelly" precisely because it was the first meeting.

Note again that the base first pair part may well have been designed in the first instance with an eye to what the answer was likely to be, and so that answer could be delivered as the preferred one. The parties to the interaction, then, must take account of what is going on in and around the talk – what it is about, what is in the turn, whether events in the setting (e.g., a sudden loud noise) might have obscured part of the talk, etc. – in sorting out whether an other-initiated repair after a first pair part portends disagreement, or whether it straightforwardly involves repair. Of course, just as it can happen that no disagreement was involved, only repair (as in the "Missiz Kelly" episode in [6.01], so it can happen that no repair is involved, only a dispreferred response.

```
(6.11) West and Zimmerman, 1983
1 A: Fb -> How wouldja like to go to a movie later on tonight?
2 B: Fi -> Huh?
3 A: Si -> A movie y'know like a flick?
4 B:        Yeah I uh know what a movie is (0.8) It's just that=
5 A:        =you don't know me well enough?
```

Here an invitation followed by a repair initiation is treated by the inviter as involving just a repair issue. But when that is asserted to be beside the point, the inviter infers on his own that it is rejection which is the issue. Still, it is through an other-initiated repair sequence that the relevance of a dispreferred response to the base first pair part is first introduced into this exchange.

One more point should be mentioned here about post-first insert sequences. In all the data excerpts displayed above (except Extract [6.08]), a single repair sequence occupies the interval following the base first pair part. But other-initiated repair can be pursued through multiple sequences, if the first effort to deal with the trouble is not successful. And multiple

repair sequences can intervene between a base first pair part and second
pair part as well, as in Extract (6.08) above and in the following instance:

```
(6.12) TG, 1:07-14
1  Ava:  F_b    -> [<I wan']dih know if yih got a-uh:m
2              -> wutchimicawllit. A:: pah(hh)khing place °th's
3                 mornin'.˙hh
4  Bee:  F_ins1 -> A pa:rking place,
5  Ava:  S_ins1 -> Mm hm,
6                  (0.4)
7  Bee:  F_ins2 -> Whe:re.
8  Ava:  S_ins2 -> t! Oh: just anypla(h)ce? I wz jus' kidding yuh.
9  Bee:  S_b    -> Nno?=
```

Here two repair sequences are initiated between the first pair part at lines 1–
3 and the second pair part at line 9 – at lines 4 and 7 respectively. Although
it is not uncommon to find two such repair sequences, it is unusual to find
more than three. If the trouble has not been dealt with in three tries, the
parties may give up and find another way of continuing the interaction.

Pre-second insert expansion

"Post-first" insert sequences are "generic" in the sense that they are
not differentiated according to the type of sequence in which they figure.
Other-initiated repair is a practice with its own characteristics and organization, fitted into a larger organization of repair which provides resources
for dealing with trouble in speaking, hearing, and understanding, talk per
se, across the topics, sequences, etc. which the talk may compose.

"Pre-second" insert expansions are (with few exceptions) type-specific,
as were some of the *pre*-expansions discussed earlier. That is, these types of
insert sequences are preliminary to some particular type of second pair part
which has been made relevant next by the type of first pair part to which it is
responding.[3] Whereas post-first inserts look backward, ostensibly to clarify
the talk of the first pair part, pre-second inserts look forward, ostensibly to
establish the resources necessary to implement the second pair part which
is pending. We will examine several such episodes.

In the first of these, two women who have not talked for a while are
talking on the telephone; an invitation is tendered and accepted.

---

[3] One exception is the "conference pass" described in Jefferson and Schenkein (1978), in
which one recipient of a first pair part invites consultation with other possibly interested
participants, and possible co-party incumbents, before undertaking a second pair part.
Such an insert is clearly pre-second rather than post-first, but is conditioned not on the
sequence type in progress but on the partitioning of the co-present participants relative to that
sequence. It is one way in which the numeric non-specificity of a turn-taking organization
can be reconciled with the organizationally two-party character of adjacency-pair-based
sequence organization.

```
(6.13) Schegloff, 1972:107
 1 Bel:          You know, I have [a house, a big garden-
 2 Ann:                          [Yes.
 3 Bel:          Why don't you come and see me some[times.
 4 Ann:                                            [I would like to.
 5 Bel:          I would like you to. Let me [just-
 6 Ann: F_b  ->                              [I don't know just where
 7               -> the- uh- this address [is.
 8 Bel: F_ins ->                          [Well where do- which part of
 9               -> town do you live.
10 Ann: S_ins -> I live at four ten east Lowden.
11               (2.0)
12 Bel:          Well, you don't live very far from me.
13       S_b  -> If you go on the State (1.0) High- no if you go out
14               past the courthouse [to Elmhurst.
15 Ann:                             [Yeah.
```

After the get-together is confirmed, A declares (at line 6) that she does not
know where the house is – in effect a request for directions. B's next turn
does not give directions, it asks a question. The question which B asks next –
the first pair part of the insert sequence – is not raising a problem in hearing
or understanding the turn which preceded; it is not the initiation of repair. It
is in search of information arguably necessary for giving directions; namely,
where the person who will be following the directions will be coming from,
so as to start the directions at that place. So this is type-specific – pre-
direction-giving, specialized as preparation for the particular type of second
pair part made relevant for the base sequence which the insert sequence
inhabits (for additional exemplars, see Psathas [1991]). When the second
pair part for the insert sequence has been delivered, the request for directions
is complied with and the directions are supplied in the base second pair part.

In the following episode, Alice and Betty are both registered nurses who
attend private patients. Alice has been trying to interest Betty in what she
refers to as a "seven day a week job case," which Betty is resisting as "too
much," given her child care responsibilities. Then:

```
(6.14) SBL 1, 10, 2
1 Ali: F_pre -> Yeah but this- this is a nice case, [an' I just-
2 Bet:                                              [Is it?
3 Bet: F_ins -> Are you on it now?
4 Ali: S_ins -> I relieve. It's the one I've been relieving on.ever
5               since March.
6 Bet: S_pre -> Oh uh what kind of case is it.
7 Ali:          Uhm (1.0) it's the uh post-brain surgery.
8 Bet:          Mm hm,
9 Ali:          And uh . . .
```

At line 1 Alice appears to be launching a renewed effort to interest Betty in
the job by proposing to describe the "case" to her. Not simply an assessment,

this utterance serves as a pre-telling, projecting a more extended account of the case – detailing its "niceness" – if given a go-ahead response. Then note that such a response is indeed forthcoming from Betty at line 6, "what kind of case is it," completing what is in effect a pre-sequence and setting up the telling which had been projected. However, in between the pre-sequence first pair part and the pre-sequence second pair part another exchange is inserted, at lines 3–5. Before "taking the bait" and aligning herself as a recipient of the telling which Alice proposes to do, Betty seeks out information on the status of what is to be told, on the authoritativeness to be attributed to it, on the authority of its teller. She arms herself with resources for how to listen, what sort of further questions she can sensibly ask, and the like, for the telling will have a different status if Alice has first-hand knowledge of the case than if she herself was told about it by someone else. Indeed, by the positioning of this pre-second insert, Betty appears to make the go-ahead response itself contingent on the authoritativeness of the telling which it would release. And it arms Betty with a key resource for "informed recipiency" before she undertakes that recipiency. In this regard it is positioned sequentially like the pre-direction-giving question before undertaking to give directions in Excerpt (6.13).

   Pre-second insert sequences are common in service encounters, especially (but not exclusively) in institutionalized, bureaucratized settings. The following episode is from a call to the police in the days before so-called 911 Emergency Services were established to deal with all such matters.

```
(6.15) IND PD: 7
 1 Cal: F_b      -> Send 'n emergency to fourteen forty eight Lillian Lane,
 2 Pol: F_ins1      Fourteen forty eight- [what sir?
 3 Cal: S_ins1                          [Yeah.
 4 Pol: F_ins2      Li[llian Lane?
 5 Cal: S_ins2        [Forteen forty eight Lillian.
 6 Pol: F_ins3      Lillian,
 7 Cal: S_ins3      Yeah.
 8 Pol: F_ins4 ->   What's th' trouble sir.
 9 Cal: S_ins4 ->   Well, I had the police out here once, Now my wife's
10                  got cut.
11 Pol: S_b    ->   Alright sir, We'll have 'em out there.
12 Cal:             Right away?
13 Pol:             Alright sir,
```

The caller makes a request (base first pair part at line 1) directly after the police answer the phone (not shown) and the police respond with an agreement to send a police car (base second pair part at line 11). In between, however, there are several insert sequences. First, several post-first repair sequences are directed to checking the police dispatcher's hearing and understanding of the address – part of the preceding turn. But after these post-first repair sequences are successful, a pre-second sequence is launched (at line 8), this one specific to request sequences to the police. Zimmerman (1984) has termed these "interrogative sequences," and finds them pervasively in service calls of various sorts. They are directed to establishing whether the conditions on granting the request (whatever they may be) have been met. These are not retrospectively addressed to the request; they are, in effect, prerequisites to the alternative possible second pair parts. Here, the second pair part to the pre-second insert is followed by a preferred second pair part to the base sequence. But the opposite outcome can also result, as in the following exchange in a lounge (from Merritt [1976:333], reproduced in Levinson [1983:304]):

```
(6.16) Merritt, 1976:333
1 Cus: F_b  -> May I have a bottle of Mich?
2 Ser: F_i  -> Are you twenty one?
3 Cus: S_i  -> No
4 Ser: S_b  -> No
```

This is perhaps as compact a base sequence with pre-second insert as one is likely to find!

Expansion of expansions

We should be explicit about a feature of adjacency pair expansion which has been exemplified in several data extracts but which has so far not been commented on.

All adjacency pairs can take expansion. Most (though not all) expansions are themselves composed of adjacency pairs. The implication is that expansions can also be expanded. And this is indeed the case. In Extract (6.14), in which one nurse was trying to interest another in a case, we saw a pre-sequence (a pre-telling) take an insert expansion (a pre-second). And insert expansions can take inserts. In the following episode, a family is having a discussion at dinner on the night of the 1988 national elections, and the 10-year-old son – Sig – is telling about something he said at school that day about the presidential race:

```
(6.17) Saunders, 3:3
1 Sig:                Now there's liberal and conservative (.) right?=
2 Dad:                =mm hmm
3                     (1.2)
4 Sig: F_b        -> Conservatives like to shoot people (and liberals don't?)
5                     (2.0)
6 Dad: F_ins      -> Conservatives like wha:t?
7                     (0.8)
8 Sig: F_insins   -> Wha:?
9 Dad: S_insins   -> Whadyu say about conservatives?   ((mouth full))
```

```
10                          (0.3)
11 Sig: S_ins      ->       Conservatives like ta shoot people en (hh) liberals
12                          don't?=
13 Mom: S_b        ->       =N::no:=
14 Dad:                     =Sh::oot people      ((sounds of eating))
15 ( ):                     (oh hh)
16 Sig:                     Yea:h.
17                          (2.0)
18 Dad:                     Whadyya mean sh:oot people.
19                          (1.0)
20 Mat:                     Sh::oo:t
21 Dad:                     Aw [Oh hh
22 Mat:                        [S-H-O-O-T      ((spelling))
23                          (1.2)
24 Sig:                     Well (.) what are conservatives (.) they're people . . .
25                          (0.4)
26 Dad:                     Who like things to remain pretty much the way they are.
```

At line 6, Dad responds to the preceding telling by initiating repair; that is, with the first pair part of a post-first insert sequence. But at line 8, instead of (or, actually, before) responding to that, Sig initiates repair on *that*, he initiates repair on Dad's repair initiator, thus inserting a second repair sequence, but not after the base first pair part, but after the insert first pair part.

In principle, if this organization were merely logical or mechanical, of course, each next embedded layer of insertion should be able to take an insert of its own, but this does not in fact seem to happen. There is rarely more than a second level of embedding, and that occurs when a base adjacency pair first pair part is followed by a repair initiation, and that repair initiation is itself followed by a repair initiation, ordinarily "huh" or "what" or "pardon me" or the like (as in Extract [6.17], line 8), that is, repair initiators which claim to have grasped little beyond that the addressee has said something.

There appear to be other restrictions on the principled availability of any adjacency pair to all expansions. Expansion sequences do not apparently themselves take pre-expansion, though all expansion sequences apparently can take at least one level of insert expansion. And, to anticipate a bit, expansion sequences can take post-expansion, i.e., expansion after the second pair part. For example, in Extract (6.13) above, after the pre-direction-giving insert sequence's first pair part and second pair part, there is another turn-constructional unit before the beginning of the base second pair part – the actual giving of directions. That is the utterance, "Well, you don't live very far from me" (line 12), an assessment which here constitutes a post-expansion of (i.e., a third turn in) the insert expansion. So also, in Extract (6.14), where we saw a pre-expansion (a pre-telling) take an insert expansion ("Are you on it now?"), we may note that the second pair part of that insert is followed by an "oh" before the response to the pre-telling ("Oh, uh what kind of case is it?"), and this is a *post*-expansion of the *insert* expansion to the *pre*-expansion! If that seems unsurmountably complicated, just go back and look at Excerpt (6.14) step by step, tracking each of the component adjacency pairs – base and expansion – and their parts.

The extent of expansions

We have noted that there can be multiple expansions both before a base first pair part (multiple pre-expansions) and between a base first pair part and a base second pair part (multiple insert expansions), and that with some restrictions these expansions can themselves be expanded. Given that the turns which compose these sequences can themselves be quite expansive (recall Ava's account of things she has to do over the weekend in the pre-invitation sequence in Excerpt [4.03] in (Chapter 4), very long stretches of talk indeed can come to occupy the positions before a first pair part and between a first pair part and a second pair part. As a case in point, consider the following extract from a telephone call from 14-year-old Bonnie to her 15-year-old, on-again-off-again boyfriend, which follows the opening of the call and a brief discussion of a youth group meeting they are expected to attend.

```
(6.18) BB Gun, 2:04-4:12 (previously [4.21])
 1 Bon:           But- (1.0) Wouldju do me a favor? heheh
 2 Jim:           e(hh) depends on the favor::, go ahead,
 3 Bon:           Didjer mom tell you I called the other day?
 4 Jim:           No she didn't.
 5                (0.5)
 6 Bon:           Well I called.(.)  [hhh ]
 7 Jim:                              [Uhuh]
 8                (0.5)
 9 Bon:   Fb ->   .hhh 'n I was wondering if you'd let me borrow
10                your gun.
11                (1.2)
12 Jim:           My gun?
13 Bon:           Yeah.
14                (1.0)
15 Jim:           What gun.
16                (0.7)
17 Bon:           Donchuh have a beebee gun?
18 Jim:           Yeah,
19                (0.8)
20 Bon:           (I'm a-) It'[s-]
21 Jim:                       [Oh]: I have a lotta guns.hehh
22 Bon:           Yuh do:?
```

```
23 Jim:    Yeah. aWhat- I meant was which gun.
24         (0.5)
25 Bon:    Tch! .hhh Oh (0.4) uh::m (0.4) t! .hhh (0.5)
26         well d'j'have a really lo:ng one,
27         (0.8)
28 Jim:    A really l:ong one.hh[h
29 Bon:                         [Yeah.
30         (0.2)
31 Bon:    't doesn't matter what ki:nd.
32         (1.0)
33 Jim:    Why:: would you like a »really long one.«
34         (0.8)
35 Bon:    Y'don' have a really long one.
36         (1.0)
37 Jim:    What?
38 Bon:    Y- Donchuh have a l- really long one?
39 Jim:    Yea::hhh. A- all I wan' to know why you want
40         a [gun,]
41 Bon:      [oh ] oh: OH::
42         (0.5)
43 Bon:    Well↑ (0.7) becu:z, I'm do[ing        ]
44 Jim:                             [You're gon]na shoot
45         your mo:m.=
46         =[Go ahead.]
47 Bon:    =[Heheh    ]
48         (0.2)
49 Bon:    .hh eheheh.hh Because I'm I'm doi- heheh (0.8).hhh
50         I am doing- a pl- a thi:ng. (0.3).hhh in drama.
51         (0.6)
52 Bon:    It's like- (.) kind of like- (.) you know what a
53         pa:ntomime is?
54 Jim:    Uhh: hhh! (0.5) Yeah: Iknow.
55 Bon:    An:- I'm doin a pantomime (.) off a record [called ]
56 Jim:                                               [Yuh gon]na
57         be doin' it up on stage in front of the whole school?
58 Bon:    No:: no no::,
59 Jim:    Nuh: [huh    ]
60 Bon:         [Jis; in]my drama class.
61 Jim:    Yeah I know.=
62 Bon:    =In front of my [drama class.]
63 Jim:                    [I mea:n:,   ] in your class when it
64         ha:: (0.2).hh like you do it at lunch?
65         (0.7)
66 Bon:    No, uhm jis' do it- during- drama period.
67 Jim:    Uhuh,
68         (0.5)
69 Bon:    Thank Go(h)d.(h)u(hh) .h[hh
```

```
70 Jim:                                            [(hheh)
71 Bon:        Uh:m, and so I'm doing it off a record called "Annie
72             Get Your ↑GUN,"
73             (0.2)
74 Bon:        and it's called "Doin What Comes Natchurly" an' she's
75             got a ↑gu:n.
76             (1.0)
77 Jim:        An' you're A:nnie.(.)hh
78             (0.3)
79 Bon:        Yea:h.
80 Jim:        ehheheh.hh
81             (0.3)
82 Jim:        You a good- (.) uh::: (1.8) a- actress?
83             (1.0)
84 Bon:        No: heheheh?
85             (0.5)
86 Jim:        Th'n how d'ju come out to be A:nnie.
87             (1.0)
88 Bon:        No- I'n- it's jis' thet-everybody in the class has
89             to do a different- (.) pantomime, you know?
90 Jim:        Uhuh,
91             (0.4)
92 Bon:        An[:]
93 Jim:   Sb ->   [Y]eah:, you can use 't,
94             (0.4)
95 Bon:        .hh Ca:n?
96 Jim:        »Yeh-«
```

The base first pair part here comes at line 9, after more than a minimal pre-expansion, but the base second pair part does not get done for a quite a while, at line 93 – eighty-two lines later in transcript terms.

This is quite a long stretch of talk, but it is analyzably coherent as the development of a single underlying adjacency pair-based sequence. It is composed of a number of insert expansion sequences, some of them post-firsts, some of them pre-seconds. (For a detailed discussion of this whole sequence, including the various types of insert expansions, see Schegloff [1990]).

All sorts of topics get taken up here (however we define that term), especially in the pre-second inserts, but it all hangs together as part of a sustained course of action, effected in the talk through the organizational framework of a single adjacency pair. This is a striking case in point of an issue mentioned in the introduction to this whole discussion of sequence organization – namely, that there is a big and important difference between "topic(ality)" as the basis for coherence – for the "clumping" of turns into a unit – and "sequence" as as unit of sequential organization. The "topics" between the base first pair part and base second pair part here in Extract (6.18) range from the gun and what type, what a pantomime is, the assignment Bonnie has to do and where and when, and to whether she's a good actress – these are quite distinct, and some of them quite unrelated. Nonetheless they are all held together by occupying in common a position in a sequence – after a first pair part and before its second. It is the sequence – and its underlying adjacency pair – which supplies the underlying structure by reference to which this coherence can be achieved (by us as analysts, but in the first instance by the participants) – with the talk understood as either operating retrospectively on the first pair part or to be considered as having prospective bearing on the second pair part which that first pair part has made conditionally relevant.

But note that the sequence does not end with the base second pair part. Lines 95–96 are clearly more of the same sequence (and they are not necessarily the end of that "more"). Here we are looking at the final type and locus of sequence expansion, post-expansion – expansion occurring after the second pair part. In several respects, however extensive the expansion that may occur before the first pair part and between the first pair part and the second pair part, the possibilities for expansion are greatest after the second pair part. Although we cannot exhaust these possibilities, we can take up some of them.

7   Post-expansion

It is the import of the conditional relevance of a second pair part given the recognizable occurrence of a first that a sequence cannot be possibly complete after a first pair part but before its second pair part. A sequence can *end* there – as, for example, when someone storms out of a room abruptly – but one major component of "abruptness" can be just this: ending the sequence before its recognizable closure. In this respect, a sequence is like a turn, a conversation, or any other recognizably structured unit which does not just end, but has a recognizable form of closure (Schegloff and Sacks, 1973).

With the production of a second pair part this constraint on sequence completion is met, and some sequences are recognizably complete (to their participants and to other observers) at the end of the second pair part turn. This is commonly the case with sequences which have no preference structure, such as greetings and leave-takings or "bye-byes." Although on occasion a third or fourth offering may be made to such sequences (especially if the first round was done in overlap), commonly enough a first and second greeting (or "bye bye") complete the exchange.

Beyond that, under a range of circumstances – for some sequence types, in some contexts, for some types of response – the parties may treat the occurrence of a second pair part as the end of the sequence, and embody this by going on to a new sequence or allowing the talk to lapse. For example, in a "continuing state of incipient talk" (see p. 26) a sequence such as a question/answer sequence may be over with the answer and a lapse may set in thereafter, a lapse which is ended with the start of a new sequence, one distinct from what preceded the lapse. For example, in (7.01) the participants have just gotten into a car for the drive to an extended-family party.

```
(7.01) Pre-Party, 1:01-16
 1              (1.0)
 2 Ann:       Baby?
 3              (1.0)  ((Engine whines and catches))
 4 Ann:       'Omi, turn around, face the front.
 5 Nao:       Wha:::
 6 Ann:       Because it's better that way when we're driving, okay?
 7 Nao:       Oka(h)ay. I don't li(hh)ke y:[ou.
 8 Mar: F ->                               [<How long dz it take
```

```
 9           -> t'get there?=hh
10 Ann: S -> Oh abou-teh- five ' ten °minutes.
11             (6.0)
12 Dic:      °(        )    (   [                    )]
13 Deb:                         [S-sure is a] y:::ukky da:y:
```

Marty, visiting from another city, asks how long the drive should be, and after the answer, a six-second lapse sets in, after which the talk turns to the sloppy weather and driving conditions. The two turn question–answer sequence has been treated by the parties as recognizably possibly complete.[1]

One sequence type that is regularly (though far from invariably) taken by participants to be closed after its second pair part is an other-initiated repair sequence. For example, Extract (7.02) is taken from a telephone call whose participants are located in a major urban center and a nearby beach community, respectively.

```
(7.02) NB II:1, 2:40-3:18 (simplified)
 1 Fra:          Whad'r y'guys doin et the bea::ch.
 2 Ted:          n:No:thin,hh
 3                    (.)
 4 Fra:          NO:the::[:n,
 5 Ted:                  [No::,
 6               (0.2)
 7 Fra:          Oh: good he[av'n.]
 8 Ted:                     [Get'n] pi:nk,
 9               (.)
10 Ted:          hh[hn,hn-hn]=
11 Fra: F ->       [H u : h?]=
12 Ted: S ->      =.hh Gitt'n↑pi:nk,
13 Fra:          Wah thoughtchu weren't goin down tel nex'seh-u-
14               th'weekeh:- ah mean the end a'the mo:nth.
15                   (0.4)
16 Ted:          No:, W'r down here fer:: two weeks,
17 Fra:          Oh:::: well yuh lucky gu::y[s.
18 Ted:                                     [Neah:::[:::
19 Fra:                                            [Oh:::::.=
```

---

[1] In as-yet-unpublished work, Federico Rossano, working on interactional environments of continuing states of incipient talk in which, unlike Extract (7.01), parties have visual access to one another, finds that the parties may withdraw from mutual gaze at the end of the second pair part turn of a base pair, thereby displaying to one another (and to us) that they take the sequence to be possibly closed at that point, and in fact actually closed; when they do not withdraw gaze, the sequence is regularly extended. And parties can be observed to withdraw gaze from interlocutor at a point of possible sequence completion, and then look up to see if interlocutor has also withdrawn gaze, thereby showing themselves to be attentive to whether possible sequence completion has been convergently treated as actual completion or not. Sequence completion or extension is thus shown to be an interactionally achieved outcome.

When Fran initiates repair at line 11 on Ted's preceding talk, his repeat at line 12 ends that adjacency pair, and Fran takes up a different tack in the larger sequence in progress.[2] Although, to be sure, this is not a *base* adjacency pair, it is a common type of adjacency pair sequence, and can be treated by the participants – and here *is* treated – as completed by its second pair part. And additional exemplars of sequences taken as complete after their second pair parts can be found in the earlier discussion of two-turn sequences (pp. 22–26).

But just as sequences can be expanded before their first pair part (pre-expansion) and between their first pair part and second pair part (insert expansion), so also can they be expanded after their second pair part (post-expansion). In this chapter, we will examine some of the ways in which parties to talk-in-interaction may expand a sequence after its second pair part.

In general, it should be said, sequences with preferred or agreeing or "+ [plus]" second pair parts are "closure-relevant," and ones with dispreferred or disagreeing or "– [minus]" second pair parts are "expansion-relevant." That is, preferred responses tend to lead to closing the sequence, while dispreferred responses regularly lead to expansion of the sequence.[3] We have already seen that much (though not all) pre-expansion and insert expansion is oriented to (the possibility of) dispreferred responses, and we shall see that the same holds true for post-expansion. And not only does this hold for the occurrence of any expansion at all, but also for the degree of expansion which may come to be involved.

We will first examine minimal post-expansions, then some more-than-minimal post-expansions and how they are brought to closure, and finally (in Chapters 8–10) other ways in which sequences can be extended which do not involve expansion of the base sequence itself.[4]

---

[2] Fran's question, "What're you guys doing at the beach?" turns out to have been ambiguous. What she means is (as revealed at lines 13–14) a request for an accounting in view of her surprise at their being there at all; she thought they were not going until later. Ted, however, hears it as a request for an account of their activities, what they are doing while they are there. His second try at that (line 8) is meant as a "joke" (see the post-positioned laugh at line 10), and Fran's "huh" is not necessarily about its being obscured by overlap, but its being not in the terms she was oriented to, given the question she thought she asked. To say, as the text does, that Fran is "tak[ing] up a different tack" is to note the contrast with the answer she has been given, but not necessarily a contrast with what she had undertaken to do with the start of the sequence.

[3] A major exception to this linkage will be discussed in Chapter 8, on 'topic-proffering sequences.'

[4] One caveat in advance: the ensuing discussion will be concerned with the forms which expansion takes after a second pair part and, subsequently, how new sequences may be related to prior ones, and it will depict occurrences within the sequence that can promote such expansion or move to end it. But there can be conduct exogenous to the dynamics of the sequence itself that can affect whether the participants actually undertake to press such expansion or not. Only one can be mentioned here, and that one only briefly. When the participants are co-present to one another, their postural configurations can embody their current distribution of attention and commitment to possible engagements in the

Minimal post-expansion: sequence-closing thirds

Minimal post-expansion involves the addition of one additional turn to a sequence after its second pair part. The import of "minimal," however, is not limited to an arithmetical count of the number of turns which happen to follow the second pair part; this is not the import of the contrast with "more-than-minimal" post-expansion. The import of "minimal" is, rather, that the turn which is added is designed not to project any further within-sequence talk beyond itself; that is, it is *designed* to constitute a *minimal* expansion after the second pair part. It is designed to move for, or to propose, sequence closing (a move which may be aligned with by recipient, or not). Given its position after a second pair part, and that the move is made by a form of turn which can *embody* the sequence closure if sustained by co-participants, we can refer to it as a "sequence-closing third" (SCT). Sequence-closing thirds are found after both preferred and dispreferred second pair parts (though they have differing interactional import in the two contexts). This minimal post-expansion, then, is less sensitive than others to the earlier-mentioned linkage of sequence closure and expansion to preferred and dispreferred responses.

Sequence-closing thirds take a number of forms or combinations of them, three of the most common of which will be briefly examined here: "oh," "okay," and assessments.

"Oh"

The core general use of the free-standing particle "oh" is to mark or claim information receipt. What Heritage (1984b) termed a "change-of-state token" is deployed to register a just-preceding utterance (or other event, perception, etc.) as an "informing," as producing a change in its recipient from non-knowing to now-knowing.

environment. They can show themselves to be primarily committed to the current interaction with the other by being fully oriented to one another with their whole (visible) bodies. Or they can show that they are simultaneously committed to other "projects" in the environment – a work task, eating, another ongoing interaction from which they have temporarily withdrawn to conduct this one, etc. They do this by a postural configuration we can call "body torque" – different orientations of the body above and below the waist, above and below the neck, and by placement of the eyes in their sockets. The orientation of lower parts of the body mark the underlying current commitment of the person, with the orientation of head and eyes (if different) indicating commitments that are more temporary. The upshot for sequence post-expansion is that it can be constrained or discouraged if one or more of the participants are in a high body torque posture relative to the others, and expansion can be promoted if parties shift posture to more directly face co-participants with minimized body torque. A similar dynamic appears to inform gaze direction; maintaining gaze at co-participant can promote sequence expansion; and withdrawing gaze can discourage it. For gaze direction, see note 1; on body torque, see Schegloff (1998).

"Oh" can be deployed after a wide variety of utterances, positioned variously within sequences. For our purposes here, however, the position of interest is after a first and second pair part (with or without pre- and/or insert expansions), where a change-of-state token can mark or propose the possible end of the sequence. By registering a state-changing receipt of information, free-standing "oh"[5] can serve as a possible sequence-closing, third position turn. This is most straightforward when the sequence in progress is directly addressed to securing information – whether through a base sequence requesting information or its confirmation – as in the two sequences in Extract (7.03) – or in repair sequences in which the information sought is the repetition or clarification of something in the preceding talk – as in Extract (7.04) below.

```
(7.03) HG, 16:25-33
 1 Nan:  F   ->  =˙hhh Dz he av iz own apa:rt[mint?]
 2 Hyl:  S   ->                          [˙hhhh] Yea:h,=
 3 Nan:  SCT-> =Oh:,
 4               (1.0)
 5 Nan:  F   ->  How didju git iz number,
 6               (·)
 7 Hyl:  S   ->  I(h) (·) c(h)alled infermation'n San
 8               Fr'ncissc(h)[uh!
 9 Nan:  SCT->             [Oh::::.
10               (·)
```

Here Nancy and Hyla are discussing one of the latter's current romantic interests, whose home in another city she has just described calling. We see here two consecutive request-for-information sequences, each of which has as its second pair part the delivery of information, followed by a sequence-closing third. (See also Extract [8.15], p. 177, another episode from the same conversation, where two consecutive sequences have sequence-closing thirds composed of "oh.")

In Extract (7.04), the participants' talk has turned to "working out," after a suggestion that they do some aerobic swimming together.

```
(7.04) SN-4, 14:01-30
 1 Kar:       One a'these nights we gotta go swim la:ps.
 2 Mar:       (°Too narrow.)/(°Dinero.)
 3            (0.3)
 4 She:       (t!) Kerin's been saying that fer two years while
 5            she's [lived here.
 6 Rut:             [uh-huh-huh-huh =
 7 Kar:       =[W h : : y.   You: sw°im.  ]
```

---

[5] "Free-standing 'oh'" refers to an "oh" designed as an utterance or utterance-component in its own right – often by being delivered under its own intonation contour (Heritage, 1984b), and is distinguished from "oh" designed to be a preliminary component of another unit of talk (as in "Oh=I don't know"), what Heritage (1998) terms "oh-prefaced."

```
 8 Mar:           =[I've been doing e:xercises] every ni̲:ght.
 9                (0.2)
10 Kar:           Y̲ou do?
11 Mar:           Every night I started- (·) about a week ago
12                doing (·) (Iyonknow) a who̲:le mess of 'em
13                <sit[ups, pull ups, °(      )]
14 She:              [I̲: thought that was an] ea:rthquake.
15                (·)
16 She:           Er you [doing ju̲]mping jacks?
17 Mar:                  [ N : o .]
18 Mar:           O̲h no no.
19 Sh?:           [ huh   huh ]
20 Kar:           [Nuh that's] prob'ly Bea [you   hear.   ]
21 Ru?:                                    [hm-hm-hm-hm-]hm
22                (0.5)
23 She:  F   ->  Prob'ly what?
24 Kar:  S   ->  Me.
25                (·)
26 She:  SCT->   Oh.
27                (0.8)
28 Mar:           No I don't do ju̲mping jacks.=I do just y'know sit ups,
29                pull u- no. not pull ups:- (·) all those things. ˙hh(hh)
30                (0.5)
```

At the arrowed turns a hearing/understanding problem is addressed with
an other-initiated repair (line 23). The proposed repair solution (at line 24)
is receipted with an "oh," which serves to close the repair sequence, after
which the larger base sequence is resumed (line 28, "doing resumption"
from lines 17–19).

"Okay"

If "oh" may be used to mark or claim receipt of information or
"informing," "okay" (and some variants, such as "alright") may mark or
claim acceptance of a second pair part and the stance which it has adopted
and embodies within the sequence.

As with "oh," "okay" is used in a variety of practices and is deployed in a
variety of positions (see, for example, Beach [1993]). Here we are focused
on its use in the turn after a second pair part in the types of adjacency pair-
based sequence for which it is appropriate (e.g., requests, offers, invitations,
etc.), with or without pre- and insert expansions.

"Okay" may serve as possible closure after "preferred" or "+ [plus]"
second pair parts, as in the offer sequence in Extract (7.05) or the request
sequence in Extract (7.06). The offer sequence in Extract (7.05) comes near
the end of a takeout Chinese dinner at John and Beth's home; Don has
brought the food, and they are beginning to finish up the meal.

```
(7.05) Chinese Dinner, 39:29-40 (simplified)
1 Don: F    -> Shall I pour it out?
2 Joh: S    -> No I rih- I don' want that much. Rea[lly.=
3 Don: SCT ->                                    [Oh okay.
4 Joh: +S   -> =I jus'wannid 'l bit (            ).
5 Don: SCT -> Okay.
6                 (0.5)
```

Don offers John the remainder of what is in one of the containers, John accepts a lesser amount and Don accepts that lesser acceptance with an "okay" (the talk that follows is by others at the table). And in the following request sequence James asks of his fellow janitor/custodian, Vic, that he help identify the culprit in a vandalism of the apartment house which is in his (James's) charge:

```
(7.06) US, 50:26-40 (partial)
 1 Jam: F    -> Yeh. Uh-I dis wantuh know de person. That's all. You
 2              point me out to im someti:me,
 3 Vic: S    -> I will.
 4 Jam: SCT -> A:lright.
 5 Vic: +S   -> I wi[ll.
 6 Jam: SCT ->      [En I w-e(hh)h! Alright, then that's all I
 7              [wantuh know.
 8 Vic:        [(Alright.)
 9 Vic:        Okay.[(I will).
10 Jam: SCT ->      [Alright. Becau:se, it's insu:red anehway,
11             when I call de office, dey'll send a man up eh
12             tuh put that glass I:N. . . .
```

In this sequence there are several cycles of accession to the request and registering/acceptance of that accession, the second of which more fully articulates its closing-relevance. (As it happens, this sequence gets extended still further at lines 11–12, but this is a contingent development on a different topic from a point which could serve as a stable closure to the sequence.)

And "okay" can serve as possible closure for sequences in which the second pair part has been dispreferred or "– [minus]." For example,

```
(7.07) Davidson, 1984:127 (previously [5.29])
1 Ali: F    -> You wan' me bring you anything?
2                (0.4)
3 Bet: S    -> No: no: nothing.
4 Ali: SCT -> AW:kay.
```

Here the offer is rejected after the slight gap common to such dispreferred responses, and the rejection is itself accepted. And in the following sequence, Mike does (at line 1) what is clearly a pre-sequence, but one which is equivocal between a pre-offer and a pre-request, expressing

an interest in a fish tank (an aquarium) which Vic is apparently no longer
using.

```
(7.08a) US, 28:09-29:07
1 Mik: Fpre -> Wuhddiyuh doing with dat big bow-puh-tank. Nothing?
2                (0.5)
3 Vic:          ((COUGH))
4 Vic:          Uh-h-h,
5                (1.0)
6 Vic: Spre ->  I'm not intuh selling it or giving it. That's it.
7 Mik: SCT ->   Okay.
8                (1.0)
```

Here again, as it happens, the sequence which is possibly complete, goes
through another round, in part devoted to clarifying whether Mike is requesting a "freebie" or is offering to buy the tank.

```
(7.08b) US, 28:09-29:07
 1 Mik: Fpre ->  Wuhddiyuh doing with dat big bow-puh-tank. Nothing?
 2                (0.5)
 3 Vic:          ((COUGH))
 4 Vic:          Uh-h-h,
 5                (1.0)
 6 Vic: Spre ->  I'm not intuh selling it or giving it. That's it.
 7 Mik: SCT ->   Okay.
 8                (1.0)
 9 Mik:          Dat wz simple. Khhhh huh-huh-heh!=
10 Vic:          =Yeh.
11                (0.7)
12 Vic:          °Teg,
13                (1.0)
14 Vic: +Spre    Becuz selling it ur giving it I::, da:t's
15                (all [there is)
16 Mik:               [Buh I din say giving it. If yer intuh
17                [selling it (I'll [take it man,)
18 Vic:          [Uh-h-h            [
19 Vic:                             [The bi:d,
20 Vic:          The bi:d is, is, (0.7) -third rate. Becuss I awready
21               r- (0.5) caught- It doesn' mattuh I'm not intuh
22               [selling it or giving it.=
23 Mik:          [F'get it.
24 Mik: SCT ->   =Oh-o[kay. ((line 24 is a "stutter" on the first sound
25 Vic:               [Clea:n, of "okay" rather than a separate "oh".))
26                (0.7)
```

Even after Mike's insistence that this is an offer to buy, Vic responds with
a vigorous rejection, one stripped of the usual insignia of dispreference

(lines 18–22). Once again, the rejection is registered and accepted with an "okay."[6]

As "oh" can serve as possible closure to a sequence in which informing and information figure centrally, then so can "okay" and its variants serve for sequences in which various other actions (in the text above featuring exchanges of various sorts) figure centrally. As we shall soon see, many sequences feature *both* of these characteristics, and parties oriented to closure in third position in such sequences may then deploy combinations of these closing "moves," most familiarly "Oh. Okay" and variations playing off it (as, for example, in Extract [7.05] at line 3). But before examining such sequences, let us introduce a third turn type whose deployment in third position in a sequence – after the second pair part of an adjacency pair-based sequence – can constitute a move to close the sequence, and that turn type is assessment.

Assessment

As "oh" registers information as having produced a change of state in its recipient and "okay" registers and accepts a responsive action, an

---

[6] Even here the sequence gets extended, but with nothing other than reflexive elaboration of the "decisiveness" of the sequence closure (whose very explication, of course, extends the sequence and makes possible alternatives to that decisiveness). The following extract follows directly after line 26 of the extract in the text:

```
(7.08c) US, 28:09-29:07
 1 Mik:      Clean,
 2 Vic:      Eh=
 3 Mik:      =jing, [tchikeh
 4 Vic:             [Eh heh heh
 5 Mie:      Tchuu!
 6 ???:      Mhhhhh
 7 ???:      hhhh
 8 Vic:      Hih! shhh
 9           (2.5)
10 Mik: ->   Dat ends dat ('ey),
11 Vic: ->   Yeh.On dat.
12 Vic:      'N, the othiz, I got rid of, 'hhh which were given tuh me.
13           Awl the tanks were given tuh me man I had, like, (0.7) uh-
14           two fawtie:s,
15           (0.7)
16 Mik: ->   If yuh evuh [get intuh selling it I'll=
17 Vic:                  [a twenny::,
18 Mik:      =[          ) tuh buy it from yuh.]
19 Vic:       [ en  two  tens  enna  fi:ve.   ]
20 Vic:      I had the sta:nds downstairs wheh you gotchur stuff,
21           'hhh en all the equipmi:nt, uh I carried a lot [upstehs,
22 Ric:                                                     [Yeh I saw
23           it.
```

assessment in third position articulates a stance taken up – ordinarily by the
first pair part speaker – toward what the second pair part speaker has said or
done in the prior turn. Such assessments are routine parts of "personal state
inquiry" sequences (Sacks, 1975) such as those reproduced in the following
fragments:

```
(7.09) TG, 1:26-37
 1 Ava: F    -> [˙hh ] How'v you bee:n.
 2 Bee: S    -> ˙hh Oh:: survi:ving I guess, hh[h!
 3 Ava: SCT+->                        [That's good,=
 4      F    -> =how's (Bob),
 5 Bee: S    -> He's fine,
 6 Ava: SCT -> Tha::t's goo:d,
 7 Bee:         °(Bu::t.)=/°(Goo:d.)=
 8 Bee:         ='n how's school going.
 9 Ava:         Oh s:ame old shit.
10 Bee:         Shhhh! hh t! ˙hh
11 Ava:         I 'av [a lotta t]ough cou:rses.
12 Bee:              [Uh really?]
13 Bee:         Oh I c'n ima:gine.=<wh'tche tol' me whatchu ta:kin.
```

In Extract (7.09) two consecutive "howaryou sequences" are closed by
having their responses receipted with assessments. And in the exchange in
Extract (7.10) Ava shows herself oriented to the use of "good" as a sequence-
closing third by starting a new sequence after it, even though she can have
heard that Bee was seeking to extend the sequence further.

```
(7.10) TG, 1:04-08
1 Bee: F    -> hHowuh you:?
2 Ava: S    -> Oka:::y?hh=
3 Bee: SCT -> =Good.=Yihs[ou:nd] hh
4 Ava: F    ->           [<I wan]'dih know if yih got a-uh:m
5              wutchimicawllit. A:: pah(hh)khing place ° th's
6              mornin'.˙hh
```

The assessment term in third position can license the start of a next sequence
even in face of its speaker's effort to override that apparent entitlement. And
this virtually canonical third position sequence closing move operates for
such "personal state inquiry" sequences even outside their most common
positioning in openings, and even with multiple answerers, as in the following sequence, initiated by a visitor some fifteen to twenty minutes into
a get-together of two couples for dinner.

```
(7.11) KC-4, 11:17-28
1 Rub:     Whenever I need a doctor for one purpose
2          or another I always give him a call.
3 Dav:     °Yeah hhe[heh°
```

```
 4 Rub:                  [And ah:: (1.2) he knows them a:ll,
 5                  (2.5)
 6 Rub: F     -> Sa howaryou people?
 7                  (1.0)
 8 Kat: S     -> We're fine,
 9 Dav: S     -> (Oh)/(No-) No complaints.
10 Rub: SCT -> Goo:d.
11                  (1.2)
12 Rub:          So listen.-Are you- uh this thing on Long Island
13              is off?
```

But "howaryou" sequences are hardly the only type which can take assessments in third position as a move to close the sequence. In the following exchange, for example, guests for dinner have just arrived and, having noticed the camera which is being used to videotape the dinner's interaction, are checking it out.

```
(7.12) Chinese Dinner, 2:20-28
1 Don: F     -> I:s this ai:med accurate enou:gh?
2                  (0.5)
3 Joh: S     -> Yes it's aimed et the table.
4 Don: SCT -> Grea:t.
5                  (1.0)
```

Nor are all assessments punchy, one-word, upbeat cheers. For example, in the exchange which was discussed in our earlier examination of insert expansions as Extract (6.13) (reproduced below for convenience), in which a prospective visitor is asking directions to her prospective host's home, the "pre-direction-giving" insert expansion is composed of more than a first pair part and a second pair part:

```
(7.13) Schegloff, 1972:107 (previously [6.13])
 1 Bel:          You know, I have [a house, a big garden-
 2 Ann:                           [Yes.
 3 Bel:          Why don't you come and see me some[times.
 4 Ann:                                            [I would like to.
 5 Bel:          I would like you to. Let me [just-
 6 Ann: F_b   ->                             [I don't know just where
 7           -> the- uh- this address [is.
 8 Bel: F_ins ->                      [Well where do- which part of
 9           -> town do you live.
10 Ann: S_ins -> I live at four ten east Lowden.
11                  (2.0)
12 Bel: SCT -> Well, you don't live very far from me.
13      S_b  -> If you go on the State (1.0) High- no if you go out
14              past the courthouse [to Elmhurst.
15 Ann:                            [Yeah.
```

At line 12, following the insert expansion's first pair part and second pair part, the insert expansion is given a sequence-closing minimal expansion, and this takes the form of an assessment: "Well, you don't live very far from me." (Note again, then, that not only base sequences can take minimal post-expansions; other expansion sequences can take post-expansion as well.)

There are other turn types (in addition to "oh," "okay," and assessments) which can be used to move for sequence closure after a second pair part as well – for example, some repeats of the second pair part turn, though many such repeats do not appear to be in the service of sequence closure, and some appear designedly equivocal in this regard. For example, the repeat at line 4 in Extract (7.14) serves to close the repair sequence and the preceding talk continues at line 5.

```
(7.14) TG, 4:12-18
1 Ava:          [Oh I ha]ve thee- I have one class in the e:vening.
2 Bee: F    -> On Mondays?
3 Ava: S    -> Y-uh::: Wednesdays.=
4 Bee: SCT ->  =Uh-Wednesday,=
5 Ava:          =En it's like a Mickey Mouse course. hh It's a joke, hh
6               ih-Speech.
```

However, the speaker whose repeat apparently serves as a sequence-closing third may then go on to extend the sequence, as in the following excerpt, which comes a moment after the exchanges reproduced in Extract (7.03).

```
(7.15) HG, 16:40-17:03
1 Nan: F    -> =Nice Jewish bo:y?
2 Hyl: S    -> O:f cou:rse,=
3 Nan: SCT ->  ='v [cou:rse,]
4 Hyl:          [hh-hh-hh] hnh ·hhhhh=
5 Nan:          =Nice Jewish boy who doesn'like tih write letters?
6               (.)
7 Hyl:          eYe::h, ·hhh En he ma:de such a big dea::l a:bout id . . .
```

And the repeat in third position can be equivocal between use as a sequence-closing third on the one hand and its use as a form of repair initiation on the other – a use which is specifically extending the sequence. In characterizing its use as "equivocal," I mean, of course, to be pointing to its equivocality for the participants, and, in particular, its recipient. For example, Mike and Vic have been discussing Vic's idiosyncratic, personal theology:

```
(7.16) US, 36:05-14
1 Mik: F   -> =W'll what are yer religious beliefs.
2              (0.8)
3 Vic: S   -> Uh, (0.7) S'preme being.
4              (0.8)
5 Mik: SCT-> Supreme being.
6 Vic:       [And,
```

```
 7 Mik:        [God
 8 Vic:        Yeh and I get confu:sed when I said supreme being en
 9             I:, `hh is- (0.5) Dat- dat's where I get fucked up.
10             (1.0)
```

After the repeat at line 5, Vic appears ready (at line 6) to continue what he was saying before Mike's question at line 1, whereas Mike appears to have treated the repeat as a way to stop and consider what to make of that usage, which he then pursues at line 7.

Composites

As noted earlier, various of the practices for moving for sequence closure in third position of a sequence can be combined, although ordinarily a third-position turn will combine no more than two of them.

A particularly common composite is "oh" plus "okay," in that order. A by-now-familiar feature of sequence organization occasions such a form of turn as a possible sequence-closing.

We noted earlier (pp. 73–78) that turn types such as question, telling, and assessment can occur not only as actions in their own right; they can also serve as the format through which other types of actions get done. We initially encountered this possibility of multiple practices embodied in a turn with respect to *first* pair parts, in the interests of delineating the possibility of multiple preference structures shaping a sequence simultaneously, and not always compatibly. Now we need to note that a similar duality can characterize second pair parts as well.

For example, although some tellings are undertaken simply to convey information, others serve to carry the materials with which rejection (to cite one example) can be conveyed. Drew (1984), for example, has described in detail how speakers may decline invitations by reporting facts that stand in the way of accepting them – a way of avoiding the explicit doing of a dispreferred second pair part. Here is an instance (not taken from Drew) of such a sequence, taken from a telephone call made by one sister to another who lives nearby.

```
(7.17) Erhardt, 1:10-21
 1 Vic: Fb   -> =I ca:lled um to see if you want to uh (0.4) c'm over
 2             en watch,the Classics Theater.
 3             (0.3)
 4 Vic:        Sandy'n Tom'n I,=
 5 Kar: Fins -> =She Sto[ops t'Conquer?
 6 Vic:              [(  )-
 7             (0.4)
 8 Vic: Sins -> Yeh.
 9             (0.3)
```

```
10 Kar: Sb   -> Mom js asked me t'watch it with her,h=
11 Vic: SCT -> =Oh. Okay,
12               (0.3)
```

Note first the gap which follows the invitation (at line 3), hinting at the possibility of a rejection, followed by an insert expansion (lines 5–8) further breaking contiguity between base first pair part and second pair part and further projecting a dispreferred response, a projection still further enhanced by another gap after the second pair part of the insert expansion. So rejection is heavily in the air here. When Karen responds at line 10, the overt form of her utterance is that of an informing: she has just been invited by their mother to watch it with her. But this conveying of information is implementing an action with respect to the invitation as well; it is, in effect, declining the invitation by offering an account for the rejection.[7]

Note, then, that in third position the inviter deploys two sequence-closing-relevant tokens. The "oh" registers receipt of the information; the "okay" registers and accepts the declining of the invitation which that information implements. And note as well that these two tokens – one addressed to the implementing format and the other to the action being formatted – occur in the same order encountered earlier (pp. 73–78) in two-component second pair parts addressed to complex first pair parts: "no, thank you" in response to a question-formatted offer deploys the format-related element first ("no" as the "answer to the question") and the action-related element thereafter ("thank you" as the "response to the offer").

Many composite third-position minimal expansion turns may be examined as indicators of such a multifaceted character to the sequence whose closing is at issue. We will briefly examine several such two-component sequence-closing thirds below. We should, however, also be alerted to a new way of inspecting single-component sequence-closing thirds which is suggested by the preceding discussion, and in particular ones composed of "oh" alone. For on many occasions the information registered by "oh" will have been implementing some other action as well, and the absence of an "okay" (or other action-accepting third-position token) may mark the only-partial character of the move to sequence closing.

In the following exchange, for example, the hosts for this dinner of take out Chinese food (Beth and John) have called attention to their new

---

[7] That this is the understanding of the parties themselves is amply displayed in the ensuing interaction, not least of all in the following launching of the conversation's closing:

```
(7.18) Erhardt, 2:22-27
1  Vic:     Oka:y well I jis ca:lled tu:h (0.4) teh:: (·) ask,=
2  Kar:     =Thanks [a    l  o:  t, ]
3  Vic: ->          [though'v cour]se I knew [the   ans]wer would be no: hnh
4  Kar:                                      [(really)]
5  Kar:     Yehhh
6           (2.0)
```

tableware, and the guests (Don and Ann) have commented on the variety of
its colors. The hostess responds:

```
(7.19) Chinese Dinner, 10:05-17
 1 Bet:        They didn' have all the colors, 'hh The orange is really
 2             nice b't they only had it in, 'hh these bowls, and uhm,
 3             (0.5) (the coffee mugs).
 4 Don:        Mmkh=
 5 Ann:        =Which is orange.
 6             (0.7)
 7 Don:        The reddy orange.
 8 Bet:        This one.
 9 Ann: ->     °Oh::.
10 Bet: ->     The reddish,
11             (1.8)
12 Ann: ->     Mimm.
13             (4.0)
```

Note first that "the orange" is introduced (at lines 1–2) as "really nice"
by Beth, an assessment which makes a second assessment relevant next
(Pomerantz, 1984) and an agreeing one preferred. Ann's launching of a
repair sequence (line 5) already adumbrates "trouble" in this regard, and
after Ann has been shown which is "the orange" by both her husband and her
hostess in the repair sequence (lines 7–8), she registers her being informed
with an "oh." But that "leaves out" the agreeing assessment which is still
relevant, and Beth's further identification of the color with "the reddish"
(line 10), which provides a further place for a second assessment, still fails
to occasion one. Here the missing assessment is really a missing response to
Beth's earlier assessment, rather than a missing component of a sequence-
closing third, but this is what such turns often look like. Extract (7.20) is a
case in point.

Vic is a janitor/custodian in New York in the early 1970s, and has been
"hanging out" with his friends in a local used-furniture store. He has been
recounting his involvement in cleaning up a vandalism to a nearby building
when his wife Carol calls him. We have encountered this exchange before
(see Extract [1.06] on p. 10 and Extract [4.27] on pp. 51–53), both for its
exemplification of a "counter" (at lines 7–9) and the generic summons –
answer pre-sequence (at lines 4–6):

```
(7.20) US, 3:13-27
 1 Mik:        Jim wasn' home, [°(when y'wen over there)]
 2 Vic:                        [ I  didn'  go  by  theh.]=
 3 Vic:        =I [left my garbage pail in iz [hallway.=
 4 Car:           [Vi:c,                      [
 5 Car:                                       [Vic(tuh),
 6 Vic:        =Yeh?
 7 Car: Fb     C'mmere fer a minnit.
```

```
 8                  (0.7)
 9 Vic:             Y'come [he:re.
10 Car:                    [You c'co[me ba:ck,
11 Vic:                             [please?
12 Vic: Sb          I haftuh go t'the bathroom.=
13 Car: SCT->       =Oh.
14                  (3.5)
15 Vic:             ((From a distance to Mike)) I cleaned'n=I left
16                  my garbage pail in the ha:llway yihknow'm I nope-I
17                  hope he don't c(h)laim it yuh kno(h)w,
18                  (13.0)
```

After Vic's counter (line 9), Carol responds (line 10) by reassuring Vic that her request is not a pretext to disengage him from his buddies, in effect re-instituting her request in response to his counter. Vic deflects this insistence not by rejecting it outright, but by providing an account for such a rejection, which in effect does the rejection (as did the declining of the invitation by offering an account in Extract [7.17] above). This account is embodied in his informing her that he has to "go to the bathroom." Note then that her sequence-closing third here (at line 13) registers receipt of his information, but not acceptance of the rejection of her request which that information is implementing. In an exchange such as this we can see that for some sequence contexts, a composite or multi-part third-position turn is relevant for sequence closing, it is not "extra." In fact, a turn like Carol's at line 13 is missing something, something with potential bearing for subsequent interaction.[8]

So we need both to examine *composite* third-position turns to see what multiple tracks the preceding sequence has been running on, and we need to examine *single component* third-position turns to see whether the preceding sequence has been running on multiple tracks, and whether therefore

---

[8] And, indeed, a few minutes later, here is how that interaction is resumed.

```
(7.21) US, 5:34-6:09
 1 Vic:  °Yeh honey?
 2 Car:  What,
 3 Vic:  You said fer me tih come tih you?=Wu:djuh want ho[ney?
 4 Car:                                                  [Yeuh.
 5       (0.5)
 6 Vic:  Wha[t.
 7 Car:     [I ash you t'take a walk across th'street with me fer
 8       a minnit=
 9 Vic:  =Okay (honey. Okay.)/(I'll be back.)     ((to Mike & Joe?))
10       (1.0)
11 Vic:  I'll be (right witchu.)/(back inna minnit.)
12       (1.5)
13 Vi?:  (                        ).
14 Joe:  (Yeh have fun.)
15       (3.5)
16 Mik:  ((whispered)) (Now they're gonna, hack it.)
17       (2.7)
```

something may be "missing" which is informative about the state of the interaction, both to the co-participants and to external observers. We have sampled both of these lines; in what follows, we can sample only a bit further.

Extract (7.22) is drawn from the earlier-cited (7.01) car trip to an extended family party. As the car draws closer to its destination, Deb voices misgivings that she had failed in months past to send a baby gift to a cousin, at whose parents' house the party is being held.

```
(7.22) Pre-Party, 11:23-30
1 Deb: F   -> [I don't think I ever sent M]arcia
2              a birth- a present for her baby did I?=or did we buy
3              something t'gether
4              (0.3)
5 Deb:         Mo:m,
6 Ann: S   -> Yeah I think we di:d.
7 Deb: SCT -> Oh:, good.
8              (1.2)
```

She seeks reassurance from her mother that a joint gift would have made her delinquency invisible to their imminent hosts. When her mother confirms the information (line 6), this at the same time serves as a reassurance about the earlier-expressed concern. This dual import is displayed in the two-part sequence-closing third – an information-receipting "oh," and a reassurance-assessing "good."

A somewhat more celebratory version of the same "oh + assessment" composite moves to close a sequence in Extract (7.23). Karen is recounting a story about a bizarre lawsuit when a phone is heard ringing (line 6) in a neighboring room in the college dormitory which is the setting here, and Karen abandons her telling mid-course (line 9) to attend to it (possibly in response to a physically embodied show of interest by one of the other participants; video is lacking for this material). The "attending" takes the form of a "negative formulation" ("I don't think that's our phone"), potentially carrying overtones of complaint (cf. Schegloff, 1988) and disappointment.

```
(7.23) SN-4, 16:29-17:20
1 Mar:         Are you serious¿ [becuss there was] yellow li:ght?
2 Kar:                          [I'm   serious.  ]
3              (0.4)
4 Kar:         This really strange light.<Yihknow, like
5              [old fashioned lights?]
6              [  ((phone rings))    ]
7              (1.0)
8 Ma?:         (°S'cuze [me°)
9 Kar: F   ->          [(A:n:: (0.2) I don't think that's our phone.
10                (0.2)
```

```
11 Rut: S    -> Oh I'll see.
12                (1.4)    ((phone rings)) ((door latch sound))=
13 Kar: F    -> =Is it?
14 Rut: S    -> Ye:p
15 Kar: SCT -> O::h. Hallelujah.
16 Ma?:         Hhh. hh
17                (1.0)
18 Mar:         W'l anyway listen I gotta go:,I gotta do alotta
19              studying,
```

The informing (line 14) that it *is* their phone is, then, not merely information,
but (as in Extract [7.22]) a kind of reassurance and neutralization of the
incipient complaint. The sequence-closing third proceeds on both fronts:
an informational change-of-state token and an upbeat assessment of its
import.

In Extract (7.24) we see a different combination of sequence-closing
tokens, "okay + repeat." Here, Fred has been recruited to bring various
items of food and convenience to the family living room, and is, in effect,
"taking orders."

```
(7.24) Post-Party, 15:29-41
 1 Fre: Fb   -> Whatchu want Naome, c'mon (I- ) come t'the
 2              ki[(tchen.)
 3 Nao: Sb   ->    [Please a glass a'milk, ]
 4 Deb: Sb   ->    [ Water fer  me   FRE:d, ]
 5 Fre:         Ajuu[shhh! ((sneeze))
 6 Mar: Sb   ->        [ En'n ash[ tray fer  ]me Fred,
 7 Fre:                  [(Scuze me?)]
 8 Fre: Fpost-> What?
 9 Mar: Spost-> A:shtray fer me,
10 Fre: Fpost-> (Two [ashtrays?)]
11 Deb: Spost->      [ Ashtray, ]water, milk.
12 Fre: SCT -> Okay. En ashtray en ennything tuh drink.
13              (0.5)
```

One order requires repetition because of Fred's sneeze and he then repeats
it himself (consolidating it with a previous order), and Deb then sums up
the order (line 11), aggregating the components of the several second pair
parts here – the answer to Fred's inquiry at line 1 and its multiplication. In
the following turn, Fred then accepts this responsive action with an "okay,"
and displays his specific task-oriented stance by again repeating (in what
turns out to be a consequentially faulted way) the task he now sets out to
execute.

In Extract (7.25), the family we have been tracking before and after an
extended family party has just left the party; line 1 reports the shutting of
the car door for the trip back home. This is quite a complicated spate of talk,

with four distinct sequences being in play, three of them involving Marty in one way or another. The letters following the speaker identifications identify the components of the several distinct exchanges, each to be examined in what follows.

```
(7.25) Post-Party, 2:25-3:11
 1              ((door slams))
 2 ???:        ahhhhhh
 3 Ann: ->a    Marty she took my ma:tches [k  i  n   I ] have a match,
 4 Fre: ->b                                [door locked?]
 5 Mar: ->a    Su:re, hmhh
 6 Fre: ->b    Mom[c'n you gitcher door?]
 7 Nao: ->c       [  E n        D a : d ]dy, hh
 8 Mar: ->c    Yea:h,
 9 De?:        [ukh!             ((cough))
10 Nao: ->c    [ho- willyuh hold this,
11 Mar: ->c    Wudiszit.
12 Fre: ->b    (mom, [            )
13 Nao: ->c          [My bracelet.
14 Mar: ->c    Oh okay hh I got it.`hh
15             (0.2)/(0.5)
16 Mar: ->a    Here's a match,
17 Deb: ->d    Boy didju know you were gonna get all those presents
18      ->d    [Naomi?] ((falsetto))
19 Ann: ->d    [ No:: ]::.
20             (0.7)
21 Fre: ->b    Mom lock yer door huh,
22                (0.8)
23 Mar: ->b    I got it,
24 Fre: ->b    °Oh thanks.
25 Deb: ->d    I didn'know you were g'nnuh g[et all those pr]esents,
26 Fre: ->b                                 [ My  paranoia. ]
27             (2.0)
```

In the first of these exchanges, marked by the letter "a," Anne asks Marty for a match (lines 3, 5, 16).

```
(7.25a) Post-Party, segment a
 3 Ann:  Marty she took my ma:tches [k  i  n  I ] have a match,
 5 Mar:  Su:re, hmhh
         (9.0)
16 Mar:  Here's a match,
```

In the second of the exchanges, marked by the letter "b," Fred asks his mother (Anne) to make sure her car door is locked and Marty eventually intervenes to see to it (lines 4, 6, 12, 21, 23, 24, 26).

```
(7.25b) Post-Party, segment b
4  Fre:   [door locked?]
          (1.0)
6  Fre:   Mom[c'n you gitcher door?]
          (5.0)
12 Fre:   (mom,[        )
          (7.0)
21 Fre:   Mom lock yer door huh,
          (0.8)
23 Mar:   I got it,
24 Fre:   °Oh thanks.
          (2.0)
26 Fre:   [ My  paranoia, ]
          (2.0)
```

In the third of the exchanges, marked by the letter "c," Naomi (aged 3–4) asks her father (Marty) to hold something of hers for her (lines 7, 8, 10, 11, 13, and 14).

```
(7.25c) Post-Party, segment c
7  Nao: F_pre ->  [ E n      D a: d ]dy, hh
8  Mar: S_pre ->  Yea:h,
   De?:            [ukh!          ((cough))
10 Nao: F_b   ->  [ho- willyuh hold this,
11 Mar: F_ins ->  Wudiszit.
                  (.)
13 Nao: S_ins ->  [My bracelet.
14 Mar: ???   ->  Oh okay hh I got it. ˙hh
                  (0.2)/(0.5)
```

In the fourth exchange, marked by the letter "d," Naomi's mother and grand-mother launch a review of the party with her, focusing on the presents which she received (lines 17–18, 19, and 25). The fourth sequence continues past the end of the extract reproduced here and will not be examined further.

Note that sequence "a" is a request sequence, but there is no sequence closing third for us to examine: there is the request itself (line 3) and a two-part response: a compliance marker to begin with (line 5) and a subsequent talk-marked delivery (line 16). But there are two turns which appear ripe for examination for our purposes here: lines 14 (in segment c) and 24 (in segment b). It will be worth analyzing line 14, if only to establish that it is *not*, in fact, a composite sequence-closing third, and line 24 to establish that it *is*, and what kind.

The exchange between Marty and Naomi (in segment c) exemplifies many of the resources we have touched on in this volume. It begins with a pre-expansion, the generic summons–answer pre-sequence at lines 7–8 ("En Daddy," "Yeah") whose preferred "go-ahead"-type response leads to the base first pair part, here a request ("ho- willyuh hold this"). Before responding to this request, Marty initiates an insert expansion, an other-initiated repair sequence directed to the repairable "it" – "wudiszit," "my bracelet," and this is followed by our target turn at line 14, "Oh okay hh I got it."

The three components of this turn are not identically positioned relative to the sequences-in-progress. The "oh" is a sequence-closing third to the other-initiated repair sequence which has been inserted into the base request sequence; it registers as "news" the information conveyed in the just-preceding turn. The "okay," however, is not another sequence-closing third for the same sequence; it is not accepting the prior turn as a response to *its* predecessor. Rather, it is itself a response to a first pair part; this "okay" is the agreement to the request at line 10; it is the base second pair part. More accurately, it is *part* of the base second pair part; it is the first part of the talk component of a second pair part turn which is composed of a talk part and a physically implemented action part which the talk accompanies (as in sequence "a," where Marty hands Anne the matches while remarking to that effect). The second part of the talk component is the "I got it," which reports accomplishment of the action which the "okay" agreed to do.

Segment b is an instructive comparison with segment c. It is also a request sequence; Fred is requesting (or trying to request of the somewhat hard-of-hearing Anne) that his mother lock her car door. His first try (line 4) is "indirect," asking whether the door is already locked as a way of prompting the locking if it is not. When this effort is ineffective – i.e., when it fails to engender a responsive action which might indicate that the request had been registered – he tries again (line 6), this time making explicit that it is a request, what the request is (though only with the idiomatic and rather anaphoric "get your door"), and who the targeted "requestee" is. When this try also fails to register, Fred apparently tries again (at line 12), although the sound is sufficiently muddled on the tape to frustrate confident transcription, though it may have been quite accessible within the confines of the car. It was apparently accessible to Marty, who intervenes and produces the second pair part although he was not the party selected to do so. Again there are two components to this second pair part: an action and talk which accompanies and remarks on the action – in this case a compliance marker whose use of the verb "get" (in "I got it") serves to connect this turn to the request to which it is responding (i.e., "get your door"), and to show thereby that it is designed to be responsive to that request. (Note that this is quite a different "got" than the one in line 14 – "oh okayhh I got it." – which, in *its* sequence, conveys that its speaker is holding the object being passed and that the "passer" can release it. It is striking that the sequence structure can allow affiliation of this word to a different usage of it by a different speaker over the same usage by the same speaker.) It is after this second pair part by other than the selected next speaker, complying with a request by other than the requestee, that the target turn is placed – "Oh thanks."

Now it is possible that, by virtue of its intonational delivery, the "oh" in this turn should not be understood as a free-standing "oh" at all, and that the turn is better understood as an "oh-prefaced response" (Heritage, 1998). On the other hand, in the terms which have been the topic of this chapter, this turn appears to be a composite sequence-closing third: its first part receipts the information that a third party has registered, and is acting on, Fred's multiple tries at his first pair part, and its second part – "thanks" – is a sequence-appropriate acceptance of a second pair part as a response to a first pair part for the sequence-type "requests" (rather than for the more-specific circumstance here, in which a third party has intervened to respond to the request).[9]

It should by now be clear that the "sequence-closing thirds" which we have been examining are all contingent possibilities. Each element of such turns – "oh," "okay," "thanks," assessment terms, etc. – can occur in a

---

[9] A nice comparison case is furnished by the following sequence, in which Don asks a child at the dinner table to pass a container of food and has the child's mother intervene to comply with the request.

```
(7.26) Chinese Dinner, 25:11-38
 1  Bet:        And things thet probly- actually mighta happened
                [tuh him.=
 2  Ann:        [Mm-hm?
 3  Bet:     =(um) in[i z      [y'know,
 4  Ann:              [Mm-hm?   [
 5  Joh:                        [((cough))
 6  Ann:                        [Mm-hm?
 7  Don:  ->  Hey Jerry,
 8  Bet:      An' it-[ he- he- i t- ]
 9  Don:  ->         [Will you pass ] that (.)
10              [(uh,)/(carton)
11  Bet:      [sort'v ra:[mbles 'n re[pea: t s , ]
12  Jer:  ->             [Uh this?     [
13  Don:  ->                           [This one he]re,
14              (0.5)
15  Bet:      Y'know?
16              (0.2)
17  Bet:      Like[I-=
18  Ann:          [ Yea[h.                    ((Ann nodding))
19  Bet:              =[I remember th[ose day:s when I use]=
20  Don:  ->                         [Oh: thank you Beth, ]
21  Bet:      =tuh[(    ) y'know?=     ((passing carton of food to Don))
22  Don:  ->      [Okay.
23  Don:  ->  =Thanks Beth.
24  Bet:      tell the same story three times o[ver.
25  Ann:                                       [Ooo.
```

Here Beth's intervention is marked by doing the requested action alone with no accompanying talk. That is, the talk she produces while passing the requested food is not "accompanying talk for the response to the request"; it is more of the talk she was already in the process of producing. Note, then, that Don's sequence-closing third includes an "oh" and "thank you Beth" as he sees her conduct project a course of action which will respond to his request – he registers the information which her body behavior has conveyed – and accepts the action which she shows herself to be undertaking. When that action is complete, he does another sequence-closing third, this time accepting the action and marking its request-complying status.

wide variety of contexts, as can combinations of them. Indeed, some "combinations of them" are better thought of as juxtapositions of them; as we have seen, in some "oh okays" the "oh" and the "okay" are parts of distinct sequence units. So, to begin with, whether any one or combination of these elements is possibly making a sequence-closing move depends on its positioning (after a second pair part, at a place in the turn's development where the second pair part turn appears designed for closure, etc.) and on its prosody (some "ohs" and "okays," to cite just those, are clearly designed as uptakes of pieces of an ongoing telling or proposal, or as launches of a just-touched-off utterance). Here, as elsewhere, what something is doing depends on both its position and its composition, and its composition may well turn as consequentially on its mode of delivery as on its lexical composition. All this goes to the very relevancy of some such forms of utterance as candidate moves for possible sequence closure.

Beyond that, however, is the contingency of such a move in its effects. The turn formats we have been examining can constitute *possible* closure for a sequence, and often enough the parties treat a turn-constructional unit composed in one of the above-described formats that way. Ensuing talk launches a new sequence, or a lapse of such duration sets in as is tantamount to sequence closure, even if it is ended by talk which turns out to be more of what preceded the lapse. This is what happens in most of the sequences examined in this chapter.

On the other hand, the import of this practice (that is, turns after an SPP and in one of these formats) as a practice for *possible* sequence closure in third position is that it may be followed by further talk which extends the sequence – often after a slight gap in which the matter may hang in the balance – by either the speaker of the possible sequence-closing third, or by the speaker of the second pair part, or indeed by another party.

Some such continuations past possible sequence closure will seem to have been "in the cards" in view of the only partial character of the composition of the move to sequence closure; an information-registering "oh" without an action-accepting "okay" may richly adumbrate the possibility of continuation within the very possibility of sequence closure. In Extract (7.27), for example, Emma and Lottie are talking about the current fishing conditions in their beach-side community. When Emma mentions a fishing trip which her husband is scheduled to go on (lines 1–3), Lottie responds with the offer of another trip which, it turns out, she is helping to organize (lines 5–6):

```
(7.27) NB I:6, 2:11-29
 1 Emm:        B[ud's goin on a trip here wih th'comp'ny=
 2 Lot:         [°Jesus°
 3 Emm:        =in a c- (.) coupla weeks: so,
 4                 (0.3)
 5 Lot: F  ->  .hhh Hey I gotta good trip if he wantstuh go it's
```

```
 6                    onna Mondee though c'n 'e go on tha[:t?]
 7 Emm: S     ->                                     [ n:] No=
 8                    =u- he's goin with the Gas Comp'n eez all booked
 9                    up. So that'll be enough fer him.
10                    (0.5)
11 Lot: SCT  -> Oh:.
12 Emm: +S   -> They're goin out yihknow they (.) charter a boat f'm
13                    San Diego.=
14 Lot:       -> =Yeah we gotta boa[t chartered too=
15 Emm:                            [mighhm
16 Lot:             =ther's gonna be js. twunny of us. It's a [big-
17 Emm:                                                       [Mm:.
18 Lot:             sixty two foot boat.
19 Emm:       -> When yuh goin.
```

Emma rejects the offer on her husband's behalf (lines 7–9), and Lottie
responds with an "oh" in sequence-organizational third position. But this
sequence-closing third is composed only of an information-registering "oh";
she does not display a stance of acceptance of the rejection of her offer. When
Emma resumes talk, it is with a continuation of her second pair part turn,
elaborating the attractive features of the trip which her husband is already
scheduled to take (lines 12–13), but this provides Lottie with an opening
to detail the attractive features of the trip she is offering, in the interests
of getting Emma to withdraw or qualify her rejection. That she has some
success in this is suggested by Emma's inquiry at line 19.

So, also in Extract (7.28), talk in a sequence continues past a sequence-
closing third directed to registering news, and comes to closure when the
responsive action of its second pair part is accepted in a further sequence-
closing third. A few minutes earlier in this conversation, Tony had been
told the news that his teenaged son Joey was flying to join him at home
in Northern California instead of driving because the convertible top had
been stolen from his car at the end of a holiday visit with his mother in
Southern California. Tony had reacted (in part) by asking (and possibly
complaining), "and he's not gonna bring it back?" Marsha (Tony's ex-wife
and Joey's mother) had answered briefly ("No") and gone on to detail the
altered travel arrangements. On their completion, at lines 1–2, Tony returns
to the issue of the car (line 1), but follows it with an expression of outrage
(lines 2 and 5).

```
(7.28) MDE-MTRAC 60-1/2, 1:35-2:22
 1 Ton: Fb  -> W't's 'e g'nna do go down en pick it up later? er
 2                    somethin like (    ) [well that's aw]:ful
 3 Mar:                                    [H i s   friend ]
 4 Mar:             Yeh h[is friend Stee- ]
 5 Ton:                  [That really makes] me ma:d,
 6                    (0.2)
```

```
 7 Mar:              'hhh Oh it's disgusti[ng ez a matter a'f]a:ct.
 8 Ton:                            [P o o r  J o e y ,]
 9 Mar:              I- I, I told my ki:ds. who do this: down et the Drug
10                   Coalition ah want th'to:p back.h ·'hhhhhhhhh ((1.0 th))
11                   SEND OUT the WO:RD.hhh hnh
12                   (0.2)
13 Ton:              Yeah.
14 Mar: Sb ->        'hhh Bu:t u-hu:ghh his friend Steve en Brian er driving
15                   up. Right after:: (0.2) school is out.En then hi'll
16                   drive do:wn here with the:m.
17 Ton: SCT->        Oh I see.
18 Mar: +S ->        So: in the long run, 'hhh it (·) probly's gonna save a
19                   liddle time 'n: energy.
20 Ton: SCT->        Okay,
21 Mar:              But Ile:ne probably (0.8) is either at the airport er
22                   waiting tuh hear fr'm in eess
23                   (0.7)
24 Ton:              O:kay.
25 Mar:              'hhhh So: yer ba:ck.
```

Marsha's efforts to address the issue of the car are frustrated (at lines 3 and 4) by this "expressive" second part of Tony's intervention, but she finally does speak to the question (lines 14–16). (Various features of the construction of this talk show it to be addressed to the earlier question across the otherwise-focused intervening talk – especially the references to "driving up" and "driving down" in response to the question's references to "go down" and "pick it up.") Tony receipts this answer (at line 17) with an "oh I see," registering the *information*, and registering that it addresses his question. Marsha, however, continues, and in her continuation addresses herself no longer to the information, but to the satisfactoriness of the *arrangement* as a solution to the problem of getting the car back to Northern California. Tony's "okay" (line 20) serves to align him with this proposal of a solution to the problem, and when Marsha continues talking after it (lines 21–22), it is no longer as part of this sequence, but rather on another still-open matter – how Joey will get from the airport back to his father's house. Here again, then, but with a tenor different from that in Extract (7.27), different usages deployed as sequence-closing moves – "oh" and "okay" – contribute differentially to the shaping of the ensuing talk and its possible closure.

In these episodes, a sequence is extended past a sequence-closing third when its speaker does not construct that turn in a fashion designed to close the sequence with respect to both information receipt and action acceptance. In other cases, the sequential *position* of third position at issue may be more to the point than its *composition*. For example, in Extract (7.29), the continuing relevance – but non-occurrence – of a base second pair part after the sequence-closing third of an insert sequence appears to prompt further talk by the first pair part speaker. Bee has asked Ava whether she is likely to "be around" during the upcoming long holiday weekend from school, and Ava responds to this pre-invitation with an extended account of the activities she may be involved in, but leaving the conclusion a hedge. Then:

```
(7.29) TG, 16:11-23
 1 Bee: Fb      ->                      [Well if yer arou:nd I'll probably see
 2                      y(hh)ou hn[hh! `hh
 3 Ava: Fins1                      [Why, whu(ts) (Bob doing)
 4 Bee: Sins1           Uh-u-uh:: goin o:ff::
 5 Ava: Fins2   ->      Where's he goin.
 6 Bee: Sins2   ->      To Wa:shin'ton,
 7 Ava: SCT     ->      Oh.
 8                      (0.7)
 9 Bee: +Sins2  ->      He asn' been there sih-since Christmas
10                      [so:. hHe's going.
11 Ava:                 [Mm.
12                      (0.5)
13 Ava: Sb      ->      Yeh w'l I'll give you a call then tomorrow.when I
14                      get in 'r sumn.
```

Note, here, that at line 5, Ava does not move to close the insert sequence which she had launched after the highly qualified move to get together issued by Bee at lines 1–2; rather she extends it with another question ("Where's he goin"). After the answer to this question (line 6), however, she does move to close the sequence with a sequence-closing third (line 7). The sequence which Ava has been promoting appears to have been an information-requesting one; though, to be sure, ostensibly in the service of the arrangements tentatively being broached. Still, no "okay" appears prima facie relevant here. But the gap of silence at line 8 is the place at which a response is due from Ava to the muted proposal at lines 1–2, and the silence represents a withholding of that response. The response had in the first instance been deferred by the insert expansion, and thereby had been made to appear contingent on it. Now, in the absence of response to the base sequence by Ava, the second pair part speaker in the insert expansion (Bee) starts up again, and builds her talk overtly as an elaboration of the preceding second pair part (the "there" building in a reference to "Washington" and the "goin" reusing an element of the question). On completion of this elaboration (actually, with a bit of delay after it), the pending response by Ava to the arrangement is received, and it is a forthcoming one (lines 13–14).

In the preceding two episodes, we have seen a sequence extended past a possible sequence-closing third. In both instances, the extension was undertaken by the second pair part speaker, in both cases by extending the second pair part. In one instance this was possibly prompted by the compositionally partial move to sequence closure; in the other, by a failure by the speaker of the sequence-closing third to proceed to the sequentially appropriate next move – a response to the base sequence underway. Other continuations past

possible sequence completion may be prompted by other aspects of the talk
in its context. We need only note that the fact that the sequence gets extended
should not be taken to subvert the claim that a move to closure was made.
It should instead prompt closer inspection of the design and placement of
that sequence-closing move and the character of the talk which passes it by,
to locate the interactional contingencies underlying these deployments.

Not all extensions of a sequence past a move to close in third position
are undertaken by the second pair part speaker; some are undertaken by the
speaker of the sequence-closing third itself (ordinarily also the first pair part
speaker). As we noted earlier in examining Extract (7.06) (a fuller version of
which is reproduced below), James is asking of his fellow janitor/custodian,
Vic, that he help identify the culprit in a vandalism of the apartment house
which is in his (James's) charge:

```
(7.30) US, 50:26-40
 1 Jam: F    -> Yeh. Uh-I dis wantuh know de person. That's all. You
 2              point me out to im someti:me,
 3 Vic: S    -> I will.
 4 Jam: SCT  -> A:lright.
 5 Vic: +S   -> I wi[ll.
 6 Jam: SCT  ->     [En I w-e(hh)h! Alright, then that's all
 7              I [wantuh know.
 8 Vic: +S   -> [(Alright.)
 9 Vic: +S   -> Okay.[(I will).
10 Jam: SCT+->      [Alright. Becau:se, it's insu:red anehway,
11              when I call de office, dey'll send a man up eh
12              tuh put that glass I:N.
13 Vic:        Well,
14 Jam:        But dis [person thet DID IT,
15 Vic:                [If I see the person,
16 Jam:        IS GOT TUH BE:: 'hh taken care of. You know what
17              [I mean,
```

We noted earlier the several rounds of sequence-closing thirds – at lines 4,
6, and 10. Actually it is the second pair part speaker, Vic, who talks further
in the sequence after its possible closing (at lines 5 and 8–9), repeating
his assurances after they have apparently been registered and accepted by
James. Eventually, however, it is James who more substantially extends
the sequence by elaborating an account for his request to have the suspect
"fingered" (lines 10ff.), and this leads to a still greater expansion of the
sequence (not shown here).

Some extensions of a sequence by the one who moved its closure are,
however, purely nominal, and involve nothing more than another sequence -
closing third. Extract (7.03), reproduced below, should already be familiar
(though the version below includes an additional turn).

```
(7.31) HG, 16:25-33
 1 Nan: F    -> = hhh Dz he av iz own apa:rt[mint?]
 2 Hyl: S    ->                         [ hhhh] Yea:h,=
 3 Nan: SCT -> =Oh:,
 4               (1.0)
 5 Nan: F    -> How didju git iz number,
 6               (·)
 7 Hyl: S    -> I(h) (·) c(h)alled infermation'n San
 8               Fr'ncissc(h)[uh!
 9 Nan: SCT ->             [Oh::::.
10               (·)
11 Nan: SCT -> Very cleve:r,hh=
```

Note here that after the first move to closure at line 3 is followed by a gap, the prior speaker (the one who moved to close) talks again, and starts a new sequence (though still roughly on the same topic – Hyla's delinquent boyfriend). When this additional sequence is brought to possible closure by its own sequence-closing third (line 9), it once again is followed by a silence, and once again it is the first pair part speaker and sequence-close proposer who breaks it, but this time she does so with another move to sequence closure (line 11) – an assessment, however ironic. (As it happens, Hyla ignores the irony, treats the assessment as a compliment, and replies with a "Thank you"!)

This last sequence is notable for the fact that, not only is its first additional turn after the second pair part (at line 9) designed to be a minimal post-expansion (i.e., potentially just a single turn following the second pair part), but when another additional turn is produced (at line 11), it also is designed to be a potentially minimal post-expansion, one that bears some similarity to the last form of minimal post-expansion we can take up.

Our examination of minimal post-expansion concludes with a much less common form of minimal post-expansion.

Post-completion musings, or postmortems

The sequentially decisive measure of sequence completion is the onset of further talk which is not analyzably part of the preceding, possibly complete sequence. As with turns, sequences – however apparently "over" – can turn out not to have been over if the next thing that happens adds to them. The best indicator that something – a turn, a sequence – is ended is the start of another, or of something else. Although the apparently ended unit can even then seem to be revived, in most cases this will be apparent as the practice which someone is deploying, and, by deploying it, they give evidence that the unit being revived is in need of reviving – i.e., to do more of it requires dealing with its otherwise apparent completedness.

There are, however, utterances which can occur after the apparent completion of a sequence which do *not* launch a new sequence or new "business" embodied in some other type of organizational unit, *do* relate in a fashion to the preceding talk, and yet do not ordinarily appear to be treated as expansions of it, even minimal ones. One way they may achieve this "non-consequential" character is by being produced as "out-louds" (Schegloff, 1988a:117), equivocally private or semi-public reflections or "musings," only equivocally making response relevant. For this reason they could be termed "post-completion musings." Because they regularly offer either some analysis/diagnosis of the prior sequence or some assessment of it (*of* it, not *in* it), they could be termed "postmortems." More often than not, they are articulated by someone who has not been a principal participant in the sequence that has come to possible completion; they are bits that a bystander or observer puts forward, drawing a moral, sympathizing or formulating the result or upshot of what appears to have been completed.

One case in point, as shown in Extract (7.32), comes from the family car trip to a party, which has been intermittently examined in this discussion. As that trip is reaching its destination (in a sequence examined earlier in another connection), Deb expresses a concern to her mother about a possibly unfulfilled obligation to a member of the family hosting the party to which they are going.

```
(7.32)  Pre-Party, 11:23-33
 1 Deb:                   [I don't think I ever sent M]arcia
 2      F     -> a birth- a present for her baby did I?=or did we buy
 3                something t'gether.
 4                (0.3)
 5 Deb:          Mo:m,
 6 Ann: S    -> Yeah I think we di:d.
 7 Deb: SCT  -> Oh:, good.
 8                (1.2)
 9 Fre: PCM  -> It's the nicest thing t'remember when yer- (going over
10                a see her)
11                (1.2)
12 Dic:          It isn't raining [very heavily (you know,)
```

Deb accepts (line 7) her mother's reassurance (line 6) in response to her concern and its possible resolution, and that (by-now-familiar) composite receipt of information and action – here "oh, good" – serves as possible closure for the sequence, a possibility not disappointed by the ensuing silence.

Note, then, that Fred's following utterance (at lines 9–10): a) concerns the prior sequence; b) does not extend the prior sequence but reflects on it (though these are not, of course, in principle mutually exclusive); c) engenders no further talk in response to itself (or as an increment to the preceding sequence whether in response to itself or not); but d) is followed by silence; which e) is broken by the potential start of a new,

unrelated, sequence. In fact, Fred's remark is an insightful (though inex-
actly formulated) observation concerning the ways in which one's orientations may turn to an incipient interaction as its onset approaches, a turning
which has here issued in a felicitous outcome (hence, "the nicest thing
t'remember").[10]

We have already had occasion to examine the episode reproduced as
Extract (7.33) for our discussions of preference, insert expansion, and
sequence closure.

```
(7.33) Erhardt, 1:10-26 (previously [7.17])
 1 Vic: F_b   ->  = I ca:lled um to see if you want to uh (0.4) c'm over
 2                en watch,the Classics Theater.
 3                (0.3)
 4 Vic: +F   ->  Sandy'n Tom'n I,=
 5 Kar: F_ins ->  =She Sto[ops t'Conquer?
 6 Vic:              [(  )-
 7                (0.4)
 8 Vic: S_ins ->  Yeh.
 9                (0.3)
10 Kar: S_b   ->  Mom js asked me t'watch it with her,h=
11 Vic: SCT  ->  =Oh. Okay,
12                (0.3)
13 Kar:           ihhh
14                (0.2)
15 Kar:           ↑˙hu:h ˙hh-hhh
16                (·)
17 Kar: PCM ->  °Gee I feel like a real nerd° you c'n ahl come up here,
18                (0.3)
19 Vic:           Nah, that's alright wil stay down here,
```

At line 11 Vicky apparently both registers the information which Karen
has just conveyed and its action-import; namely, a declining of the invitation which Vicky had tendered to Karen. Such a combination of sequence-
closing thirds can effectively do "marking the end of a sequence," and the
"silence" which follows does nothing to counteract that.[11] After almost
a second of such aspirated silence, Karen ("the rejector") offers a "musing," delivered as such in part by the sharply reduced volume in which it is
offered. Then, as if prompted by her own musing, Karen extends the project
("getting together"), though not the sequence, by launching a reciprocal

[10] It may be remarked as well that such postmortems may especially issue from parties not
   involved as primary participants in the sequence on which they remark – though, as will
   be seen shortly, this need not be the case.
[11] I put the word "silence" in quotes to register that this is interactionally ostensible silence,
   i.e., nothing being said, even though things are hearably happening, such as the in- and
   out-breaths which are surely subject to interpretation by co-participants.

sequence (see below at pp. 195–207), in which she invites Vicky and co to her place instead, an invitation which is itself declined.

Extract (7.34), from the pre-party car ride again, comes just after the apparent resolution of a dispute (only partially mock) between a mother (Ann, in her fifties) and her daughter (Deb, in her early thirties) following the daughter's complaint, "How come I never got a trousseau." While Ann takes on the complaint directly with a challenge, Deb's father Dick tries to desensitize the situation with a pun, responding to Deb, "Because you had a falso." This tactic is ineffective in defusing the incipient clash, and Ann and Deb work through – with some feeling– the question of whether or not Deb had gotten a trousseau. As the dispute is apparently coming to closure, Dick comments (lines 2–3) on his earlier pun/wisecrack to Marty, Deb's husband.

```
(7.34) Pre-Party, 7:01-40
 1                (0.8)
 2 Dic:     (Men-) Mendel I like(d) that quote.
 3          It wasn' a trousseau it was a falso.
 4 Deb:     Oh:[:.
 5 Dic:        [I like(d) tha'one.
 6 Deb:     fa:ther.=
 7 Mar:     =[Y i h     d o:,]
 8 Ann:     =[Well yer the o]nly one that likes it.
 9 Mar:     °Ahh
10 Dic:     Alright.
11                (4.2)
12 Mar:  -> Fi(h)ne sensibilities are never wi:despread.
13                (0.4)
14 Deb:     ehh!
15 Fre:     Mhh=
16 Ann:     =[Wha::t.
17 Fre:     =[hmm hmm,
18 Deb:     hah [hah hah hah, huh,]
19 Dic:         [Uh  repeat   that,]
20 Deb:     .ah-h-h. ah-h-h
21                (1.5)
22 Dic:     I:, missed it.
23                (0.4)
24 Deb:     He's talking for posterity.
25 Mar:     No:,
26                (0.4)
27 Deb:     hhh
28 Mar:     'a wz a:, perfectly good commend=yer father said he
29          liked it'n nobody else liked it so I said. 'hh Fine
30          sensibilities are not widespread.
31 Deb:     [ °Hmmm,
32 Di?:     [Aww::
```

```
33              (0.9)
34 Dic:         Tha'ss very good.
35              (.)
36 Dic:         I appreciate (it).
37 Fre: PCM -> A joke with an escape hatch.=
38          -> (I)[gotta  r e m e m ]ber dat.=
39 Mar:            [((clears throat))]
40 Fre:         =Hu:h
41              (5.0)
```

Self-praise (just like self-deprecation) is a problematic action (see Pomerantz, 1978, 1984), and Dick's venturing such a sequence (lines 2–3 and 5)
meets with a common fate for sequences of this sort – disagreement and
rejection, though here administered not by the addressee (his son-in-law)
but (in muted exasperation) by his daughter (lines 4 and 6) and (robustly)
by his wife (line 8). Dick's acceptance of this rejection (line 10) potentially closes the sequence, a possibility apparently sustained by the ensuing
silence (line 11), substantial even in this continuing state of incipient talk.
Marty's subsequent comment (line 12) is equivocal between being a post-
mortem and being a compliment to counter-balance the direct rejection of
Dick which had preceded.[12]

Note further that, after the sequences which Marty's remark turns out to
have engendered have run their course and the "compliment" upshot has
been registered and appreciated by Dick, Fred (at line 37) offers another
post-completion musing and assessment, one which does not add to the
otherwise possibly complete sequence. Here, then, is another possible post-
mortem.

---

[12] Deb's comment (line 24) "He's talking for posterity," although in the first instance most
likely referring to the tape recording which is in progress, may partially reflect the understanding that Marty's remark was not designed to engender further talk in this sequence.
This is suggested by its placement – after other initiated repair first pair parts at lines 16,
19, and 22, the last of these after a long failure to respond to the first two, by two different
parties. Such other-initiated repair displays its speakers' felt need to grasp what has been
said so as to be able to respond, and where no response is relevant it can be taken to display
a misunderstanding. If this is what prompts Deb's remark, it reflects her understanding
that Marty's remark was designed as a post-mortem. For another instance in which other-
initiated repair displays a ill-grounded understanding of the sequential character of its
repairable, consider a sequence from the start of the TG conversation:

```
(7.35) TG, 1:07-13
1 Ava:            [<I wan]'dih know if yih got a-uh:m
2            wutchimicawllit. A:: pah(hh)khing place°th's mornin'.'hh
3 Bee:     A pa:rking place,
4 Ava:     Mm hm,
5          (0.4)
6 Bee:     Whe:re.
7 Ava: -> t! Oh: just anypla(h)ce? I wz jus' kidding yuh.
```

Here the utterance at lines 1–2 is apparently meant non-seriously, which the other-initiated
repairs (at lines 3 and 6) show their speaker failed to grasp and may therefore be gearing
up to respond to inappropriately.

Although in Extract (7.33) the post-completion musing is articulated by one of the protagonists of the preceding sequence, in Extracts (7.34) and (7.35) the musings are articulated by Fred, who is in both cases a non-participating observer of the sequence in question.[13] This is, as remarked earlier, a regular feature of post-completion musings, and not an idiosyncrasy of Fred's. One more case in point can serve to secure this observation.

```
(7.36) Virginia, 3:23-4:8
 1 Vir:      Can I please get that dre:ss, please mom¿
 2           Lemme g[et that-
 3 Mom:           [Dreh(ss)-?
 4 Vir:      >You know that [one-<
 5 Mom:                     [OH VUHginia, we('ve) been through this
 6           befa[wh, you've got enough summa d[resses now I think=
 7 P??:          [hhhh! ((laughter?))            |
 8 Vir:                                      [uhhh!(("pained" sound))
 9 Mom:      =you just wait an' get- some'uh'the'new fa:ll stuff when
10           it comes in.
11 Vir:      tch!
12           (0.5)
13 Pru: ->   I[t's   s o| frustrat|ing havin'  a| mothuh]
14 Mom:       [If you s|aved yer-| if you saved| yer al]lowan[ce,
15 Pru: ->                                                   [hhh `hhh
16 Mom:      [(if you) save yer allowance, an:' um: you could get=
17 Pru: ->   [w(h)ith a °sho(p)°°    ((° = mid-word trailoff))
18 Mom:      =these little extr[a things.
19 Vir:                        [A(h)llo::wan(h)ce? I o(h)nly g(h)et
20           fi(h)ve d(h)ollars a week.That's rid(h)i(h)c(h)ul(h)ous.
```

In this conversation at the dinner table, 14-year-old Virginia, having just heard that her mother is having a sale at the women's clothing store that she

---

[13] This is not to say that post-completion musings by protagonists of the sequence are rare. Recall, for example, Extract (7.08b), reproduced here for convenience:

```
(7.08b) US, 28:09-29:07
 1 Mik: Fpre->   Wuhddiyuh doing with dat big bow-puh-tank. Nothing?
 2               (0.5)
 3 Vic:          ((COUGH))
 4 Vic:          Uh-h-h,
 5               (1.0)
 6 Vic: Spre->   I'm not intuh selling it or giving it. That's it.
 7 Mik: SCT->    Okay.
 8               (1.0)
 9 Mik: PCM->    Dat wz simple. Khhhh huh-huh-heh!=
10 Vic:          =Yeh.
11               (0.7)
12 Vic:          °Teg,
13               (1.0)
```

In Extract (7.33) the post-completion muser was the one doing the rejection (and having misgivings about it), but here (at line 9) it is done by the one rejected.

runs, has asked (apparently not for the first time) to get a certain dress that she has seen there. Her mother rejects the plea to Virginia's considerable distress (the sequence is examined in greater detail in Schegloff [2005]). The sequence has come to a point of possible completion at line 11, and the silence that develops there betokens that possibility. Into that silence, Prudence (the fiancée of Virginia's older brother) introduces what appears to be a post-completion musing – in this case, a sympathetic reflection on Virginia's disappointment, "It's so frustrating having a mother with a shop" (at lines 13, 15, and 17). As it happens, just as she is starting this post-completion musing from the vantage point of an observer, Mom elects to use this exchange as the occasion for a renewed lecture on the virtues of saving one's allowance (at lines 14, 16, and 18),[14] and in the overlap with Prudence Mom wins out, and the sequence, with its newly introduced theme, is extended on and off for virtually the entire meal. Observers may, then, offer post-completion musings, but they are at risk of the principals renewing the sequence and rendering the musing out of bounds and out of attention.

When a minimal post-expansion fails to close a sequence, the sequence is opened to non-minimal expansion, and that is a development of quite a different order. Non-minimal post-expansion occurs not only when a minimal post-expansion fails to achieve closure; it is also the main alternative to minimal post-expansion in the first instance. When a second pair part is not taken itself to be the end of a sequence, or is not followed by some form of sequence-closing third, what follows is some continuation which not only serves to expand the sequence *itself*, but serves as well to provide for – to project – *further increments* to the sequence. And it is to such non-minimal post-expansion that we turn next.

Non-minimal post-expansion

What makes some stretch of talk a post-expansion is its occurrence after a second pair part of an adjacency pair while still being part of the same sequence. Minimal post-expansions get their character from being

---

[14] This is a somewhat prejudicial way of putting it. As noted earlier (pp. 137ff.), when an SPP speaker extends the SPP past the possible close of a sequence (as Mom does here), it invites analytic scrutiny. So we can note: Mom's construction of her dispreferred SPP, rejecting Virginia's plea, is nicely designed to end on an upbeat note – an allusion to a future purchase when the new season's clothes come in to the store. One tack Virginia could have taken (at line 11) was to brighten at the prospect, and exit the sequence on an amicable note. Instead, the most she manages is a reduction in the degree of the anguish she had expressed at the earliest sign of rejection in Mom's turn. That it is this extension of anguish that Virginia is doing with the "Tch!" of her exit from the sequence that prompts Mom's extension of the sequence is shown by her using that extension to redirect the "blame" for the outcome ("no dress") back onto Virginia herself, and her (mis-)management of her allowance.

designed to be possibly finished with a single turn following that second pair part. Non-minimal post-expansions are different in that the turn following that second pair part is itself a first pair part, and thereby projects at least one further turn – its responsive second pair part – and thereby its non-minimality.

We cannot undertake here to examine the substantial range of types of post-expansion sequences awaiting description. By touching briefly on a few of these types, and more extensively on several of special importance, we can enrich our alertness to yet other forms which an attentive observer of talk-in-interaction can surely come to notice.

Other-initiated repair

In our earlier discussion of insert expansion (in Chapter 6) we noted that efforts to deal with troubles of hearing and understanding which were launched by recipients of the problematic talk (recipients of the "trouble-source") were almost invariably initiated in the turn after the trouble-source turn. And, because anything in the talk could come to be a trouble-source or be treated as one, such other-initiation of repair could occur after any turn-at-talk. When such repair initiation occurs after a first pair part, it constitutes the beginning of an insert expansion. When it occurs after a second pair part, it constitutes the beginning of a post-expansion. Because such a repair initiation is itself a first pair part and makes conditionally relevant next a responsive second pair part, it constitutes the beginning of one type of non-minimal post-expansion.

Extract (7.37) displays a simple and limited instance. Connie is discussing travel plans related to her employer.

```
(7.37) Connie and Dee, 9
 1 Dee: F_b    ->   Well who'r you workin for.
 2 Con: S_b    ->   'hhh Well I'm working through:: the Amfat Corporation.
 3                  (0.8)
 4 Dee: F_post ->   The who?
 5 Con: S_post ->   =Amfah Corpora[tion. (.) 'ts a holding company.
 6 Dee: SCT    ->               [Oh
 7 Dee: SCT    ->   Yeah
 8 Con:              'hhhh But uh:: (0.5) they're bik(h) (0.2) holders in
 9                  uh of property en h Honolulu.
10                  (0.8)
11 Conn               'hhhh A:n' uh so anyway, I wannida go (0.5) toward the
12                  end of summer . . .
```

When Connie answers (at line 2) Dee's question (at line 1), he has trouble with the answer, and responds by initiating repair (line 4). The repair sequence itself gets expanded after its second pair part, with two minimal

post-expansions (lines 6 and 7).[15] With closure of the repair sequence as a
post-expansion of the question–answer sequence, the larger telling sequence
which was in progress is resumed (lines 8–10).[16]

In the extended sequence with which we ended our discussion of insert
expansion (see Extract [6.18], pp. 111–14), we noted that there was more
talk in the sequence after the base second pair part, and if we now re-
examine that portion of the sequence we can see that it is a non-minimal
post-expansion in which other-initiated repair is launched.

```
(7.38) BB Gun, 2:04-4:12 (partial; previously [6.18])
 1 Bon:          But- (1.0) Wouldju do me a favor? heheh
 2 Jim:          e(hh) depends on the favor::, go ahead,
 3 Bon:          Didjer mom tell you I called the other day?
 4 Jim:          No she didn't.
 5               (0.5)
 6 Bon:          Well I called.(.) [hhh ]
 7 Jim:                             [Uhuh]
 8               (0.5)
 9 Bon: Fb   ->  .hhh 'n I was wondering if you'd let me borrow
10               your gun.
11               (1.2)
12 Jim:          My gun?
13 Bon:          Yeah.
14               (1.0)
15 Jim:          What gun.
16               (0.7)
17               .
18               . [Roughly 70 lines omitted; see pp. 111-13 for text]
19               .
20               (0.4)
21 Bon:          An[:]
22 Jim: Sb   ->    [Y]eah:, you can use 't,
23               (0.4)
24 Bon: Fpost->  .hh Ca:n?
25 Jim: Spost->  »Yeh-«
```

---

[15] Note the careful calibration of these minimal post-expansions. Dee registers the repeat of
the company's name as news with his "oh," but when Connie goes on to offer a further
description of the company, Dee receipts it with a sequence-closing third – "yeah" – which
treats what has preceded as not constituting new information (cf. Heritage, 1984b).

[16] Arguably the beginning of the talk at lines 8–10 is an addition to Connie's description of
the company, perhaps as an afterthought. That is, the big in-breath at the start of line 8
and the "but" which follows suggest the shift into a new talk activity, one differentiated
from what has just preceded. The "uh" may suspend this, the use of "holders" connecting
this talk back to the preceding "holding company." On completion of this TCU, there
is again a big in-breath and a sequential marker – "anyway" – regularly used to mark a
return to an activity or undertaking which came before the immediately preceding one (a
usage which, if memory serves, Sacks termed some years ago a "right-hand parenthesis
marker").

After a modest pre-expansion at lines 1–8, Bonnie makes a request of Jim (line 9), asking if she can borrow his gun. A long insert expansion issues eventually in his acceding to the request, the second pair part occurring on line 22 (line 93 in the full version of the sequence at p. 113). Clearly the talk which follows (at lines 24–25) is part of the same larger sequence; it follows the base second pair part of that sequence; it is designed to occupy more that a single turn; it is aimed at checking Bonnie's hearing/understanding of what the response to her request has been. It is, then, an other-initiated repair sequence which constitutes a non-minimal post-expansion. (Unlike the preceding instance, this post-expansion does not itself get post-expanded. As we shall see later, this may have to do with subsequent talk which is still related to this sequence.)

Disagreement-implicated other-initiated repair

When we noted earlier that *insert* expansion "repair" sequences often served as pre-disagreements, this could, at least in part, be attributed to the fact that, by intervening between a first pair part and its second pair part, they served to violate the preference for contiguity which ordinarily obtains in adjacency pairs whose parts are in a preferred relationship. But other-initiated repair sequences often serve as vehicles for the expression of disagreement, or for introducing its relevance, even when placed elsewhere in talk-in-interaction. Just as questions, tellings, and assessments can accomplish not only those actions themselves but can serve as vehicles for the accomplishment of other actions as well, so can this particular form of question – other-initiated repair – do so. And when other-initiated repairs serve to implement some other undertaking in interaction, that undertaking is most often disagreement-implicated.[17]

A variety of features of other-initiated repair sequences makes them apt and suitable instruments for addressing disagreement-implicated talk. For example, by not quite "getting" what was said, they raise the possibility that it was "not quite right," often leaving the respects in which it was not quite right unexplicated. More to the point for the actual working out of the "problem," they provide a place in the very next turn in which the prior speaker can make some adjustment in what was said – to make it more accessible, and perhaps more "acceptable." If the "problem" is straightforwardly a problem of hearing/understanding, then that adjustment may involve repetition, clearer articulation, selection of an alternative wording, addition of some explanation, etc. Where the "problem" can be understood to involve

---

[17] Sacks noted some years ago that the cliché that "if we understood one another better we would disagree less" might as well be reversed. For one basic way that humans have of dealing with disagreement and conflict is to treat it as a problem in hearing or understanding, and try to "fix" *that* problem. Not, then, that misunderstanding breeds conflict; but that conflict is handled by trying to treat it as a problem of misunderstanding. And the instruments for so treating it are the practices of repair.

the possibility of disagreement or other forms of dispreferred response, then
the adjustment may take the form of some backdown, in the direction of
possible compromise, as a way to resolve the misalignment. Or a withholding of such a backdown or move toward compromise. In either case, such
disagreement-implicated post-expansions are prime instances of the earlier
observation that preferred second pair parts are sequence-closure-relevant,
while dispreferred second pair parts are sequence-expansion-relevant. Post-
expansion is one place where the consequences of dispreferred second pair
parts get played out.

   Extract (7.39) reproduces Extracts (6.12) and (6.05) from our discussion
of insert expansion and adds several turns following the base second pair
part (as well as the preceding talk from the beginning of the conversation,
to which we shall soon return). We noted before that the insert expansion
provides an opportunity for Bee to back away from the assessment "happy,"
which the other-initiated repair (at line 20) treats as problematic. Bee, however, stays with that assessment and, as projected, Ava then disagrees with
it in the base second pair part (at line 23).

```
(7.39)  TG 1:01-26
 1                      ring
 2 Ava:                H'llo:?
 3 Bee:                hHi:,
 4 Ava:                Hi:?
 5 Bee:                hHowuh you:?
 6 Ava:                Oka:::y?hh=
 7 Bee:                =Good.=Yihs[ou:nd ] hh
 8 Ava:                           [<I wan]'dih know if yih got a-uh:m
 9                     wutchimicawllit. A:: pah(hh)khing place °th's
10                     mornin'. hh
11 Bee:                A pa:rking place,
12 Ava:                Mm hm,
13                     (0.4)
14 Bee:                Whe:re.
15 Ava:                t! Oh: just anypla(h)ce? I wz jus' kidding yuh.
16 Bee:                Nno?=
17 Ava:                =[(°No).]
18 Bee: Fb     ->      =[W h y ]whhat'sa mattuh with y-Yih sou[nd HA:PPY,] hh
19 Ava:                                                       [  Nothing.]
20 Ava: Fins   ->      u- I sound ha:p[py?]
21 Bee: Sins   ->                     [Yee]uh.
22                     (0.3)
23 Ava: Sb     ->      No:,
24 Bee: Fpost  ->      Nno:?
25 Ava: Spost  ->      No.
26                     (0.7)
27 Bee:                hh You [sound sorta cheer[ful?]
28 Ava:                       [°(Any way).      [ hh ] How'v you bee:n.
```

Having declined to be dissuaded from the assessment before its overt rejection, Bee now questions the rejection itself (at line 24), providing yet another opportunity for Ava to take a less outright, rejecting stance. When Ava again declines to do so (line 25), it is Bee who does the backdown (at line 27), lowering the level of her positive assessment of Ava's mood from "happy" to "sorta cheerful," and the talk turns to a new sequence.

It may be useful to explore for a moment the interactional grounds which Bee may have for pursuing this sequence, one which might ordinarily be taken as just part of the routine ritual of conversational openings (Schegloff, 1986). But the forms of sequence organization are not mere formal tokens being played with on an interactional checkerboard; they are the resources through which real interactional concerns are pursued. Though we cannot detail the interactional dynamic embodied in every extract offered to instantiate the sequential practices we are concerned with, we can do so occasionally.

At the very outset of this conversation, Ava has answered Bee's "howaryou" inquiry (at line 5) with an unusually drawn out "okay:::," which prompts a response from Bee (at line 7), which is interrupted, "Good. Yihsound-" The interruption turns out to be a bit of "kidding" by Ava, and it is from this kidding sequence that Bee is returning the talk (in line 18) to the previously aborted "you sound [happy]." Ava has, in a very few moments at the start of this conversation, "given off" or "exuded" (to use Goffman's [1969] terms) several indications of being in a "positive personal state" (Sacks, 1975). And giving such inexplicit indications is one way parties to conversations can try to mesh the agendas they respectively bring to a conversation (especially a telephone conversation, in which they are not visually accessible to one another) to avoid awkward juxtapositions of one another's good or bad news (Jefferson, 1980; Schegloff, 1986). Without saying so explicitly, one party can give off indications of being in especially good or bad shape (e.g., by the intonation of their talk, and just such playfulness as "kidding around"), allowing the other to elicit a telling of what that is about, if they choose to do so, and leaving it unexplicated (or becoming more explicit on their own initiative) if they do not. And here Ava may well appear to Bee to have done just that – with both her "playful" initial "OK" response and her "kidding." On this understanding, Bee is pursuing bait which Ava seems to have set, and Ava is just "playing hard to get" in resisting a bite on "you sound happy" and the account which it would occasion.[18]

Extract (7.40) (which previously appeared as Extract [6.07]) in the chapter on insert expansion, and is reproduced here with the ensuing turns) features two young men who had apparently served as counselors at a summer

---

[18] There is, of course, the possibility that Ava *is* happy that Bee has called, but is reluctant to say so because of a drifting apart between these two young women (an estrangement indicated in many other aspects of this conversation). Later on, when Bee tries to arrange a get-together with Ava over the long holiday weekend from school (see Extract [4.03] at

camp; here they are discussing one of the campers with whom they had had
to deal. The sequence runs off similarly to Extract (7.39): an assessment
("wouldn't behave for anything" at lines 2–3) is followed by an other-
initiated repair (line 4) which indicates some problem in responding with
the preferred agreement. The first pair part speaker does not back down
from the problematic assessment (line 5), which is then disagreed with in
the SPP ("she behaved okay" at line 6).

```
(7.40) Schegloff et al., 1977:368
1 Sta:          That's all. But you know what happened that night
2       F_b   -> we went to camp. Forget it. She wouldn't behave for
3               anything.
4 Ala: F_ins  -> W-when.
5 Sta: S_ins  -> When we went to camp.
6 Ala: S_b    -> She behaved okay.
7 Sta: F_post -> She did?
8 Ala: S_post -> Yeah. She could've been a lot worse.
```

Here again, after the base second pair part, the sequence is expanded: the
disagreeing second pair part is itself questioned (line 7). But, whereas in
Extract (7.39) the second pair part speaker "stands firm" and its recipient
backs down, here in (7.40) the second pair part speaker, after initially confirming his stand (line 8, "yeah"), then backs down from it – "could've been
a lot worse" being considerably weaker than "behaved okay."

   The preceding extracts display post-expansion repair sequences which
are disagreement-implicated: the base second pair part in each case is
clearly marked as a dispreferred one within its sequence, it is questioned
on its production, and the misalignment of the parties (and the parts)

pp. 32–33, only part of which is reproduced here), Ava resists making arrangements until
Bee answers, "what's Bob doing."

```
(4.03) (partial)
 1 Bee: F_b?                              [Well if yer
 2            arou:nd I'll probably see y(hh)ou hn[hh! `hh
 3 Ava: ->                                       [Why, whut's (Bob
 4      ->    doing)
 5 Bee: ->    Uh-u-uh:: goin o:ff::
 6 Ava: ->    Where's he goin.
 7 Bee: ->    To Wa:shin'ton,
 8 Ava: ->    Oh.
 9            (0.7)
10 Bee: ->    He asn' been there sih-since Christmas [so:. HHe's going.
11 Ava: ->                                           [Mm.
12           (0.5)
13 Ava: S_b?  Yeh w'l I'll give you a call then tomorrow.when I get in
14            'r sumn.
```

Ava, it appears, thinks she is only second in line behind Bee's boyfriend, in which case
she may be loath to appear to seem enthused over a phone call. In any case, underlying
this stretch of talk appears to be just that orientation to the preference for noticing over
announcement sketched above (see Chapter 5, n. 17 and the text which it accompanies).

is "resolved" by one of the parties backing down in the direction of a compromise (which remains tacit in both cases), with a different party backing down in each case (speaker and recipient of the second pair part respectively).

But disagreement-implicated other-initiations of repair may also be deployed after – and in response to – a second pair part which was *not* designed as a dispreferred second pair part, but nonetheless is coming in for disagreement by a recipient. Extract (7.41) comes from the very beginning of a therapy session for teenaged boys in the 1960s; Ken, Roger, and Al are "the patients"; Dan is "the therapist":

```
(7.41) GTS, 5:3
1 Ken: F_b    -> Is Al here today?
2 Dan: S_b    -> Yeah.
3                (2.0)
4 Rog: F_post-> He is? hh ehheh
5 Dan: S_post-> Well he was.
```

Here, although the very asking of the question may imply the possibility of a negative response, the design of Ken's question appears to project a positive answer as preferred, and this is what Dan produces. The 2.0-second silence following the preferred second pair part appears to mark the sequence as thereby complete ("preferred second pair parts are closure-relevant"). Still, Roger at least appears to think otherwise, and his questioning of Dan's second pair part prompts a backdown by Dan to a position of agnosticism about Al's current whereabouts. Here the disagreement-implicated post-expansion is not prompted by a disagreeing base second pair part, but by an incipient disagreement *with* the base second pair part.

Topicalization

Several of the turn types which can be used for other-initiation of repair can also be used to mark some utterance or utterance part as of special interest, and worthy of further on-topic talk (what Jefferson [1981] terms "news marks"). Among these forms are repeats or partial repeats, "pro-repeats" (such as "he is?" in Extract [7.41] above), and "really," all with or without a preceding "oh" (although these forms may work quite differently with and without the "oh"; see Heritage [1984b:339–44]). Various of these forms, positioned after a base second pair part, serve to initiate a post-expansion, and one which is designedly non-minimal, though the extent of the ensuing expansion can be shaped both by the form used to launch it and by the moment-to-moment practices of the participants as the expansionary talk develops.

In Extract (7.42), Mark has just arrived for a visit with Sherry, Karen, and Ruthie at their dormitory: the sequences through which this interaction

gets launched are marked to the left, but are neither identified by sequence
type nor parsed into sequence components; by now these should be readily
recognizable by the reader.

```
(7.42) SN-4, 1:01-2:10
 1       a->   ((knock knock knock knock))
 2             (1.0)
 3 Rut: a->   Tch. C'mi::n.
 4             (1.4)        ((door squeaks))
 5 Mar: b->   Hi Sherry, hi Ruthie,
 6 Rut: b->   Hi Ma:rk.
 7 She: b->   Hi Ma:rk.=
 8 Mar: c->   =[How're you guys.
 9            =[((door slams))
10            (0.2)
11 Rut: c->   Jis' fi:ne.
12            (0.2)
13 She: c->   Uh:: tired.
14 Mar: c->   Tired, I hear yih gettin' married.
15            (0.6)
16 (?):       °((sniff))
17            (0.3)
18 She: c->   Uh:: you hear right.
19            (0.2)
20 Mar: c->   (Ih) shah-I hear ri:gh[t.
21 Sh?:                             [mmhh [(heh  hh])
22 Mar: d->                               [Didja e-] by the way
23            didja ever call up uh: Century City Hotel 'n
24            (1.0)
25 She: ->   Y'know h'much they want fer a wedding¿ It's
26           incredible.
27            (0.5)
28 She: d->  We'd 'aftuh sell our house 'n car 'n evryt(h)hing
29           e(h)l(h)se [tuh pay fer the wedding .]
30 Mar: d->            [Shhh'er house 'n yer car.]
31 ???: d->             [(hh  heh theh  huh   huh )]
32 Mar: e->  'hh What about the outside candlelight routine izzat
33           still gonna go on?
34 She: e->  No yih can't have outside candlelight it's a fi:re
35           hazard.
36            (0.5)
37 Mar: e->  Oh really?
38            (˙)
39 She: e->  Yes[:  :  .   ]
40 Kar: e->     [C'n have] it insi:de,
41            (0.8)
42 Mar: e->  You c'd have 'm inside though?
```

```
43 Kar: e->   Yeah
44            (0.4)
45 She: e->   Yeh but who wants t'get married inside in the
46            middle a' the summer when it's still light till
47            n[ine   o'clock. ]
48 Mar: e->    [Gunnuh be beau]tiful outsi:de.
49            (0.2)
50 She: e->   Ye:ah.
51 Mar: e->   W'll (jat'll) jus' be fanta:stic.
```

Note first Mark's uptake at line 37. He has asked an updating question about Sherry's forthcoming wedding (at lines 32–33) and has gotten back a disagreeing response, i.e., one not aligned with the designed preference of the question (at lines 32–33). As we have seen, an "oh" might register this as information, and move thereby to close the sequence. By contrast, "oh really?" marks the answer as "news," and provides for further expansion of its telling (Maynard, 2003). As it happens here, Sherry has no sooner confirmed it than another form of post-expansion is introduced by Karen (to which we will return in a moment), which pre-empts the expansion which Mark's "oh really?" might have engendered.[19] That expansion has been prompted by Mark, the recipient of the base second pair part, but left for its speaker to direct.

---

[19] There are intimations in the literature (Heritage [1984b:340], citing Jefferson [1981:62–66]; the discussion here is addressed to the Heritage text because of its greater accessibility) that "oh really?" regularly engenders limited expansion, in which reconfirmation is followed by assessment ". . . which is generally terminal or topic curtailing." Although this does, in fact, describe Extract (7.42) in the text (allowing for the Karen-engendered exchange), it does not characterize the instances cited on its behalf in the literature. Thus:

```
(7.43) NB IV:7, 4:35-5:11
 1 Bar: Fb      ->   =e-How m'ny cigarettes yih had.
 2                   (0.5)
 3 Emm: Sb      ->   ↑↑NO:NE.
 4 Bar: Fpost-> Oh rea↑lly?
 5 Emm: Spost-> NO:.
 6                   (.)
 7 Bar: SCT     ->   ↑Very ↑goo↓*:d.
 8 Emm: SCTup-> VERY good.=
 9 Emm: Fb      ->   =.hhh ↑WILL YOU ↓AH'LL k- hAh'll CALL [YIH DUH]MORROW 't=
10 Barb                                                   [Wuddit-]
11 Emm:               =NI↓:N[E
12 Bar: Fb      ->          [How m'ch weight ev yih gained.
13 Emm: Sb      ->   uRe:ll I'm abou'two pou:nd ss.h
14 Bar:              Oh: God I've sure put it on
15                   .h[h
16 Emm:                [nYeah, .t.h W[illyuh HELP M]E OU:TTA [THI:S:, ]
```

The literature (Heritage, 1984b; Jefferson, 1981) stops the transcript at line 7 (of this later retranscription by Jefferson). Although Emma resists it – by launching a possible closing section of the conversation at, line 9 – it is clear that the sequence is pressed further by Barbara with the follow-up question at line 12, Barbara being the news recipient whose

Note, by contrast, Mark's move at line 14. Here he is following Sherry's second pair part ("uh tired") in response to "How are you guys." He does a repeat of her answer ("tired") and uses it to pursue the matter, to find what it permits the topicalization of ("I hear you're getting married"), and thereby undertakes to direct the topical post-expansion himself, rather than leaving it for the speaker of the second pair part which is its source to do (a tack which leaves one vulnerable to rejection, as Mark is here).

Another type of post-expansion, then, often initiated with forms of utterance similar to those used to initiate repair, is the topicalization of something done or mentioned in the base second pair part. Such expansions then become subject to the organizational contingencies of topic-talk.

"oh really?" and assessment are the purported sources of curtailment on this view. The other instance seems even less in keeping with the "curtailed expansion" account:

```
(7.44) NB II:2, 3:01-30
 1 Emm:    Hey that wz the same spot we took off fer Ho:nuhlulu
 2         (0.3)
 3 Emm:    Where they puut. him o:n,
 4         (0.6)
 5 Emm:    et that chartered pla:[ce,
 6 Nan:                         [Oh: ri→ll[y?
 7 Emm:                                   [y:::Ye::ah,
 8 Nan:    ↑Oh: fer ↓heaven sa:[kes.
 9 Emm:                        [ExA:Ctly it says on West Imperial
10         Booleva:rd i[n  :   u h ]
11 Nan:                [°°Mm hm?°°]
12         (.)
13 Emm:    u.-theh I c'd see the bui:lding en then the Wo:rld Airways
14         wz uh: .hhh on the side there whur it comes in en that's ↑is
15         where ↑we took o:ff
16 Nan:    W'l ↓ah'll be ↓da[rned ]
17 Emm:                     [↑↑Ye::]ah, .hhhh[hh
18 Nan:                                      [Oh:: ((nasal))
19 Nan:    Well I'm glad ih didn'ha:ppen while you were tryin tih get
20         o:ff,
21 Emm:    hOh: my Go:[:d hh
22 Nan:               [God that w'd'v been a mess you'd a'never got'n
23         tuh Hawaii,
24         (.)
25 Emm:    n:No ↑wouldn'that a'been sum[°p'n°
26 Nan:                                [°Jeemunny Ch::rismus.°
27 Nan:    °No kidding.°
28 Emm:    °°Mm[hm,°°
29 Nan:        [.hhhhhh Yeah it's been a rough week ah everbuddy is (.)
30         youknow
```

Here the sequence is stopped at line 8, but it seems clear that the topic is extended rather further. It might be argued that the "oh really" speaker subsequently produces a sequence-closing third, which is a move toward curtailment of the topic, even though the sequence is expanded nonetheless. This argument appears to work better for Extract (7.44) than for Extract (7.43), but further work is clearly in order to establish whether, or under what conditions, "oh really?" provides for a curtailed expansion of telling on a mentioned matter.

Rejecting/challenging/disagreeing with the second pair part

We have already noted one disagreement-implicated form of post-expansion – other-initiated repair which can serve as a way of circumventing overt disagreement by providing an opportunity for the other to back away from that which is to be disagreed with. But sometimes the disagreement is not approached gingerly but is expressed forthrightly, and this provides a distinct form which post-expansion can take.

Looking again at Extract (7.42), line 40, we can see such a tack being taken up. Sherry has, in answer to Mark's question, said that the "outside candlelight routine" is no longer possible outside, because it is a fire hazard, and it is this which Mark has received with a newsmark. On the heels of Sherry's confirmation, however, Karen intervenes with "You can have it inside." In effect, then, Karen is rejecting the account of, or the grounds for, the basis of Sherry's dispreferred response. If "oh really?" is the expansionary alternative to the sequence-closing "oh" with respect to information, then Karen's rejection is the expansionary alternative to "okay" with respect to acceptance or not of the action being done in the second pair part turn.

Here Mark takes over Karen's intervention as his own (lines 40 and 42), his addition of the "though" lexicalizing the opposition which in Karen's turn had been accomplished through the contrastive stress on the first syllable of "inside." Sherry is then obliged to respond to this rejection of her account for canceling the "outside candlelight routine" (lines 45–47) as the post-expansion is further extended, to end with Mark's apparent acceptance of her retort. Assessments figure in the closure of this sequence in a fashion somewhat familiar by now, although the form they take here is different – a single assessment does not bring this sequence to a close. We will discuss sequence-closing sequences in Chapter 9.

Extract (7.45) is taken from the same data source, but from a separately encapsulated episode within it, touched off by the arrival of Carol, who had apparently been expected to return with an ice-cream sandwich.

```
(7.45) SN-4, 5:01-40 (previously examined as Extract [5.30])
 1               ((door squeaks))
 2 She:      Hi Carol.=
 3 Car:      =H[i : .]
 4 Rut:        [CA:RO]L, HI::
 5 She: Fb -> You didn' get en icecream sanwich,
 6 Car: Sb1-> I kno:w, hh I decided that my body didn't need it,
 7 She:   ->  Yes but ours di:d=
 8 She:      =hh heh-heh-heh [heh-heh-heh [`hhih
 9 ???:                      [ehh heh heh [
10 ???:                                   [(    )
11 Car: Sb2-> hh Awright gimme some money en you c'n treat me to
12              one an I'll buy you a:ll some [too.]
```

```
13 She:    ->                                    [I'm ] kidding, I don't
14                    need it.
15                    (0.3)
16 ???:               (hih)
17 Car:               I WA:N' O:N[E,
18 Ru?:                         [ehh heh-hu[h
19 Car:                                    [hheh-uh `hhh=
20 Car: Sb3->         =No they [didn' even have any Ta:(h)b.=
21 Ru?:                        [°hheh
22 Car: Sb3->         =This is all I c'd find.
23                    (·)
24 Rut:    ->         Well then there's ez many calories ez that prob'ly
25                    in en ice cream sa:nwich=so yih jis':, yih know.
26                    (`)
27 Car: Sb4->         I know(,) an icecream sanwich is better, but I di'n
28         ->         feel like going down tuh P²⁰ an seeing all those weird
29         ->         people.an have them st[a:re at   me.   ]
30 Rut:                                     [In yer slipper]s¿
31                    (0.2)
32 Car:               Yes.
33                    (0.8)
34 Car:               I don't want them tih see me when I l(h)ook t(h)his
35                    good.
36                    (0.2)
37 R?C:               ((cough)) (H) (H)UH `hhhh=
38 Car:               =N(h)o one des(h)erves it. ((hoarse voice))
39                    (0.2)
40 ???:               (Tch `hh=)
41 Car:               I'll see you all later,
42 Rut:               Awri:ght,
43                    (1.4)     ((door opening))
```

After a round of greetings, Sherry notices what Carol has *not* brought (note
that she *has* brought something of the same general sort – a snack from
a vending machine; see line 22), and by doing so in effect lodges a complaint. Various types of second pair part are made relevant by complaints
and, where possible, remedies or offers of remedy appear to be preferred
(as is agreeing with, or joining, the complaint). What Carol does here (at
line 6), however, is to justify the action that has been complained of, and by
reference to her own interests at that.[21] This account, and the claim it makes
to being an adequate response to the complaint, is simply rejected outright
at line 7. This is a clear exemplar of the type of post-expansion at issue

[20] "P" in line 28 refers to the "Parking Level" in the dormitory building.
[21] There is quite a bit more going on here which cannot be taken up in this discussion – for
example, the self-deprecation woven into this response, which requires a response of its
own (but see the partial discussion, in Chapter 13, of sequence as practice). For a fuller
treatment, see Schegloff [1988a:118–31].

here – overt (rather than projected) rejection of, or challenge to, the second pair part (in both instances by rejecting or disagreeing with the account which it incorporates), perhaps a clearer exemplar than was offered in Extract (7.42).

In the aftermath of rejection of the base second pair part we can see various orderly and describable ways in which sequences can get expanded. In Extract (7.42), the second pair part speaker undertook to respond to and neutralize the turn(s) which had rejected her second pair part, and such a tack provides one trajectory for subsequent post-expansion. In Extract (7.45), we see a different trajectory of response. Instead of defending her second pair part against the rejection of it, the second pair part speaker accepts that rejection (line 11, "awright") and provides a new, alternative second pair part to the initiating first pair part – here an offer to get ice-cream sandwiches (lines 11–12). As it happens, this *second* second pair part is rejected as well (line 13), and the sequence is still open: a first pair part and no acceptable second pair part. Carol then offers yet a third possible second pair part, another account (at lines 20 and 22),[22] but this too is rejected as inadequate (lines 24–25) and this rejection is also accepted by Carol (beginning of line 27), who goes on to give yet another account, this one neither accepted nor rejected.

Here, then, are two diverse practices for responding to an overt rejection of a second pair part, practices implemented by the second pair part speaker, which yield quite different forms of post-expansion, quite different trajectories of interaction, and result in quite different shapes of sequence structure. More surely await description.[23]

---

[22] Before this, at line 16, Carol produces a mock, whining complaint of wanting an ice-cream sandwich after all, but then marks that as a joke, and returns to serious mode with her third try at a response to the complaint, as described in the text. This bit of the sequence is taken up in Schegloff (2001).

[23] One of these should be at least mentioned here, for it is another trajectory which could be described by the phrase "multiple second pair parts," but which is inter-actionally quite different from what has been examined in the text. That is the circumstance in a multi-person conversation in which more than one person responds – by design or by self-selection – to a first pair part framed by another; for example, when one party asks a question which several co-participants answer one after the other, with or without sequence expansion following each of the second pair parts.

Looking back at Extract (7.42) in the text, at lines 5–7, Ruthie and Sherry respond separately and consecutively to Mark's greeting, and at lines 8–13 they respond separately and consecutively to his "Howaryou" inquiry, the second of these leading to a post-expansion. But the post-expansion aside, each of the first pair parts has taken two second pair parts and this embodies longer sequences independent of the forms of expansion which have been discussed here. Here clearly is a potential source of substantial sequence expansion, depending on the sequence types involved and number of participants in the interaction who might relevantly and appropriately participate.

Once the possibility of multiple second pair parts has been registered, we should note as well the possibility of multiple first pair parts, in effect the endorsement of a first pair part by other than its original speaker, as described by Egbert (1997) for the other-initiation of repair or as in the following episode – from Lerner (2002) – in which M compliments H

First pair part reworkings post-expansion

In the preceding sections of this chapter, we have taken note of various tacks which the recipient of a second pair part can take toward it – from simple receipt with a sequence-closing third, to various types of turns which project further expansion of the sequence, in most instances by raising problems of hearing/understanding or adequacy/acceptability of the second pair part. Sometimes these problems can be addressed adequately to the parties and the second pair part stands; in other instances, the questioned second pair part is abandoned and alternative responses are offered, expanding the sequence through a series of second pair parts.

But sequences can be expanded not only by an elaboration or multiplication of second pair parts, but also through renewals, reworkings, repetitions, modifications, enhancements, inducements, etc. of the first pair part by reference to the second pair part which was its response.[24]

We have already seen exemplars of such practices and the sequence expansion which they produce. Extract (7.47), for example, reproduces an Extract (5.38), displayed earlier in Chapter 5 on preference organization, where it was offered as a possible instance of a request camouflaged as an offer.

```
(7.47) SBL 1,1,1
 1 Bet:          And uh because I'm s'pposed to be hostess Sunday,
 2 Ali: F_pre->   Oh uh didju want relief on that.
 3 Bet: S_pre->   Well I don't know, there's nobody else down with me,
 4                I spoke to uhm
 5 Ali: F_b->     Well, I'll- I can help you,
 6 Bet: preS_b->  Uh well, I probably it's only between twelve and twelve
 7                thir[ty,
 8 Ali: F_b->         [Yes, so that's r- I can help at that time,
 9 Bet: preS_b->  Uh because uhm I think what's her name? uhm (0.4)
10 Ali:          Oh
11                (0.2)
12 Bet:          that's on in the morning?
13                (0.2)
14 Ali:          Sue?
15 Bet:          Uh Sue Brown, I-she usually stays till eleven.
16 Ali:          Yeah, mm hm,
17 Bet: S_b->     Uh and uh so uhm but I think uh that it will work out
```

on the meal being served, and A endorses that compliment, in effect adding a second first pair part to the sequence, another source of sequence expansion:

```
(7.46) Smith-Thanksgiving (Lerner, 2002)
 1 M:    Oh Helen this looks wo:nder:[f u l :. ]
 2 A: -> [>Sure doe]s.<
 3       (.)
 4 H:    W'll let's hope.
```

[24] Davidson (1984) and (1990) are given over largely to such developments and display relevant data. The account offered in this chapter departs from Davidson's treatment in various respects.

```
18              alright, uh well, I don't know, I (thought) I would
19              call Maryanne, I thought I'd let her call me, because
20              (she hadda) day yesterday. [And-
21 Ali: F_b->                            [Well if you- If you want
22              help Sunday, I'll do it.
```

What is, at least on the face of it, designed as a pre-offer is first articulated at line 2 and is met with an equivocal response at best in the second pair part at lines 3–4. This second pair part is followed by an overt offer at line 5, which is followed by a pre-rejection at line 6. Alice's turn at line 8 re-does the offer in a fashion suited to the terms of the pre-rejection, but this try is also deflected by Betsy at lines 9, 12, and 15, ending with rejection again at lines 17–20, and another re-doing of the offer at line 21. Here, then, the first pair part speaker does not argue with or reject the dispreferred (or less-than-preferred) second pair parts offered in response to the initial offer, but reworks the first pair part, in some instances in a fashion aimed at the particulars of the prior second pair part (as at line 8, "I can help at that time," fitted to the hours mentioned in the preceding response).

Extract (7.48) displays not a repetition or re-doing of the first pair part but a follow-up inducement, following the declining of an invitation (actually a counter-invitation, after Karen had declined Vicky's; see Extract [5.14] above).

```
(7.48) Erhardt, 1:26-33
1 Kar:    °Gee I feel like a real nerd° you c'n all come up here,
2             (0.3)
3 Vic:    Nah, that's alright wil stay down he[re,
4 Kar: ->                                      [We've gotta
5       -> color T.V:,
6 Vic:    ˙tch˙hh I know but u-we're watchin:g The Ascent'v Ma:n,
7         ˙hh en then the uh phhreview: so: y'know wil miss
8         something if we come over.
9 Kar:    °'khay°
```

After Vicky's reciprocal declination (line 3), Karen in effect reinstitutes the invitation (line 4) by articulating an inducement which might make it more attractive.

And Extract (7.49) displays yet another form of "reworking:" re-doing the offer with different particular things being offered – first at lines 7–8 changing what is on offer from the beauty parlor to "the store" or the supermarket, then adding "Richard's" at line 10 after the start of Emma's turn at lines 9–10 projects upcoming rejection.

```
(7.49) NB IV:10, 41:17-35
1 Lot: F  ->   ↑Don't chu want me tih come dow:n getchu
2              dihmorr'en take yih dow:n dih the beauty parlor?
3              (0.3)
4 Emm: S   -> What fo:r I ↑jis did my hair it looks like pruh- a
```

```
 5                       perfess↓ional.
 6                          (0.3)
 7 Lot: F_redo-> ↑I mean uh: you wanna go 'd the store er anything over
 8                    et the Market[Ba:sket]er an]ything?]
 9 Emm:                         [.hmhhh ].thhh].hhh .h]h W'l
10                    ↑HO[NEY]AH]
11 Lot: F_add->     [or ]Ri]chard's?
12                          (0.2)
13 Emm: S   ->  I've bou↑:ghtEVrythai:ng?
14                          (0.9)
```

This surely does not exhaust the range of practices on which first pair part
speakers may draw in undertaking – after a problematic second pair part –
to expand the sequence by reworking the first pair part so as better to achieve
a preferred response.

   An extended sequence with multiple re-doings or reinstitutions of the first
pair part will provide exemplars of various of these practices, a first pair
part counterpart to the multiple second pair part episode displayed several
pages ago (Extract 7.45). After a pre-invitation sequence initiated by Bee
has been brought to an indeterminate conclusion (see Chapter 4, section
on pre-invitation, on pp. 29–34), Ava and Bee are just concluding making
arrangements to speak on the phone to make arrangements to possibly get
together when Bee mentions (lines 1–2 below) that she might "go t'the
city" (i.e., to Manhattan, from Long Island where Ava and Bee live with
their families), and Ava seizes on this (lines 3–4) to launch a sequence
proposing an alternative possibility:

```
(7.50a) TG, 16:31-17:15
 1 Bee:            [Well] when]ever. I'll poh I-I might go t'the
 2                 city in the mo:rning ·any[way,
 3 Ava:                                     [It depends on how (tough
 4      F_pre  -> the)=So what time y'leaving f'the city,
 5 Bee: S_pre  -> Oh:: probly about ten ten thirdy eleven,
 6                 er-[n-d-ih-] `hh
 7 Ava: F_b    ->    [O    h ] if you wanna leave about eleven I'll walk
 8                 down with [you.]°Cz I haftuh go] t'school]
 9 Bee: +S_pre->             [I t ]  de p en :d s ]how I ro:]l outta bed
10                 tom(h)orr(h)uh![`hh!]
11 Ava: F_b    ->               [Well] le'[s see-eh-so ] lemme give=
12 Bee: +S_pre->                          [how I fee:l.] hh
13 Ava: +F_b   -> =you a call about ten thi:rdy.
14 Bee: S_b    -> `hh Yeeuh.
15 Ava:           [A'ri:ght?]
16 Bee:           [I'll  see] w'ts-
17 Bee:           Yeah. [See what's going o:n.]
```

To Ava's pre-sequence first pair part at line 4 (whether pre-invitation, pre-offer, or pre-proposal is indeterminate), Bee responds with what in the end emerges as a hedge,[25] at lines 5, 9, and 12, which is designed to be understood as a single, through-produced response. Note that the response – the pre-expansion second pair part – initially just offers a range of times (lines 5 and 7), but when Ava takes this as a go-ahead response and proceeds to an offer/proposal base first pair part (lines 7–8), Bee resumes talking as it approaches possible completion with what is designed to be a post-positioned characterization of the range of times with which "her turn" had begun – which reconstitutes its design as a single, through-produced turn despite the long break between its parts. This second part of the turn underscores the hedging character of the response.

The hedging response to the initial version of the first pair part prompts a backdown by Ava from the offer/proposal to walk to the train station together to an arrangement to call about doing so (lines 11–13). (This, then, is another practice of "reworking.") This proposal is met with a "weak agreement" and a further hedge (lines 14 and 16),[26] a response which is re-asserted (line 17) even when an opportunity is provided to upgrade it (line 15). This is an unstable response at best for the next day's course of action which Ava is proposing, and Ava proceeds with a series of further re-doings of the base first pair part.

```
(7.50b) TG, 17:15-18:11
 1 Bee:            Yeah. [°See  w h a t ' s  g o i n g  o:n.]
 2 Ava: F    ->         [Maybe you wanna come downtuh school] see what
 3                 the new place looks like,
 4                 (0.5)
 5 Bee: S    -> Yih may:be. (N)a::[h,  b't I  hadn'- ]
 6 Ava: +F   ->                   [You c'n come innoo] a cla:ss
 7                 with m[e.
 8 Bee: S    ->         [I haven' thought about that la(h)tely hh huh
 9                 eh-[huh!
10 Ava: F_{again}->     [Why donch[a I mean you won' haftuh do any]thing,
11 Bee: F_{ins} ->               [.hh   You   know   I   wu-u-u] I wonder
12                 if Do:nna went back tuh school, i'z
13                 [I wz curious tuh  know,]
14 Ava: S_{ins}   [I n- Y'know- Fridays is] a funny day. mMost a' the
15                 people in schoo:l, `hh that's why I only have classes
16                 on Tuesday en Fri:day `hh (0.3)°u- one cla:ss, because
17                 most a' them have o:ff those days. Yih kno[w like=
```

---

[25] Much as Ava had earlier done to Bee's pre-invitation, cf. the discussion of Extract (4.03), at pp. 32–33 above.

[26] See Pomerantz (1984), who uses the term "weak agreement" to characterize responses to assessments which may implicate *dis*agreement in a semi-covert way. Davidson (1984, 1990) proposes to adapt this notion to responses to offers, invitations, requests, and proposals.

```
18 Bee:                                                          [Ye::h,
19 Ava:        =if yih kuh work yer schedule out that [way=I cuutn't.
20 Bee:                                                 [Right.
21             (0.7)
22 Ava:        Tch! But if you wanna-uh:m (0.2) come in en see.
23 Bee:        Tch! I wouldn' know wheretuh look fuh her(hh)
24             hnhh-hnh[h!˙hh
25 Ava: Fagain->        [Well you know, you know, come along with me,
26             (0.7)
27 Ava:        A:nd uh:m,
28             (0.7)
29 Ava:        °Wuhwz I gonnuh say.
30             (0.7)
31 Ava: Fagain-> You c'n come in the class with me, it's a logic class=I
32             think yih gonna see a pitcher o:n on something good
33             tomorruh in that class anyway so it's n[o ha:ssle,
34 Bee:                                                [°Nnh,
35 Ava: +F   -> hh 'T's only f'f'fty minutes anyw: ,
36             (0.6)
37 Ava:        [A:nd uh,
38 Bee: Shedge-> [˙hh W'l I'll see. hhYih[know
```

Although we cannot work our way through the whole of Extract (7.50b) in
the same detail as has informed our examination so far, we can take note
of some of the major sequence-organizational points of reference. So note
that at lines 2–3 Ava puts forward another proposal, perhaps meant as an
inducement, and that is an invitation/offer for Bee to come visit the new
campus of the college which they used to attend together, but from which
Bee has transferred to another school. In the face of weak agreements and
hedged responses (lines 5 and 8–9) by Bee, Ava continues to modify the
terms of the offer/proposal (line 6), and re-institutes the first pair part (line
10, "why doncha") with inducements, even if negative ones ("ya won't have
to do anything"). After Bee introduces contingencies which appear to derail
the sequence (lines 11–24), Ava nonetheless finds her way back, and again
re-institutes the general proposal (line 25) and then the most recent specific
one (line 31, reprising line 6 and re-setting the sequence to that point) but
with new inducements ("a pitcher on something good" at line 32, and, just
in case it is not, "only fifty minutes anyway" at line 35). All of these re-
doings, detailings, and inducements end up eliciting only the same hedging
response which Bee had previously given (line 38).

```
(7.50c) TG, 18:11-19:01
  1 Bee:       [˙hh W'l I'll see. hhYih[know
  2 Ava: +F  ->                        [Maybe if yih come down I'll
  3             take the car (then)/(down).
  4 Bee: Shedge-> t! We:ll, uhd-yihknow I-I don' wanna make any- thing
```

```
 5                   definite because I-yihknow I jis:: I jis::t thinkin:g
 6                   tihday all day riding on th'trai:ns hhuh-uh
 7                   ˙hh[h!
 8 Ava:                 [Well there's nothing else t'do.<I wz
 9                   thingin[g of  taking  the  car  anyway.] ˙hh
10 Bee:                     [that I would go into the ss-uh-]=I would go
11                   into the city but I don't know,
12 Ava: F     ->     Well if I do ta:ke it, this way if- uh-if- y'know uh::
13                   there's no pa:rking right away I c'n give you the car
14                   en you c'n look aroun a li'l bit.
15 Bee: S_hedge->    Mye::[:m ,    ]
16 Ava:                   [y'know] en see what happens.
17                   (0.4)
18 Bee: S_hedge->    Wel[l I'll see I] don'know ah, yihknow it's just u:n=
19 Ava:                 [if you want,]
20 Bee: S_alt  ->     =idea, I n-I wanniduh go to uh- (0.7) t!˙hhhhh the:
21                   Hallmark card shop on fifty seventh en fifth,
22 Ava:              (Oh:)=/ (Mm:)=
23 Bee:              =I wanniduh look aroun fuh some cards,
24 Ava:              (Oh:.)/(Right.)
25 Bee:              Tch! I'll get some advance birthday cards, hhm hmh!
26                   (0.6)
27 Bee:              ˙hhh A:n:d uh, (0.5) Me:h,
28                   (0.2)
29 Bee:              Oh Sibbie's sistuh hadda ba:by bo:way.
```

Ava is not finished. With the continued hedging by Bee, Ava now offers another "inducement" (lines 2–3) – an offer to "take the car" contingent on Bee's coming along (recall that this sequence began with an offer to walk together to the train station!). When this too elicits a hedging response (lines 4–7 and 10–11), the contingency aspect is dropped from the offer (lines 8–9, "I was thinking of taking the car anyway."). And then a new "offer" is articulated, one which may betray that underlying the "offer" sequence which has developed there is another "agenda," which lends it rather the cast of a "request." What Ava is now proposing, it appears, is a solution to her parking problem at school; if there is no parking, Bee can take the car and "look around a little bit" (line 14), a questionable undertaking in Manhattan even in the late 1960s, when this was recorded.

Bee's response ends the sequence, at least temporarily. First, she considers (lines 10–11 and 18) canceling the possibility which was used to launch the sequence in the first place (Extract [7.50a], lines 1–2, "I might go t'the city in the mo:rning anyway,"), and second, she hints at the esteem in which she holds Ava's proposal by entertaining as her alternative the prospect of shopping for "some advance birthday cards," i.e., cards which she does not need now but might need in the future (Extract [7.50c], line 25). When Ava has no response to this, no new reworking of her first pair part, Bee uses the resource of her last utterance to jump off into a sequence-organizationally unrelated new matter (line 29).[27]

It seems quite clear in the case of this episode that the elaborate moves made by Ava are parts of a single sequence, one whose base first pair part undergoes a series of transformations, specifications and other reworkings to secure a different – an aligning – response from Bee. There are other similar episodes which are less clear in whether they are built as a single, multiply expanded sequence or as a series of linked sequences – an alternative form of sequence organization to be examined in Chapter 10.

---

[27] But it is not over. When the announcement sequence about "Sibbie's sister" is over, Ava resuscitates the sequence, going back to its original proposal, or rather the first reworking of it (Extract [7.50a], lines 7–8).

```
(7.50d) TG, 19:29-20:07
 1 Bee:         [Awright so,
 2 Ava:  F   -> [Well if you wan' me (to) give you a ring tomorrow
 3              morning.
 4 Bee:  Shdg-> Tch! 'hhh We:ll y-you know, let's, eh- I don'know, I'll
 5 Bee:         see (h)may[be I woon' even be in,]
 6 Ava:  F                [Well when yih go intuh] the city y'gonna
 7              haftuh walk down t'the train a[n y w a y.]
 8 Bee:                                       [ r-Ri:ght.]
 9 Ava:  +F  -> So might ez well walk with some[buddy. 'hh
10 Bee:                                        [Right. So I'll
11              s-Alright. so gimme a call,
12 Ava:         Bout ten thirdy.
13 Bee:         Ri:ght.
14 Ava:         Okay th[en.
15 Bee:                [A'right.
16 Ava:         [A'ri[ght.
17 Bee:         [Tch![ I'll (s-)/(t-) I'll talk tihyou then t'mor[row.
18 Ava:                                                          [O:kay.=
19 Bee:         =Okay [buh buy,
20 Ava:               [Bye bye.
```

When Ava seeks (lines 2–3) to re-establish that earlier proposal, Bee again resists (lines 4–5), and Ava once again expands the sequence, and warrants her proposal in what could be taken to be quite a self-demeaning way: Bee might as well walk with somebody on the way to the train; Ava offers herself as that "somebody." The drifting-apart of this relationship of past friends could come to no more poignant an expression than the self-reduction of one of them to no more than an anonymous "somebody" to walk with, given the failure of Bee to align herself to any of the previously offered possibilities. This one, however, she does align with. She agrees with Ava's warrant (line 8, "Right"), and accordingly the proposal which it was offered to warrant (line 11, "Alright, so give me a call"), and even goes so far as to volunteer (in first position, not reactively) the next day's prospect (line 17, "I'll talk t'you then tomorrow).

8   Topic-proffering sequences: a distinctive adjacency pair sequence structure

The post-expansions discussed so far are ones that have developed in a sequential environment in which (as noted early on) preferred responses are sequence-closure-relevant and dispreferred responses are sequence-expansion-relevant. With the exception of minimal post-expansions and simple repair sequences, the post-expansions we have examined are generally implicated in disagreement and misalignment.

It is possible, however, to have a sequential environment in which there is a systematic reversal of the ordinary differential expansion relevance of preferred and dispreferred second pair parts. *Specifically, in topic-proffering sequences, as we will see, preferred responses engender expansion and dispreferred responses engender sequence closure.* In this distinct sequence type, expansion has a very different interactional import, and poses sequential problems of a different character, so much so that the development and extension of these sequences can not be assimilated to what we have been referring to as post-expansion.

We have already had occasion to register the fact that some turn types may do "double duty," both enacting their own action (questioning, assessing, telling) and serving thereby as the vehicle or instrument for another action. The same utterance (or, more technically, TCU) which does questioning can be doing requesting, or offering, etc. The same utterance which does telling can, by what is told or how, constitute a complaint. The TCU which conveys an assessment can thereby accomplish a compliment or an insult.

One type of action which a question can possibly accomplish, and can be understood by its recipient to be engaged in doing, is "topic proffering," and it is therefore something deserving of an account here, even though we are not otherwise systematically dealing with the organization of topic and topic talk. Topic proffering is a distinct mode of entering into topic talk, contrasting with (among disjunctive new topic starts) topic solicitation (such as the "itemized news inquiries" proposed by Button and Casey [1984, 1985] and Button [1988/89]) and unilateral topic initiation (or "nomination," Button [1988/89]) among others, and with the wholly different modality of topic change represented by step-by-step topic shift (Sacks, 1987[1973]; Jefferson, 1984).

With a topic proffer (ordinarily after the just-prior talk has been brought to possible sequence closure), a speaker *proposes* a particular topic (as compared to a solicitation, in which the speaker invites the *recipient* to propose a topic), but does not actively launch or further develop the proposed topic (as in a unilateral topic initiation). By "proffering" the topic, the speaker makes it available to recipient(s) to embrace or reject, to "buy into" or decline. Our account of topic-proffering sequences ought to provide characterizations of the proffering, of the response(s) to the proffering, of the form the common trajectories of this sequence take, and how such sequences engender successful launching of a topic or coordinated non-uptake of the topic. We cannot here take up the organization of the topic talk once launched.

We begin with two characteristic features of topic proffers. First, one type of topic which is commonly put forward this way can be characterized as "recipient-oriented topics"; that is, ones about which the recipient is, or is treated as being, an/the authoritative speaker. The topic may concern something which is specifically, differentially, or even exclusively within the recipient's experience, or on which their view has special weight or authority. In that regard, the projected topic-talking sequence, if it does in fact develop from the proffer, will be one in which the recipient is likely to carry the burden of the talking – either because they are the only ones who could do so, or because they are the ones who *properly* do so. This projected differential division of labor is clearly relevant to the profferer doing *only* a proffer, for the recipient to take up or to decline. In the exemplars of topic-proffering sequences examined here, look at the initial topic proffers and who the prime speakers on the proffered topic are projected to be.

A second common feature of topic proffers is that they are most often implemented by so-called "yes/no"-type questions (Extracts [8.01]–[8.03] and [8.05] below), though they can be carried by other types of questions (as in [8.04] below) or by utterances in an assertion format which can have the sequential force of questions, for example, in soliciting confirmation (as in [8.06] below).

```
(8.01) TG, 14:1-3
1 Ava:     °That's goo[d,
2 Bee: ->            [Dihyuh have any-cl- You have a class with
3      ->  Billy this te:rm?

(8.02) TG, 10:2-3
1 Bee: ->  °(I 'unno)/°(So anyway) °hh Hey do you see v- (0.3)
2      ->  fat ol' Vivian anymouh?

(8.03) TG, 4:35-36
1 Bee: ->  Eh-yih have anybuddy: thet uh:? (1.2) I would know from
2      ->  the English depar'mint there?

(8.04) Auto Discussion, 5:16
1 Cur: ->  (W'll) how wz the races las'night.
```

```
(8.05) SN-4, 16:02
1 Mar: -> So ('r) you da:ting Keith?

(8.06) Stolen, 2:22
1 Mar: -> ·hhhh So: yer ba:ck.
```

In the turns following these topic proffers – that is, in second position – the key issue is whether the recipient displays a stance which *en*courages or *dis*courages the proffered topic, embraces it or rejects it, accepts or declines what has been proposed, and does so in a type-conforming way or not. Several features of the response turns are regularly relevant here.

One is the inclusion (often in turn-initial position) of positive or negative response tokens, sequentially relevant by virtue of the turn being one which follows a "yes/no"-type question.

A second, related feature of the response turns is whether the response does or does not align with the polarity of the question which, at one level, it is answering. (This is related to the presence of "yeses" and "nos" but is not identical with it, because the form for *aligning* with a negatively formulated question may be "*no*" – as in [8.09] below, at lines 7–8, whereas a "yes" may be the way of *denying* alignment with it.)

A third feature, and often the key one, is whether the response turn is constructed to be minimal (or minimized – i.e., analyzably kept short, even if not as short as possible) or expanded. Here turn organization plays a strategic role; response turns composed of a single TCU, and a brief one, or several brief TCUs (especially if they are redundant or repetitive) are ways of embodying minimal responses. Turns built of more than one TCU, and including one whose grammatical composition is more elaborate or inflected and designed to add to what the prior TCU has done, are ordinarily ways of doing expanded responses.

But none of these work mechanically. They are all ways in which the recipient of the topic proffer can display a stance toward it, and the key facet of that stance is recurrently (though not invariably) that of "access." The recipient's deployment of positive and negative response tokens, alignments and non-alignments, minimal and expanded turns, is in the service of claiming access to the topic or denying access; that is, claiming the resources (the knowledge, the experience, etc.) for sustaining the talk they are being invited to take up or *dis*claiming them. For example, even if the response turn is *not* built to be minimal, even if it has a second turn-constructional unit and that unit is sentential and richly informative, if it is being used to disavow access to the topic, the responder will be understood to be *declining* the topic (for lack of access), not embracing it. Compare, then, the responses to the topic proffers in Extracts (8.07) and (8.08):

```
(8.07) TG, 14:01-06 (building on [8.01])
1 Ava:      °That's goo[d,
2 Bee:                 [Dihyuh have any-cl- You have a class with
```

```
3           Billy this te:rm?
4 Ava: ->   Yeh he's in my abnormal class.
5 Bee:      mnYeh [ how-]
6 Ava: ->         [Abnor]mal psy[ch.
```

Note here that Ava's response is an agreement with that facet of the prior turn which constitutes a "yes/no" question, that this agreement is indicated directly in turn-initial position with a type-conforming "yes" token, and that this response is multiply built as an expanded and not minimal turn – first, in the production of a second TCU ("he's in my abnormal class"); and then in the post-completion repair ("Abnormal psych"), which expands the turn still further (although it could be argued that this is a subsequent turn, not an expansion of the same one). Note, finally, that all of these resources are deployed here to claim access to the topic which Bee is proffering – talk about Billy.

On the other hand,

```
(8.08) TG, 10:02-05 (building on [8.02])
1 Bee:    °(I 'unno     )/°(So anyway) ·hh Hey do you see v- (0.3)
2         fat ol' Vivian anymouh?
3 Ava: -> No, hardly, en if we do:, y'know, I jus' say hello
4      -> quick'n, ·hh y'know, jus' pass each othuh in
5         th[e hall.]
```

Here, Ava's response is built to take up a quite different stance toward the proffered topic. As an answer to the question, her response disagrees with the premise on which the question is built. This disagreement is displayed in turn-initial position with the negative (though type-conforming) token, "No." And, although the turn is built to be not minimal but expanded, its expansions are designed to display a negative stance toward the proffered topic, and do so in two ways. First, Ava shows herself to have "reached for" this "no," for she immediately backs down from it to "hardly," which might be translated as "yes, but not much," which could have led to an answer of "yes," were Ava inclined to embrace the topic. Responding with "no, hardly" is then a way of showing one is *choosing* "no," rather than simply "reflecting the facts." Second, note that the further expansion of Ava's response turn is designed to disavow whatever access to the topic ("Vivian") her answer-so-far might seem to have suggested. Whatever "seeing" she has done with Vivian (clearly this is meant as a sociable encounter and not merely a visual one) has not led to the sort of interchange on which she could now report.

The important point being exemplified here is that, even though expanding the response turn is regularly a way in which the recipient of a topic proffer can indicate an inclination to take it up, this default understanding can be superseded by what is actually said in the expansion, and *that* can indicate that the very expansion itself was mobilized to discourage the topic.

As with other sequence types in which accepting and rejecting/declining are the alternative responsive stances, accepting or embracing the proffered topic is ordinarily the structurally *preferred* response type, and the one done in the manner of preferred responses, and rejecting is the dispreferred alternative.[1]

One way in which the preference for acceptance of a proffered topic shows itself is that, with very rare exceptions, a topic profferer will essay *two tries* at proffering the topic. Of course, if the initial proffer is embraced, the next "try" may have as much the character of the pursuit of an already-going topic as that of a try, although often enough the "follow-up" is still a try in that it moves to steer the talk toward a particular facet of the topic domain first broached. This is the case in Extract (8.01) and its continuation.

```
(8.09)  TG, 14:01-08 (building on [8.07])
1 Ava:      °That's goo[d,
2 Bee:               [Dihyuh have any-cl- You have a class with
3             Billy this te:rm?
4 Ava:      Yeh he's in my abnormal class.
5 Bee:      mnYeh [ how-]
6 Ava:            [Abnor]mal psy[ch.
7 Bee: ->                       [Still not gettin married,
8 Ava: ->  ·hhh Oh no. Definitely not.[married.]
```

Note that the "second try" at line 7 is steering the talk in a direction quite different from the one employed to proffer the topic at lines 2–3. The first proffer located Billy in an academic context; the second moves the talk toward a discussion of romance.

Note also the response to this second try. It is built as an agreement (even an upgraded agreement, "definitely not married"); here the agreement is articulated through a negative token, because what is being agreed with was formulated in a negative. And, by being expanded, together with the emphatic upgrade which alludes to different, new, and possibly newly gained information, it again displays an embracing stance to the topic, and even indicates a direction of pursuit.

---

[1] It is worth remarking as well that, even though rejecting Bee's topic proffer, Ava may be in some respects aligning with her. Note that Bee self-interrupts her topic-proffering utterance to insert an apparently unflattering descriptor of Vivian; what starts to be "V-[ivian]" is changed into "fat ol' Vivian." And the word "anymore" in the topic proffer is what linguists call a "negative polarity item"; it displays an orientation to a negative answer, just as "still" may display an orientation to a positive one (see Extract [8.11] below, at lines 6–7). Ava's rejection of the topic may thus be partially attuned to a negative stance which Bee has herself displayed. Bee's topic proffer may be understood to embody a kind of ambivalence that puts Ava in an interactional quandary. Perhaps this has something to do with the mixed messages in her response; "no" and "not no"; and "in the 'not no' still not enough to talk about." All this in place of "no," or "not really" – and all of it contiguous to its first pair part.

```
(8.10) TG, 14:01-16 (building on [8.09])
 1  Ava:        °That's goo[d,
 2  Bee:                   [Dihyuh have any-cl- You have a class with
 3              Billy this te:rm?
 4  Ava:        Yeh he's in my abnormal class.
 5  Bee:        mnYeh [ how-]
 6  Ava:              [Abnor]mal psy[ch.
 7  Bee:                            [Still not gettin married,
 8  Ava: ->     ·hhh Oh no. Definitely not.[married.]
 9  Bee: ->                                [No  he's] dicided
10              [defin[itely?]
11  Ava:        [·hhh [O   h ] no.
12  Bee: ->     ·hh Bec'z [las'] time you told me he said no: but he=
13  Ava:                  [No. ]
14  Bee:        =wasn't su:re,
15  Ava:        n:No definitely not. He, he'n Gail were like on the
16              outs, yihknow¿
```

And the topic talk continues along these lines.

But if the initial topic proffer is declined, a second try more clearly takes
on the cast of an extended effort to achieve an outcome not achieved by the
first proffer. It should hardly be surprising that second tries which follow
rejection of the first proffer are also vulnerable to rejection. Consider the
sequel to Extracts (8.02) and (8.08):

```
(8.11) TG, 10:02-08 (building on [8.08])
 1  Bee:        °(I 'unno     )/°(So anyway) ·hh Hey do you see v- (0.3)
 2              fat ol' Vivian anymouh?
 3  Ava:        No, hardly, en if we do:, y'know, I jus' say hello
 4              quick'n, ·hh y'know, jus' pass each othuh in
 5              th[e hall.]
 6  Bee: ->       [Is  she] still hangin aroun (wih)/(with) Bo:nny?
 7  Ava: ->     Ah:, yeh hh yeh,
```

Here again the second try shifts the focus of the topic proffer from access
to sociability, but this is very likely an artifact of both of these topic-
proffering sequences being of the "updating" or "catching up" variety, in
which two acquaintances get updated on what has transpired in the interim
since they last talked. (It may even reflect a matter of personal style, since
both sequences are initiated by the same speaker to the same recipient.) It
does not appear to be a feature of topic-proffering sequences per se.

The response to this second try (at line 7) is hardly more encouraging
than was the response to the first. Although in this case the answering to
the question is an agreement and this is implemented by a "yes" token, the
response is still minimized, if not minimal. That is, it is not minimal insofar
as the first TCU is followed by another, so the turn is, in a literal or technical
sense expanded, but the second TCU does no more than literally repeat the

first, with no elaboration, or even expansion in the minimal, lexical form of
the TCU.

```
(8.12) TG, 10:02-14 (building on [8.11])
 1  Bee:       °(I 'unno       )/°(So anyway) ·hh Hey do you see v- (0.3)
 2             fat ol' Vivian anymouh?
 3  Ava:       No, hardly, en if we do:, y'know, I jus' say hello
 4             quick'n, ·hh y'know, jus' pass each othuh in
 5             th[e hall.]
 6  Bee:         [Is  she] still hangin aroun (wih)/(with) Bo:nny?
 7  Ava:       Ah:, yeh hh yeh,
 8  Bee: ->    Hmh!
 9       ->    (0.7)
10  Ava: ->    ·hhh Bud uh I- I- n-like this term I don' have hardly
11             any breaks. I made it, up that way.
12  Bee:       Mmm.
13  Ava:       Like, the only break I have is like t'day. En like,
14             we . . .
```

After the second try at proffering the topic (at line 6) is also discouraged
(the minimalist reply at line 7), in the third position to that adjacency pair
(at line 8) the profferer "passes"; that is, Bee makes no further efforts to
press the topic and leaves it to the recipient to make the next move. Ava
then deflects the talk in a tangential direction, offering what can ostensibly
be taken as an account for not encountering Vivian, and thus apparently
staying "on topic," but beginning a step-by-step shift to a quite unrelated
topical focus.

But second tries are not hopeless undertakings. Sometimes second tries
are embraced after initial topic proffers were rejected. Thus the sequence
beginning with a topic proffer in Extract (8.03) develops like this:

```
(8.13) TG, 4:35-5:05 (building on [8.03])
 1  Bee:       Eh-yih have anybuddy: thet uh:? (1.2) I would know from
 2             the English depar'mint there?
 3  Ava: ->    Mm-mh. Tch! I don't think so.
 4  Bee: ->    °Oh,=<Did they geh ridda Kuhleznik yet hhh
 5  Ava: ->    No in fact I know somebuddy who ha:s huh [now.
 6  Bee:                                                [Oh my got
 7             hh[hhh
 8  Ava:         [Yeh en s' he siz yihknow he remi:nds me of d-hih-ih-
 9             tshe reminds me, ·hhh of you, meaning me:.
10             ((continues on topic of Kuhleznik and other teachers))
```

The initial topic proffer at lines 1–2 is rejected at line 3. The answer is in
"disagreement" with the premise of the question, and this is conveyed with
the negative response token "mm-mh." Although the turn is expanded with
another TCU, and the additional TCU does weaken the disagreement, it

does so only by weakening the confidence with which it is asserted; it does not change the substance of the assertion, whose upshot is to disclaim access to the matter being proffered as the topic – teachers known in common that they could talk about. This topic is being rejected.

As with the other topic-proffering sequences we have examined, this one also gets a second try, at line 4, and this second try gets quite a different reception. Even though the turn begins with a "no" and thus may sound like the start of another rejection, Ava rushes to include a second TCU, an expansion which augurs well not simply as an expansion, but also for what is asserted in it; namely, a claim of access – *mediated* access, but access nonetheless, and a display of a move to embrace the topic. (Note, by the way, the "yet" in Bee's second try, another "negative polarity item," displaying an orientation to a negative response, with which Ava's answer is then aligned.) This acceptance of the second try gets a rather more engaged and animated uptake by the topic profferer ("Oh my God" at line 6) than did the rejection of the second try in Extract [8.12] ("Hmh" at line 8), and talk continues on the now-launched topic.

Other trajectories are also possible. On some occasions, the rejection of the initial topic proffer may be taken to be so abrupt and unyielding, or so hostile in context, as to discourage the very articulation of a second try. Such single-try topic proffer sequences can sound starkly dramatic and painful. Extract (8.06) above is taken from a conversation between a divorced/separated couple discussing a hitch in the return of their teenaged son to the custody of the father after a holiday stay with the mother, while the father was on a trip. After the son's new travel plans have been described by the mother and apparently settled, the talk develops as follows:

```
(8.14) Stolen, 2:18-25 (building on [8.06])
1   Mar:        But Ile:ne probably (0.8) is either at the airport er
2               waiting tuh hear fr'm in eess
3               (0.7)
4   Ton:        O:kay.
5   Mar: ->     ·hhhh So: yer ba:ck.
6   Ton: ->     Yah.
7               (1.0)
8   Mar: ->     I see. So you'll- you'll hear fr'm im,
```

Lines 1–4 represent the closing down of the preceding arrangements-making sequence, and at line 5 Marsha proffers as a new topic Tony's recent trip. Although his answer is in agreement with the premise of the question and this is expressed with a "yes" token, and there is no question of Tony's access to the proffered topic, the utter and stark minimality of the response, and its unyieldingness within the full second of silence which follows it, in which there are multiple opportunities for Tony to resume talking and expand the turn, are understandable as a rejection by Tony of the proffered topic (and perhaps of *any* non-instrumental topic), and are apparently so understood by Marsha. She makes no second try, and repeats in a closing-relevant way the upshot of the arrangements which have already been concluded. But such one-try topic-proffering sequences are relatively rare, and markedly dramatic and telling when they occur.[2]

The sequences examined so far have all been drawn from telephone conversations, and thus have involved only the profferer and the addressed recipient, and they have been conducted entirely through the hearable talk. With co-present interactions involving more than two participants, other possibilities inform the interaction. Only two will be mentioned here, as a kind of principled alert to a range of matters which cannot be taken up here in detail.

One of these possibilities is that, after a topic-proffer sequence has run its course between the profferer and the addressed recipient (or even before it has run its course), other parties to the interaction may involve themselves, and extend the talk beyond the trajectory which had been imparted to it by the principals.

The sequence initiated by the utterance reproduced as Extract (8.05) above is taken from a conversation between three young women and a young man in the women's suite in a private college dormitory. Mark had earlier in the conversation voiced a mock complaint about one of the women,

---

[2] The following instance is a bit more expansive. In reflecting on the import of the abrupt response, the participants make it more explicitly accessible for analytic purposes as well. Hyla and Nancy have just been discussing the prospects of a date Hyla will be having with a young man from out of town, and the possibility of a mutual attraction being frustrated by his having to return home. On completion of that topic/sequence, Nancy poses a question to Hyla about the mail – an allusion to a *current* male interest from whom mail has been due for a while.

```
(8.15) HG, 14:26-38
 1  Nan:   Didja a'ready get the mai:l,=
 2  Hyl:   =·hhhh Yes, hh-hh-h[h,
 3  Nan:                      [Oh, hhhmhh[hh
 4  Hyl:                                 [hh-hh
 5                  (·)
 6  Nan:   Sorry I brought it u(hhh)p
 7                  (·)
 8  Hyl:   Yeah,
 9                  (·)
10  Nan:   [·hnnnn,
11  Hyl:   [So em I-:-:.  ·hhhh[hhhhhh-h-h-h-h
12  Nan:                      [Oh::::,
13                  (·)
```

Nancy's post-expansion comment on this minimally expanded sequence makes explicit that she took herself to be proffering a topic ("bringing it up"), and that she understood Hyla *not* to have aligned with that move (despite the "yes" answer) and to have declined it sufficiently strongly to make an apology relevant. Hyla in turn confirms this by not even accepting the apology, but seconding Nancy's expression of regret. We have here, then, data-internal evidence that a positive and "agreeing" response to a topic proffer – even when there is no issue of access to the topic – can by its designed minimization convey vigorous rejection of that topic proffer, to the point that no second try is undertaken.

Karen, having gone out with "Keith" and not with him. Some ten minutes
later, just after a topic/sequence has been brought to closure, Mark proffers
new topic talk keyed to Keith.

```
(8.16) SN-4, 16:02-20 (building on [8.05])
 1  Mar:      So ('r) you da:ting Keith?
 2             (1.0)
 3  Kar:      'Sa frie:nd.
 4             (0.5)
 5  Mar:      What about that girl 'e use tuh go with fer so long.
 6  Kar:      A:lice? I [don't-] they gave up.
 7  Mar:                [ (mm) ]
 8             (0.4)
 9  Mar:      (°Oh?)
10  Kar:      I dunno where she is but I-
11             (0.9)
12  Kar:      ↑Talks about 'er evry so o:ften, but- I dunno where she is.
13             (0.5)
14  Mar:      hmh
15             (0.2)
16  She: ->   Alice was stra::nge,
17             (0.3)      ((rubbing sound))
18  Mar:      Very o:dd. She usetuh call herself a pro:stitute,='n I
19             useteh- (0.4) ask 'er . . .
```

Mark's initial topic proffer at line 1 is met with disagreement, with
correction; the response is delayed as befits and often marks dispreferred
responses, and implies a more attenuated access than is proposed by the
question. The second try (at line 5) shifts the topical focus, and gets a
somewhat more forthcoming response. At the very least this response turn
is multiply expanded and somewhat informative. But the upshot, when all
is said and done, is a denial of access ("I dunno where she is"), which is
received (at line 14) with a minimal receipt much like that in Extract (8.12)
above, at line 8, after rejection of the second try in that sequence. But here,
a third party – Sherry – enters (at line 16) and revives the otherwise dying
topic, which Karen subsequently rejoins (in a sequel not shown; for further
discussion, see Schegloff [1996c]).

   The sequence launched by Extract (8.04) comes from a conversation at a
backyard picnic in Ohio in the early 1970s. Curt is the host, and one of his
guests, Mike, had gone to the automobile races the prior evening.

```
(8.17) Auto Discussion, 5:16-36 (simplified) (building on [8.04])
 1  Cur:      (W'll) how wz the races las'night.
 2             (0.8)
 3  ???:      (Ha-[u h)     ]=
 4  Cur:          [Who w'n][th'feature.]
 5  Mik:               =[A l w o n,]
```

```
 6            (0.3)
 7  Cur:      [(Who)]=
 8  Mik:      [ A l.]=
 9  Cur:      =Al did?
10  Cur:      Dz he go out there pretty regular¿
11            (1.5)
12  Mik:      Generally evry Satur[dee.
13            (1.2)
14  Phy:      He wins js about evry Saturday too.
15  Cur:      He- he's about the only regular <he's about the
16            only go[od regular out there'z, Keegan still go out?
```

For present purposes, there is one main point which is important to register about this very rich sequence (in which, by the way, can also be seen the joining by a third party when a topic-proffering sequence may have petered out – see Phyllis's entry [line 14] after the long gap at line 13). After the initial topic proffer at line 1, there are various apparent indications that Mike (who is the targeted addressee) is declining the topic. There is, for example, the long gap at line 2, followed by the apparently minimal response at line 5. However, when the transcribable talk is re-examined together with the visible conduct which co-occurs with it, it turns out that this "silence" at line 2 is not an interactional vacuum, but is a place at which Mike is nodding. In the sequential position after a question requesting an assessment, such nodding can constitute a determinate response – a positive assessment. If that is registered, and is understood as the whole of Mike's response, it still appears minimal. Curt's line 4 then appears to be a second try. On the other hand, Mike's nodding at line 2 can be understood as the first part of an expanded response to the initial topic proffer, the first part gesturally accomplished, the expansion done in talk – namely, "Al won." On that understanding, Mike's response to the initial topic proffer is *encouraging*: it is forthcoming with an aligning second pair part, it is filled with affirmative tokens, it is expanded, and embodies Mike's known access by giving information, and information beyond what was requested.

It is not possible here to work through a resolution between these two analyses of this topic-proffering sequence (for an extended treatment, see Schegloff [1987, 1996d]). What is central, however, is to register the observation that, in working through the development of such sequences, with the response contingencies which are conditionally relevant at the several junctures, the participants may deploy the full range of resources available to them as interactants in that setting, and the outside analyst who wishes to understand what is going on as the co-participants might understand it will do well also to attend to the whole range.

What, then, is special and different about this sequence type as compared to others which have been discussed? We have seen before that, generally speaking, preferred second pair parts are "closure-relevant" and dispreferred second pair parts are "expansion-relevant." That is, after production of a preferred second pair part, sequence closure generally follows quickly. Dispreferred second pair parts, on the other hand, often generate expansions in anticipation of them and to avoid them (pre-expansions and insert expansions), and expansions in their aftermath to reconcile the divergences. It is in this respect that topic-proffering sequences are different. For it is precisely after a *preferred* response – when the proffered topic is *accepted* or *embraced* – that one finds substantial sequence expansion; that is, the topic-*talking* sequence itself. And it is after *dispreferred* responses – when the topic proffer is rejected, and re-rejected after a second try – that the sequence faces incipient closure. Talk may develop in an ostensibly related way, by the prior recipient or by a third party, but this is largely a cover-up for what is in effect a failed, and closed, sequence.

This divergence from the ordinary structural format poses a sequential problem. The closure-relevance of preferred responses provides a "natural way" for sequences to come to closure: either they get preferred responses or, in the wake of dispreferred responses, various trajectories of compromise, backdown, or reconciliation are pursued, often to some form of agreement or acceptance of divergence. But if agreement/preference engenders *expansion*, how is the expanded sequence brought to closure? The solution to this problem is also a solution for other "long sequences"; that is, sequences with extensive post-expansion. We will call it "the topic/sequence-closing sequence."

9   Sequence-closing sequences

As sequences get expanded, their structuring can become progressively less determinate. But this indeterminateness is not evenly distributed across a sequence's trajectory. Specifically, as sequences get expanded *after their base second pair part*, their structuring can become increasingly unconstrained. There are fairly straightforward reasons for this.

Pre-expansions are disciplined by the projected first pair part by reference to which they get their import. Their growth is always under the shadow of the parties' orientation to the sequence which the pre-expansion foreshadows.

Similarly, insert expansions are constrained by the relevant and impending base second pair part which has been made conditionally relevant by the base first pair part, a relevance which each element of insert expansion renews, as it defers its realization. The growth of insert expansions is under the shadow of the parties' orientation to the response to which they are preliminary.

However, post-expansions have no such projected structural component by which they are disciplined or constrained. Although some sequences do appear to require some third-position object to achieve closure (Jefferson and Schenkein, 1978), "third position" is a much less determinate position than second. The turn following a second pair part is a place ready for a third-position object to be recognized as such, as is the slot after a small post-expansion. But if there is a substantial expansion of the sequence after its base second pair part, then no next turn position can accommodate an "oh" or "okay" which will directly be recognized as closing the sequence.

How, then, do such longer sequences get closed, both those whose lengthy post-expansion is a sign and product of trouble (e.g., disagreement) and those which represent success, such as the topic-talk following a topic-proffering sequence?

Unilateral and foreshortened sequence endings

There are, of course, various ways a sequence can get ended. Some of these are unilateral, or virtually unilateral. One party can, for example, abandon an utterance-in-progress, and disjunctively launch a new topic

or new sequence, perhaps under the auspices that it has been touched off
by something in the talk or in the interaction's environment. The above-
mentioned qualification – "*virtually* unilateral" – is meant to recognize that
such disjunctive shifts do require the collaboration of co-participants, at the
very least their willingness not to insist on resumption of the abandoned
topic or sequence.

In Extract (9.01), Frieda and her husband Rubin are having dinner at the
home of Kathy and her husband, Dave (Frieda and Kathy – who weaves in
her spare time – are long-standing friends). Frieda has just introduced an
awkward matter, their having offered their country home (which in the past
had been made available to Dave and Kathy) to someone else.

```
(9.01) KC-4, 13:22-14:31
 1 Fri:    But uh[m as a matter of fact y'know uh th' thee- thee=
 2 ???:        [(y'know)
 3 Fri:    =uh my girlfriend. who uh (1.0) I: -offered the house
 4         to up in the countr[y.
 5 Dav:                       [Mhhm
 6 Fri:    She has a- an invalid m:othah.
 7 Dav:    Mhhm
 8 Fri:    Who's be:d ridden.
 9 Dav:    Mhhm
10 Fri:    They still haven't figured out, (·) how they're gonna
11         get to the country:<who's gonna take care of huh mo:thah.
12         while [they're- y'know 'p in the country.on the weekends.
13 Dav:          [Mm
14         (0.2)
15 Fri:    So: (·) you know,
16         (0.8)
17 Fri:    An besides tha[:t,
18 Rub:                  [You c'n go any[way
19 Dav:                                 [Don'- Don' git- don [get ]
20 Fri:                                                       [they]
21         won't be:
22 Dav:    Y'know there- there's no- no long explanation is
23         necessary.
24 Fri:    ↑Oh nono↑no: I'm not- I jus:: uh-wanted: you to know that
25         you can go up anyway.=
26 Rub:    =Yeah:.
27         (0.2)
28 Fri:    You know.
29         (0.2)
30 Fri:    Becaus-ah
31         (3.3)
32 Rub:    They don mind honey they're jus not gonna talk to us
33         ever again.=
34 Dav:    =(hehem)/(ri:(h)ight)
```

```
35              (0.8)
36 Kat:         We don mind<[we jus ne:ver gonna talk to you e:ver(hh heh)
37 Dav:                       [(No, b't )
38 Rub:         heheheheh
39 Kat:         [No::] that's awright
40 Fri:         [So::]
41 Dav:         [(                             ) ]
42 Fri:         [You know what we're gonna-] in fact I'm- she I haven't
43        ->    seen her since I spoke to you but I'm going to talk
44        ->    to=whatayou making?
45              (0.2)
46 Kat:         It's a ↑bla:nket.
47 Fri:         Did yu weave tha[t yourse:lf]
48 Kat:                         [ I w o : ]ve this myself.=
49              ((continues on the blanket))
```

The awkwardness and sensitivity of the matter are oriented to overtly by
the participants themselves – for example, in the utterances at lines 22–
25, 32–33 and 36, which, by their very apparent levity and mock outrage,
suggest some ongoing turbulence underneath. Note, then, Frieda's move
at the arrows (lines 43–44), by which she abruptly drops the utterance-in-
progress, which is concerned with the country house, and remarks on a
piece of weaving ("what are you making") which she thereby claims to
have just noticed, i.e., a disjunctive topic/sequence shift prompted by the
environment, and a diversion with which Kathy (and, a bit later, Dave as
well) collaborates. This, then, is one device for exiting long or expanded
sequences.[1]

There are less abrupt topic-shifting practices, practices for shifting topic
step-by-step, either accomplished by a single speaker or participated in by
more than one (see Sacks, 1987[1973]; Jefferson, 1984; Schegloff, 1996d),
but these are relevant in the first instance to topicality and topic-talking
sequences, and less so to other types of action sequence.

The preceding paragraphs all concern variations on a single theme – ending a sequence by starting a different one. It is notable that efforts simply
to pre-emptively shut down a sequence in which post-expansion is sequentially motivated by a dispreferred SPP do not seem viable. If one party does
make an overt move to foreshorten the sequence, it regularly fails, even if
the other party or parties overtly agree to it. This happens more than once
in Extract (9.03a), taken from the by-now-familiar upholstery shop data.
Mike has asked Vic about an aquarium that he has, and Vic is detailing the
many such "tanks" (as he calls them) which he has accumulated.

---

[1] Such sharp shifts from one sequence to another can be prompted not only by "trouble" but
by perceived opportunity. For example, we have several times, and for various interests,
examined a long segment from the TG conversation, whose latter part is preoccupied with
arrangements for possibly meeting. This portion of the conversation is started by Bee with
a pre-invitation, and, after a bumpy development to a precarious arrangement, suddenly

```
(9.03a) US, 28:1—22
1                  (1.2)
2 Vic:            Uh::-˙hh I'm intuh, I got one tank which is a f-forty
3                 or a fifty. (0.7) 'T's a lo:ng, (0.5) Y'know about so
4                 high en about this long. En I got a::::, (0.7) a
5                 fishbowl in the center of it, 'n fixed up like it was
6                 a regular fish but the fi- gol'fish. One gol'fish.
7                 (0.7) I had- three. But I had the, ˙hh the floppy
8                 tail ki:nd yihknow duh:: angel type [(    ) fish.
9 Mik: Fpre->                                        [Wuhddiyuh doing
10                with dat big bow-puh-tank. Nothing?
11                (0.5)
12 Vic:          ((COUGH))
13 Vic:          Uh-h-h,
14                (1.0)
15 Vic: Sb ->    I'm not intuh selling it or giving it. AThat's it.
16 Mik: SCT->    Okay.
17                (1.0)
18 Mik: *        Dat wz simple. Khhhh huh-huh-heh!=
19 Vic: *        =Yeh.
20                (0.7)
21 Vic: *        °Teg,
22                (1.0)
```

shifts into a proposal by Ava. Here is the point of shift from the first of these sequences to
the second.

```
(9.02) TG, 16:22-17:03
 1 Ava:    Yeh w'l I'll give you a call then tomorrow.when I get
 2         in 'r sumn.
 3              (0.5)
 4 Bee:    Wha:t,
 5 Ava:    <I'll give yih call tomo[rrow.]
 6 Bee:                            [Yeh: ] 'n
 7         [I'll be ho:me t'mor]row.
 8 Ava:    [When I-I get  home.] I don't kno-w- I could be home
 9         by-˙hh three, I c'd be home by two [I don't] know.]
10 Bee:                                       [ Well  ] when ]
11         ever. I'll poh I-I might go t'the city in the mo:rning
12         any[way,
13 Ava: ->    [It depends on how (tough the)=So what time
14      ->    y'leaving f'the city,
15 Bee:    Oh:: probly abou-t ten ten thirdy eleven, er-n-d-ih-
```

Ava's talk at the start of line 13 is a continuation of the talk at lines 7–9, in which she
is offering an account of her having to estimate the time at which she will try to call
Bee (very likely she is in the process of invoking "it depends on how tough the [traffic
is]"). Note, then, that she simply slides from that utterance-in-progress into a new one
which concerns not her arrival home but the time of Bee's departure the next day, and
is doing a pre-expansion to some next sequence – by its incorporation of "the city,"
Ava's modified turn shows itself to have been prompted by the just-preceding talk by Bee.

One common locus for such abrupt shifts is when something in the talk triggers for either
the speaker or some co-participant a locally tellable story. Such occurrences are discussed
in Jefferson (1978a).

Mike's question at lines 9–10, especially given its proposed candidate answer "Nothing?," is readily understandable as a pre-expansion. Although it is not entirely clear what action it is leading up to, it does seem clear that it is an acquisitive one on Mike's part. The long gap at lines 11–14 projects a dispreferred response to come, and, when it comes at line 15, it turns out to be an SPP not to the pre-sequence but to the as-yet-unarticulated base SPP which Vic shows himself to figure is a request to buy or be given the aquarium. And then he moves peremptorily to end the sequence right there; that is, to pre-empt the sequence expansion that is made likely by the dispreferred SPP. Although I have characterized Mike's turn at line 16 as a sequence-closing third, it could as well be treated as an alignment or acceptance of Vic's move to shut off any further pursuit of the matter. Although there is a bit more to the sequence (lines 18–22), it does not extend the matter the sequence was concerned with; it is addressed to the way in which the exchange was ended. But, it turns out that it was not ended. Here is what happens next:

```
(9.03b) US, 28: 22–29: 03
 1 Vic: +Sb        Becuz selling it ur giving it I::, da:t's (all [there is)
 2 Mik:                                                          [Buh I din
 3      Fb         say giving it. If yer intuh [selling it (I'll [take it man,)
 4 Vic:                                         [Uh-h-h           [
 5 Vic:                                                           [The bi:d,
 6 Vic:            The bi:d is, is, (0.7) -third rate. Becuss I awready r-
 7      Sb         (0.5) caught- It doesn' mattuh I'm not intuh [selling it or=
 8 Mik: Fbretract                                               [F'get it.
 9 Vic:            =giving it.=
10 Mik: SCT        =Oh-o[kay.
11 Vic: *               [Clea:n,
12                 (0.7)
13 Mik: *          Clean,
14 Vic:            Eh=
15 Mik: *          =jing, [tchikeh
16 Vic:                   [Eh heh heh
17 Mik: *          Tchuu!
18 ???:            Mhhhhh
19 ???:            hhhh
20 Vic: *          Hih! Shhh
21                 (2.5)
22 Mik: *          Dat ends dat ('ey),
23 Vic: *          Yeh.On dat.
```

Vic now adds to his SPP what appears to be an account, which, as we have seen, is common way in which dispreferred SPPs are packaged and expanded. This re-opens the sequence, and Mike now disavows asking for a handout, and, in effect, re-institutes his FPP by naming it as an economic transaction. Vic reiterates his rejection (line 7), and Mike retracts his FPP (line 8) before the rejection is even finished, then moves to close with a sequence-closing third. Note, then, that the sequence now has a familiar, simple way of closing, but in the ensuing turns (lines 11–23) both Vic and Mike replay the post-hoc commentary they had engaged in after the previous, peremptory move to end. In fact, it turns out, the sequence is still not finished; Vic resumes telling about his tanks, Mike reiterates his interest in buying the tank, but Vic ignores the offer and redirects his attention to Rich, a tenant in his building who had earlier questioned his ownership of the tanks.

The upshot is that unilateral and foreshortened endings are not a viable way of ending sequences. How, then, can sequences be closed?

Dedicated sequence-closing sequences

One resource for closing an extended or long sequence collaboratively and interactionally is a sequence designed for just this use – a little sequence used to close long sequences or topics. Because they need to be adaptable to a virtually unlimited range of sequence and topic types and "contents," such topic/sequence-closing sequences are flexibly composed and deployed and can take a range of variant forms. Only some of this variation can be captured here, but from the account which is offered below it should be possible to glean the underlying workings of this practice and resource, and one can be alerted to other forms of its application.

The basic form of the sequence-closing sequence is composed of three turns.

1. The initial turn, whatever form it takes, serves in effect to propose the possible closing of the sequence or topic-in-progress in the just-preceding talk. Among the most common initiating turn types which serve to introduce this possibility are: returns to the start of the sequence or topic (often re-addressing it and incorporating words from it), summaries, assessments, idiomatic or aphoristic formulations of the upshot or outcome of the sequence or topic (see Drew and Holt, 1998), and jokes which trade on, or are symbiotic with, the topic/sequence. Many, if not most, of these represent practices for taking up and displaying a stance toward that which may be ending – whether "cognitive," i.e., an appropriate "grasp" of it (e.g., "They have a problem.", Extract [9.06] below) or lack thereof (e.g. "Eh who knows," Extract [9.07] below), "evaluative," i.e., a summary assessment of some evaluative dimension (e.g., "But uh I hope it gets better as it goes on," Extract [9.04a] below, or "That's too bad," Extract [9.05] below), or "affective," i.e., an emotional take on what has preceded (e.g., ".hhh It gets sickening a(hhh)fte(hhh)r aw[hi(h)le-.hhh]"; Appendix 2, 13:39).

2. The recipient of such a turn may undertake to collaborate in closing down the topic/sequence or to withhold or even resist compliance. Collaboration is implemented by producing whatever response to the prior turn would achieve agreement or alignment with the action/stance displayed in it; that is, a preferred response. Resistance is embodied straightforwardly, by the recipient simply continuing talk on the sequence/topic whose closure had otherwise been made relevant. Withholding collaboration while not actually resisting can be implemented by withholding agreement/alignment, e.g., by silence, which leaves it to prior speaker to continue, if there is to be continuation, or by responding with something other than agreement/ alignment, which may provide for expansion of the sequence- closing sequence itself, or (thereby) return to the talk which had been in progress.

3. Any of the non-collaborative responses can in effect abort the sequence-closing sequence. However, if the recipient of the closing initiation has aligned with it, then in a third turn the initiator of the sequence-closing sequence may produce a third "move," a final closing token or assessment, in effect a ratification of the recipient's alignment with the closing proposal. In this third turn, as well, its speaker may add to this closure completion the initiation of a new topic or sequence.

Across the three turns, it is common[2] for the successive turns to be pro- duced with declining volume and pitch, with the new sequence/topic start in the second part of the third turn to be produced in sharply increased volume and pitch.

Thus the sequence-closing sequence is itself adjacency-pair-based, and ordinarily takes the form of a minimally expanded pair, one which (when "successful") may be followed directly by the start of a new sequence/topic. Here are two instances of such a sequence in its basic form. In each, the letters "a," "b," and "c" point to the three components of the sequence respectively, the "c" arrow calling attention ordinarily to just the first part of the turn to which it is pointing. In Extract (9.04a), Bee is bringing to a close her account of one of the courses she is taking in the recently begun winter term at the college she attends.

```
(9.04a)  TG,  8:03-14
  1 Bee:       Yeh we[ll y'know it's true we can't hear him::=
  2 Ava:          [(                      ).
  3 Ava:       =[ye:ah.
  4 Bee:       =['nd uh,
  5 Ava:       Yeah. [hhhh!
  6 Bee: a->         ['n:: he wz too much::
  7 Ava:       [(                ),
```

---

[2] And consistent with similar findings in Goldberg (1978) and Couper-Kuhlen (2004).

```
 8 Bee: a-> ['hh Bu:t uh I hope it gets bettuh. as it goes o:[n.
 9 Ava: b->                                                    [Well
10       b-> you nevuh know.
11 Bee: c-> Nye::h, en my u- my two ar' classes 'r pretty good I
12          en- I'm enjoying them b't=
```

The two initiations of the sequence-closing sequence in Extract (9.04a) may
be understood by reference to the sequence which they seek to close; the
course whose account is here being brought to a close was introduced as
follows:

```
(9.04b) TG, 7:01-09
1 Bee:-> 'hhh Becaw but uh, Oh my, my north american indian
2          class 's really, (0.5) tch! It's so boring.
3          (0.3)
4 Ava:   Ye(h)e(h)ah!
5          (0.2)
6 Bee:-> I-ah- y-yihknow this gu:y has not done anything yet
7          thet I unduhsta:nd. En no one eh- no one else in the
8          class unduhstands him eethuh. 'hhh We all sit there en
9          'hhh we laugh et his jokes, hhh hmhh=
```

First the course was introduced and assessed (lines 1–2) and then the instructor (lines 6–9). The sequence-closing sequence begins with an assessment
of the instructor (line 6 in [9.04a]), who was introduced as a sort of sub-
ordinate topic of the sequence, and then a stance toward the course itself
is taken up (line 8 in [9.04a]). The structure of the topic/sequence is thus
echoed in the initiation of the move to bring it to closure.

   In Extract (9.05), Bee is bringing to a close her account of one of the art
classes which was being launched in lines 11–12 of Extract (9.04a) above;
she is complaining about the unavailability of some of the required reading
("she" in line 1 apparently refers to the course instructor).

```
(9.05) TG, 9:30-10:03:
 1 Bee:      'hhhh So she tol' me of a place on Madison Avenue 'n
 2           Sevendy Ninth Street.=
 3 Ava:      =M[mm.
 4 Bee:        [tuh go en try the:re. Because I als- I tried Barnes
 5           'n Nobles 'n, (0.6) they didn' have any'ing they don'
 6           have any art books she tol' me,
 7 Ava:      Mmm
 8 Bee:      So,
 9 (Ava):    'hhhh
10 Bee: a-> °That's too bad,
11 Ava: b-> hhhh!
12          (0.5)
13 Bee: c-> °(I 'unno )/°(So anyway) 'hh Hey do you see v- (0.3)
14          fat ol' Vivian anymouh?
```

The response turns in these closing sequences can be quite "indexical"; that is, virtually contentless, and interpretable in various ways. For example, in Extract (9.05), at the "b" arrow, the response to the move to close is a long, loud out-breath. This is hearable as a laugh, as a sigh, perhaps of commiseration, etc. It is, very likely, the minimal form of collaboration in closing the topic/sequence, less than an articulate agreement/alignment with what has been said in the initiating turn, yet still a produced "something," which permits understanding as alignment, and often gets it as the preferred response. However, if the closure proposal includes something potentially controversial, an indexical response may not be allowed to pass unremarked. In Extract (9.06), Ava and Bee are discussing the state of the relationship of a couple they both know.

```
(9.06) TG, 14:23-37
 1 Bee:        There's only one time that I r-hh `hh- thet they really
 2             looked happy wz the time they were etchor hou(h)se.
 3 Ava:        Oh:. Yea:h. Didn' they look ha:ppy.=
 4 Bee:        =[Uhhh huhh! `hhh
 5 Ava:        =[Ho ho ho,
 6 Bee:        hhhunh [hunhh.hh
 7 Ava:               [Tha wz about ez happy ez they ge:t. Eh-hu:h,
 8 Bee:        `hh Really (now)=
 9 Ava: a->    =They have a prob'm.
10             (0.4)
11 Bee: b->    Mm.
12             (0.5)
13 Ava: a->    Definite pro:b'm,
14 Bee: b->    We:ll, `hh (0.3) I don'know.
15 Ava:        YOU HO:ME?
```

At line 9, Ava moves to close by offering her summary assessment of the relationship. After a delay, Bee's response, "mm" (at line 11) is fully as indexical as the "hhhh!" just discussed (Gardner, 1997, 2002). Here, however, Ava does not let it pass, and displays her understanding of it as a demurrer by repeating, in upgraded, emphatic terms, her prior assessment. The problem here is one we have encountered before, one of cross-cutting preferences. Bee has to deal both with a move to close the topic/sequence and with the particular turn type and turn through which that move is being implemented. Pressed by the upgraded assessment to respond in a less indexical fashion, she confirms Ava's suspicion (perhaps grounded in the delay which preceded it) that her "Mm" betokened a reservation, and expresses this in a more explicit way (at line 14), but still as a reservation (an "epistemic" caution) rather than an explicit disagreement. That the underlying issue here was, however, closing the sequence can be seen in Ava's next turn. The effort to accomplish topic closure collaboratively having failed to come to fruition, she shifts topic unilaterally and disjunctively.

Extract (9.06) exemplifies an effort to close which does not run off smoothly, but there are other variants of the sequence that do not represent "trouble." Rather, they provide for flexibility in the deployment of this device which circumvents what could otherwise be an untoward consequence of it. Invariant operation of the three-turn format would entail that the one who initiated closure of a topic/sequence would inherit the right (and perhaps a default obligation) to determine the next topic/sequence if the closing sequence ran off successfully. This sort of unilateral assignment of determinative capacity is ordinarily checked in the structure of conversational interaction, ordinarily by the availability of countervailing practices to other parties. (For example, just as pre-expansions provide a prospective first pair part speaker a resource for avoiding dispreferred responses, so do insert expansions provide such a resource to prospective second pair part speakers. So also are there "checks and balances" in the organization of overlap resolution.)

In the collaboration on closing long sequences with the dedicated sequence-closing sequence being described here, there are two-turn and four-turn trajectories of the sequence which have next topic initiated by other than the party who initiates closure of prior sequence. In the four-turn version of the sequence, the closing-sequence initiator ratifies (at the "c" arrows in third position) the recipient's alignment with closure, but does not proceed directly to initiate a new sequence or topic, as can be seen in Extracts (9.07) and (9.08).

```
(9.07) TG, 3:26-4:01
 1 Bee:      Tch! (M'n)/(En) they can't delay much lo:nguh they
 2           [jus' wannid] uh-`hhh=
 3 Ava:      [ O  h  :  . ]
 4 Bee:      =yihknow have anothuh consulta:tion,
 5 Ava:      Ri::ght.
 6 Bee:      En then deci::de.
 7           (0.3)
 8 Bee:      B[ut u]h,
 9 Ava:       [Oh:.]
10 Bee: a->  Eh:: who knows,
11           (0.5)
12 Ava: b->  I know,
13           (0.3)
14 Bee: c->  °You know.
15           (0.4)
16 Bee: d->  So, <I got some lousy cou(h)rses th(hh)is te(h)e(h)rm
17           too.

(9.08) TG, 5:32-6:03
 1 Bee:      =Eh-ye:h, ih-a, She wz rea:lly awful, she ha-duh, (`hh)
 2           she's the wuh- She ha:duh southern accent too.
```

```
 3 Ava:       Oh:.
 4 Bee:       A:nd, she wz very difficul'tuh unduhstand.
 5 Ava: a->   No, she ain't there anymoh,
 6 Bee: b->   No I know I mean she, she's gone a long t(h)ime
 7             (h)a'rea(h)[dy? hh
 8 Ava: c->                 [Mm, [hhmh!
 9 Bee:                          [`hhh
10             (0.2)
11 Bee: d->   nYeeah, `hh This feller I have-(nn)/(iv-)"felluh"; this
12             ma:n. (0.2) t! `hhh He ha::(s)- uff-eh-who-who I have
13             fer Linguistics [is real]ly too much, `hh[h=     ]
```

In both of these excerpts, the third-position ratification of closure is followed by a brief gap, in which it remains to be determined which party will initiate the move to shape the talk to follow. In Extract (9.07), Bee initiates closure of the "grandmother sequence" and seals that closing sequence, but leaves open what will follow, and who. As it happens, Ava passes the opportunity afforded her at this juncture; "afforded her" because there is something of an asymmetry of opportunity in this silence at line 15, Bee's prior turn leaving the default assignment of next turn position to Ava. In Extract (9.08), Ava initiates closure of the sequence by an observation whose obviousness underscores that its articulation is serving a use other than informativeness. It in effect (re-)answers the question asked by Bee several minutes earlier (about whether there were any teachers left from the time when she attended Ava's college) as the utterance which launched the topic/sequence which Ava is now moving to close. Once again, after the initiator of the closing sequence ratifies its closure (at the "c" arrow at line 8), a silence provides a possibility for the other to shape the ensuing talk, and here it is in fact Bee who does so.

   In these sequences, then, we see an uncoupling of the closing of a prior sequence from the initiation of a next sequence (the "d" arrows in the two sequences). In these exemplars, however, this uncoupling is enabled by the initiator of the closing sequence, by the withholding of a new sequence start after ratification of the prior sequence closure. But is the uncoupling dependent on their generosity? Not necessarily, for the *recipient* of the move to close a topic/sequence can pre-emptively launch a new one in the very turn in which they align with the move to close. The same two-TCU turn structure which we have already observed in the third turn in the sequence (complete closing sequence plus start new sequence) can be deployed in the second turn as well, as in Extract (9.09), in which Nancy and Hyla have been discussing recent episodes in the "Dear Abby" advice column.

```
(9.09) Hyla II, 23:25-24:08
 1 Hyl:     =Abby says `hh we::ll, (0.2) you haftih give yer
 2          mother chance tuh(r) (·) to: u. (·) realize thet
 3          she: `hh hass- thet she c'n respectchu'n that c'n
```

```
4              only be by you acting matu:re. `hh en not c'mplaining
5              about the way she- m- yihkno:w=
6 Hyl:         =[what] ru[:le she se[t s   [do:wn,]
7 Nan:         =[Oh:,]    [Come  o n [are y[ou  se]riou[s,]
8 Hyl:                                            [I ]
9              s:swea[r.tih Go:d.]=
10 Nan:              [`hhhawhhhhh]=
11 Hyl:        =°`hh-`hh°
12             (0.5)
13 Hyl:        a-I wz [°shho hhh [ma:d]°
14 Nan:                [Ihh don't [buh]]ieve- I don't read her,
15             (·)
16 Nan:        co[l'mn] that much,hh en ah'm ne(h)ver g'nna=
17 Hyl:          [ehh!]
18 Nan:        =r[ead it [again.]
19               [`uh`uh [`uh`eh] `eh[`eh
20 Nan:                              [`hh
21             (0.7)
22 Hyl:        `hh[hhh]
23 Nan:           [Yeh] that's ah:ful advi:ce,=
24 Hyl:->       =I kno:w.=
25 Hyl:->       =`hh Maybe we c'n go out fer a drink t'night.
26             (·)
27 Nan:        Ye::ah. That soun- Yeh I owe y'a dri:nk.
28             (·)
```

At lines 24–25, Hyla, the recipient of closing initiation, both aligns with the
proposed sequence closing by agreeing with the assessment and launches
a new sequence in the same turn. The result of the systematic availability
of such a practice is that the initiator of closing does not automatically or
mechanically get to control the launch of the next sequence.

It is worth repeating that the sort of sequence/topic closure and new
topic/sequence start described above is not the canonical form of organization, either for sequences in general or for topic-talk sequences in
particular. For topic talk, step-by-step topic shift appears the more common form of organization for moving "effortlessly" from topic to topic,
rather than the sharply bounded topic delimitation which these sequences
produce. And, for sequence structure more generally, the canonical trajectory is for sequence starts to get preferred response types and for these to
provide for quick sequence closure, with the orientation to first and second pair parts serving to control and minimize sequence expansion before
them.

The resource described here is thus specialized and localized in character, however generous its provenance. Once sequences get substantially
expanded after their second parts, and after topic-talk sequence structure
(with or without stepwise shifts) has led to a substantial extension of topic

talk, the job of closure can present itself with few structural resources indigenous to the talk available to guide it to closure.

This issue is especially pointed in settings organized for continuously sustained talk rather than "continuing states of incipient talk." Talk in the latter
is organized in a fashion which provides for lapses, in which silences are collaboratively allowed to develop into what amount to potential sequence ends
("potential" because the post-silence talk can revive the topic or sequence
which preceded the lapse). The preceding discussion has not explored the
range of practices and resources brought to bear in such trajectories, nor
the interactional developments which can occasion them. But the sequence-
closing sequences described here are among those practices and resources,
as can be seen in the following exchange.

```
(9.10) SN-4, 12:15-40
 1 Mar:      Yih know my stomach after every meal now feels r:ea:lly
 2           weird 'n its been giving `hhh Mi:les got Digel tablets?
 3           'n stuff like tha:t?
 4           (0.4)
 5 ???:      [ °henh
 6 Mar:      [A:nd uh: like-(·) 't's r:ea:lly weird, (      too).
 7           `hh- I find one thing.don't eat their pineapples. They
 8           make yer stomach imme:diately after dinner really feel
 9           lousy.<'t least mi:ne.=
10 She:      =Their pineapple's ca:nned.
11           (1.5)
12 Mar:      (°I 'on't care,) it's still terrible.
13 Sh?:      mmh-
14 Mar:      hhhh HUH-HUH `hhhh hh they really- just turn my
15           stomach. Sump'm after dinner [(ih)('s)]°turning in=
16 ???:                                   [hhhh `hh]
17 Mar:      =yer stomach .hh
18           (0.5)
19 Mar: ->   But u:m:
20           (1.2)
21 Kar: ->   C'est la vie, c'est la vie,=
22 Mar: ->   °=eyeh°
23           (1.2)
24 Mar: ->   That's about it hell I haven't been doing anything but-
25           (·) s-(Well,) (0.2) going out [actu]ally.
26 Ka?:                                    [mmh ]
27           (0.7)
28 Mar:      I 'aftuh start studying no:w
```

When the sequence in progress fails to secure co-participation at lines 18 and
20 (after earlier trouble, e.g., at line 11), Karen provides the sort of aphoristic
summing up which can launch an overt sequence closure (line 21). Mark's
response aligns him with that project, and he leaves it for someone else to

launch a next sequence or topic (line 23), before continuing himself in the absence of any takers. The closing relevance of what has preceded – for the most recent topic/sequence and potentially for the occasion as a whole – is displayed at the start of the next turn.[3]

In settings in which the type of overall structural organization provides for continuously sustained talk, the development of more than transient silence at possible sequence boundaries can make closing of the conversation – or of the occasion – relevant, and a conversation-closing sequence may be the relevant one to initiate next. In such a conversational environment, in which strategically positioned incipient silence is not an available resource for sequence/topic closing, sequence-closing sequences are an available and locally adaptable resource which can organize the parties' collaboration in bringing to closure just that talk which is in progress, whatever its particulars and whatever its import for them, benign or malign.

---

[3] That turn ends with a return to a much earlier sequence. Several minutes earlier, after the close of an encapsulated, interrupting conversation (the one displayed as Extract [7.45] and taken up at pp. 159ff.), the following "resumption" occurred:

```
(9.11) SN-4, 6:01-06
1 Mar: Where were we.
2      (0.5)
3 She: I dunno.='ve you been studying lately¿
4 Mar: No,°not et aw-° not et a:ll:. I hafta study this whole
5      week.<every ni:ght, {(˙hhhh)/(0.8)} en then I got
6      s'mthing planned on Sunday with Lau:ra,
```

That talk then segued, step-by-step into other matters, ending with the sequence closing displayed in the text, and the return to the sequence representing the earlier resumption of this interaction after its interruption by another.

10 Sequences of sequences

When a sequence is brought to a close, whether by its second pair part, by a sequence-closing third, after a more-than-minimal post-expansion, or with a sequence-closing sequence, some new sequence is ordinarily launched, either "next" or after a lapse of some length, whether of silence or of intervening activity. In introducing our discussion of sequence organization we noted that successive turns have a shape to them, relations of mutual relevance and positioning, coherence and orderliness that makes of them not merely a *series*, but a *sequence* of turns. Although successive sequences may often be less closely linked than successive turns are, there can be particular ties of relevance between several sequences that serve to extend our sense of the coherence and organizational relatedness of a stretch of talk beyond the boundaries of a single base sequence and its expansions which have so far been sketched. Here we will examine just a few of these types of organization of more than one sequence, or sequences of sequences.

Reciprocal or exchange sequences

By reciprocal or exchange sequences we refer to episodes in which a sequence which has just been initiated by A to B (that is, in which A is the first pair part speaker and B is the second pair part speaker) is then (after it has run its course) reciprocated – initiated by B to A. Same sequence type; reversed speaker/recipient participation.

In some respects, then, this sequence of sequences is akin to "counters." In counters, it may be recalled (pp. 16–19), the same action which A has just directed to B is redirected by B back to A *in the next turn* – that is, before otherwise responding. Counters, we suggested early in our account of basic adjacency pair organization, "reverse the direction of constraint." In exchange sequences, on the other hand, the recipient of a first pair part *does* respond to it with a second pair part, with or without insert expansion. And the sequence may undergo post-expansion as well. Unlike the preemptive effect of counters, then, exchange sequences are forthcoming, and *furthermore* reciprocal.

Generally the reciprocal or return sequence is done "next," but because the first sequence in the exchange may be expanded the second can end up being separated from that which it reciprocates. Whether the second sequence is next or deferred, it can be done *as* a reciprocal, that is, marked as such (as in "How about you," which may lexically and intonationally mark its reciprocal status) and locating the initial sequence as its point of reference. Or the second sequence can be not marked as a reciprocal; that is, while occurring (for example) directly after the initial sequence of the exchange, it can be designed and delivered in a way which does not otherwise underscore that it is reciprocating and direct attention to that which it is reciprocating.

Perhaps the most common exchange sequence type is the "howaryou," especially as it appears initially in interactional openings.[1]

```
(10.01) Two Brothers, 1:01-07
1              ((ring))
2 Kar:        Hello:
3 Cla:        Hi: Karl:
4 Kar:->      Yeah hey Clarke How're you.
5 Cla:->      Good: How're you doing.
6 Kar:        Ahm alright.
7 Cla:        Good?
8 Kar:        What's up.=
```

```
(10.02) HG, 1:01-11
 1              ((ring))
 2 Nan:        H'llo:?
 3 Hyl:        Hi:,
 4 Nan:        ↑HI::.
 5 Hyl:->      Hwaryuhh=
 6 Nan:->      =↓Fi:ne how'r you,
 7 Hyl:        Oka: [y,
 8 Nan:             [Goo:d,
 9              (0.4)
10 Hyl:        ·mkhhh[hhh
11 Nan:              [What's doin,
```

In Extracts (10.01) and (10.02) we see the two component sequences of the exchange done consecutively, with the same turn (at line 5 in Extract [10.01] and line 6 in Extract [10.02]) used to do both the response to the first sequence and the initiation of the reciprocal. This is the tightest positional fitting of the second sequence as a reciprocal to the first, and seems to be the most common. It is not, however, the only form which successive placement can take.

---

[1] Versions of "Howaryou" may recur over the course of an occasion of talk-in-interaction. Because this three-worded question – "How are you" – has become collapsed into a virtually single term, I have represented it in the text in this collapsed form, and will therefore refer to "howaryou" sequences.

As with other sequences of sequences, two consecutive sequences can be positionally related to each other in at least two ways – serial organization and interlocking organization (Schegloff, 1986:130–33). Extracts (10.01) and (10.02) exemplify the latter of these, with two sequences being interlocked by having a multi-unit turn be composed of one unit from one (the prior) sequence and another unit from a different (the new) sequence. Consecutive sequences, including consecutive "howaryou" sequences, can also be positioned *serially*, with the second sequence beginning in the turn after the first sequence is closed, often with a sequence-closing third. Extract (10.03) offers a case in point.

```
(10.03) Schegloff, 1986:115
 1                    ((ring))
 2 Ida:      Hello,
 3 Car:      Hi Ida¿
 4 Ida:      Yeah
 5 Car:      Hi,=This is Carla
 6 Ida:      Hi Carla.
 7 Car:->    How are you.
 8 Ida:      Okay:.
 9 Car:      Good.=
10 Ida:->    =How about you.
11 Car:      Fine. Don wants to know . . .
```

Here the answer to the first "howaryou" sequence occupies its turn alone (line 8), and is followed (line 9) by an assessment serving as a sequence-closing third. In the next turn (line 10), the recipient of the first sequence initiates its reciprocal. Note that this is a *new* sequence, which follows closure of the prior sequence, but is nonetheless related to the prior sequence in sense, in activity, in relevance, and in design.

Several observations will have to suffice on how the reciprocal status of the second sequence in these exchanges is and is not marked.

First, of two common ways in which the inquiry "howaryou" is intonationally shaped, one appears to differentiate between first and second delivery and the other does not. "Howaryou," it appears, can be used as *either* a first or a second inquiry in an exchange without marking that inquiry positionally (see, for example, line 4 in Extract [10.01], where it is first, and line 6 in Extract [10.02], where it is second). On the other hand, "howaryou", with the main stress on the second syllable, is used for initial inquiries (as in Extract [10.02] at line 5), or for "big" ones – that is, for ones designed to show "specialness," either because a long time, or because time with extraordinary events, has passed since the last encounter. Note: this does not mean that "howaryou" cannot appear in the second of an exchange of "howaryous" (or cannot do so without being a "big" one). It can be deployed as a resource by speakers to bring off interactionally the firstness of their inquiry, bypassing thereby recognition of a prior inquiry by interlocutor (for example, if it was obscured by overlap or otherwise compromised).[2]

The main point here is that the stress on the final syllable of "howar*you*" is not treated by interactants as necessarily contrastive and thereby second, or marked as reciprocal. In Extract (10.01) above, the initial inquiry is not understood that way, but neither would the second have been, had it just been "howar*you*." What marks it as a reciprocal-by-design is the addition of "doing." Another common form for designing the second inquiry as a marked reciprocal is "How about you," as at line 10 in Extract (10.03) above.

As noted above, production of a reciprocal first pair part can be delayed from occurring in close proximity to an initial one. One way this can happen, part and parcel of how sequences get composed by interactants, is by the expansion of the first of the sequences, and by topic offshoots which it can engender. Consider, for example, the start of the TG conversation.

```
(10.06)  TG,  1:01-31
1                 ((ring))
2 Ava:       H'llo:?
3 Bee:       hHi:,
4 Ava:       Hi:?
```

---

[2] For example, in the following opening of a telephone conversation, Rita's initial inquiry about the arrival of Les's house guests not only follows an apparent problem on his part in recognizing her (lines 3–4 and 6–7), but it disrupts the usual order of sequences in the opening (Schegloff, 1986).

```
(10.04)  Berkeley, 1:2-19
 1                  ((ring))
 2 Les:      hello:.
 3 Rit:      hi le::s
 4                  (0.7)
 5 Rit:      yur c[ompany there?]
 6 Les:           [(I'm   sorry) ] Rita?
 7 Rit:      ye:ah.
 8 Les:      how are ya.
 9 Rit:      pretty go:od.
10                 (0.2)
11 Rit:      didjur company arri:ve?
12                 (0.7)
13 Les:      lay-=oh yeah, las' night.
14 Rit:      okay good.how are you:.·
15                 (0.6)
16 Les:      oka:y(hh)=
17 Rit:      okay, that's good.
18                 (0.4)
19 Rit:      well, I wan'ed tuh thank you fer . . .
```

Rita then finds herself the recipient of a "howaryou" (line 8) while she still has retrieval of her earlier sequence from overlap as a possibly relevant task. After responding to the "howaryou," then, she does this retrieval (lines 11–14) rather than the exchange "howaryou," and when finally she does the latter (line 14) , she does it as a first.

There can be constraints of recipient design on doing the *first* "howaryou" rather than a reciprocal. For example, in the following extract, Penny is calling Pat at someone else's home because there has been a fire at Pat's.

```
 5 Bee:->     hHowuh you:?
 6 Ava:       Oka:::y?hh=
 7 Bee:       =Good.=Yihs[ou:nd  ] hh
 8 Ava:                  [<I wan]'dih know if yih got a-uh:m
 9            wutchimicawllit. A:: pah(hh)khing place °th's
10            mornin'.`hh
11 Bee:       A pa:rking place,
12 Ava:       Mm hm,
13                     (0.4)
14 Bee:       Whe:re.
15 Ava:       t! Oh: just anypla(h)ce? I wz jus' kidding yuh.
16 Bee:       Nno?=
17 Ava:       =[(°No).]
18 Bee:       =[W h y ]whhat'sa mattuh with y-Yih sou[nd HA:PPY,] hh
19 Ava:                                              [ Nothing. ]
20 Ava:       u- I sound ha:p[py?]
21 Bee:                      [Yee]uh.
22            (0.3)
```

```
(10.05) Houseburning, 1:01-21
 1            ((ring))
 2 Ans:       Hello:,
 3 Pen:       .pt .hhh hhHi, this is Penny Rankin from:Lincoln I'm a
 4            friend'v Pa:t's. ken I speak t'her et all?
 5 Ans:       She:ur.
 6 Pen:       [Okay.    ]
 7 Ans:       [Just one] sec'nd.
 8            (4.0)
 9 Pat:       Penny?
10 Pen:       .khh-HHI:[:
11 Pat:                [Hi::.. How are you. hh [(hh)
12 Pen:                                        [I'm awri:ght that's
13            w't I hhwz gunn(h)uh a:sk you:.
14            (0.2)
15 Pat:       Um, pretty-g-I'm much bettih this aftihnoo:n.
16            [(then) I] wa:s.=
17 Pen:       [ Ye:h,  ]
18 Pat:       =Yeah.
19 Pen:       [Yeah.
20 Pat:       [I wiz bad (la-st i-) night'n this morning
21            (b't )/(though) I feel m- really a LO:T better
22            right now. hhhhh=
23 Pen:       =(0.0)/(.hh-) Yea:h,
24 Pat:       Yeah.=
```

Of the two, Pat is the one with special claims to concern about her well-being, but it is she who does the first "howaryou" (at line 11). Penny displays the interactional anomaly of finding herself in "reciprocal" position given the recipient design considerations in which they find themselves at the moment, while thereby bringing off that very reciprocal character of her inquiry. Yet Pat's move to do the first "howaryou" is compatible with a common practice for positioning oneself as recipient of the second "howaryou," where there is a greater openness for expansive replies, an expansiveness relevant to her current circumstances. On these practices for positioning first and second "howaryous" in the opening, cf. Schegloff, 1986:130–33.

```
23 Ava:        No:,
24 Bee:        Nno:?
25 Ava:        No.
26             (0.7)
27 Bee:        `hh You [sound sorta] cheer[ful?]
28 Ava: ->            [°(Any way).]          [`hh ] How'v you been.
29 Bee:        `hh Oh:: survi:ving I guess, hh[h!
30 Ava:                                          [That's good, how's
31             (Bob),
32 Bee:        He's fine,
33 Ava:        Tha::t's goo:d,
34 Bee:        °(Bu::t.)=/°(Goo:d.)=
```

Note only a few points here. First, the "How'v you been" at line 28 is the "long-time-no-see" version of "Howaryou" which is "routine" (as compared to the special or "big" version, "Howaryou"). This "how'v you been" thus serves as Ava's reciprocal of Bee's inquiry at line 5.[3] Second, this reciprocal is not consecutive with the initial sequence in the exchange, but has been displaced by intervening talk, specifically the "parking place" sequence (lines 8–17) and the expansion of the initial "howaryou" sequence (begun at line 7, "y'sound", and resumed at lines 18–28). Still, on completion of the latter, what Ava does next is start her part in the exchange of "howaryous." Third, she does not specifically mark this as a reciprocal, as she might have, for example, with a stress on the "you." (Unlike in the "howaryou" form, this *would* have underscored contrast, and thereby reciprocity.) Rather, the light stress here is on the "been," the element which marks this as indexed for a long-time-no-see contact.

It can happen, of course, that expansion of the first "howaryou," or other contingencies of the conversation's opening have the consequence that the reciprocal is rather more substantially delayed, or never done at all. For example, the conversation between Marsha and Tony which we have already consulted a number of times begins as follows.

```
(10.09a) MDE-MTRAC 60-1/2, 1:01-07
1                    ((ring))
2  Mar:        Hello:?
3  Ton:        Hi: Marsha?
4  Mar:        Ye:ah.
5  Ton:        How are you.
```

---

[3] More generally, recipient design considerations can enter into selection of, or construction of, a form with which to do a reciprocal. In monitoring the talk for a possible reciprocal, then, interlocutors (and academic observers) properly cast a broad net for an utterance which can be heard to be doing that job – addressing some aspect of its recipient's current personal state in a fashion appropriate for this speaker to this recipient on this occasion.

This can be made into a locus of playfulness and joking as well. In the following extract, a young boy, Jerry, and then his mother, announce to their dinner guests the appearance of

```
6  Mar:          Fi::ne.
7                (0.2)
8  Mar:          Did Joey get home yet?
```

As is common in openings, there is much delicate interactional business
packed into this opening, not least of all at the momentary silence at line
7, and we cannot take it up here. But do note that among the things which
are possibly relevant here – and accordingly possibly missing here – is a
reciprocal inquiry by Marsha to Tony. The sequence which has its origin in
line 8 carries, with its expansions, well into this relatively brief conversation.
When this sequence, with its major issues, has been brought to closure by
Tony's acceptance of the arrangements for the transport of both Joey and
the car back home (see the discussion in the section on sequence-closing
thirds, pp. 118–47, and pp. 135–37 in particular), the conversation proceeds
as follows.

Jerry's first loose tooth. (One of the guests, Don, is shown fetching and delivering knives
to the table at lines 2, 3, 5, 12, and 13.)

```
(10.07) Chinese Dinner, 29:14-28
 1 Jer: ->    Guess what I have a[loo:se t]ooth.
 2 Don:                       [Hey Ann?]
 3 Don:       Dju wa[nt a knife?]
 4 Bet:             [   O   h   ]yea:h.=
 5 Ann:       =[Nyeh,
 6 Bet: ->    =[Jerry's r- has a mi:lestone to announce he's
 7      ->    go[tta loose tooth.
 8 Ann:         [Oh::! You gonna getta big tooth?= ((breathy))
 9             =a regular big tooth?
10 Jer:       Uh huh?
11 Ann:       Which one[is looth.
12 Don:                [°John, (              ).
13 Joh:       °Oh thanks.
14 Ann:       Ooo:::::::::::::
15 Bet:       Just think ih wz[only yes-
16 Ann:                       [WooEEhOOOO!    ((squeal))
```

The sequence develops with talk of tooth-fairy gifts and continuous manipulation of the
tooth by Jerry to the (probably feigned) consternation of the guests. And then Ann launches
a "reciprocal":

```
(10.08) Chinese Dinner, 30:31-37
1  Ann:->    My teeth are loose too.but it's too (h)la(h)te,
2  Bet:      °Mhh hmh hm hm
3            (1.5)
4  Don:      Nothing (will grow in).
5            (0.5)
6  Jer:      You[mean you still get ba:by tee?
7  Ann:         [Nope,
```

This is a nice exemplification of the notion of sequence organization as practice, rather than
as fixed structure (see Chapter 13).

```
(10.09b) MDE-MTRAC 60-1/2, 2:11-22
  1 Mar:      ˙hhh Bu:t u-hu:ghh his friend Steve en Brian er driving
  2           up. Right after:: (0.2) school is out.En then hi'll
  3           drive do:wn here with the:m.
  4 Ton:      Oh I see.
  5 Mar:      So: in the long run, ˙hhh it (·) probly's gonna save a
  6           liddle time 'n: energy.
  7 Ton:      Okay,
  8 Mar:      But Ile:ne probably (0.8) is either at the airport er
  9           waiting tuh hear fr'm in eess
 10           (0.7)
 11 Ton:      O:kay.
 12 Mar:->    ˙hhhh So: yer ba:ck.
```

Though much delayed from the first sequence of the exchange pair, this
reciprocal is delivered at a place which is analyzably the first opportunity
after the completion of what had analyzably, and accountably, delayed it.
And the reciprocal is recipient-designed for the interlocutor, and in a way
that registers the occasion for this very conversation (i.e., now that Tony has
returned home, Joey can/must return home).

"Howaryou" sequences are surely not the only "exchange type"
sequences in talk-in-interaction, nor have we by any means exhausted their
relevance. A few additional observations, and one more empirical explo-
ration, may serve to indicate the directions in which attention to exchange-
type sequences may lead analysis (and see also Schegloff, 2002:250–62).

The exchangeability status of various sequence types (or topic types) is
subject to recipient-design considerations, and may turn on the category
of person the participants relevantly are, relative to one another for that
conversation. For example, "howaryou" sequences are not relevant in certain types of institution-specific conversations (Schegloff, 1986; Whalen
and Zimmerman, 1987), and in some work settings they may be relevant
in one direction of status relations but not the other, and hence be non-
reciprocal. Similarly, some sequences are potentially reciprocal if the participants are both (or all) members of the same category of persons, and
that category membership is (or can properly be made) relevant for that
conversation.

For example, if a student is asked by their parent, "How's school going?",
this is ordinarily not understood as a potentially reciprocatable sequence –
unless, of course, one of the interlocutors can be re-identified (correctly)
not as "parent" but as "student," if, for example, that person has "returned
to school."

The point is that, for interlocutors who are relevantly students, at an
appropriate time of year, the inquiry "How's school going?" is the start
of a possibly exchange-relevant sequence. And, indeed, one party who

has something to tell may elect, as their way of coming to tell it, not to launch a telling sequence themselves, but to launch an inquiry sequence of a reciprocatable sort. They then rely on their recipient eventually to reciprocate their inquiry, and thereby to provide an opportunity to tell their tellable as a response to a question, rather than as something told on their own initiative. That is, exchange sequences can supply a resource for a particular form of conversational practice, a practice for *telling*.

This resource rests in part on a feature of exchange-type sequences which has not yet been made fully explicit, and that is that reciprocating the exchange of certain sequence types is not just something which "happens to happen," it can have some normative constraints driving it. It is, then, not only that someone *can* reciprocate a certain sequence type. If their interlocutor has made that sequence type relevant by launching a first such sequence, then a reciprocal has been made relevant and there is a normative onus to do the reciprocal. Failure to do so is not as glaring, or as consequential, as the failure to produce a second pair part in response to a first pair part. But it figures nonetheless, and it undergirds the practice of using an inquiry as a route to doing one's own telling by eliciting a reciprocal inquiry from recipient; that practice rests on the normativity of doing reciprocals when relevant. (Reciprocals, that is, can invoke relevance rules.)

As observers of talk-in-interaction, we need to be alert to such practices and the structural and normative resources which they deploy and on which they rely, else we will fail to understand what is going on at critical junctures in the talk.[4]

Consider, for example, the "How's school going" inquiry initiated by Bee in Extract (10.10a) below, and the long trail of relevances and consequences which it engenders.

```
(10.10a)  TG, 1:32-2:11
 1 Bee:->  ='n how's school going.
 2 Ava:    Oh s:ame old shit.
 3 Bee:    Shhhh! hh t! ˙hh
 4 Ava:    I 'av [a lotta t]ough cou:rses.
 5 Bee:    [Uh really?]
 6 Bee:    Oh I c'n ima:gine.=<wh'tche tol' me whatchua
 7         ta:kin(.)/(,)
 8 Ava:    Oh Go:d I have so much wo:rk.
 9 Bee:    Tch!
10         (0.4)
11 Bee:    Mmm.
12         (0.5)
13 Ava:    [°B't asi]de fr'm that it's a'right.
```

___

[4] This may be an aspect of the organization of practices of talk-in-interaction on which the variability of languages/cultures could be heightened.

```
14 Bee:     [So what-]
15          (0.4)
16 Bee:     Wha:t?
17 Ava:     I'm so:: ti:yid. I j's played ba:ske'ball t'day since
18          the firs' time since I wz a freshm'n in hi:ghsch[ool.]
```

The initial inquiry sequence (and possible topic proffer) comes to possible completion at or after line 6 (which registers that Bee has already heard about Ava's courses), and then again at line 8, which can be heard as a possible closing-relevant assessment, with which the "tch!" in line 9 aligns. At or after either of these places, Ava could have reciprocated the inquiry. She does not.[5] From the temporizing embodied at lines 10–12, it appears that something is being awaited. More specifically, it is Bee who does the temporizing (at line 11), and who may be waiting for Ava to do something, something whose relevant doing she (Bee) has already provided for. I mean, of course, the reciprocal inquiry.

Eventually, they both undertake to break the logjam at the same time (lines 13–14), thereby reproducing it. Ava's utterance here moves to show more decisively that the first inquiry sequence is over. Her "it's a'right" is the "bottom-line" answer to "how's school going," and it is the type of response that discourages further expansion (Sacks, 1975; Schegloff, 1986). But when Bee tries to retrieve that utterance from its possible interference by overlap, Ava neither repeats it nor uses the opportunity to launch the reciprocal sequence which the end of the first inquiry sequence could occasion. Instead, and quite oddly, she launches a telling about playing basketball.

As that telling comes to a conclusion, a sequence boundary may be projected, and with it another place for the reciprocal inquiry.

```
(10.10b) TG, 2:31-37 (not continuous with Extract [10.10a])
1  Ava:     En, I had- I wz- I couldn't stop laughin it wz the
2           funniest thing b't y'know you get all sweaty up'r
3           en evrything we didn' thing we were gonna pla:y,
4           'hh en oh I'm knocked out.
5  Bee:     Nhhkhhhh! 'hhhh
6  Ava:     Ripped about four nai:ls, 'n okhh!
7  Bee:     Fantastic.=
8  Ava:->   =B't it wz fun-You sound very far away
```

But when the story is brought to a close, its teller rushes through the transition space following its final component (line 8, "But it wz fun-") and starts a new sequence ("You sound very far away")! Again, no reciprocal. But this new sequence is very brief.

---

[5] Actually, line 8 could be taken as equivocal in this regard, being hearable as a possible complaint, and a preface to an extended telling which will detail that complaint. However, line 10 appears to subvert that analysis.

```
(10.10c)  TG, 2:37-3:02 (overlaps with last turn of Extract [10.10b])
1  Ava:    =B't it wz fun-You sound very far away
2          (0.7)
3  Bee:    I do?
4  Ava:    Nyeahm.
5  Bee:    mNo? I'm no:t,
6  Ava:    Yer home? ˙hhh=
7  Bee:    =[(Mnuh,)]
8  Ava:->  =[Oh my] mother wannduh know how's yer grandmother.
```

Brief though it may be, a component utterance of this sequence touches
off a separate inquiry, and launches a whole new sequence – about Bee's
grandmother. It is this sequence whose closure is implemented by one of
the "sequence-closing sequences" examined in Chapter 9.

```
(10.10d)  TG, 3:26-40 (not continuous with Extract [10.10c])
 1  Bee:    Tch! (M'n)/(En) they can't delay much lo:nguh they
 2          [jus' wannid] uh-˙hhh=
 3  Ava:    [ O h  :  . ]
 4  Bee:    =yihknow have anothuh consulta:tion,
 5  Ava:    Ri::ght.
 6  Bee:    En then deci::de.
 7          (0.3)
 8  Bee:    B[ut u]h,
 9  Ava:     [Oh:.]
10  Bee:->  Eh:: who knows,
11          (0.5)
12  Ava:->  I know,
13          (0.3)
14  Bee:->  °You know.
15          (0.4)
```

Bee initiates the sequence-closing sequence (at lines 8 and 10), Ava aligns
with it (at line 12) and Bee ratifies the alignment (at line 14) . . . and then
waits. Rather than herself initiating a next sequence, she holds off, allowing
Ava to do so. Here again is a place for the still-relevant reciprocal sequence,
made relevant by that long-ago inquiry "how's school going" to be initiated. But again it is not forthcoming from Ava. What Bee does next shows
that the reciprocal *has* been relevant to her, and that the formulations of its
"absence" in our tracking of this sequence have not been external, imag-
ined impositions, but capture Bee's continuing orientation to a sequential
structure she has set in motion.

```
(10.10e)  TG, 3:35-4:01 (overlaps with Extract [10.10d])
1  Bee:    Eh:: who knows,
2          (0.5)
3  Ava:    I know,
4          (0.3)
```

```
5 Bee:      °You know.
6           (0.4)
7 Bee:->    So, <I got some lousy cou(h)rses th(hh)is te(h)e(h)rm
8           too.
```

Bee now launches her telling without the reciprocal inquiry from Ava to occasion it. Note especially the "too" at the end of her utterance at line 8. This "too" appears to connect back to the origins of this sequential trajectory (at Extract [10.10a] above), where Bee had asked a reciprocatable question, "how's school going," and had gotten as part of Ava's answer, "I have a lotta tough courses." Now, after the most recent failure by Ava to reciprocate that inquiry at an opportunity to do so, Bee launches her reciprocal telling on her own, without benefit of a question, but ties her "answer" (what would have been "her answer" had she been asked the question) back to Ava's answer ("have a lotta tough courses"), thereby marking her telling as a reciprocal telling, even if bereft of the reciprocal question to license it, and she does it with this "too."[6]

Although the initial "how's school going" sequence had come to a conclusion, its sequence-organizational relevance had not necessarily been exhausted. It had a bearing on a possible sequence of sequences; in this instance, a reciprocation of the sequence which had been done. There are several junctures in this stretch of talk which cannot properly be understood without taking into account the continuing relevance of that earlier inquiry sequence, even though it had come to closure. We cannot understand the temporizing going on in the segment extracted as (10.10a), or the significance of the rush-throughs in Extracts (10.10b) and (10.10c) without attention to the continuing relevance (at least to Bee) of a reciprocal inquiry.

Reciprocal or exchange sequences, then, constitute one type of sequence of sequences which can shape the trajectory of the talk in ways sensitive to a sequence even after that sequence is closed, and without re-opening it. Because their normative sequential force is weaker, they may be harder for non-involved observers to spot. Most importantly, their normative sequential import can supply and support a texture of relevancies running through the talk which can undergird the occurrence of negative events (i.e., things which relevantly do not happen), and which can accordingly license negative observations (observations of and about things that did not happen). We know that things that do not happen can be as consequential for the conduct of the interaction as ones which do. But the weaker normative force of these extra-sequence constraints makes it harder to spot events whose import remains important to spot. And because the parties' surfacing of

---

[6] Even then Bee does not get to tell how school is going for her. Shortly after she launches her telling, Ava "steals the topic" by starting to tell about one of *her* courses, and several other topics largely centered on Ava get taken up before Bee manages to sustain talk on her school preoccupations.

these relevancies may be less obtrusive than in other normatively specified loci, a greater onus of discovery lies on the external analyst.

Action-type sequence series

In the exchange sequences we have just been discussing, the same sequence type is done again with a change in speakership and recipientship of its key parts. In action-type sequence series, the same sequence type is done again – more precisely, another instance of the same sequence type is done, with the same parties as first pair part and second pair part speaker, but with a change in topic or target of the sequence (the "item" depending on the type of sequence involved). Various sequence types can enter into an extended series – question series, request series, offer series, etc. We will examine briefly only two of these.

First, question series. Here again "howaryou" sequences provide a readily available and familiar case in point. Consider the end of Extract (10.06), reproduced below as Extract (10.11).

```
(10.11) TG, 1:26-30
1 Ava:->        [°(Any way).]           [˙hh ] How'v you bee:n.
2 Bee:     ˙hh Oh:: survi:ving I guess, hh[h!
3 Ava:                                    [That's good, how's
4          (Bob),
5 Bee:     He's fine,
6 Ava:     Tha::t's goo:d,
```

We noted earlier (pp. 198–200) that Ava's "How'v you been" is a reciprocal to Bee's earlier "howaryou" sequence. Note that it is brought to closure (line 3) with a sequence-closing third-positioned assessment. Although what follows is clearly related to what comes before, it is also clearly a separate sequence – as compared, for example, to a more-than-minimal post-expansion (e.g., "Why, what's the trouble that you're surviving?").[7] It is, rather, another sequence of the same type, initiated by the same speaker to the same recipient, but about a different item. The two sequences are thus within one another's orbit or scope of mutual relatedness. The inquiry about "Bob" (which is at least as much an inquiry about the relationship – Bob being Bee's "boyfriend," appropriate answers may include such as,

---

[7] Jefferson (1980) examines what she calls "trouble-premonitory responses to inquiry," and shows how responses like (and, indeed, including) "Oh surviving I guess" can be a way of giving an indication that there is trouble to be told about which the speaker is not proposing to undertake the telling of here (cf. also Heritage, 1998). Of course, that can be the occasion for co-participant to pursue such a telling, a course of action not undertaken by Ava here. Note, then, that minimal post-expansions – sequence-closing thirds like Ava's "That's good" at line 3 – can be done specifically as alternatives to otherwise possibly relevant, interactionally grounded *non*-minimal post-expansions.

"Oh, we're not together anymore") gets part of its sense and import from appearing in a series after an inquiry about recipient (as compared, for example, to being separately inquired about, which may be an accountable inquiry, "why is she asking about him?"). And once a series of inquiries is seen to have been addressed to some social organizational unit (e.g., the family, the household, the office, the friendship group, etc.), it may become relevant, and noticeably absent, if some member of the unit is *not* made the object of a sequence in the series.[8]

But "howaryous" are not distinctive in their capacity to give rise to a question series. Extract (10.12) displays the start of an interaction beginning as the initial greetings and "howaryou" inquiries are ending, with Sherry's response to "howaryou" being "uh tired."

```
(10.12) SN-4, 1:13-2:19
 1 She:      Uh:: tired.
 2 Mar:      Tired, I hear yih gettin' married.
 3           (0.6)
 4 ???:      °((sniff))
 5           (0.3)
 6 She:      Uh:: you hear right.
 7           (0.2)
 8 Mar:      (Ih) shah-I hear ri:gh[t.
 9 Sh?:                             [mmhh [(heh hh])
10 Mar: ->                               [Didja e-] by the way didja
11         -> ever call up uh: Century City Hotel 'n
12           (1.0)
13 She:      Y'know h'much they want fer a wedding¿ It's
14           incredible.
15           (0.5)
16 She:      We'd 'aftuh sell our house 'n car 'n evryt(h)hing
17           e(h)l(h)se [tuh pay fer the wedding .]
18 Mar:                 [Shhh'er house 'n yer car.]
19 ???:                 [(hh   heh   heh   huh   huh )]
20 Mar: ->   ·hh What about the outside candlelight routine izzat
21         -> still gonna go on?
22 She:      No yih can't have outside candlelight it's a fi:re
23           hazard.
24           (0.5)
25 Mar:      Oh really?
26           (·)
```

---

[8] And, note, the later "howaryou"-type inquiry – "Oh my mother wanted t'know how's yer grandmother" (Appendix 2, 3:02ff.) – is not assimilated to the series in the opening; it is asked separately, and disowned as Ava's own inquiry, being attributed instead to Ava's mother. There appear, then, to be constraints on what or who properly enters into a series – whether people in a "howaryou" series, or targets in a request or offer series. And what is included as alternatives or combineables in such series can be taken as revelatory of how the speaker sees things as grouped or disparate in the world as they understand it.

```
27 She:      Yes[: : .    ]
28 Kar:         [C'n have] it insi:de,
29           (0.8)
30 Mar:      You c'd have 'm inside though?
31 Kar:      Yeah
32           (0.4)
33 She:      Yeh but who wants t'get married inside in the
34           middle a' the summer when it's still light till
35           n[ine  o'clock. ]
36 Mar:       [Gunnuh be beau]tiful outsi:de.
37           (0.2)
38 She:      Ye:ah.
39 Mar: ->   W'll (jat'll) jus' be fanta:stic.'hh So what've
40      ->   y'called any other hotels ('r) anything?
41           (·)
42 She:      Y:eah I called thee Embassader 'n stuff. I've go so
43           much work that I don't believe it.so I'm j'st not
44           even thinking about that [°now.
45 Mar:                               [In schoo:l yih mea[:n?
46 She:                                                  [Ye:ah,
47              (0.2)
48 Mar:      (Y')haven't been 'n school in five weeks doesn' matter.
```

Briefly, after Mark's initial move (line 2) to launch topic-talk on Sherry's
approaching wedding is rebuffed (line 6), he nonetheless initiates a topic-
proffering sequence with a question (lines 10–11) warranted, in the face of
the rebuff, by being cast as an updating of a matter he is already privy to; this
is specifically the upshot of the "ever" in the question at 10–11. Note that,
although Sherry does not explicitly answer the question, her responsive turn
embraces the topic proffer in various ways – most importantly by claiming
access and by being substantially more than minimal; indeed, she responds
by reporting what was ostensibly the outcome of the event Mark has inquired
about.

After the possible completion of this sequence, Mark's ensuing talk (at
lines 20–21) is clearly related to, but also not part of, the prior sequence.
It is another first pair part; it is also marked as an updating question (by
the "still" in "izzat still gonna go on?"), and it is from the outset built
as in continuity with the prior exchange via the "What about X" format,
commonly used to re-invoke one or more elements of a prior exchange
while varying another.[9] This, then, is a next-in-a-series not only by virtue of

---

[9] Cf. Roth and Olsher (1997), in which the authors examine the use of this format by mod-
erators of news interview programs, and describe instances in which the practice takes
forms such as "What about that, Mr./Ms. X?" in which the moderator indexes a previously
articulated position by one interviewee and confronts another interviewee with it; or "What
about Y?" where an interviewee who has just taken a position on one issue is confronted
with another issue on which they are asked to take a position.

being a topic-proffering, updating question–answer sequence after such a one has already been worked through. It is designed in its very constitution as a subsequent-in-a-series sequence.

And so is the first pair part which follows the closure of this second sequence in the series. Here, in the same turn which seals the closure of the prior sequence, Mark asks another question, not bearing the overt mark of an updating sequence, but in effect cross-referring to a previous first pair part in the series for part of its sense. In asking "have you called any other hotels" (lines 39–40), this topic-proffering question is again, but differently, built to co-inhabit a sequence of such sequences by being made partially parasitic on an earlier one of them. Here, then, we have quite a different type of question series than we saw in the "howaryous."

But questioning is not the only action type of sequence of which a series of sequences can be built. In the episode partially represented in Extract (10.13), Betsy is planning a card party at her home, and Alice "wants to help out." What develops is an offer series the whole of which is too extensive to reproduce in its entirety, but substantial chunks of which will be displayed in order to provide a sense of the extent of talk which can be occupied by a sequence of sequences such as an offer series, especially when some of the component sequences themselves get expanded.

```
(10.13) SBL T2/C6 (partial)
 1 Bet:        And uhm I:: won't get it 'ntil the last minute, because
 2             I haven't room fer too much in- you know,
 3 Ali:        [Oh.
 4 Bet:        [I wasn'- I wasn' going to get it until late tomorrow
 5             afternoon, anyway.
 6 Ali: ->a    Do you need any silver.
 7 Bet:        Uh no, because . . .
 8
 9             ((12 lines of transcript deleted))
10
11 Bet:        So I'll put out the dessert spoons for the ones that
12             want them, and then there're plenty of teaspoons,
13             (1.0)
14 Bet:        And uhm
15 Ali: ->b    An' you don't need a fork.
16 Bet:        Uh- Uh no,
17 Ali:        [No.
18 Bet:        [That- that's the reason I made this kind of thing I
19             did.
20 Ali:        Uh huh,
21 Bet:        I w- I used . . .
22
23             ((31 lines of transcript deleted))
24
```

```
25 Ali:          But uh then uh what time shall we be o- shall I-
26        ->c1   Is there- eh- nothing- hh Do you want any pots for
27               coffee, or any[thing?
28 Bet:                        [Well, I have-
29 Ali: ->c2     You know, I have that great big glass coffee m-maker,
30               it makes nine cups.
31 Bet:          Well, say, now that's an idea, Yes. I would like to use
32               [that.
33 Ali:          [Now I c'n- I'll bring the inside to it, y'see, I just
34               use powdered s-coffee, [but-
35 Bet:                                 [Uh- Well, you . . .
36
37               ((30 lines of transcript deleted))
38
39 Bet:          And- I have over half of it to throw away every time.
40 Ali:          [Uh huh,
41 Bet:          [I'm going to quit doing it.
42 Ali: ->c3     Well, if you'd like it honey, I'll bring it.
43 Bet:          Well, I-I don't uhm Come to think of it, I think I can
44               manage uh:: otherwise.
45 Ali:          Well . . .
46
47               ((12 lines of transcript deleted))
48
49 Ali: ->c4     But yer welcome to [it (Bea),
50 Bet:                             [Yeah.
51 Bet:          Well, thanks a lot but don't bother, because y-it-
52               I won't need it [that much.
53 Ali: ->d                     [Do you need any cards, I have- I have
54               a coupla decks that have never been opened.
55 Bet:          So have I, I got a couple [(               )-
56 Ali:                                    [Alright, honey,
57 Bet:          Uh huh,
58 Bet: ->       But thanks a lot,
59 Ali:          [heh heh heh,
60 Bet: ->       [And uh I don't think I need anything,
61 Ali: ->       Money's all you want, is it?
62 Bet:          That's all,
63 Ali:          heh heh heh [heh heh!
64 Bet:                      [Uh huh,
65 Ali:          Alright-
66 Ali:          Say I had a very busy day I didn't get away yesterday
67               until four thirty.
68 Bet:          Oh:: Uh huh,
```

For present purposes it is not necessary to examine this partial transcript
in detail. It is a long stretch of talk, even longer than appears from this

substantially edited transcript. But we should be able to see clearly in it two main points: first, the sense in which an "action-type series" like an "offer series" is composed of a number of sequences of the same type, by the same initiating party to the same recipient party,[10] with a change in item or target; and second, that it can be sometimes straightforward – and sometimes not – to distinguish between post-expansion of a single sequence (e.g., via re-doing or reworking of its first pair part) and a sequence of sequences of the action-type series sort.

Note, then, that the activity of "offering" here begins with the offer at arrow "a" (line 6), an offer which is declined with an account. This account is just the start of a post-expansion, the bulk of which is not shown, which is brought to possible closure at lines 11–12. At line 13, where a sequence-closing third could accept the rejection to seal the closure, Alice the offerer is silent, and Betsy (at line 14) intervenes to break the silence with a form of utterance commonly used to re-complete a turn, in effect, by showing there is nothing further to say.[11] The offer of "silver" has been rejected with respect to "spoons"; Alice now (at line 15) raises the possibility of forks. When we add to the prior observation about her failure to participate in the closing of the preceding sequence-so-far the observation that the matter of forks is a) categorically a sub-type of silver, b) marked by the turn-initial "and" as an added increment, and c) treated as an inferably negative outcome (by the phrasing "you don't need") given Betsy's previous response, an initial inclination to treat this as a next offer sequence in a series (same sequence type, same parties, different item/target) may yield to treating it as a further post-expansion of the prior sequence – a reworking of its first pair part. Either way, the offer of forks leads to a longish response, in part used to segue from the offer to a description of what the hostess has prepared for the dessert which she is to serve.

On completion of that exchange, and as a self-interruption of what appears to be an inquiry about the proper time to come, Alice presents another offer (at arrow "c1," lines 26–27) – this one clearly the same sequence type, by same first pair part speaker to same second pair part speaker, with different

---

[10] I put it this way to allow for occurrences in which several members of one multi-person party initiate the several sequence initiations in a series to the same recipient, or in which a sequence initiator directs several such sequences to several members of a recipient-party, etc. For example, in a now-classic analysis of an "initiation ritual," Sacks (1992a) examined an episode in a group therapy session with teenaged boys following the arrival for the first time of a new "patient." The "veteran" patients – the ones who had already been members of the group – collectively address a series of observations/guesses/questions to the newcomer, displaying how much they figure they can know about him simply by virtue of his coming to attend this therapy group. For the conduct of this sequence, the participants are formed up into two parties – the newcomer and the old-timers, and the observation/guess/question series is deployed by first pair parts by one or another of them as members of the "oldtimers" party to him as sole member of the newcomers party. It is still an activity-type series.

[11] Notwithstanding the construction which appears semantically and syntactically to be launching a next installment of talk.

item/target. At the first sign of incipient rejection (the turn-initial "well" at line 28), Alice intervenes with a follow-up (arrow "c2" at lines 29–30) which is clearly a reworking of the same offer, not a next sequence-start in an offer series. This reworked offer appears initially to meet with a warmer reception, but eventually (lines 39–41) Betsy's stance cools, and when Alice reinvokes the offer (at arrow "c3," line 42) – again, clearly the same offer, reworked as part an expansion of the same sequence – it meets with a dispreferred response (lines 43–44). Alice once again does not accept the rejection but responds to it (starting at line 45), and ends with yet another re-offer (at arrow "c4", line 49), which meets with same fate.

Alice tries again. Note that at arrow "d" (line 53) the offer is of a wholly new target, and thus appears to be another in the offer series, even though here again Alice has not responded to the rejection of the prior offer by accepting it. This by itself is not decisive for whether a next "offering" is more of the prior sequence or a next sequence in a series of sequences. When this offer is rejected as well (line 55), Alice accepts the rejection with a sequence-closing third, and this marks her preparedness to abandon the offer series as well, and prompts recognition of the activity of offering which has been sustained throughout the series.

Successive parts of a course of action

We have examined two kinds of relationships which can obtain between two sequences when the second follows closure of the first and is not an expansion of it and yet is kindred to it. One kind of relationship is another sequence of the same type but with reversed participatory alignment; the second kind of relationship is another sequence of the same type, with the same participatory alignment but a different item/target/topic. A third way in which a next sequence following a sequence close can be related yet separate is that it implements a next step or stage in a course of action, for which the just-closed sequence implemented a prior stage. A brief segment of data, which follows a long sequence already familiar, can serve to exemplify this point.

Extract (10.14) displays again the very end of a sequence in which Jim has acceded to Bonnie's request to borrow his gun, after a substantial pre-expansion and a lengthy insert expansion (see pp. 111–14).

```
(10.14) BB Gun, 4:02-40
 1 Jim:        Th'n how d'ju come out to be A:nnie.
 2             (1.0)
 3 Bon:        No- I'n- it's jis' thet-everybody in the class has
 4             to do a different-(.) pantomime, you know?
 5 Jim:        Uhuh,
 6             (0.4)
```

```
 7 Bon:              An[:]
 8 Jim: S_{b,req}->   [Y]eah:, you can use 't,
 9                    (0.4)
10 Bon: F_{post}->   .hh Ca:n?
11 Jim: Sp_{post}->  »Yeh-«
12 Bon: F_{b,req}>   .hh 'dju bring it to the meeting?
13                    (.)
14 Bon:              The lo:ngest one you [ h a ]ve.
15 Jim: S_{b,req}->                       [»Sure«]
16                    (0.4)
17 Bon:              [An']
18 Jim:              [The]lon:gest one?
19 Bon:              The lon::gest one.
20                    (0.8)
21 Jim:              I tell ya what I'll bring ya my good one.
22                    (0.2)
23 Jim:              Oh:: no:.
24 Bon:              No:, if you're- I mean don't gim- your- [gimme (    )
25 Jim: F ->                                                 [Say why
26        ->         don'tchuh come over.
27                    (0.2)
28 Bon:              .hhh Uh::m
29                    (0.5)
30 Jim:              Cause my: uh:: (·) tch! hh it's a good beebee
31                    hehheh.hhh shootinwise, b't it doesn't look all that
32                    good. really.
33 Bon:              .hhh Okay w[ell-              ]
34 Jim:                         [»whaddya think« ]
35                    (1.2)
36 Bon:                  [Uhh
37 Jim: F ->         Why ['onchu come over, I've got two gu::ns an'
38        ->         why'onchuh pick one.
39                    (0.5)
40 Bon: S ->         Tch! Alright well I'll have to bring my friend because
41        ->         she is coming to the meeting and then I have to take
42                    her home.
43 Jim:              Okay.
```

The base second pair part to the request sequence (at line 8) is followed
(as we saw in our discussion of non-minimal post-expansions doing repair,
pp. 150–51) by a brief other-initiated repair sequence (lines 10–11). On
confirmation that Jim's response was indeed favorable, Bonnie initiates a
new sequence (lines 12 and 14). We can note that it is another request,
launching another request sequence, but we will not capture a key element
of the relationship between them if we see these as simply two requests in a
request series. The request sequence initiated at line 12 seeks to implement
the outcome of the prior sequence; there is a different sort of contingency

holding between them than obtained in the previously considered sequences of sequences. Although this sequence turns out also to be preoccupied with the selection of a particular item to serve as the requested/granted object (lines 18–35) and this leads to a counter-proposal on how the item is to be conveyed to Bonnie (lines 37–43), it remains the case that the subsequent sequence is made relevant as a next step in the course of action triggered by the outcome of the prior. They represent the steps in an unfolding trajectory of action, not a number of tries at some outcome.

There are respects, however, in which both same activity-type series and successive parts of a course of action may figure similarly in an interactional episode. This is exemplified in the findings of Heritage and Sorjonen (1994), who found that questions which implement a continuing course of activity across sequence boundaries – precisely as in a question series or in steps in a course of action – are regularly prefaced with an "and," which marks not coordination with immediately preceding talk, but with the larger continuing activity whose next increment the new question begins to implement. The relationship between sequences – and between the expansion of single sequences and the ties of sequences of sequences – can, then, have consequences for the very turn design of the sequence parts which compose them.

Other relations between sequences of sequences: multi-part tellings

There are, of course, other aspects of the way talk-in-interaction is conducted which can issue in very long stretches of talk being properly understood as being organized under the scope of a single sequence. Some are quite straightforward. For example, a speaker may launch a simple telling sequence, but one in which what is to be told about has many "parts." Then a very long spate of talk indeed can be occupied with what amounts to a list-organized telling, in which the "parts" are taken up one by one, each of them subject to "sequence expansion" of its own, each followed upon its completion by a turning to the "next" item on the telling's agenda. Though we will not reproduce the lengthy transcript here, the reader may wish to track – through the transcript of the TG conversation in Appendix 2 – the "telling about her courses" which Bee eventually manages to accomplish after many blockings and digressions by Ava.

As was noted earlier (pp. 203–06), Bee launches the telling about her situation in school on her own initiative (after Ava fails to reciprocate Bee's inquiry) at TG, 4:01, "So I got some lousy courses this term too." But Ava promptly diverts the talk onto one of *her* courses, and a series of step-by-step topic shifts leads the talk in different directions rather than back to

Bee's courses. When this line of development is closed off with a sequence-closing sequence (5:37–6:01), Bee starts again, directly on one of the courses (6:01), and then sustains a long stretch of telling which is finally brought to closure by another sequence-closing sequence (at 9:37–10:02). That very long stretch of talk is composed of Bee's tellings about "her courses," and the courses serve as "the parts" of the telling, each organizing a spate of talk including Ava's participation (such as it is),[12] each brought to closure as a sub-part, each closure followed by the initiation of telling about the next part of the "agenda." But, although this is a very long stretch of talk to be sustained by a single teller, the underlying sequence structure is very simple. There is a single first pair part which informs the whole telling; it is not re-done or reworked for each next "part." There is very little sequence expansion (as compared to turn expansion), most of it being constituted by small sequence/topic-closing sequences to bring each part of the telling to closure before moving on to the next.

Long stretches of talk do not necessarily imply sequence expansion, then. This long telling by Bee might better be understood as sequence-organizationally simple, and as well understood by reference to *topic* as by reference to *sequence* structure.

---

[12] The linguistics course and its instructor at 6:01–42; the "north american indian class" and its instructor at 7:01–8:13; and the two art classes and the problem of getting books from the bookstore at 8:13–10:02.

11   Retro-sequences

In contrast with adjacency pair-based sequences, which operate prospectively – i.e., a first pair part makes something prospectively relevant so that it is missing if not there – there are sequences which operate retrospectively. We will call them "retro-sequences."

These are sequences *activated from their second position*, which invoke what can be called a source/outcome relationship. What surfaces in the interaction as their first effective component turns out not to have been temporally the first thing in them to have occurred. Rather, the first recognizable sign that such a sequence is in progress generally displays that there was "a source" for it in what preceded, and often locates what that source was. But note that the source engendered nothing observable – indeed, was not recognizable as a "source" – until the later utterance/action, billing itself as an "outcome," retroactively marks it as such. Their "firstness" follows their outcome, though their occurrence preceded it. These are sequences *launched* from their *second* position.

One common instance is that of other-initiated repair. Consider the following sequence examined earlier (as [6.01], on p. 97) as an instance of post-first insertion.

```
(11.01) SBL 2,1,8 (Schegloff et al., 1977:368)
1 Bet:   F_b ->  Was last night the first time you met Missiz Kelly?
2               (1.0)
3 Mar:   F_i ->  Met whom?
4 Bet:   S_i ->  Missiz Kelly.
5 Mar:   S_b ->  Yes.
```

In describing a canonical exemplar of other-initiated repair like this, one needs to relate three elements which will figure in any instance: a trouble-source, a repair initiation, and a candidate repair solution. (A sequence-closing third is an optional component of such a sequence; none is present in this specimen.) Looking with the hindsight of professional analysis, it seems clear that the trouble-source is "Missiz Kelly," the repair initiation is "Met whom?" and the candidate repair solution is "Missiz Kelly." But how do we as analysts determine that the trouble-source is "Missiz Kelly?" We know that nothing can in principle be excluded from the category "trouble-source" or "repairable" (Schegloff et al., 1977:363). So if anything on line 1 could be the trouble-source, how do we come to say that it is "Missiz

Kelly?" We do so because Mary's turn at line 3 locates the trouble-source by framing it with the repeat of the just-preceding word ("met") and putting in its place a question word that shows that she (Mary) heard that it was a reference to a person, but didn't "get" who the person was that was referred to. Without Mary's having located the trouble-source as part of the job of initiating repair on it, no one could know that there even *was* a trouble-source. So the repair sequence does not begin with Beth's turn at line 1, or any part of it. It begins at line 3, with Mary's initiation of it. Mary's turn is, in that sense, the start of the repair sequence; but it locates something that occurred earlier as its source – here, its "*trouble*-source." At the same time, of course, the repair initiation launches a (proactive) sequence, projecting the relevance of a second pair part addressed to repairing the trouble whose existence has been brought to attention or whose source has been located.

It is important to register that there are two different types of sequence construction at work here. It is tempting to think of the repair sequence as beginning with the repairable or trouble-source, which engenders the repair initiation, which makes the repair operation relevant next. But this conflates two quite different kinds of sequential operation, each of which is grounded in the repair initiator. One of these serves to locate the source of the trouble; the other to engender dealing with it. The trouble-source itself, however, is not sequentially implicative of the repair initiation; the trouble-source itself does not make anything relevant next, even though the repair initiation locates it as its source. It is this "backward" operation of locating the source of some outcome that the term "retro-sequence" is meant to capture.

Another common exemplar of the source/outcome configuration involves some occurrences of laughter, though not all laughter marks a retro-sequence. Obviously, parties may tell jokes or in some fashion indicate that they are doing something "funny" which projects the relevance of laughter, after which the absence of laughter may be found to amount to the laughter being "missing," and consequentially so. But there can be an alternative development: laughter may "break out" (whether from a single participant or more) and thereby occasion the relevance of a search by co-present parties for the laugh *source*. "What's so funny," the non-laughers may say, or their conduct may show them to entertain. The laugh-source will be understood to have preceded the laugh, but its relevance – as laugh-source or as anything – has in such cases been activated by the laugh which announces itself as its outcome.

For example, in Extract (11.02) (presented as [1.05] on p. 10),[1] the only sound hearable in what appears to be a simple passing of a plate is a slight laugh by the man at the head of the table who is watching as the food is being put on to his plate prior to passing. The woman seated to his right quickly looks up from her plate and at the laugher to her left (11.02a); finding him looking at the server, she quickly swivels her head in the opposite direction

---

[1] References to Extracts (11.02a) to (11.02d) refer to video clips that are available online (see p. 2) and will need accessing in order to follow the argument presented here.

to look at the server as well (11.02b), in search there for what might be the source of the laughter (11.02c). She apparently finds nothing amusing, and gradually returns her head to a straight ahead position (11.02d).[2]

The most general formulation of the type of sequence which sets into play the operation of a source/outcome relationship is "noticing." In a sense, both repair initiation and laughter can be understood as specialized types of noticing, but "noticing" – as an action-in-conversation – can be done in ways that do not invoke trouble-relevance or laughter-relevance. Doing a noticing makes relevant some feature(s) of the setting, including the prior talk, which may not have been previously taken as relevant. It works by mobilizing attention on the features which it formulates or registers, but it treats *them* as its source, while projecting the relevance of some further action in response to the act of noticing. There can be a delicate equivocality in some cases between "provocation" which is taken to be designed to engender noticing and which may then be cast as proactive, and a noticing which is taken as the effective agent for bringing its object into relevance (see Chapter 5, fn. 17).

But the central point here is to discriminate two different ways in which a series of turns/actions which are sequentially related are to be understood. Some sequences are anchored by their temporally first component (the proactive sequences like adjacency pairs); other sequences are anchored by a subsequent component, and it is only by their subsequent component that some prior is rendered a first (retro-sequences).[3]

---

[2] "Crying" can also trigger such a search, and possibly all of those expressions which Goffman (1978) termed "response cries." See also Jefferson (1978a) on "touched-off" stories, which regularly display as part of their launching what just-prior event – something said or some occurrence in the environment – triggered the telling.

[3] There is a related practice that should be mentioned here, though without the elaboration that it invites. Some utterances get built in a fashion that locates something prior as their source, but without depicting the earlier event as precipitating the current talk. I offer two instances here. One is taken from Sacks' discussion (1992a) of an utterance in his group therapy data which occurred in the aftermath of the reception accorded a newcomer. One of the long-standing participants says, after the "welcoming" phase of the arrival, "I still say, though . . ." and resumes an earlier discussion. Sacks points out that an utterance constructed in this manner is self-positioning, and positions itself as third in a sequence – the "first" being this speaker's initial statement of his stance on the matter being discussed, the second being someone else's disagreement with that stance, and now, in third position, the original speaker's reassertion of his stance in the face of the disagreement. The earlier utterances are thereby not cast as the immediate prompters of the current talk (as is the case with laughter and repair), but as earlier events in the light of which the current utterance is being said, and what it can be understood to be doing in light of its relation to these sources. The effective agent here is "still say." Another instance comes from the TG conversation, and the talk set off by Bee's inquiry about whether the teacher "Kaleznick" had been gotten rid of (Appendix 2, 4:35ff.). In Ava's response, she mimics Kaleznick's manner of speaking by overlaying on to her New York City accent a "Southern accent" (Appendix 2, 5:08–13). Later in this spate of talk, Bee describes a teacher that *she* had had when she attended that school as "having a southern accent too" (Appendix 2, 5:32–33). Here the effective agent is "too"; it sends the recipient in search of what in the preceding talk the current utterance is locating as, in some respect, its predecessor or source. Again, it is a source that is being marked, but not a generative source; not something that has prompted the current saying, but which, having occurred, makes it necessary for the current saying to register its speaker's awareness of – something like a conversational citational footnote.

12 Some variations in sequence organization

Although the account of sequence structure built on the underlying resource of the adjacency pair has considerable scope and robustness, it should not be understood as an inflexible template which mechanically generates "parts" assigned to various participants. Rather it should be understood as an organizational resource – a kind of convergently oriented-to set of possible routes – which the participants draw on in charting and incrementally building a joint course of action.

There is, then, an underlying range of orderly structures and a set of practices for suiting those structures to the particulars of the moment in which the participants are acting. Because sequences are a major resource in implementing courses of action, we should expect their forms and trajectories to reflect (among other sources of variation) the contingencies of the courses of action being pursued through them. And because particular settings may be the site of distinctive activities and courses of action, variants of the sequence organization and practices we have been describing may show up with special clarity in "specialized settings," whether specialized by virtue of the work which gets done in them (which will be our focus here) or by reference to other characteristics (e.g., the population which they specially mobilize and their interaction-relevant characteristics, the non-work activities specially pursued there, etc.).

This is not a vapid and shapeless "adaptation to context," not an undisciplined "anything will do," or "anything goes." Various aspects of the practices of sequence construction and their underlying organization of pairs and expansions (as well as the organization of the turns in which the elements of a sequence are regularly accomplished) may vary from the account offered above. It is our job to be alert to these possibilities, to detect them, and to describe their character, whether as variants of familiar practices or as counter-evidence on the accounts previously developed (and, if the former, to illuminate what prompts or is achieved by the variant practice being examined).

Here we will discuss just three aspects of sequence organization whose variation by reference to their social location and the activities being pursued in it may be suggestive of the range of such variation remaining to be explored and specified. One of these is the form taken by minimal post-expansion of sequences. A second concerns sequence types or configurations so setting-specific that they become virtually iconic for that setting. The third concerns a situated reversal of a preference mentioned earlier concerning responses to self-deprecation. Because the first two of these are well treated in easily available sources, our discussion of them will be brief.

Sequence-closing thirds

First, then, minimal post-expansion. We noted in Chapter 7 that, in ordinary conversation and many other settings, minimal post-expansions take a very few forms. "Sequence-closing thirds" get done by information-registering "oh," by action-accepting "okay," by assessment terms, and by relatively few other forms. But it turns out that this sequence-organizational third-position is a significant locus of variation.

To begin with, Heritage (1985) has noted that in news interviews, third-position "oh" is virtually never done. Here is a setting thoroughly occupied by question–answer sequences (Heritage and Roth, 1995), and thus full of third positions which might appear ripe for information-registering "ohs." But because the questions asked by interviewers are designed to be treated as asked on behalf of an overhearing audience, it is not the interviewer who is meant to be informed by the answers. Furthermore, to the degree that "oh" can be heard as accepting and thereby validating the "answer," it can pose problems for the interviewer's mandate to remain "neutral." Various aspects of the activity of conducting news interviews, then, and of the speech-exchange system (Sacks et al., 1974) which has developed to support this activity, serve to effect a modification in this aspect of how the parties together fashion sequences.

In legal proceedings of various sorts, related variations of questioner conduct in third position may be observed. In formal legal settings, attorneys' examinations of witnesses regularly omit third-position receipts as well (Atkinson, 1992; Drew and Heritage, 1992b), whether because the attorneys in direct examination ask only questions they already know the answers to, because they avoid validating answers on cross-examination, or because – as in news interviews – the questioning is conducted on behalf of an overhearing audience, the jury, and it is their informedness which is relevant. But Atkinson describes informal legal proceedings in which an officer of the court who adjudicates disputes also serves as the one eliciting the conflicting positions by asking questions of the disputants. Here there is no "overhearing audience," and the question-asking is "authentically" after information rather than enabling its articulation. Still, receipting answers with an "oh" may be beset by already-noted disabilities, such as implying validation. It turns out, Atkinson reports, that there are sequence-closing thirds in this setting, but they are embodied in forms other than the ones

which predominate in less (or differently) specialized settings and tasks –
forms such as "yes" or "certainly," as in the following exchange, taken from
Atkinson.

```
(12.01) Atkinson, 1992:200-01 (Arb=Arbitrator, Pln=Plaintiff)
 1 Arb:       So (0.2) you explained the design (0.3) that you
 2            wanted?
 3 Pln:       In very general terms, I said I had thiis kind of thing
 4            in mind and what did he think of it, and so on and so
 5            on -- he drew the thing and said "Well that's OK. I can
 6            put that together for you" kind of thing.
 7            (0.3)
 8 Arb: ->    Certainly (0.3) And (.) did you specify any (0.4)
 9            particular material for the (1.0) sh- uh sandals?
10            (.)
11 Pln:       No I didn't.
12            (1.4)
13 Arb:       You left that up to his judgement?
14            (.)
15 Pln:       Yes (0.2) He showed me some of the materials he had in
16            the shop, but actually I had no view about the
17            materials used -- I merely wanted a pair of wearable
18            sandals.
19            (0.7)
20 Arb: ->    Certainly (1.2) And when you talk about a 'bespoke
21            sandal' (0.2) this is one made (0.3) to your (0.3)
22            order.
23            (0.5)
24 Pln:       Uh (0.4) when you say to my order, ehm I would expect
25            to get a wearable pair of sandals out of it -- ehm ah
26            -- it was done in discussion with Mr (NAME) he and I
27            talk about it uhh (1.8) I think yes it's fair to say
28            that he said that the sandals would be (0.3) acceptable.
29 Arb: ->    Certainly (0.6) eh- can we now (0.3) look at the (0.2)
30            uh (0.7) dispute between the two of you about fittings
31            (1.0) You say that there was only one.
```

Although this arbitrator appears to use only "certainly," Atkinson displays
other data in which other items are used for sequence closure (note the
absence of "certainly" at line 13, where the sequence is in fact being
expanded rather than being closed), but these also are different forms than
those used in other settings.

It is worth remarking that sequence-organizational third position appears
to be a recurrent locus of variation across a range of work settings – medical consultations (e.g., ten Have, 1991) and classrooms (e.g., Mehan, 1979,
1985) are among the other settings which have been discussed in the literature (see also Drew and Heritage, 1992b). At the relevant junctures, the

special contingencies of the task activities which characterize the settings prompt participants to do the interactional and sequential job of possible sequence closure in ways adapted to the interactional features of the local context.

Distinctive sequence and expansion types

A second kind of variation may be found in the very character of the sequence types employed, or in the distinctive ways in which sequence types get expanded. As some have noted (e.g., Levinson, 1979), some sequence types are so tied to specific activities and the settings in which they are largely conducted that, even in the absence of factual information, they prompt inferences about the source of exchanges in which they figure. They are virtually identified with those activities and settings even when actually implemented elsewhere.

A prototype of such a sequence type is what is sometimes called the "test question," but might more suitably (and generally) be termed "known-answer questions." These, of course, are conventionally understood as being tied to classroom – or, more generally, instructional – settings. Extract (12.02) offers a short stretch of a longer exemplar of such sequences (taken from Levinson [1979 (1992):89–90], citing Brazil et al., 1980), although such sequences will be experientially familiar to any reader of this book.

```
(12.02) Levinson, 1992 [1979]:89-90
 1 T:  Now tell me: why do you eat all that food? Can you tell
 2     me why do you eat all that food?
 3     Yes
 4 C:  To keep strong.
 5 T:  To keep you strong. Yes. Why do you want to be strong?
 6 C:  Sir, -- muscles.
 7 T:  To make muscles. Yes. Well what would you want to do
 8     with your muscles?
 9 C:  Sir, use them.
10 T:  You'd want to--
11 C:  Use them.
12 T:  You'd want to use them. Well how do you use your
13     muscles?
14 C:  By working.
15 T:  By working. Yes. And . . .
```

Although ordinarily identified with the classroom setting, known-answer questions are common, specialized resources in other settings as well, for example in celebrity profile interviews, in which the interviewer elicits for an audience's benefit (and the celebrity's!) information already known to the interviewer – a kind of "staging" operation. Still, it is of classrooms that such questions are most commonly reminiscent (Levinson, ibid.; Mehan, 1979), and persons finding themselves addressed with such questions in other settings may complain (whether jokingly or seriously) of being demeaned or being "put-down" by such a questioner.

Of course, it is not always apparent from the question itself that a known-answer question sequence is in progress (Heritage, 1984a:280–90). In an exchange such as, "Do you know what time it is? Three o'clock. That's right," it is not until the third turn that this is revealed, and with its revelation, that the sequence is being used to do some activity other than asking the time, such as cuing or triggering a departure or some other, previously scheduled matter.

Here again third position is a locus of significant variation, for although we earlier noted that sequence-closing thirds may be implemented by assessments, the assessments (or "evaluations," as they are commonly referred to in the literature on classroom settings) which known-answer question sequences take in third position are of a different character, and embody a very different stance in and to the interaction than the third-position assessments in other adjacency pair-based sequences. In fact, third-position evaluation is an organic part of such sequences in a fashion quite different from third-position assessment in most other adjacency pair-based sequences. Whereas in other contexts it makes analytic sense to ask what the addition of a third-position turn is doing (e.g., moving for sequence closure), with known-answer question sequences (and in the settings for which they are the indigenous resource) the more cogent analytic issue often appears to be what the *withholding* of a third-position evaluation is doing.[1]

It will almost certainly repay the effort to work through the mutual bearing of the distinctive sequence structure of known-answer question sequences, the distinctive interactional stances which they impart to the first pair part and second pair part speakers respectively, and the close connection of this sequence type to particular settings and environments of use, i.e., what makes for the elective affinity between this sequence type and the social settings which specially exploit it.

Similarly, pursuit of an extended series of questions (Atkinson, 1992), especially ones which seek to make explicit what would ordinarily be treated as warranted presuppositions of, and inferences from, prior answers (Levinson, 1992), may be closely identified with legal settings, and with cross-examination in particular. Again, the appearance of such post-expanded question sequences, and series of such sequences, in other settings (e.g., at the dinner table) may prompt in the recipient of the sequence of sequences remarks about being "cross-examined." Here, then, both a sequence type (question sequences of a distinctive sort) and an expansion

---

[1] Recall that this issue was first broached at the beginning of this discussion of sequence organization, with respect to the underlying two-partedness or three-partedness of basic sequence structure; see Chapter 2, fn. 1; Chapter 3, fn. 1.

type (extended post-expansion) become symbiotic with, and symbolic of, a distinct activity type and a setting which is specialized for that activity. They exemplify another kind of variation in sequence organization.

Preference organization

Self-deprecation is not all that common an occurrence. Nonetheless, the sequence which it engenders has figured importantly in accounts of sequence organization because it supplies an accessible exemplar of an exceptional sequential environment, one in which, in contrast to the common preference organization, agreement is *dis*preferred and disagreement is preferred. The case for this claim has been made by Pomerantz (1984), who noticed that, after self-deprecations, disagreements were done in a fashion characteristic of preferred responses, not dispreferred ones – whatever the forms used to implement them (negations, partial repeats, compliments, challenges, etc.). Extracts (12.03) to (12.06), taken from Pomerantz (1984), offer cases in point.

```
(12.03) Pomerantz, 1984:84
1 R:      Did she get my card.
2 C:      Yeah she gotcher card.
3 R:      Did she t'ink it was terrible.
4 C: ->   No she thought it was very adorable.

(12.04) Pomerantz, 1984:83
          ((L, the hostess, is showing slides.))

1 L:      You're not bored (huh)?
2 S: ->   Bored?=No. We're fascinated.

(12.05) JG, C & D (Pomerantz, 1984:83)
1 C:      . . . c(h)ept in my old age I'm slowin down
2         considera[bly. ]  .hhhhhh]=
3 D: ->           [He:ll] Old age.]=
4 D: ->   =[What'r you thirdy fi:v]e? ]
5 C:      =[hheh - heh-heh-heh-heh]e-h] hY(h)e(h)e(h)es
6 D:      hh-hh hhh-hhh!
7 C:      .t.hhhhhhhh[hhh
8 D: ->             [But a young thirdy fi:ve.

(12.06) SBL 2,2,2,3R, 51 (from Pomerantz, 1984:85, retranscribed)
1 Chl: -> En I n:ever was a gr(h)ea(h)t br(h)idge [play(h)er]=
2 Cla:                                            [ Y e :: h]
3 Chl:    =Cl(h)a [ heh? ]
4 Cla: -> =.hhh   [Well I] think you've always been real good . . .
```

In such instances the responses come without delay, they are early in their turn (or whatever is early in the turn participates in the disagreement with the self-deprecation), they are not mitigated, and are not accompanied by accounts, etc. – all features of preferred responses. An additional feature which Pomerantz noted was that, if there is a delay (i.e., a gap of silence) after a self-deprecation, then it may be understood as an indication of a *dis*preferred response in the works, but in this case that means evidence of *agreement* – although, given its dispreferred status, often qualified agreement, as in Extract (12.07).

```
(12.07) Pomerantz, 1984:91-92
1 W:       . . . Do you know what I was all that time?
2 L:       (no).
3 W:       Pavlov's dog.
4     ->   (2.0)
5 L:  ->   (I suppose).
```

Pomerantz describes additional features of this reversal of the otherwise characteristic preference for agreement and dispreference for disagreement, and the proposal is quite compelling.

However, there are settings in which this account turns out to be problematic, and using it as a tool of analysis can be misleading. In studying language assessment interviews, in which non-native speakers of English are assessed for their eligibility for English as a second language (ESL) classes and evaluated for the level of class suited to their competence, Lazaraton (1991, 1997) noted that often the first utterance containing an assessment of English language competence was made not by the interviewer but by the student being assessed. Often this self-assessment would be part of the response to the interviewer's initial inquiry, designed to elicit a spate of talk which displayed the student's competence, "Why don't you tell me a little bit about yourself," or words to that effect. Extracts (12.08) to (12.10) display cases in point of responses which included self-assessments.

```
(12.08) Lazaraton, 1991:126-27
 1 Int:     psk! so: Hakiu: why don't you tell me something about
 2          yourSELF.
 3          (0.8)
 4 Stu:     myself? ((sniff out)) [.hhh!
 5 Int:                           [mmhmm?
 6          (0.2)
 7 Stu: ->  uh: I came he:re (0.5) uh:: (1.0) uh:::: nineteen eighty
 8      ->  ni:ne: summer. (.) a:nd (0.5) still I have been here
 9      ->  .hhh h: uh: about uh: ine n half years (0.5) but (0.5) I
10      ->  cannot sp(huh!)eak .hhh English (0.2) e:m (0.8) uh:::
11      ->  FlueNTly, (0.2) so I: ha:ve ma:ny uh: (0.5) I feel many
12      ->  uh troublesome: (0.5) uh: to: CONversate- (.) to
13      ->  converse with m- my: PRO:fessor .hhh (mm)
14          (1.0)
15 Int:     psk! (m)- wu- WHERE are you from.
```

```
(12.09) Lazaraton, 1991:129-30
 1 Stu:        n also next quarter maybe I like to: mm (0.8) I haff to
 2             take the: (0.2) I haff to: give a seminar in: my
 3        ->   department n: .hhh (0.5) so: this- (0.2) I feel my oral
 4        ->   English is not good hhh! heh! .hhh [so: that's why I=
 5 Int:                                          [o:ka:y
 6 Stu: ->     =li(ke) to: improve my oral English
 7        ->   (0.8)
 8 Int:        (akay)
 9        ->   (0.8)
10 Int:        tch! alright .hhh wu- u- IS: what is: your native
11             LA:Nguage.

(12.10) Lazaraton, 1991:131
 1 Stu: ->     O(hh):K(h)AY. eh:: (0.5) psk!.hhh I thi:nk I:- I needed
 2        ->   to improve my English, (1.2) *eh* (0.2) AS SOON as
 3             possible.
 4 Int:        eh(h) (h)eh!
 5 Stu: ->        you [know I'm going to take many: seminars cla:ss (.)
 6 Int:               [why
 7 Stu: ->     in the coming: ye:a:r. .h[hh (0.8) en uh: (1.5) I'm=
 8 Int:                                 [mm
 9 Stu: ->     =afraid that (0.2) uh it is beyond my ability. (0.5) to
10        ->   join the discussion h(hh)ardt discussion.
11             (1.0)
12 Int:        mmhmm
13 Stu:        huh huh! heh! heh! heh! .huh!
14             (1.5)
15 Stu: ->     so:- .hhh if I- if I ca:n't improve my English I: (0.5)
16        ->   I think I- I'm going to da(hh!)de hhh! hah!
17        ->   I [c(hh!)an't (be) survive,
18 Int:          [((sniff))
19             (0.2)
20 Int:        psk! oka:y of the two: courses that ma:y be
21             offered(t), . . .
```

In each of these exchanges, the students/applicants offer self-critical assessments of their English language competence, and this is not met with disagreement from their interlocutor. In Extract (12.08) there is no uptake at all, but – after a gap of 1.0 seconds (at line 14) – simply a proceeding to a next question. In Extract (12.09) there is a quick uptake, but the uptake "okay" (at lines 5 and 8) is not so much an agreement with the assessment as it is a receipt of the requested language sample, and again the interview proceeds to the next question. In Extract (12.10), the student's self-assessment comes in several bursts, the first of which is met (at lines 4 and 6) by an appreciative chuckle and request for an account, the others of which are met with silence or continuers. In none of these exchanges, then, is self-deprecation met with

the preferred response we have been led to expect – disagreement. Furthermore, on some occasions when the self-deprecation is disagreed with, the
response can have special, apparently delicately designed characteristics,
as in Extract (12.11).

```
(12.11) Lazaraton, 1991:140
 1 Stu:        =um- (.5) a:n- in- EVERY- (.8) like everyday I talk to
 2       ->    lots of (.) American friends of mi:ne n they(re) all
 3       ->    saying you really have so much problem in (Eng)lish: n=
 4 Int: ->     =[oh I can't [believe they say th[at
 5 Stu:        =[.hhh          [um:                    [no: thu- that's
 6             becau:se I'm a grad student
 7 Int:        mm[hmm?
 8 Stu:           [n there's so: much topics (.) that we have to talk
 9             about=
10 Int:        =y(hh)eah(hh)
11 Stu:        n: espeshal politics an:d (.5) social issue: .hhh which
12             is really unfamiliar for me
```

As Lazaraton (1991:141) notes, the disagreement (at line 4) avoids offering a
counterbalancing compliment of the student/applicant's language ability; it
simply questions the conduct of the friends. Furthermore, the disagreement
is itself disagreed with, the student justifying the negative assessment the
friends had offered, in effect re-introducing the thrust of their evaluation.

But is it correct, using Pomerantz's work as a guide, to treat silences
after negative self-assessments as incipient agreements, i.e., as incipient
*dis*preferred responses? Is agreement with a self-deprecation actually to
be taken as a dispreferred response? Or is the preference structure here
re-reversed, with agreement preferred as it is in most sequences? Not
really. In fact, in a few instances in which the applicants make self-
deprecating remarks about matters other than their English language competence, the Interviewer is quick to disagree, and the reassurance is warmly
accepted.

But these occasions of talk-in-interaction are designed to do a job, sorting
out language capacity in the interest of deciding which courses to offer and
whom to admit to them. English language competency is the applicants'
"ticket of admission" to an ESL class, or rather their *lack* of competency
is (and most applicants appear fervently to wish to be admitted). Their
self-deprecation constitutes, in this context, given this activity as the preoccupation of the interaction, a bid or claim by the applicants for admission.
And agreement with that assessment, in promoting the applicant's bid to a
"successful" outcome, stands as a preferred response. By the same token,
disagreement by the Interviewer can be heard as tantamount to rejection of
their application, or preparing the ground for such an outcome, as can be
seen twice in Extract (12.12).

```
(12.12) Lazaraton, 1991:160-61
 1 Stu:       . . . en: I have so many seminars I rea(hh!)lly.hhh
 2            [(I really am) to] be scared about that=I mean I-
 3 Int:       [yah:
 4 Stu:       [I I've HAD] seminars la:st quarter too en I could=
 5 Int:       [no: (you:)]
 6 Stu:       =manage .hhh but [I always] felt (.) some- (.)
 7 Int:                        [ (good) ]
 8 Stu:       uncomfortable [sometimes=
 9 Int:                     [((sniff))=
10 Int: ->    =yeahm [it seems to me that that it would be] more it's
11 Stu:             [ .hhh e:nd uh:                         ]
12 Int: ->    =a question of (0.2) confidence.
13            (0.2)
14 Stu:       ye:s.
15 Int: ->    because yur la:nguage is really, (.) not (.) the
16            problem,
17 Stu: ->    hhh! th(hh!)ank y(h)ou [s(h)o m(h)uch]
18            ((twelve lines omitted))
19 Int:       okay=.hhh there's only ONE thing tha I wanna sa:y about
20            tha:t en it's you see how many people are applying
21 Stu:       mmhmm=
22 Int: ->    =.hhh so there are some people who really NEE:D
23            [not just    [the confidence .hhh but the ]<LA:nguage>=
24 Stu:       [.hhh I KNOW [[but it's it's not .hhh! hhh]
25 Int: ->    =end [the (y'know)
26 Stu:            [it's not
```

In the exchange at lines 10–16, the Interviewer compliments the applicant's language ability and this compliment is appreciated, but a bit later on (lines 21–23, and note that some intervening transcript has been omitted at line 18) a rejection is prepared which relies precisely on the terms of the earlier compliment. Indeed, applicants can be quick to infer such projected rejections from appreciations of their language competence, as in Extract (12.13).

```
(12.13) Lazaraton, 1991:163
1 Int: ->    now what is you:r issue. your pro:blem is: you are
2      ->    MU:ch better than (0.5) the average.
3            (0.5)
4 Stu: ->    y'mean I will [be (kinda) Kicked out from (.)=
5 Int:                     [participant
6 Stu: ->    =[thirty four?
7 Int:       =[see you may be kicked OU:T because you are too good.
8            (1.5)
```

The connection between not being bad enough and rejection could hardly be clearer.

By the same token, ready agreement by the Interviewer with an applicant's linguistic self-deprecation can be taken as in effect endorsing their credentials, and projecting admission to the course(s). This is a reading the Interviewers prefer to avoid in any given case, because (as they readily say in response to applicants' questions and entreaties) they may not yet know the distribution of competency and incompetence in the applicant pool, and, in fact, do not know which level of course will actually be offered that term, until the competence distribution in the applicant pool overall is known and the budgetary allocations for instructors are finalized. Given the import of assessments at this opening stage of the interview, then, virtually no stance toward an applicant's negative self-assessment is tenable for the Interviewer. In these language assessment interviews, it is not that the preference structure of self-deprecations is reversed, as much as it is neutralized by being implicated in quite a distinct, instrumental course of action. The withholding of response displayed in Extracts (12.08) to (12.10) reflects this neutralization insofar as it is not interpretable either as agreeing or disagreeing with the assessment. The usual operation of preference structure which can serve to ground inferences about the import of a gap such as this does not work here.

So, positive and negative assessments of language competence – linguistic compliments and self-deprecations – implement context-specific other actions in this setting, and are parts of a specially focused course of action. They are not the same objects that are described by Pomerantz (1984), and the divergence of Lazaraton's (1991) observations from Pomerantz's do not serve, in these respects, to call the latter into question; nor is Pomerantz's account mechanically applicable to Lazaraton's data. Rather, we have here a quite specifically calibrated variation in preference structure, fitted to just (and only) those assessments which in this context have a different action import. This variation testifies not to the looseness of preference organization or these studies of it, but, on the contrary, to the precision of fit of this element of sequence organization to the specific context of its use and the course of action it is being employed to implement.

13 Sequence as practice

The sequence structures we have been describing are the outcome of practices of sequence construction. They are the product of a convergence between practices for implementing a course of action-in-interaction through talking, and the structures of talking through which such a course of action can be implemented. The fact that there are robust, recurrent forms and structures of sequences which are precipitated out by these practices testifies to the recurrence of certain interactional and sequential contingencies which press for solution and resolution, and which, given the way in which talk-in-interaction is otherwise organized (its turn-taking and turn-constructing practices, the availability of the resources and practices of repair and the structuring they appear to have, etc.), recurrently get resolved in ways embodied by these sequence structures. They document interactants' recurrent solutions to exigencies of interaction, of talking-in-interaction, and of building courses of action.

Still, these structures are not rigid prescriptions. Who would have prescribed them? Who would enforce them? If they are the precipitate of recurrently employed practices, we must expect that there will be occasions on which interactional and sequential contingencies occasion or invite the use of different practices, or different uses of the same practices, yielding organizational or structural outcomes that vary from the most commonly observed ones. These provide opportunities to sort out what in our observations displays the underlying driving contingencies and their solutions, and what is better understood as the common, but not deeply rooted, surface manifestation or realization of the practices-as-responses-to-contingencies.

Non-canonical forms

Consider, for example, the sequence structure of the focal sequence/topic of the "Stolen" conversation, starting at line 8.

```
(13.01)  MDE-MTRAC 60-1/2 Stolen, 1:01-35
 1          ((ring))
 2 Mar:   Hello:?
 3 Ton:   Hi: Marsha?
```

```
 4 Mar:  Ye:ah.
 5 Ton:  How are you.
 6 Mar:  Fi::ne.
 7       (0.2)
 8 Mar:  Did Joey get home yet?
 9 Ton:  Well I wz wondering when 'e left.
10       (0.2)
11 Mar:  ˙hhh Uh:(d) did Oh: .h Yer not in on what ha:ppen'.(hh)(d)
12 Ton:  No(h)o=
13 Mar:  =He's flying.
14       (0.2)
15 Mar:  En Ilene is going to meet im:.Becuz the to:p wz ripped
16       off'v iz car which is tih say someb'ddy helped th'mselfs.
17 Ton:  Stolen.
18       (0.4)
19 Mar:  Stolen.=Right out in front of my house.
20 Ton:  Oh: f'r crying out loud,=en eez not g'nna eez not
21       g'nna bring it ba:ck?
22 Mar:  ˙hh No so it's parked in the g'rage cz it wz so damn
23       co:ld. An' ez a matter fact snowing on the Ridge Route.
24       (0.3)
25 Mar:  ˙hhh So I took him to the airport he couldn' buy a et.
26       (·)
27 Mar:  ˙hhhh Bee- he c'd only get on standby.
28       (0.3)
29 Ton:  Uh hu:[h,
30 Mar:        [En I left him there et abou:t noo:n.
31       (0.3)
32 Ton:  Ah ha:h.
33       (0.2)
34 Mar:  Ayund uh,h
35       (0.2)
36 Ton:  W't's 'e g'nna do go down en pick it up later? er . . .
```

Several observations can help us fix the circumstances of this sequence's inception.

First, Marsha's inquiry at line 8 is pre-emptive. It is a launch of the first topic/sequence by the recipient of the contact, in the face of a default weak entitlement of the initiator of the contact to that prerogative in order to introduce the reason for the contact, if one is to be introduced (Schegloff, 1986). Further, here Marsha's introduction of it comes where there is an alternative action which is possibly relevant, and that is a reciprocal "howaryou" inquiry. The gap of (0.2) at line 7 is, in the first instance, analyzably the result of Tony's withholding of talk in a turn position which is his, in view of Marsha's having brought a preceding turn to possible completion. His withholding is projectably a withholding of "the reason for the contact" on behalf of a reciprocal "howaryou," and Marsha exploits the opening to do a pre-empting sequence launch of her own. In effect, this appears to reverse the initial allocation of topic/sequence initiative provided in the overall structural organization of talk-in-interaction to the initiator of the contact, if there is one (Schegloff, 1986).

It is within this sequence-organizational context that we should understand Tony's response (line 9), which amounts to a counter. Although it is true that his response conveys what is, in effect, an answer to Marsha's question (if Tony is wondering when Joey left, then surely he has not yet arrived), the turn which he produces, and the action which it implements, are not designed as answers, or to "do answering." Rather, his turn is designed as a counter, to put a question of his own in the place of Marsha's as the source of sequential relevance constraining what should happen next (the grammatical question is embedded within a frame in the turn's design), and he does so before, or without, himself doing an answer to her question. In effect, he thereby reverses the pre-emption of sequential initiative which her question had embodied. As of the end of his turn (at line 9), what is conditionally relevant next is an answer to the question: "When did Joey leave?"

Note, then, that by the end of the proximate response (at line 32), what has been conveyed is that Marsha does not know when he left (and she returns subsequently to this matter, to say that the airport was not too crowded when she left Joey there, so his wait to get on a plane on standby status – i.e., to leave – should not have been too long), but that his trip has changed from what had been planned in ways previously unknown to Tony. But this is not done as a straightforward second pair part; there is no single-turn "answer." Rather, Marsha addresses the conditionally relevant next action as involving a telling, and sequentially formats the telling in a *telling sequence*, rather than an answering turn.

But even this omits a key aspect of the exchange. It appears that Tony's counter triggers an alarm in Marsha's understanding. She hears in it a reference by Tony to a determinate "leaving," subject to the decision of the traveler, when she knows that she left Joey at the airport at about noon without a ticket and on standby status, i.e., a status whose departure time is indeterminate. This was in fact the source of her question to Tony, "Did Joey get home yet?" She had left him at the airport not knowing when he would leave, and (as she later tells Tony) having asked Joey to call "when he got in." It appears that Marsha has understood this phone call as Tony's call to let her know that that has happened – a prophetic anticipation, as it happens, because later on, when Joey *has* arrived, it is Tony who ends up having to call Marsha to inform her, as Joey has gone off to the movies with his girlfriend without doing so. Marsha's pre-emptive question at line 8 appears in this light to have been designed as an anticipation of that "news," as providing a sequential niche for the telling which she figured Tony had called to do.

So Tony's question "rings false" for Marsha, and she appears to be starting to ask whether Joey has not called to alert Tony to the change in plans (line 11, "Uh did"), when she registers out loud that Tony does not know the changed circumstances. Her articulation of this diagnosis ("Oh, you're not in on what happened") serves, in sequence structural terms, as a pre-announcement or pre-telling, to which Tony's confirming "No" (line 12) serves as a go-ahead response.[1] The telling which Marsha does, then – first the terse announcement ("He's flying") and then the elaborated narrative account (lines 15–30) – ends up being packaged in telling-sequence format (i.e., pre-telling sequence plus telling) which is embedded into the second pair part position in a question–answer sequence.

Although this is not the type of recurrent, virtually canonical, sequence structure which has been described elsewhere in these pages, it is the product of the same practices of sequence construction as yield those structures, but whose deployment here, given the particularities implicated in this "misunderstanding" and the specific sequential juncture at which it was revealed (after the pre-emptive question and the pre-emption-redressing counter), yields a less familiar, ad hoc configuration of otherwise familiar sequence-constructional resources.

However ad hoc, the "pre-telling plus telling" configuration in the episode we have been discussing remains analyzable as anchored in a larger base sequence in progress; it is located in the second pair part position, and is responsive to the constraints put on that position by the preceding first pair part. It simply deploys practices for sequence construction not ordinarily found in that position. Although not anchored by reference to an adjacency pair structure in the same fashion as pre-, insert-, and post-expansions, it is nonetheless positioned relative to an underlying adjacency pair armature.

---

[1] Note that Marsha here abandons a form (projectable as "Did Joey call you?") which is likely to force a disagreeing response, at least on the level of turn design, in favor of one which permits an agreeing response (albeit a negative, to agree with the negative cast of her assertion). Compare the following exchange, eerily similar not only in turn re-organization but in topical focus:

```
(13.02) Sacks, 1987 [1973]:64
1  A:      Uh I am surprised he didn't call you
2  B:      Well's alright
3  A:->    ((laugh)) Did he- he didn't evidently
4  B:->    No
```

The suggestion that Marsha's "Did" may be the start of "Did Joey call?" or even "Didn't Joey call?" is, of course, speculative. But this is a judgment informed by an understanding of the context under examination in the Marsha/Tony interaction, as well as data (such as the exchange cited in this note) which appear to approximate this context, and in which such an utterance was articulated further before being cut off. Although in the end this is speculation, it is well-grounded speculation.

Nor is this possibility limited to second pair part position. In Extract
(13.03), Lila has called Reginald with what she takes to be a delicate task.
His father has had a stroke while away from home, and his wife (Reginald's
stepmother, called Venus) has been in touch with Lila (apparently a friend
or neighbor) to prepare the house for their return by buying a hospital bed
and wheelchair, cleaning up, etc. Lila has called Reginald to clear this with
him – he being a family member and left uninvolved, and she being the one
turned to.

```
(13.03) MC II:2
 1 Lil:     Say, uh-Reginald,.mhh I uh I'm in a kind of a-hh (.)
 2          . hh hh a little, hh unhappy position but nevertheless
 3          I'll: go ahead 'n make the best of it. <.hh um uh what
 4          I wan'duh ask you about .hh uh b-uh- Venus wrote me: an
 5          a:sked me: if I would order a hospital bed, .hhh and a
 6          <chai:r .hh> For her. .Mhh Becuz she wannid me tuh be
 7          here,.hh I imagine thet she felt thet probably ih
 8          would save you some trouble, u- u- having t'come up
 9          here en have somebuddy (0.4) have'm put it where it
10          belonged. .Hh.mhh Now. .hh uh: tuh [make-
11 Reg:                                        [You have the
12          key:s to the place¿=
13 Lil:     =Yes I do,
14 Reg:     (Mm hm, o[kay)
15 Lil:             [.hhm.hh And um-I-I-I called um (0.8) I hadtuh
16          call 'er long distance buh-cause she didn't make .hh
17          specify properly about this wheelchair and this bed.
18          .hh And, in doing so, I very stupidly asked- forgot
19          tuh ask her what roo:m she expected tuh putcher father
20      Fb  in. .hh Now d'z she- d'you think she expects tuh put im
21       |  in that back bedroom where he was before:¿
22       |  (1.5)
23 Lil:  |  'Cuz I'll haftuh get Mister Bush tuh go over there with
24       |  me en clea- .hh an' take that bed outta there, .hh
25       |  becuz the-uh-they-they expect the place to be ready
26       |  y'know.
27 Reg:  |  Mm hm,
28 Lil:  |  I d- I been all through this with my brothers so I- I
29       |  know what they expect.
30 Reg:  |  Uh huh,=I see. .hh uh,
31 Lil:  |  Or do you think it would be better tuh put- uh-put it
32       |  in the- in the front bedroom ahl- I mean .hh not- not
33       |  the one on the corner but- .hh where yer mother usetuh
34       |  sleep.
35       |  (1.5)
36 Reg:  |  I know where you mean.=
37 Lil:  |  =[Mm hm
```

```
38 Reg:  |  =[Uh, Golly I hadn't thought a' that either, I [suppose
39 Lil:  |                                                 [Of
40       |  course that's easy to uh-transfer't, to the ba:ck, .hh
41       |  eh-uh with a coupla men tuh do it, .hh because it's
42       |  gonna be en electrical one, .hh eh-but uh-I've-uh
43      Fb  thought I better talk tuh you first,
44          (1.0)
```

There are some familiar practices deployed at the start of Lila's launch
here. First, an indication of the delicateness of her position and what she
has to do (lines 1–3). Then a pre-pre at lines 3–4, projecting the eventual
asking of a question, but alerting the recipient that what is coming next is
not that question but some preliminary, but necessary, preparation for it. The
preliminaries begin in the middle of line 4, and continue to line 20. At lines
20–21, it appears that the base FPP is produced. After a gap of 1.5 seconds,
Lila resumes with an account of what would be entailed if that was going to
be the plan. Together with the design of the question at 20–21 ("d'you think
she expects to put him . . ." as compared to, for example, "does she want to
put him . . ."), the burdensomeness of what would be entailed suggests that
Lila has presented first the alternative that she does not favor, and that there
is more to come – an alternative that she prefers.[2] Just as Reginald appears
to be starting a reply (at line 30), Lila begins talking again, constructing her
talk to embody a continuation of what she was saying before. By doing this,
she allows the propriety of his continuer "uh huh, I see," but pre-empts any
further talk that might involve answering a question which she now shows
has not yet been fully articulated. And so, at lines 31–34, we find more
FPP, and before Reginald can answer she adds the observation that if this
second alternative is chosen and does not turn out well, it can be reversed
(a possibility not mentioned with regard to the first alternative). And then,
having made her case by the way she "asked" about the alternatives, she
announces the end of the base FPP at line 43.[3]

In Extract (13.01) we encountered an answer, an SPP, that exhibited many
of the features of a sequence in its own right. Here, in Extract (13.03), we
have a question, an FPP, that occupies the better part of 23 lines of transcript,
though, unlike (13.01), it gets constructed as a single, multi-unit turn, and
not like an adjacency-pair formatted sequence. The upshot of this discussion
is that, although the forms of FPP and SPP that we have encountered for the
most part – packaged in single TCU turns – may be the most common way
these pillars of adjacency pairs are designed, but they are not the only way.
Astute analysis therefore requires that attention be paid to longer stretches

---

[2] Recall Sacks' observation (1987 [1973]) that, if there are two FPPs in a turn, the second
will be responded to first. One consequence is that FPP speakers can place the option they
favor second, where it is most accessible for favorable response.
[3] There is too much of this sequence to take up here. It is not until some 150 seconds later
(90 lines of transcript) that the question gets an answer – indeed, gets *the* answer that Lila

of talk for the possibility that, taken as a whole, they serve to implement an FPP or SPP of an adjacency pair, a structure which underlies its sequence just as the more compact forms encountered more commonly do.

There are, however, practices for sequence construction whose position does *not* appear to be occasioned by reference to an underlying base adjacency pair at all. The sequences which result are thus "unanchored" and "incidental" in that sense (and no implication of unimportance is attached to this usage), and are occasioned ostensibly by reference to other ongoing sequential and interactional structures. As with much else in this book, what can be offered here are only several cases in point. More surely remain to be described, and a systematic assessment of their organization and import awaits that description.

Incidental sequences

Perhaps the clearest exemplar of the underlying practice base of sequence organization is the practice of "try-marking" – a common sort of reference to persons in conversation (Sacks and Schegloff, 1979; Schegloff, 1996c). A brief account will suffice for our purposes here.

A great many of the references to persons in talk-in-interaction, and especially in conversation, are to persons the speaker knows the recipient to know, and there are determinate forms of person reference which serve to alert a recipient that the person being referred to is (figured by speaker to be) someone they know. Personal name, and especially first name, is a particularly common "recognitional reference form," but not the only one.

favored – which is immediately followed by a sequence-closing third, and quick transition to a new topic-talk sequence.

```
(13.04) MC II:2 (82 lines omitted)
 1   Reg:              [(I wonder) where she would like the darn
 2                     thing.
 3   Lil:              What?
 4   Reg:              I wonder where it would be best tuh put it.
 5   Lil:              .hh Well that's what's got me stumped. .hh Now fer he:r
 6                     ihhm .hh uh-tuh be helpful fer he:r, I would say, it
 7                     would be easier tuh have him in that front bedroom. .Hh
 8                     En I know the hospital uh-bed will fit in there. En it
 9                     [could-
10   Reg:  Sb         [Put it in nere nen, en nen go ahead 'n ifuh .hh if
11         |           they haftuh change it why:: I c'n go up 'n help'm
12         Sb          change it 'r ( Dean ) 'n I can, ['r (somebody)
13   Lil:  SCT                          [Okay sweetie, I dis- I
14         New seq.    just- .hh I tell you I had .hh When I first got word
15                     from her,
16   Reg:              Mm [hm,
17   Lil:                 [I went down to- .hh to talk to Evelyn . . .
```

And it continues along this line.

Indeed, as we shall see, it is not only that such "recognitionals" *are* used; there is a preference for using them, if possible.

On some occasions, however, a speaker may *figure* that someone about to be referred to is a person known to recipient, but is not certain of this. Then the speaker may use the appropriate recognitional form – like a name – but deliver it in a specially marked way, commonly with upward intonation followed by a brief pause. That is, they mark the reference as a "try" to achieve recognition with that reference form; if delivered in that way, we will speak of the reference form as "try-marked."

If the recipient does in fact recognize who is being referred to, they ought to so indicate in that brief pause, and if they do so the speaker then goes on with what they were in the process of saying. If the recipient does not so indicate, the speaker may provide an additional indication or clue as to whom they mean to be referring to, often again with upward intonation, and again awaiting some sign of recognition from recipient. This cycle may be repeated several times, but if no recognition is secured within those several tries the effort may be abandoned and the talk configured in a different way.

A clear example of this try-marked usage of a recognitional reference is displayed in Extract (13.05). Sherry, Ruthie, Karen, and Mark have been telling stories of friends who have recovered insurance compensation for damage to their property. Sherry is just launching her part in this round of telling at the beginning of the extract (where "La Mancha" refers to the private dormitory which she, Karen, and Ruthie live in, and where the conversation is taking place).

```
(13.05) SN-4, 11:28-12:08
 1 She:    Luhma:ncha had something dri:pping on the fronta my car
 2         last year but I never got tuh colle:ct on it.
 3         (0.6)
 4 She:    Yihknow when it- (·) came from thee:: I think (a) air
 5         conditioning system.it drips on the front of the ca:rs?
 6         (·)
 7 She:    if you park inna certain place?=
 8 Ru?:    =[mm hmm]
 9 She:->  =['hhhh] (·) Peter.
10         (0.2)
11 She:->  Legget?
12         (0.5)
13 Kar:->  [ O h       y e a h. ]
14 She:->  [(Y'know who) I'm tal]king about? Yeah.'hh He collected
15         a fo:rtune fer that. He claimed all k(h)i:nds of
16         damages.
17         (1.1)
18 Ru?:    huh huh-huh=
19 Kar:    =From Lama:ncha:?
20 She:    Yeah.
21         (1.4)
```

Commonly, try-marked references have their recognition validated in passing, for example with a head nod, because speakers make correct suppositions about their recipients' capacity to recognize. But on occasion, even when eventually validated, enough of a hitch develops to get the reference-try elaborated into a full-fledged question in its own right. In Extract (13.05), Sherry's initial reference to the protagonist of her next story (line 9) is not delivered with upward intonation, but is followed by a pause in which recognition can be marked or claimed. Apparently (there are no video data for this material), no such indication is given (at line 10) and Sherry adds another "clue," the last name, this time with upward intonation added to the pause to mark it as a try (at line 11). Again there is a problem. Even though Karen does eventually (claim to) recognize who is being talked about (at line 13), she has apparently given no indication of this in the pause at line 12, leading Sherry to bring the matter out of tacit treatment into articulate focus. Because Karen is signifying her recognition even as Sherry is asking the question, Sherry repeats the answer herself, but it is nonetheless clear that we have here a question–answer sequence, prompted by (and positioned relative to) not the environing sequence structure (which in this case happens to be a round of story-telling, rather than adjacency pair-based), but by a reference practice she has employed, a word which she has used to refer to someone.

It is worth noting that the person reference which Sherry is try-marking is designed to be the "subject" of her sentence, and with a timely recognition token from a recipient – even after the *supplementary* clue – the telling's start could emerge as a straightforward clause, embedded in which would be, in effect, something like a question–answer adjacency pair, with its question intonationally accomplished and its answer gesturally accomplished (e.g., "Peter. [0.2] Legget? [0.5, with nod] . . . collected a fortune for that.")

In such an *en passant* exchange we could see sequence organization as practice, with none of the surface "precipitate" as product. As it happens, a collapsed adjacency pair is actually produced ("collapsed" in that the question asker herself articulates the answer); still, only a "he" (line 14) breaks the otherwise grammatically smooth line of narrative.

A rather fuller sequence development can be seen in Extract (13.06), a sequence nonetheless also occasioned by, and positioned relative to, the exigencies of securing recognition of a person reference, not by otherwise ongoing sequence structures, relative to which it is "incidental."

```
(13.06) SBL T2/S2/C4, 9:08-29
 1 Amy:      Well this friend who really knows about it will be
 2           back, she was going through here, and they uhm (1.0)
 3           uh the friend she stops with, uh called some of her
 4           C.F.O. friends here in San Bosco,
 5 Bea:      Oh[h.
 6 Amy:         [And uh for a little tea yesterday, well I was the
```

```
7               only one other than- [than the uhm -- tch Astons.
8 Bea:                              [(       )
9 Amy:  ->   [Uh Missiz Basil Aston?
10 Bea:      [(                ),
11 Bea:      N[ow-
12 Amy: ->   [You know, uh [the-the cellist?
13 Bea: ->                 [Oh yes.
14 Bea: ->   She's- she's the cellist.
15 Bea: ->   Yes. Ye:[s.
16 Amy:              [Well she and her husband were there, an' it
17           seems they're old friends of this friend,
18 Bea:      Oh.
19 Amy:      who uhm [was from- is from Vista.
20 Bea:              [I-
21 Bea:      Ye:[s,
22 Amy:         [And she wuh- they were interested too she was
23           telling about them,
```

Here again the person reference figures in a telling sequence; here the hitches
in securing validation of recognition induce a somewhat greater disruption
of the grammatical structure of the telling apparently in progress. (It apparently was on the way to being – at lines 6–7, and 22 – "Well I was the
only one other than the Astons . . . who [was] interested," but gets more
elaborated than that.)

Particular words or usages, and ones other than recognitional reference,
can occasion sequences incidental to the ongoing sequence structure in
other ways as well. Sometimes, for example, the speaker may not be able to
retrieve the word when needed, and may launch a sequence to try to "find"
it, often mobilizing their recipient on behalf of the search (see Goodwin,
1983; Goodwin and Goodwin, 1986), but occasionally looking outside the
interaction they are in for help, as Rita does in Extract (13.07), in which
she turns to her husband at her end of this telephone interaction for help in
finding the name of the place they traveled to to see a movie (in a sequence
not fully hearable on tape).

```
(13.07) Berkeley, 5:05-12 (simplified)
1 Rit:      . . . ya know, we: went to the mo:vies.=
2               =we went to:uh:m. uh- to:- uh(hh)
3         -> what's °the name of the° (      ) ((to someone off line))
4         -> ((2.0 seconds, off line))
5 Rit:  -> (°Millbrae°) ((off line))
6           (0.3)
7 Rit:      Millbrae:. which is o:ver: past Burlingame.((on line))
8           (.)
```

Word search sequences, then, are also incidental to the sequence structure in
which the talk which occasions them is embedded. So also are the sequences

which can be engendered by "anticipatory completions" by a recipient of what a current speaker is saying – what Lerner (2004) terms "collaborative turn sequences."

Or the issue may be neither trouble in what is supposedly recognizable to recipient nor in what is not retrievable by speaker, but a usage which comes "naturally" to speaker, who then addresses the possibility that it may not be understandable to recipient. In Extract (13.08), Kathy has deflected a compliment about something she has hand-woven by saying that "it wove itself once it was set up," and she is asked to explain.

```
(13.08)  KC-4, 16:15-35
  1 Rub:      Whaddyou mean it wove itself once it w's set up.=
  2           =[What d's that] mean.=
  3 Kat:       [ O h    i -   ]
  4 Kat:      =Well I mean it's ve:ry simple, (`hhh)
  5           (0.8)
  6 Kat:      It's exac[tly the same in the we]:ft as it is in the=
  7 Dav:               [ She also means th't- ]
  8 Kat:      =warp.
  9           (0.2)
 10 Kat:      That is if the warp has sixteen greens an two blacks
 11           an two light blues and two blacks an sixteen greens
 12           an:sixteen blacks an sixteen blues an so on,
 13      ->   `hh y'know the warp are the long pieces.
 14           (0.5)
 15 Fri: ->   Mhhm
 16 Kat:      The weft has exactly tha:t.
 17 Fri:      Yah.
 18           (0.5)
 19 Rub:      Oh. So [its square,] °in o[ther words.°
 20 Kat:             [Y a  s e e?]      [
 21 Kat:                           [It's perfectly sq[uare yah.=
 22 D?R:                                             [Mm hmm
```

Here she has incorporated the use of the (mildly) technical terms "weft" and "warp" in her account, and then interpolates into the as-yet-incomplete account and incomplete turn-constructional unit (at line 13) an explanation of the term "warp." But note that she takes this to be subject to confirmation, to a show of understanding, and withholds completion of the turn-constructional unit and of the account until this is forthcoming. In effect, then, she has prompted the interpolation of what we can call *a parenthetical sequence* into the middle of her extended turn.

This incidental sequence is somewhat different from the ones just examined. Those were produced in the face of overt trouble – the failure (or anticipatable possible failure) to secure recognition for something which solicited it, or the failure to be able to produce an item when its time for articulation in the turn had arrived. The parenthetical, however, is not prompted by signs

of failure. If anything, this parenthetical is a prophylactic to pre-empt the
possibility of failure. But this is not endemic to parenthetical sequences.
For example, in Extract (13.09), a parenthetical insert is designed to specify
an aspect of context which (given that it is from a telephone conversation)
might otherwise not be available, and which could have an adverse bearing
on the outcome of the sequence.

```
(13.09) Stalled, 1:7-18
  1 Don:        Guess what.hh
  2 Mar:        What.
  3 Don:        ˙hh My ca:r is sta::lled.
  4             (0.2)
  5 Don:  ->    ('n) I'm up here in the Glen?
  6 Mar:  ->    Oh::.
  7             {(0.4)}
  8 Don:        {˙hhh }
  9 Don:        A:nd.hh
 10             (0.2)
 11 Don:        I don' know if it's po:ssible, but {˙hhh}/(0.2)} see
 12             I haveta open up the ba:nk.hh
```

Again, the parenthetical is designed to get a response – i.e., to be a
sequence, not a clause in a turn. It conveys information possibly not known.
This one, unlike Extract (13.08), may well have a bearing on the business
of the larger base sequence, yet it is not positioned relative to it – as pre-
expansion, or insert expansion (see the earlier discussion of insert sequences
in Chapter 6). And, unlike the instances examined so far, it does not appear
to be occasioned by, or directed to, a word or usage which has otherwise
figured in the talk.

There is a likely independence here, then, between two matters we have
been considering together. One, that incidental sequences can be rooted in
problems with words or usages which figure in the surrounding utterances;
the other, that speakers can launch parenthetical sequences to introduce
information into the talk without situating that introduction as part of the
expansion of the base sequence. The two can converge, as we saw in
Extract (13.08), but they need not. Usage problems can be dealt with in
non-parenthetical sequences, which are nonetheless not structurally part of
the local sequence structure. Parenthetical sequences can be used to address
usage-focused problems, but need not be used for that alone.

Two more episodes will allow us to stretch further our sense of the ways
in which sequences incidental to the underlying armature of action in a base
adjacency pair can be introduced into interstices of the talk or as an overlay
to it.

Note then that in Extract (13.10), which we have examined before in
Chapter 7, a complaint sequence (line 4) is responded to with an account of
the omission which has been complained of (line 5).

```
(13.10) SN-4, 5:01-09 (previously [7.45])
1  She:       Hi Carol.=
2  Car:       =H[i : .]
3  Rut:         [CA:RO]L, HI::
4  She:       You didn' get en icecream sanwich,
5  Car: ->    I kno:w, hh I decided that my body didn't need it,
6  She: ->    Yes but ours di:d=
7  She: ->    =hh heh-heh-heh [heh-heh-heh [`hhih
8  ???:                       [ehh heh heh [
9  ???:                                    [(      )
```

But there is more to be said about this base second pair part. It not only offers an account for not bringing an ice-cream sandwich. That account appears to incorporate (by barely veiled allusion) a self-deprecation on Carol's part, apparently concerning her weight. The ensuing talk continues to develop the underlying base sequence along lines which have been sketched throughout the earlier discussion (this second pair part is rejected, and a succession of other second pair parts is offered by Carol, each of which is rejected except the last, which remains unaddressed altogether). But overlaid onto this underlying structure is another texture of relevance – the self-consciousness about her appearance displayed in the self-deprecation (a relevance which surfaces in later interpolations by Carol, such as "I don't want them tih see me when I look this good. No one deserves it"). Far from disagreeing with the self-deprecation, the rejection of the second pair part at line 6 is built by pejorative contrast with it. When (later on) Carol makes, as a second try at a second pair part, an offer to get ice-cream sandwiches for everyone, Sherry declines specifically by returning to this theme – "I don't need it." Although it is not the self-deprecation sequence which organizes this stretch of talk, its interactional contingencies play off the surfaces of the complaint sequence which does so, and inform the talk as practice, if not as sequence structure (see Schegloff, 1988a:118–31 for a fuller treatment of this episode).

Extract (13.11) should also be familiar by now. Here a pre-offer of information about a bargain is met with a blocking response, which sets off a series of post-expansions, each addressing the dispreferred second pair part of the pre-sequence (see Extract [4.07]).

```
(13.11) Debbie and Nick, 1:34-2:12
1  Deb:     `hhh Um:: u- guess what I've-(u-)wuz lookin' in the paper:.
2           -have you got your waterbed yet?
3  Nic:     Uh huh, it's really nice °too, I set it up
4  Deb:     Oh rea:lly? Already?
5  Nic:     Mm hmm
6           (0.5)
7  Deb:     Are you kidding?
8  Nic:     No, well I ordered it last (week)/(spring)
```

```
 9                 (0.5)
10 Deb:           Oh- no but you h- you've got it already?
11 Nic:           Yeah h! hh=                      ((laughing))
12 Deb:           =hhh [hh ˙hh]                    ((laughing))
13 Nic: ->             [I just] said that
14 Deb: ->        O::hh: hu[h, I couldn't be[lieve you c-
15 Nic: ->                 [Oh (°it's just) [It'll sink in 'n two
16      ->        day[s fr'm now (then      ) ((laugh))]
17 Deb:              [          ((l a u g h ))        ] Oh no cuz I just
18                got- I saw an ad in the paper for a real discount
19                waterbed s' I w'z gonna tell you 'bout it=
```

Eventually, in his response to the third of these post-expansions, Nick not
only reiterates his response; he remarks on the reiteration (line 13). This is in
effect a complaint, one which is derivative from the sequence which has otherwise provided the sequential matrix for this interactional trajectory. That
underlying sequence continues – note the "would have been" version of the
base first pair part at lines 17–19, which gets responded to in the ensuing
turns. But the complaint sequence – which is incidental to the base sequence
though prompted by features of its development – runs simultaneously with
it. Although in a literal sense it occurs in the midst of the pre-expansion, it
is not *of* the pre-expansion; it plays no role in the effort to get the telling
done. It is incidental to the sequence in whose environment it occurs.

Interactional projects, thematic threads, committed lines, etc.

If "incidental sequences" can occur in and around the basic structural components of a sequence without being moored to them and have
recurrent and describable uses, there is a counterpart that transcends the
boundaries of a sequence, does not constitute any of the familiar composite constructions we have called "sequences of sequences," and yet is an
orderly interactional feature that can shape what goes on in interaction and
can be demonstrably oriented to by participants. No single term seems to
capture its variety, so I will vacillate between several terms – an interactional
project, a course of action, an interactional line or stance, a thematic thread.
Under whatever term, what is at issue here is a course of conduct being
developed over a span of time (not necessarily in consecutive sequences)
to which co-participants may become sensitive, which may begin to inform
their inspection of any next sequence start to see whether or how it relates
to the suspected project, theme, stance, etc.

We took notice earlier (see Chapter 4, fn. 1) of participants being oriented to any utterance for the omnirelevant "why that now" question, and
by reference to that inquiry understanding what project a question was

in the service of – most obviously in the case of pre-sequences, even if
it was not clear what they were pre- to. In addressing here the notion of
"sequence as practice," we take seriously the observation that parties to
interaction are *always* interrogating the conduct of others for "why that
now"; pre-sequences are just recurrent instances that yield over time, as a
kind of precipitate, the recurrent, apparently stable structures we have called
"pre-invitations," pre-announcements," etc. The most we can do here is to
examine in a sketchy way several episodes which can alert analysts to the
diverse lines or projects or courses of action being extended or prosecuted
or being prefigured by some current bit of talk, and constitute a kind of
thread surfacing now and again as a persistent theme or project of the
talk.

Extract (13.12) was recorded at a retirement home in Southern California.
Hank, Betty, and Tom are sitting and having coffee. A brief lull has set in,
and is ended by Hank's question at line 2. He has noticed the video camera
being used to make the recording from which this datum is drawn. Betty
explains how it came to be set up, and prefaces her response with "well."

```
(13.12) Coffee Chat, 8
 1                (0.5)
 2 Han: ->    Wut is that cam:era set up for?
 3 Bet: ->>   Well they- she came over and she ask'd* if we minded if
 4            she took (.) our conversation they're jist doing it for
 5            a school proj:ect.
 6 Han:       Mm hm.=
 7 Bet:       =And we said we _didn't mi:nd<and we all sign:ed it.
 8            (ap)proving we didn't mind so(h)=
 9 Tom:       =heh=heh=
10 Bet:       =heh heh .hh hh
11                (1.6)
```

Although Hank's question may well be innocent, its target is potentially
trouble. People "snooping" is a complainable, and Betty apparently under-
stands the possibility of this question leading in that direction; she orients to
the possible project being incubated here. Instead of simply delivering the
answer that ends up being embedded in her response – "they're just doing
it for a school project," she builds a story which provides for the potential
complaint targets having made an appropriate inquiry to the people then
seated at the table, having secured the agreement of the people being video-
taped, including their signed testament to their agreement. Indeed, Betty
seems to have begun a more direct response ("Well they-") before aban-
doning it for the less straightforward one. Here, then, the respondent does
deal with an incipient line of action which she spots as potential trouble, but
does so in a way that includes an answer to the question asked, even though
embedded in a non-straightforward response turn. And, at the end, she

triumphantly returns the turn to Hank (with her "so" at line 8; see Raymond [2004]), virtually defying him to make trouble now that she has detoxified the situation, and Tom joins her in a slight giggle.

The second specimen is drawn from the "Chicken Dinner" material from which we have drawn before. When material from this interaction was first introduced as Extract (1.02), it was described like this: "Vivian and Shane (seated to the left) are hosting Nancy and Michael for a chicken dinner, and are recording it for use in a college course. Vivian has prepared the meal, and her boyfriend Shane has been teasing her by complaining about this or that claimed inadequacy."

For present purposes we need to decompose my formulation of this "theme" or "line" or "project" or "thematic thread" which I referred to as "has been teasing her." Extract (13.13a) occurs just 45 seconds into the start of the meal, after Vivian has turned on the recorder and sat down with the others.

```
(13.13a) Chicken Dinner, 2:29-38
 1 Sha:  Dju cook this all the way through?
 2       (1.0)
 3 Viv:  ↑Ye:s.
 4       (0.2)
 5 Sha:  Think there's still ice on it.
 6       (1.3)
 7 Viv:  I:[ce:?
 8 Sha:    [°kheh-heh-heh-h[eh°
 9 Viv:                    [They weren'even[frozen.
10 Sha:                                    [.k-h-h-h
11
```

We cannot take up the practices of teasing that run through these sequences, tempting though it may be. Suffice it to say that, with his question at line 1, Shane raises an issue about the competence of the cooking, although a presupposition of his observation at line 5 – that this was frozen chicken – turns out not to be true.

About a minute and a quarter later, there is another episode – the one previously examined as Extract (1.02), an expanded version of which is here reproduced as Extract (13.13b).

```
(13.13b) Chicken Dinner, 4:28-5:06
 1       (1.1)
 2 Sha:  Ah can't- Ah can;t[get this thing ↓mashed.
 3 Viv:                    [Aa-ow.
 4       (1.2)
 5 Nan:  You[do that too:? tih yer pota]toes,
 6 Sha:     [This one's hard ezza rock.]
 7 Sha:  ↑Ye[ah.
 8 Viv:     [It i:[s?
```

```
 9 Sha:              [B't this thing- is ↑ha:rd.
10          (0.3)
11 Viv:  It's not do:ne? th'potato?
12 Sha:  Ah don't think so,
13          (2.2)
14 Nan:  Seems done t'me how 'bout you Mi[chael,]
15 Sha:                                  [Alri' ]who cooked
16          this mea:l.
17 Mic:  ·hh Little ↓bit'v e-it e-ih-ih of it isn'done.
18 Sha:  Th'ts ri:ght.
19          (1.2)
20 Mic:  [°('T's alright)°
21 Sha:  [No it's a(h)lr(h)i(h)ght['t's (h)air(h)i(h)ght]
22 Nan:                           [The h:   F u_c k  t h e]m it's
23          goo:d.o[kay?
24 Sha:           [he-he
25          (1.8)
26 Mic:  Nah ah'm ah:'m:
27          (1.9)
28 Viv:  They were bi:g.That's ↓why. I[mean rilly bi]g.
29 Sha:                              [Y a y  yea:h.]
30          (0.4)
31 Nan:  Yeah where'dju git tho:se. Gah ther hu:[ge.
32 Viv:                                         [Well w't happ'n
33          was we picked'p a ba:[g
34 Sha:                         [Oh yeh it wz ba:[:d
35 Viv:                                          [en they w'r
36          ro:tt'n.
37          (0.7)
38
```

The exchange starts with a complaint by Shane at line 2. Nancy, who had not participated at all in the previous episode of mock-complaining, has apparently registered that Shane is building a course of action, one in which he complains about his girlfriend's cooking (perhaps because he knows she still lacks confidence in it). Nancy undertakes to divert the exchange into "shared ways of eating potatoes" (at line 5), but Shane is insistent at lines 6 and 9, and Vivian is taken in by the ruse at lines 8 and 11. After Shane reinforces (at line 12) Vivian's concern that the potatoes are "not done," insufficiently cooked (at line 11), Nancy joins in on the other side at line 14. As noted earlier, she answers Vivian's question at line 11 in a fashion designed specifically to disagree with, or contest, the answer previously given by Shane, and reassures Vivian that the potato has been properly cooked. She then tries to recruit Michael to the side of reassurance, with at best mixed success; Shane triumphantly treats Michael's reply as vindication (line 18).

Then, at line 21, Shane calls a halt to the charade. His "no" marks a transition from a "joking" to a "serious" stance (Schegloff, 2001), and offers reassurance that is thoroughly implicated in laughter (which can, of course, be taken to subvert the claim of now being serious). Nancy's reassurance (at line 22), on the other hand, is delivered defiantly, and the episode appears to be framed as a gender battle. But reassurance does not heal as quickly as teasing injures. Although they have all now said that the potatoes are fine, Vivian (at line 28) is still treating the episode seriously, offering an account for why they were not cooked through, even though the claim to that effect had already been recanted. Nancy, who had "smelled a rat" from the very outset and had tried to divert the sequence, now exploits Vivian's observation about the size of the potatoes to move the talk on to safer ground.

About one minute later:

```
(13.13c) Chicken Dinner, 6:32-7:17 ((lines 4-7 belong to prior
sequence, not shown))
 1             (1.3)
 2 Viv:       hhah=
 3 Nan: ->    =Vivia[n,
 4 Viv:           [Yeah. (Plai[n to evryo[ne)
 5 Sha:                    [(        [   .)]Yeah. ]
 6 Mic:                             [She's]probly]
 7            hidin[g  i t]b'[t
 8 Nan: --        [(Viv)-]  [The chicken is rilly goo:d.
 9 Viv: ->    You li[ke it?
10 Nan: ->          [Very very good.
11 Viv: ->    °O↓kay[good.↓°
12 Sha: ->>        [Yuwuh (.) g'ss I g'd say ih same abaht
13           p't[atoes.
14 Nan:          [↑Mm::.
15            (0.8)
16 Sha: ->>   whhh-hh huh-hh-hh-hh-hh
17 Viv:       ↑Fine I'll nevuh cook f'you again.
18 Mic:       Mm:.
19            (0.6)
20 Nan:       Mm:.
21 Mic: ->    It is good.
22            (0.7)
23 Viv:       Like it?
24            (0.6)
25 Viv:       (↓G'd.)
26 Mic:       Yeh
27            (1.8)
```

At lines 3 and 8 Nancy launches the conventional complimenting of the cook's craft, here made more poignant by the preceding rounds of teasing critique. But after the initial round, in which only Nancy offers a compliment, Shane once again enters with a critique, once again subsequently marked as a tease by the laughter at line 16. It should by now be clear what is meant by a party to the interaction pursuing a project, a thematic thread throughout the occasion, surfacing and then disappearing, only to surface again and recurrently over the continuing course of the interaction. It is this sort of development, one may conjecture, that Betty succeeding in thwarting from its outset in Extract (13.12).

Sequence as practice: the bottom line

The point, then, is that other things can be going on within the stretch of talk organized around the twin poles of the first pair part and the second pair part of a base adjacency pair besides turn expansion and/or multiplication of those anchoring elements, and the several types of expansion in the several positions for sequence expansion which we have been trying to sketch. And sequence-organizational designs can be worked out on a canvas that transcends particular, well-structured sequences of the sort we have been describing. The anatomy of sequence organization which we have been describing supplies a framework, a scaffold, for the implementation of courses of action through talk, but it does not exhaust the resources which parties to interaction can draw on, nor the innovations of practice which they can deploy on behalf of the projects which they pursue separately and together. What has been described here may serve the analyst as points of reference, as clues and reminders about sorts of things which have been observed to recur, or at least occur, within the trajectories of action sequences in talk. They may help the achievement of insight, but they should not pre-empt it. One thing is certain: there is much which goes into the composition of sequences, or which is played off of them, which has not yet been properly understood and described, and much that has not even been glimpsed. And yet everything which occurs there – in the environment of a sequence-in-progress – is in principle accountable by reference to it. Parties will in the first instance seek an answer to the omnirelevant question "why that now" by reference to its relationship to the course of action – the sequence – which is possibly in progress.

And there is a converse point to be made here, as well. It is not only that more can be going on within a sequence than has been described here, and different; it is also that much of what goes on in an adjacency pair-based sequence does not go on only there. There are a number of features, resources, and practices of talk-in-interaction which we have been examining within the context of adjacency pairs which appear to have an extraordinarily broad provenance.

Because the turn-taking organization for conversation is a local system, distributing just a next turn over the course of any given turn, growing incrementally through a series of such "nexts," and because much of what is *in* the talk is shaped by this local organization of practice (in contrast, for example, with speeches, etc., which are prepared in advance of the interaction, or the moment in the interaction, at which they are to be delivered), the relationship of *adjacency* matters widely and often decisively in conversation. Though its consequentiality is not restricted to the ways in which it figures in adjacency pairs, it turns out that it is mobilized in them with a special force and efficacy, and with a distinctive consequentiality.

Similarly, there is a range of places in conversation in which a next turn takes up some stance to, or relative to, a prior turn, and that stance is roughly characterizable as "plus" or "minus", aligned or misaligned, preferred or dispreferred. And there are practices of utterance production which can display and embody the "stance-capacity" in which some utterance is put forward – mitigation, deferral, etc. on the one hand; upgrading and promptness on the other. Again, as with the feature of adjacency and its deployment in the practices of talk-in-interaction, though the consequentiality of preference/dispreference is not restricted to the ways in which it figures in adjacency pairs, it is mobilized in them with a special force and efficacy, and with a distinctive effect. It can come to be stabilized in certain sequence types as a property of the sequence structure of that sequence type, or of the sequence type on that class of occasion, and not as simply a locally occasioned practice.

"Pre-ness" is another. We have already seen that it can work within adjacency pairs both to project (albeit defeasibly) the prospect that a sequence is to begin, and what sort of sequence, and to project the type of response that such a sequence start is about to meet with. But this is a more generally available resource in talk-in-interaction: parties can make moves, and can understand what another has done as constituting a move, which contingently projects a direction for further interactional development – whether or not that development will be constructed from the building blocks of adjacency pairs as described in the preceding pages. And again, in the adjacency pair, this more generally available conversational practice and resource is mobilized on behalf of somewhat more formally organized sequential structures, structures which have a recurrency – though not a rigidity – which we have tried to characterize in this volume as built out of limited sequence-constructional resources.

14 Summary and Applications

The organization of sequences is one of the central forms of organization that gives shape and coherence to stretches of talk and the series of turns of which stretches of talk are composed. The focus of this organization is not, in general, convergence on some *topic* being talked *about*, but the contingent development of *courses of action*. The coherence which is involved is that which relates the action or actions which get enacted in or by an utterance to the ones which have preceded and the ones which may follow. The very root of the word "interaction" underscores the centrality of action to the commerce between people dealing with each other, and this aspect of their conduct is a central preoccupation informing what people do in the turns in which they speak, and informing as well what they are heard to be doing.

We have focused on what is very likely the basic unit of sequence organization – the adjacency pair. There *are* other types of sequence in conversation, but a very broad range of the sequences we find organized as systematic expansions of adjacency pairs. And at least some sequences which may not be *based* on adjacency pairs nonetheless have some of their parts constituted by these sequence-constructional units.

We started by considering the basic, minimal form of the adjacency pair and its constitutive features – two turns, by different speakers, adjacently positioned, one recognizably a first pair part (FPP, or F), the other recognizably a second pair part (SPP, or S), with the two drawn from the same pair (or sequence) type. We noted that most sequence types can take more than one type of SPP, though not all; that there are turn types or moves alternative to SPPs which can be done in the turn after an FPP, most of which are understood by the parties to simply defer the SPP (and for good cause), but at least one of which – the counter – works differently and reverses the directionality of the sequence.

We sketched the relevance rules informing the operation of adjacency pairs, and how they can work in the environment after an FPP to provide for the parties (and for us as external observers) what someone is *not doing* when they are silent, and which shape in a major way what recipients of an FPP will be taken to be doing in its aftermath if they *do* talk (or otherwise provide analyzably responsive conduct). Adjacency pair organization is a major locus of relevance rules – a major source for the interpretive "meaning" which parties to talk-in-interaction accord one another's utterances, and much other conduct as well. First pair parts set relevance constraints on the next turn position, and those constraints are used to understand immediately following conduct, whatever it is – coughs, words, raised eyebrows, a fixed stare, etc. Doing a relevant SPP is the prime way a recipient of a prior turn can show their understanding of what the prior turn was doing and what it made relevant to be done next, and thereby grounds that turn's efficacy as an action.

We saw that adjacency pairs can occur in the basic, minimal form of two turns, but that they more often get expanded, and can be expanded in one or more of the three places made available by a two-turn structure, and we described a variety of pre-expansions, insert-expansions, and post-expansions. The consequence of such expansion possibilities (and of the ties which can bind a succession of sequences into a *sequence* of sequences) is that very long stretches of talk indeed can develop, which are constructed in their course by the participants – and are understood in their course by the participants – by reference to the expansion of a basic adjacency pair. For us as external analysts, as a consequence, they cannot be otherwise properly understood.

How to use this book, part 1

The single most troublesome misunderstanding harbored by those just exposed to conversation analysis, or still coming to terms with it, is that the work of analysis is done when a bit of data is recognized as belonging to some category, and the category term is applied to the data fragment. But that is a taxonomic act, not an analytic one. It locates one possible feature of the event being examined, but not how that event was achieved in its particularity – in *those* words or physical actions, by *that* participant, at *that* point in the interaction, understood in *that* way by co-participants, produced by some *specifiable practices* of conduct. The formal features do not add up to an analysis until they are filled out by the particulars that constituted that achieved event and relate it to what has come before and what interpretive shadow is cast on what is to follow.

To show what this means, let us take a stretch of talk, some of whose parts should be recognizable by a reasonably careful and serious reader of the book to this point. Let us use the analytic resources that have been developed here to reconnoiter the data, to characterize its formal shape and course, and thereby prepare it for an analysis of the actions that compose it in detail, and whose details make it what it is. And then we will have one pass, however partial and rough, at analyzing in detail how the particulars of the contributions of the parties to this stretch of talk constitute it as an instance of the sequence-organizational character we have attributed to it, and how these particulars add new understanding of what is going on over and above the formal characterization of its sequence-organizational structure. Such an analysis of the actions and their sequencing – encompassing both their formal trans-situational character and its local, particularizing realization – is needed for the episode to be understood properly by us as analysts, and, if we are right, as they were understood by the participants.

In Extract (14.01), Arthur has called Rebecca, both of them young aspirants to places in the movie/television world based in Los Angeles. In the seven or so minutes preceding the start of the transcript below and its associated sound, they have talked about their respective career trajectories since they last talked (which, from the manner of their talk, was not very long ago). Both of them seem to be doing well, and when the talk turns to a project they would both be involved in (together with other friends) but for Arthur's continuing hesitancy about making a commitment, he exits the topic by talking about how gratifying it is to have a steady source of income, and they both celebrate their good fortune. This leads to talk about a project at a major studio where Arthur has recently been hired, and it is with the latter part of that recounting by Arthur that the transcript below begins.

```
(14.01) Arthur and Rebecca, 9:27-11:17
 1 Art:  . . . , (0.8) and then now thee: thee new owner's ABC wan
 2       thirty hours.
 3       (0.5)
 4 Art:  >So they c'n s-< sell more ti:me;
 5       (0.2)
 6 Art:  um:.hhh <So anyway they're fighting about budget
 7       now an:: w'll find out October twenny eighth.
 8       (0.8)
 9 Art:  and then if- if it's a yes:: October twenny eighth,
10       (0.2) then- u:m:::: (0.8) then I can work there until
11       nineteen eighty eight °if=
12       =[I wan to huh huh .hhh hah hah hah hah
13 Reb:  =[.hhh huh hah hah hah .hhh hah hah hah .hhh hhh
14 Art:  ( ) but then if it's no::, then: everybody goes that
15       da:y.
16 Reb:  [Oh god
17 Art:  [(Everybody) goes ho:me.
18       (.)
19 Art:  uh But they've already spent like several million
20       dollars already.
21 Reb:  Uh huh
```

```
22 Art:  So ugh: uh: s- this is now playing with numbers.
23 Reb:  Yeah
24 Art:  °So: (.) I dunno.=
25 Reb:  =Listen I've gotta go cuz I'm gonna go t'dance class;
26 Art:  Okay:=
27 Reb:  =But um (.) I'll be home- <What're you doing this
28       evening.
29 Art:  Uh: nothing, (.) What d'yuh do- do somet'n?=
30 Reb:  Um sure I w's j's thinking we c'd talk (0.2)
31 Art:  Okay=
32 Reb:  =some mo:re, or: (.) or maybe we could go out to
33       movie or something.
34 Art:  Oh okay
35 Reb:  °(        )=
36 Art:  =Sure
37 Reb:  [So- ]
38 Art:  [I'm-] I'm going over to Laurie's right now.
39 Reb:  Oh good=
40 Art:  =Give her some t'matoes.
41 Reb:  Oh how ni:[c e   ]
42 Art:            [You w]ant some tomatoes?
43 Reb:  [Um: (0.8) [S u:re ]
44 Art:  [( )       [Y'have-] -ehhhh sh::(h)ure. .hhh
45       And green beans? 'e got lots of green beans.=
46 Reb:  Su:re. .hhh Anyway um see if she wants to do
47       >something.u-I gotta go< tuh: UCLA::. en study
48       French? uh fer the afternoo[:n
49 Art:                             [Okay,
50 Reb:  And I oughta be home about five thirty or si:x.
51 Art:  Oh okay so I'll talk to you later.
52 Reb:  [Okay
53 Art:  [see what happens
54 Reb:  Grea:t
55 Art:  kay b[ye  ]
56 Reb:       [<Or] maybe we can just have um (0.5) some in-
57       enchiladas andum °what are those things
58 Art:  Oh tamales?=
59 Reb:  =Tamales huh [huh huh
60 Art:               [hhh But then yih have to get them now
61       though. [so that's a has[sle=
62 Reb:          [°oh-            [(Oh)/(So) forget it
63 Art:  So forget it.=
64 Reb:  =Okay I'll talk to you later
65 Art:  Okay
66 Reb:  Okay=[bye
67 Art:       [Bye
68       ((Hang up))
```

To go to work on this using the resources of sequence organization as what we can call "the key" – the technical instrument which we use to enhance our technical access to the data – there are basically three ways to proceed.

One of them might start by marking all the smallest sequences and then building up from there to see what larger structures they compose. So, we might register simple, two-turn adjacency pair sequences at lines 25–26, 27–29a (if there are two distinct turn-constructional units in a turn, we will refer to them as "a" and "b"), 29b–30a, 42–43, and so forth. In doing so, we might recognize that at line 32 Rebecca is continuing her utterance at line 30 and that at line 34 Arthur is re-receiving that utterance by Rebecca.

We might then try to characterize the actions or courses of action in which each of these sequences is engaged or implicated. So Rebecca's line 25 is an announcement in basic format, though it surely seems to be the vehicle for some other action(s) as well, and Arthur's reply exhibits not so much receipt of news as alignment with an action. The sequence at lines 42–43 invites recognition as an offer sequence, with a rather ambivalent response – a preferred acceptance token delivered as if dispreferred in being delayed by both the "um" and the pause. And so forth.

A second way of proceeding starts by finding the largest units that can be identified and then finding the smaller sequences which are organized by it and within it. So we might begin by noting that Rebecca's turn at line 25 appears to be launching a closing of the conversation, an action that gets its initial response in Arthur's line 26, and its final disposition with the hanging up at line 68. But we might note next that relatively little of the talk between those two boundaries is overtly addressed to closing the conversation, and look further to find the next largest (or just large) sequence we can.

We might then note that Rebecca's turn at lines 30b–32–33 looks like an FPP proposing an arrangement for getting together that gets an aligning SPP at line 34, and that after what looks like an intrusion of unrelated talk, gets re-issued with modification at lines 46–47–48–50 (with a further extension after the initial "bye" of a closing exchange). There are smaller sequences that are components of this larger one, but notice that *their* boundaries may be drawn differently here than they were using our first line of approach – for example, whether the utterances at lines 31 or 34 are correctly understood as an SPP or as SCT.

A third way of proceeding starts by registering things that present themselves as familiar and recognizable to the analyst (if the preceding alternatives had not), and then seeing where that leads. So, for example, we might note that Rebecca's turn at lines 27–28 has the familiar profile of a pre-expansion FPP, and that Arthur's turn at line 29 has the familiar profile of a preferred, go-ahead response.

What kind of pre-expansion is it? Well, it is not entirely clear whether it is a pre-invitation or a pre-arrangement-making, but it may not be necessary at this point to resolve the matter; its ambiguity may be a designed feature of the turn, so "clarifying" what/which it is would be just the wrong thing to do by insisting on making clear something that had been designed to *not* be clear.

In any case, whichever of the possible alternatives we consider, it seems clear that "nothing" would be the preferred SPP, advancing the progress of the projected sequence. And that is what Arthur delivers in line 29a; and he goes on to display his understanding of the action import of Rebecca's turn (as if his "nothing" had not already done so) by articulating it himself in the form of a question, hastily spoken but apparently designed to be something like "y'wanna do something?"

We are thereby brought to a different analysis of lines 29b–30 and 31 than the one we arrived at using our first way of proceeding. There we took note of the question in the second TCU of Arthur's turn at line 30 and treated it as an FPP; Rebecca's next turn was then seen as an SPP, and Arthur's at line 34 as possibly an SCT. In this third way of approaching the analysis, Rebecca's turn at lines 27–28 is understood as a pre-sequence FPP, and Arthur's at line 29a as a go-ahead SPP. Arthur's addition of the second TCU at 29b makes fully explicit his understanding of the action import of Rebecca's preceding turn, and Rebecca's virtually redundant response at line 30a confirms that understanding. The continuation of her turn at lines 30 and 32–33 is, then, the base FPP, with Arthur's lines 31, 34, and 36 as the base SPP.

The last of these analyses is the most satisfactory, but this does not mean the third path of analysis will always be the best. Indeed, they are not mutually exclusive alternatives. Starting with any of them will get an analyst into a position to examine the data technically, and may enhance one's capacity to see technically on any of the three paths I have described, and alternatives to them that others may find more congenial.

That said, the task of this chapter being set before you, the reader, has barely begun. The goal here is to make clear how the kind of *formal* analysis of sequence organization which this book has been designed to present – analysis which is of necessity maximally trans-situational – needs to be complemented by examination of the idiosyncratic, contextually specific details that make this *kind* of action sequence into this *singular* sequence of that kind – in *its* context, with *these* parties, at *this* point in the interaction, doing actions inflected by *these* circumstances, etc.

This is no more a separate task from the one that has occupied most of the pages of this book than the "heads" side of a coin is a separate thing from the "tails" side. But it cannot be given the same amount of space here; that must be reserved to a separate publication. Still, we should do enough here to make clear and accessible the character of the relationship between "sequence organization" as a formal structure and the interactional analysis of actions done in turns and courses of action done through sequences of turns. The following paragraphs are meant to deliver on this commitment.

How to use this book, part 2

We can begin with the exchange at lines 25–26, which we remarked on earlier as a minimal adjacency pair. We noted then that the basic design of the FPP is that of a telling or announcement, but the uptake in the SPP conveys an alignment with an action, not a receipt of news. Now we can add that the action the FPP is doing is moving to close the conversation. It does so in a fashion available to call recipients, though not exclusive to them. Ordinarily, it is *callers* who broach the possibility of closing, by making it clear that they there is nothing further that they are committed to taking up in the conversation, and that they are prepared to close unless the call recipient has something they want to take up (Schegloff and Sacks, 1973; Schegloff, 1986); the recipient can then elect to introduce some new sequence or topic, or can align with the caller's preparedness to proceed to the closing of the conversation; this way of proceeding is, then, designed to be consensual. When call *recipients* move to close, on the other hand, they are much more likely to do so unilaterally by invoking some reason that prompts the relevance for them of closing *now*. (Callers may, of course, also invoke such grounds for moving to close, but it is a more marked practice for them.) This practice is embodied in Rebecca's turn at line 25 first, by casting it in the language of necessity or constraint ("I've gotta go") and, second, by offering an account of the basis for this necessity or constraint.

In addition to these compositional features of Rebecca's turn, its positioning also figures in the action she is doing. In the just-preceding turns, the topic on which Arthur had been holding forth – the imminence of a decision by the company he has gone to work for that could either entail work for a long time or a quick exit – is brought to possible completion by way of a sequence/topic-closing sequence: the aphoristic summing up (at line 22) of what has preceded, the aligning response by Rebecca at line 23, and, continuing the gradient to lower volume, the closure with a free-standing "so" (Raymond, 2004) and an epistemic "shrug" ("I dunno") at line 24.

A sequence having been brought to possible closure, this is a place, then, that is ripe for the launching of a new topic or sequence. And it is in this place that Rebecca hastens to claim the turn (note the latching of her turn start at line 25 to the end of the prior turn) to block the start of something new by Arthur, and to use that turn position to launch a new sequence that makes relevant as the next thing to be done movement toward closing the conversation. In the next turn Arthur aligns with this move by Rebecca.

What might one expect next? One possibility is immediately ending the conversation by an exchange of "bye byes," as in Extract (14.02):

(14.02) Closings #139
```
1 Ann: Weh then call me back when yer finished.=I gotta get
2      Ronnie off t'the market mother, it's si[x thirty. ]
3 Bon:                                        [Yeah I (wi]ll)=
4 Ann: =Guh by:e:.=
5 Bon: =Bye.
```

But, as is exhibited even in this quick closing, it is common to include
some reference to future interaction. One virtually formulaic usage is some
version of "(So) I'll talk to you." This sort of element, and such an expression
of it, is not special to "gotta go"-initiated closings, whether launched by
caller or recipient, but it does occur in them, as can be seen in Extracts
(14.03) to (14.05).

(14.03) Debbie and Shelley, 6
```
1 Deb:       [And that's-] that's the only thing I'm
2       ->   sayin,<anyway, I gotta get goin,<'cause
3            I'm at work.
4 She:  ->   °okay° ((whisper voice))
5 Deb:  ->   So: I'll talk to ya later.
6 She:       okay
7 Deb:       bye
8 She:       bye
9            ((hang up))
```

(14.04) Closings #124
```
1 Ali:->  . . . >I gotta hurry en make a telephone call becu' it's
2         almost five an' I gotta call these people by five,< =
3 Bet:->  =.hhh Okay baby well I'll be down there t'morrow so
4         I'[ll talk to you (to) the store:.            ]=
5 Ali:->    [Okay. (I'll be talking to you tomorrow.)]=
6 Bet:    =EeYeah.
7         (.)
8 Ali:    Oka:[y:.
9 Bet:        [Bye sweetie.
10        (.)
11 Ali:   Buh bye.
```

(14.05) Closings #1
```
1 And:    But they were so tasty. Hih!
2 Bel:    Yea:[:h. ]
3 And:        [huh!] huh!
4         (0.2)
5 Bel:->  E::u::l.=.hhh Well I haftuh go huhhh [huh huh]=
6 And:->                                       [ Y e s ]
7 Bel:->  =[huh! So]:: (.) [I'll tal]k to you lader.=
8 And:     [(    )]        [(goo:d) ]
9 And:    =O[kay.]=
10 Bel:     [.hhh]=
```

```
11 Bel      =Okay.
12          (.)
13 And:     Buh bye,=
14 Bel:     =Buh bye,
```

And, indeed, we find it in the Arthur and Rebecca call as well – at line 51, at line 64, and, very likely, incipiently at line 37. But that is not what follows Rebecca's "gotta go" and Arthur's alignment with it.

```
(14.06) Arthur and Rebecca, 10:10-12 (previously [14.01])
25 Reb:  =Listen I've gotta go cuz I'm gonna go t'dance class;
26 Art:  Okay:=
27 Reb:  =But um (.) I'll be home- <What're you doing this
28       evening.
```

It is in this place that what we earlier recognized as a pre-expansion (whether pre-invitation or pre-arrangement-making) is articulated – the place after a unilateral move to close the conversation at a place where one topic-talking sequence had been brought to a close, and another might have been started. But, actually, this is *not* where the "What're you doing this evening" has been placed; two other things have been placed there first. And, just as the prior occurrence of the unilateral move to close can inform the understanding of "What're you doing this evening," so can the other components of the turn that precede it.

For example, the "But um" moves immediately to project a counterbalance to the imminent and unilateral rupture in the interaction which Rebecca has just announced; and noticing that can lead us to notice as well the equivocal intonation contour at the end of the turn at line 25, marked with a semicolon – that is, both a comma and a period – to register its hearability either as possibly final or as continuative. That is, the projected counterbalance has been delivered as a hearable continuation of the same utterance, and thereby as an already available incipient remedy for the utterance's first part.

So, in a place where a vague and virtually formulaic invocation of future communication could go ("So I'll talk to you later" in Extracts [14.03] to [14.05]) and quickly advance the course of the talk toward a terminal exchange, "But um" prefigures a quite different sequel in the works. That sequel's next element starts to be an announcement of later availability (when re-done to completion at line 50, it announces the time of availability), but it is cut off mid-course, but far enough into it to make plainly accessible what it is doing. Before committing herself to being home and available to do something, Rebecca first moves to get on the record *Arthur's* availability; yet getting "I'll be home" said first (line 27) shows that the question "What are you doing?" is not being asked idly; she "has something in mind"; and having projected imminent closure of the conversation, she has shown that no extended account of "what he is doing this evening" is in order. So this saying of "What're you doing this evening" (lines 27–28) carries with it all the inflections, constraints, and promissory possibilities afforded by this specific context in which it occurs and by which, and *for* which, it has been shaped.

Let us take a moment to take stock of the foregoing pages. We recognized in the form of the utterance "What are you doing this evening?" a practice of sequence construction. Earlier in this book we had characterized the class of practices (of which this is one) as "pre-expansions." By this we meant that by the production of an utterance of this form in an appropriate sequential environment, a speaker can show, and a recipient can understand, that the utterance – in this case, a question – is being said not on its own behalf, so to speak, but on behalf of something else, whose production is contingent on the response to this utterance. So it is not simply a question requesting information; it is a sounding board for the recipient's likely stance toward an action of a determinate sort – here, making an arrangement or broaching a possible arrangement already planned. All this is part of a formal account of this sort of practice, type-specific pre-expansion, and this particular variety of, pre-invitation/arrangement-making. Put this way, it takes no note of the particular place in a particular interaction, the particular participants, and the particular proposal. And yet any real occurrence of such an utterance, embodying such a practice, will be said in a real place (the form of whose characterization itself remains to be specified), by a real speaker, standing in a determinate relationship to its targeted recipient, etc. This is the research specification of one of the epigraphs to this book, taken from Goethe: "The general and the particular converge; the particular is the general, appearing under various conditions."

In "How to use this book, part 1," and in the earlier section on pre-expansion, we were concerned to provide an account – a formal, trans-situational account, a "general" account in Goethe's terms – of this practice. But even in those discussions, in providing exemplars of what was being described the practice was inhabited by the local particulars of the circumstances from which the exemplar was taken. Because we were there trying to depict the formal aspects of the practice, we minimized attention to that order of detail. But the general always in real life (as compared to invented or roughly remembered examples for academic convenience) presents itself infused with its particulars, and it is not thoroughly understood without them. Of course, some of the details that we treat as particularizing aspects of the context may themselves be describable formally as the embodiment of some other practice. For example, in characterizing the placement of Rebecca's pre-expansion, we had occasion to remark on the launching of a closing of this conversation, and, as it happens, that set of practices – practices for closing conversation – is also amenable to more formal characterization (see, for a start, Schegloff and Sacks, 1973).

The upshot of these remarks is, again, to emphasize that saying of some turn (or turn-constructional unit, or series of turns) that it is a pre-invitation, or an insert expansion, or a repair sequence, etc. is not the *end* of analysis; indeed, it is not even the *beginning* of analysis. It is the *preparation* of a bit of the target data for analytic inspection, with a candidate possible direction of analysis ready for assessment. The last several pages were meant to make clear the difference between a simple labeling of something as "pre-expansion," and the particularized specification of what is going on interactionally here. The next several paragraphs will extend this specification of the actions getting done in this sequence to provide at least a modicum of closure.

```
(14.07)Arthur and Rebecca, 10:10-22 (previously [14.01])
25 Reb:  =Listen I've gotta go cuz I'm gonna go t'dance class;
26 Art:  Okay:=
27 Reb:  =But um (.) I'll be home- <What're you doing this
28       evening.
29 Art:  Uh: nothing, (.) What d'yuh do- do somet'n?=
30 Reb:  Um sure I w's j's thinking we c'd talk (0.2)
31 Art:  Okay=
32 Reb:  =some mo:re, or: (.) or maybe we could go out to
33       movie or something.
34 Art:  Oh okay
35 Reb:  °(    )=
36 Art:  =Sure
37 Reb:  [So- ]
38 Art:  [I'm-] I'm going over to Laurie's right now.
```

Arthur's "uh nothing" (at line 29) responds to what Rebecca ended up having said and done, and he could have stopped there. But, although his reply of "nothing" is the preferred go-ahead SPP to the pre-sequence, it has been produced with a tinge of dispreference – the delaying "uh" that precedes it. His addition of a second turn-constructional unit to the turn is a more proactive move to advance the sequence to its base FPP, and to show that he had heard not only what Rebecca had said, but also what she was *doing* by the saying of it, and that he was aligning with the project that it pre-figured.[1]

"What d'yuh do- do som'ng?" seems to be an amalgam of "Whuddiyuh wanna do" and "Y'wanna do something?" except the "wanna" gets lost. Rebecca's "sure" (at line 30) shows her to have had (at least) the latter hearing. The "um" that precedes it registers that there is some trouble here, something that has for the moment retarded the progress of the sequence. There is no lack of candidates for what this may be: perhaps a bit of trouble in unscrambling the grammar, perhaps the redundancy entailed by Arthur's offering for confirmation the "plain" import of Rebecca's prior turn. The simplest and most straightforward form for this kind of sequence

[1] Note that "Y'wanna do something," in showing *his* understanding that her turn was doing a pre-invitation or pre-planning move, thereby grounds *our* analysis along those lines.

construction is the minimal one: pre-expansion FPP, pre-expansion SPP, base FPP. Anything more is possible trouble, and is accountable; and here there is something more: more in the pre-expansion SPP – namely, an FPP; and that in turn makes relevant something more in the base FPP turn – namely an SPP. Here again we are dealing with local, contextual particulars, not incorporated in the general or formal organization of sequences, but requiring and getting local management – which is marked by the "um."[2]

What was projected to be Rebecca's base FPP now has the cast of a response to Arthur's question whether she wants to "do something," and we now can see that, however ill formed a part of the sequence, Arthur's question casts a persistent shadow over what follows. Rebecca answers first with a something that is *not* a something – "talk . . . some more"; then she offers a possible "something" – a movie; and then she provides a place for him to offer another alternative – "or something." What this suggests is that this course of action was launched with an eye toward redressing the rupture introduced at line 25 by proposing the resuming of the talk – a possibility grounded in her addition of "some more" to the first option in her three-part list (Jefferson, 1990). Her starting this TCU with "I was just thinking" can then be understood as conveying almost literally what was being pre-figured in her question "What are you doing this evening," in its exact positioning – that is, asked after saying "I'll be home"; after saying, in effect, we have to stop this conversation. But Arthur's question about "doing something" makes relevant a different class of possibilities – "things one does" – of which "movie" is more or less a prototype.

And here we have another possible trouble that can have figured in the "um sure" that preceded this proposing of arrangements. Now, it appears, we can in fact entertain what had previously seemed improbable – that Rebecca would be marking as dispreferred what Arthur had offered as forwarding "her sequence." His asking about "doing something" has upgraded the character of what she meant to be proposing from simply continuing the conversation she now had to break off to engaging in the kind of activity that counts as "doing something" – like going to a movie or going out to eat. It is this untoward upgrading whose rejection it would be awkward to bring off that she marks as problematic by her "um sure."

There is more that can be said about the elements of this sequence we have partially addressed, and obviously much to be said about the elements we will have to leave unaddressed. Dealing with them would require, as the preceding pages have required, blending the formal structuring of sequence organization with the particulars of this sequence in this place. It would also

---

[2] Note that it would miss the mark to insist on deploying here the common analysis of such a delay of an SPP discussed earlier in the discussion of preference/dispreference (at p. 68); namely, that Rebecca, by delaying her "sure" with "um," is displaying a disinclination to "do something."

require analytic tools that have informed the preceding discussion without having been named as such – the organization of turns and their component turn-constructional units; the overall structural organization of the unit "a single conversation," of which closings are a component and which therefore figures centrally in understanding this sequence; the organization of word selection which underlies the import of "doing something" as it figures in this sequence, etc. These analytic tools are taken up elsewhere. But there is more that can be done before seeking out those other tools in those other places.

Re-beginning

Anyone who has re-read a novel, seen a movie more than once, listened again and again to a piece of music, or followed a sustained argument from start to finish knows that it is one thing to read or see or hear for the first time – not knowing what lies ahead and how it turns out – and it is quite another to engage the work from its beginning while knowing from the outset where it is going, what one only learned eventually the first time through. It is no different with this work.

While it is still fresh in mind, it will repay the effort to go back to the start and work through what has been presented here with the overview and sophistication that has been acquired from the first pass. On the subsequent pass(es), read with the critical edge supplied by previous exposure. Analyze the data for yourself and find where the analysis in the text seems problematic. Most importantly, use what was learned from the later pages in re-examining the earlier pages, and, in particular, using what has been gleaned from this chapter and its focus on the contextual particularity that inescapably complements the formal organization, to (re-)analyze for yourself the data extracts throughout this book.

And then get your own data, and do it again, and again, and again.

What, then, when all is said and done, is sequence organization all about? The organization of practices for turn-taking serves to provide for the *distribution of opportunities to talk* among parties to an interaction. The organization of practices for constructing turns-at-talk serves to shape *what is said in those opportunities, and how*. The practices of action formation allow the *composition* of a turn (or of a TCU, or of a part of a TCU), in the *position* in which it is placed, to constitute *some possible recognizable action*, and to be understandable as some possible action – that is, *what is* done *in those opportunities*. Sequence organization – organized around its core sequential practice and unit, the adjacency pair – relates a series of these productions into *coherent courses of action*, and thereby harnesses the resources of talk-in-interaction to getting things done. More specifically, because of its prospective operation, the adjacency pair is the prime resource in conversation for getting something to happen, because it provides a determinate *place* for it to happen – next.[3]

The bearing of sequence organization is, of course, not limited to the end point of what I have made to sound like an assembly line; its structures and practices inform the distribution of opportunities to talk and what is made of those opportunities as much as *they* constitute *it*. All of these organizations of practice (turn-taking, turn organization, action formation, and sequence organization) and others (repair, word selection, and overall structural organization) operate together all the time to inform the participants' co-construction of the observable, actual conduct in interaction that is the prima facie, bottom-line stuff of social life. Only by observing them all together will we understand how the stuff of social life comes to be as it is. Only by understanding them one by one will we get into a position to observe them all together.

---

[3] As we wrote over thirty years ago (Schegloff and Sacks, 1973:297):

> The type of problem adjacency pairs are specially fitted for, and the way they are specially suited for its solution, may very briefly be characterized as follows. Given the utterance by utterance organization of turn-taking, unless close ordering is attempted there can be no methodic assurance that a more or less eventually aimed-for successive utterance or utterance type will ever be produced. If a next speaker does not do it, that speaker may provide for a further next that should not do it (or should do something that is not it); and, if what follows that next is "free" and does not do the originally aimed-for utterance, it (i.e., the utterance placed there) may provide for a yet further next that does not do it, etc. Close ordering is, then, the basic generalized means for assuring that some desired event will ever happen. If it cannot be made to happen next, its happening is not merely delayed, but may never come about. The adjacency pair technique, in providing a determinate "when" for it to happen, i.e., "next", has then means for handling the close order problem, where that problem has its import, through its control of the assurance that some relevant event will be made to occur.

Appendix 1: Conversation-analytic transcript symbols

This set of notational conventions was first developed by Gail Jefferson (1978a, 1983a, 1983b, 1985, 1996). It continues to evolve and adapt both to the work of analysis, the developing skill of transcribers, and changes in technology. Not all symbols have been included here, and some symbols in some data sources are not used systematically or consistently. An online module with sound illustrations is available at http://www.sscnet.ucla.edu/soc/faculty/schegloff/TranscriptionProject/.

Temporal and sequential relationships
Overlapping or simultaneous talk is indicated in a variety of ways.

⌈
⌊   A left bracket bridging two lines indicates a point of overlap onset, whether at the start of an utterance or later.

[
[Separate left square brackets on two successive lines with utterances by different speakers indicates the same thing.

⌉
⌋   A right bracket bridging two lines indicates a point at which two overlapping utterances both end, where one ends while the other continues, or simultaneous moments in overlaps which continue.

]
]   Separate right square brackets on two successive lines with utterances by different speakers indicates the same thing.

//   In some older transcripts (cited in some papers you will read), a double slash indicates the point at which a current speaker's utterance is overlapped by the talk of another, which appears on the next line attributed to another speaker. If there is more than one double slash in an utterance, then the second indicates where a second overlap begins, the overlapping talk appearing on the next line attributed to another speaker, etc. In transcripts using the //

*   notation for overlap onset, the end of the overlap may be marked by right brackets (as above) or by an asterisk.

So, the following are alternative ways of representing the same event (TG, 1:35–36):

```
35  Ava:  I 'av [a lotta   t]ough cou:rses.
36  Bee:        [Uh really?]
```

```
35  Ava:  I 'av [a lotta   t]ough cou:rses.
36  Bee:        [Uh really?]
```

```
35  Ava:  I 'av // a lotta t*ough cou:rses.
36  Bee:  Uh really?
```

Bee's "Uh really?" overlaps Ava's talk starting at "a" and ending at the "t" of "tough."

=   Equals signs ordinarily come in pairs – one at the end of a line and another at the start of the next line or one shortly thereafter. They are used are used to indicate two things:

   1. If the two lines connected by the equal signs are by the same speaker, then there was a single, continuous utterance with no break or pause, which was broken up in order to accommodate the placement of overlapping talk. For example, TG, 2: 18–23:

```
18 Bee: In the gy:m? [(hh)
19 Ava:              [Yea:h. Like grou(h)p therapy.Yuh know
20      [half the grou]p thet we had la:s' term wz there en we=
21 Bee: [O h : : : .  ]˙hh
22 Ava: =[jus' playing arou:nd.
23 Bee: =[˙hh
```

   Ava's talk at lines 20 and 22 is continuous, but room has been made for Bee's overlapping talk at line 21.

   2. If the lines connected by two equal signs are by different speakers, then the second followed the first with no discernible silence between them, or was "latched" to it.

(0.5) Numbers in parentheses indicate silence, represented in tenths of a second; what is given here in the left margin indicates 0.5 second of silence. Silences may be marked either within an utterance or between utterances, as in the excerpts from TG, 3:03–04 and 3:15–17 below:

```
 3 Bee: ˙hhh Uh::, (0.3) I don'know I guess she's aw- she's
 4      awright she went to thee uh:: hhospital again tihda:y,
```

```
15 Bee: Tch!.hh So uh I don't kno:w,
16      (0.3)
17 Bee: En:=
```

(·) A dot in parentheses indicates a "micropause," hearable but not readily measurable; ordinarily less than 0.2 second.

Various symbols and combinations of symbols are used to represent various aspects of speech delivery, such as some aspects of intonation.

. The punctuation marks are *not* used grammatically, but to indicate intonation. The period indicates a falling, or final, intonation contour, not necessarily the end of a sentence.

? Similarly, a question mark indicates rising intonation, not necessarily a question, and a comma indicates continuing intonation, not necessarily a clause boundary. In some

, transcript fragments, a combined question mark and comma indicates a rise stronger than a comma but weaker than a question mark. Because this symbol cannot be produced by

¿ the computer, the inverted question mark (¿) is now used for

: : this purpose. Colons are used to indicate the prolongation or stretching of the sound just preceding them. The more colons, the longer the stretching. On the other hand, graphically stretching a word on the page by inserting blank spaces between the letters does *not* necessarily indicate how it was pronounced; it is used to allow alignment with overlapping talk. Thus in TG, 3:26–31,

```
26 Bee: Tch! (M'n)/(En ) they can't delay much lo:nguh they
27      [jus' wannid] uh- `hhh=
28 Ava: [ O h   :   . ]
29 Bee: =yihknow have anothuh consulta:tion,
30 Ava: Ri::ght.
31 Bee: En then deci::de.
```

the words "right" in line 30, and "decide" in line 31, are more stretched than "oh" in line 28, even though "oh" appears to occupy more space. But "oh" has only one colon, and the others have two; "oh" has been spaced out so that its brackets will align with the talk in line 27 with which it is in overlap.

word Underlining is used to indicate some form of stress or emphasis,
word either by increased loudness or higher pitch. The more
WOrd underlining, the greater the emphasis. Therefore, underlining
wOrd sometimes is placed under the first letter or two of a word, rather than under the letters which are actually raised in pitch or volume. Especially loud talk may be indicated by upper case; again, the louder, the more upper case. And, in extreme cases, upper case may be underlined.

° The degree sign indicates that the talk following it was markedly
°° quiet or soft. When there are two degree signs, the talk beween them is markedly softer than the talk around it.

-          A hyphen after a word or part of a word indicates a cut-off or
           self-interruption.

Combinations of underlining and colons are used to indicate intonation
contours.

_: If the letter(s) preceding a colon is underlined, then there is a
           falling intonation contour.
:   If a colon is itself underlined, then there is a rising intonation
           contour, or inflection. So, in TG, 2:18-29,

```
18 Bee:  In the gy:m? [(hh)
19 Ava:               [Yea:h. Like grou(h)p therapy.Yuh know
20        [half the grou]p thet we had la:s' term wz there en we=
21 Bee:  [ O h : : : . ] ˙hh
22 Ava:  =[jus' playing arou:nd.
23 Bee:  =[˙hh
24 Bee:  Uh-fo[oling around.
25 Ava:       [˙hhh
26 Ava:  Eh-yeah so, some a' the guys who were bedder y'know wen'
27        off by themselves so it wz two girls against this one guy
28        en he's ta:ll.Y'know? [˙hh
29 Bee:                         [ Mm hm?
```

           The "Oh" at line 21 has an upward inflection while it is being
           stretched (even though it ends with falling intonation, as
           indicated by the period). On the other hand, "tall" on line 28 is
           inflected downward ("bends downward," so to speak, over and
           above its "period intonation").
↑↓   The up and down arrows mark sharper intonation rises or falls
           than would be indicated by combinations of colons and
           underlining, or may mark a whole shift, or resetting, of the pitch
           register at which the talk is being produced.
> <   The combination of "more than" and "less than" symbols
           indicates that the talk between them is compressed or rushed.
           Used in the reverse order, they can indicate that a stretch
< >   of talk is markedly slowed or drawn out. The "less than" symbol
           by itself indicates that the immediately following talk is
           "jump-started," i.e., sounds like it starts with a rush
<   (sometimes referred to as a "left push").
hhh   Hearable aspiration is shown where it occurs in the talk by the
           letter "h" – the more "hs," the more aspiration. The aspiration
           may represent breathing, laughter, etc. If it occurs inside the
(hh)   boundaries of a word, it may be enclosed in parentheses in order
           to set it apart from the sounds of the word (as in TG, 2:12–13,
           below). If the aspiration is an inhalation, it is

· hh   shown with a dot before it (usually a raised dot).

```
12 Bee:                                          [Ba::]sk(h)et=
13        b(h)a(h)ll? (h)[°Whe(h)re.)
```

{}   Curly braces are sometimes used to indicate the duration of a
           breath or other sound when its effect can be heard as a pause or
           gap of silence. Both the breath or other sound and the duration
           are in parentheses separated by a slash, the whole enclosed in
           curly braces, as in:

```
I don' know if it's po:ssible, but {(°hhh)/(0.2)} see I
haveta open up the ba:nk.hh
```

           Here the in-breath can be heard as a pause of 0.2 seconds

Other markings

(( ))   Double parentheses are used to mark transcriber's
           descriptions of events, rather than representations of them.
           Thus ((cough)), ((sniff)), ((telephone rings)), ((footsteps)),
           ((whispered)), ((pause)), etc.

( )   When all or part of an utterance is in parentheses, or the
           speaker identification is, this indicates uncertainty on the
           transcriber's part, but represents a likely possibility. Empty
           parentheses indicate that something is being said, but no
           hearing (or, in some cases, speaker identification) can be
           achieved.

(a)/(uh)   Alternative hearings of the same strip of talk are displayed
           by putting the alternative hearings in parentheses, separated
           by a single oblique or slash, as in TG, 1:31:

```
31 Bee: °(Bu::t.)=/°(Goo:d.)=
```

           Here, the degree marks show that the utterance is very soft.
           The transcript remains indeterminate between "But" and
           "Good." Each is in parentheses and they are separated by a
           slash.

Appendix 2: Transcript of a telephone call

This transcript is provided to allow the reader to put various brief data extracts into a more generous context than was feasible in the text, and to allow discussion of longer sequences without filling pages of text with pages of transcript. The sound for which this is the transcript is available at http://www.cambridge.org/9780521532792.

TG

```
1:01  Ava:  H'llo:?
1:02  Bee:  hHi:,
1:03  Ava:  Hi:?
1:04  Bee:  hHowuh you:?
1:05  Ava:  Oka:::y?hh=
1:06  Bee:  =Good.=Yihs[ou:nd ] hh
1:07  Ava:            [<I wan]'dih know if yih got a-uh:m
1:08        wutchimicawllit. A:: pah(hh)khing place °th's mornin'. ˙hh
1:09  Bee:  A pa:rking place,
1:10  Ava:  Mm hm,
1:11        (0.4)
1:12  Bee:  Whe:re.
1:13  Ava:  t! Oh: just anypla(h)ce? I wz jus' kidding yuh.
1:14  Bee:  Nno?=
1:15  Ava:  =[(°No).]
1:16  Bee:  =[W h y ] whhat'sa mattuh with y-Yih sou[nd HA:PPY,] hh
1:17  Ava:                                         [ Nothing. ]
1:18  Ava:  u- I sound ha:p[py?]
1:19  Bee:                 [Yee]uh.
1:20        (0.3)
1:21  Ava:  No:,
1:22  Bee:  Nno:?
1:23  Ava:  No.
1:24        (0.7)
1:25  Bee:  ˙hh You [sound sorta] cheer[ful?]
1:26  Ava:         [°(Any way).]      [˙h ] How'v you bee:n.
1:27  Bee:  ˙hh Oh:: survi:ving I guess, hh[h!
```

270

```
1:28  Ava:                                  [That's good, how's (Bob),
1:29  Bee:   He's fine,
1:30  Ava:   Tha::t's goo:d,
1:31  Bee:   °(Bu::t.)=/°(Goo:d.)=
1:32  Bee:   ='n how's school going.
1:33  Ava:   Oh s:ame old shit.
1:34  Bee:   Shhhh! hh t! `hh
1:35  Ava:   I 'av [a lotta  t]ough cou:rses.
1:36  Bee:         [Uh really?]
1:37  Bee:   Oh I c'n ima:gine.=<wh'tche tol' me whatchu ta:kin(.)/(,)

2:01  Ava:   Oh Go:d I have so much wo:rk.
2:02  Bee:   Tch!
2:03         (0.4)
2:04  Bee:   Mmm.
2:05         (0.5)
2:06  Ava:   [°B't asi]de fr'm that it's a'right.
2:07  Bee:   [So what-]
2:08         (0.4)
2:09  Bee:   Wha:t?
2:10  Ava:   I'm so:: ti:yid.I j's played ba:ske'ball t'day since the
2:11         firs' time since I wz a freshm'n in hi:ghsch[ool.]
2:12  Bee:                                               [Ba::]sk(h)et=
2:13         b(h)a(h)ll? (h)[(°Whe(h)re.)
2:14  Ava:                  [Yeah fuh like an hour enna ha:[lf.]
2:15  Bee:                                                 [`hh] Where
2:16  Bee:   didju play ba:sk[etbaw.   ]
2:17  Ava:                   [(The) gy]:m.
2:18  Bee:   In the gy:m? [(hh)
2:19  Ava:                [Yea:h. Like grou(h)p therapy.
2:20         (.)
2:21  Ava:   Yuh know [half the grou]p thet we had la:s' term wz=
2:22  Bee:            [ O h : : : . ] `hh
2:23  Ava:   =there- <'n we [jus' playing arou:nd.
2:24  Bee:                  [`hh
2:25  Bee:   Uh-fo[oling around.
2:26  Ava:        [`hhh
2:27  Ava:   Eh-yeah so, some a' the guys who were bedder y'know wen'
2:28         off by themselves so it wz two girls against this one guy
2:29         en he's ta:ll.Y'know? [`hh
2:30  Bee:                         [Mm hm?
2:31  Ava:   En, I had- I wz- I couldn't stop laughin it wz the funniest
2:32         thing b't y'know you get all sweaty up'r en evrything we
2:33         didn' thing we were gonna pla:y, `hh en oh I'm knocked out.
2:34  Bee:   Nhhkhhhh! `hhhh
2:35  Ava:   Ripped about four nai:ls, 'n okhh!
2:36  Bee:   Fantastic.=
```

```
2:37  Ava:  =B't it wz fun-You sound very far away
2:38        (0.7)
2:39  Bee:  I do?
2:40  Ava:  Nyeahm.
2:41  Bee:  mNo? I'm no:t,
2:42  Ava:  Yer home? `hhh=

3:01  Bee:  =[(Mnuh,)]
3:02  Ava:  =[Oh   my] mother wannduh know how's yer grandmother.
3:03  Bee:  `hhh Uh::, (0.3) I don'know I guess she's aw- she's
3:04        awright she went to thee uh:: hhospital again tihda:y,
3:05  Ava:  Mm-hm?,
3:06  Bee:  `hh t! `hh A:n:: I guess t'day wz d'day she's supposetuh
3:07        find out if she goes in ner not.=
3:08  Ava:  =Oh. Oh::.
3:09  Bee:  Becuz they're gonna do the operation on the teeuh duct.
3:10        f[fi: rs]t. Before they c'n do t[he cata]ract ]s.
3:11  Ava:   [Mm-hm,]                        [ Right.]Yeah,]
3:12  Bee:  `hhh So I don'know I haven:'t yihknow, she wasn' home
3:13        by the t-yihknow when I lef'fer school tihday.=
3:14  Ava:  =Mm hm,
3:15  Bee:  Tch!.hh So uh I don't kno:w,
3:16        (0.3)
3:17  Bee:  En:=
3:18  Ava:  = °M[hm.
3:19  Bee:      [Well my ant went with her anyway this time,
3:20  Ava:  [Mm hm,]
3:21  Bee:  [My  mo]ther didn't go.
3:22  Ava:  Mm hm,
3:23  Bee:  t! `hhh But uh? I don'know=She probably haf to go in
3:24        soo:n though.
3:25  Ava:  Yeah.
3:26  Bee:  Tch! (M'n)/(En ) they can't delay much lo:nguh they
3:27        [jus' wannid] uh-`hhh=
3:28  Ava:  [ O h  :  . ]
3:29  Bee:  =yihknow have anothuh consulta:tion,
3:30  Ava:  Ri::ght.
3:31  Bee:  En then deci::de.
3:32        (0.3)
3:33  Bee:  B[ut u]h,
3:34  Ava:   [Oh:.]
3:35  Bee:  Eh:: who knows,
3:36        (0.5)
3:37  Ava:  I know,
3:38        (0.3)
3:39  Bee:  °You know.
3:40        (0.4)
```

```
4:01  Bee:   So, <I got some lousy cou(h)rses th(hh)is te(h)e(h)rm too.
4:02  Ava:   Kehh huh!
4:03  Bee:   ˙hhh[h  m-]
4:04  Ava:       [W-whe]n's yer uh, weh- you have one day y'only have
4:05         one course uh?
4:06  Bee:   mMo[nday en Wednesday:[s right.] That's ] my linguistics=
4:07  Ava:      [ ˙hhhh          [ O  h.  ] that's-]
4:08  Bee:   =course [hh
4:09  Ava:          [O[h, oh[ : . ]
4:10  Bee:            [ ˙hhh [This i]s (a)-/(w)- This course is a winnuh
4:11         (hh)ih really i(h)[ : s . ]
4:12  Ava:                     [Oh I ha]ve thee- I have one class in the
4:13         e:vening.
4:14  Bee:   On Mondays?
4:15  Ava:   Y-uh::: Wednesdays.=
4:16  Bee:   =Uh-Wednesday,=
4:17  Ava:   =En it's like a Mickey Mouse course. ˙hh It's a joke, hh
4:18         ih-Speech.
4:19         (0.2)
4:20  Ava:   ˙hh[hh
4:21  Bee:      [Sp[e   c  h, ]
4:22  Ava:         [It's the big]ges' jo:ke.going.=it really is.
4:23         (0.3)
4:24  Bee:   ((S[niff))
4:25  Ava:      [I figyuh I'm gonna star' talking with a lis:p en by the
4:26         end a [the term I'll get en A [because I haf to impro:ve.
4:27  Bee:         [hhhhmhh!               [ ˙hhh
4:28  Bee:   rRi::gh[t. hh
4:29  Ava:         [Yihknow I mean it's really stupidyih go up there
4:30         en jus' slop anything up en anything from there kuh be en
4:31         impro:vemint.Yih[know, it's a real Mickey Mou:se thing.=
4:32  Bee:                   [°Mmm.
4:33  Ava:   =It's really stupid. ˙hh
4:34         (0.4)
4:35  Bee:   Eh-yih have anybuddy: thet uh:? (1.2) I would know from the
4:36         English depar'mint there?
4:37  Ava:   Mm-mh. Tch! I don't think so.
4:38  Bee:   °Oh,=<Did they geh ridda Kuhleznik yet hhh

5:01  Ava:   No in fact I know somebuddy who ha:s huh [now.
5:02  Bee:                                            [Oh my got hh[hhh
5:03  Ava:                                                         [Yeh
5:04         en s' he siz yihknow he remi:nds me of d-hih-ih- tshe
5:05         reminds me, ˙hhh of you, meaning me:.
5:06         (0.4)
5:07  Bee:   Uh-ho that's [a- that's a s[wee:t co:mplimint,  ] ˙hh-
5:08  Ava:               [Kuhleznik.=  [=I said gee:, tha:n]ks a
```

```
5:09          lo:[t honeh,
5:10  Bee:       [ hhhhhhuh huh=
5:11  Ava:   ='hh [ Said ] yih all gonna gitch' mouth shuddup fih you=
5:12  Bee:           ['hhhh!]
5:13  Ava:   =yih don't sto:p i[t.]
5:14  Bee:                     [°M]mmyeh,
5:15  Bee:   I think evrybuddy's had her hm[hhh!
5:16  Ava:                                 [Ohh, [she's the biggest=]
5:17  Bee:                                       [-fih   something, ]
5:18  Ava:   =pain in the a:ss.
5:19          (0.3)
5:20  Bee:   °Yeh,
5:21  Ava:   .T She's teaching uh English Lit too, no more composition,
5:22  Bee:   Oh:::, She's moved up in the wor[ld ]
5:23  Ava:                                   [She] must know somebuddy
5:24          because all those other teachers they got rid of.hhhh
5:25          (0.3)
5:26  Bee:   Yeh I bet they got rid of all the one::Well one I had, t!
5:27          'hhhh in the firs' term there, fer the firs'term of
5:28          English, she die::d hhuh-uhh ['hhh
5:29  Ava:                                 [Oh:.
5:30  Bee:   She died in the middle of the te:rm?mhhh!=
5:31  Ava:   =Oh that's too ba:d hha ha!=
5:32  Bee:   =Eh-ye:h, ih-a, She wz rea:lly awful, she ha-duh, ('hh)
5:33          she's the wuh- She ha:duh southern accent too.
5:34  Ava:   Oh:.
5:35  Bee:   A:nd, she wz very difficul'tuh unduhstand.
5:36  Ava:   No, she ain't there anymoh,
5:37  Bee:   No I know I mean she, she's gone a long t(h)ime
5:38          (h)a'rea(h)[dy? hh
5:39  Ava:              [Mm, [hhmh!
5:40  Bee:                   ['hhh
5:41          (0.2)

6:01  Bee:   nYeeah, 'hh This feller I have-(nn)/(iv-)"felluh"; this
6:02          ma:n. (0.2) t! 'hhh He ha::(s)- uff-eh-who-who I have fer
6:03          Linguistics [is real]ly too much, 'hh[h=     ]
6:04  Ava:                [Mm   hm?]                 [Mm [hm,]
6:05  Bee:                                               [=I didn' notice it
6:06          b't there's a woman in my class who's a nurse 'n. 'hh she
6:07          said to me she s'd didju notice he has a ha:ndicap en I
6:08          said wha:t. Youknow I said I don't see anything wrong
6:09          wi[th im, she says his ha:nds.=
6:10  Ava:     [Mm:.
6:11  Bee:   ='hhh So the nex' cla:ss hh! 'hh fer en hour en f'fteen
6:12          minutes I sat there en I watched his ha:n(h)ds hh
6:13          hh['hhh=
6:14  Ava:      [ Why wha[t's the ma[tter] owith (his h'nds)/(him.)
```

```
6:15  Bee:              [=She      [meh-]
6:16  Bee:  ˙hhh t! ˙hhh He keh- He doesn' haff uh-full use uff hiss
6:17        hh-fin::gers or something en he, tch! he ho:lds the chalk
6:18        funny=en, ˙hh=
6:19  Ava:  =Oh[:      ]
6:20  Bee:     [hhHe-] eh-his fingihs don't be:nd=en, [˙hhh-
6:21  Ava:                                           [Oh[::      ]
6:22  Bee:                                              [Yihknow] she
6:23        really eh-so she said you know, theh-ih- she's had
6:24        experience. ˙hh with handicap' people she said but ˙hh
6:25        ih-yihknow ih-theh- in the fie:ld.
6:26        (0.2)
6:27  Ava:  (Mm:.)
6:28  Bee:  thet they're i:n[::.=
6:29  Ava:                  [(Uh [huh)
6:30  Bee:                       [=Yihknow theyd- they do b- (0.2)
6:31        t! ˙hhhh they try even harduh then uhr-yihknow a regular
6:32        instructor.
6:33  Ava:  Righ[t.
6:34  Bee:      [˙hhhh to uh ins(tr)- yihknow do the class'n
6:35        evr[ything.] An:d,
6:36  Ava:     [Uh huh.]
6:37  Bee:  She said they're usually harder markers 'n I said wo::wuhh
6:38        huhh! ˙hhh I said theh go, I said there's- there's three
6:39        courses a'ready thet uh(hh)hh[hff
6:40  Ava:                               [°Yeh
6:41  Bee:  I'm no(h)t gunnuh do well i(h)n,
6:42  Ava:  hhhh!

7:01  Bee:  ˙hhh Becaw but uh, Oh my, my north american indian class
7:02        's really, (0.5) tch! It's so boring.
7:03        (0.3)
7:04  Ava:  Ye(h)e(h)ah!
7:05        (0.2)
7:06  Bee:  I-ah- y-yihknow this gu:y has not done anything yet thet
7:07        I unduhsta:nd. En no one eh- no one else in the class
7:08        unduhstands him eethuh. ˙hhh We all sit there en ˙hhh we
7:09        laugh et his jokes, hhh hmhh=
7:10  Ava:  =Ye:h. [ I kn[ow. ]
7:11  Bee:         [˙hhh [en w]e no:d when he wants us tuh say ye:s?=
7:12        =(h)e[n ] ˙hhh
7:13  Ava:       [Ye]ah,=
7:14  Bee:  =We raise ar ha:nds when he wantsuh take a po:ll?=
7:15  Bee:  ='n[ : : ]
7:16  Ava:     [Ye:h.]
7:17  Bee:  ˙hh Yihknow buh when we walk outta the cla:ss.=
7:18  Ava:  =nobuddy knows wh't [wen' on,]
7:19  Bee:                      [Wid- ˙hh]h=
```

```
7:20  Bee:  =Li(hh)ke wu- 'hh Didju n- Didju know what he wz talking
7:21        about didju know wh't [structural paralysis was=
7:22  Ava:                        [dahhhhhh!
7:23  Bee:  =I sid no I sid but we're supposetuh know what it is
7:24        (fuh Weh-)'hh yihknow fuh tihday's [class. 'n,
7:25  Ava:                                    ['hhh Mmm.
7:26  Bee:  He nevuh wen' o:ver it 'n, t! 'hhhh
7:27        (0.2)
7:28  Ava:  [hh h h h!]
7:29  Bee:  [He (dih-)]=/(geh-)]=
7:30  Bee:  =Oh he-he's too much.He doesn't- en he put- they put us
7:31        in this gigantic lectchuh hall.
7:32  Ava:  Mmm.
7:33  Bee:  Tch! An::!(0.2) He doesn't speak- (0.2) very lou:d anyway.=
7:34  Ava:  =Mm hm,
7:35  Bee:  Tch! An:', bo:y oh boy hhhhihhhnh! ['hhhh!
7:36  Ava:                                     [(There a lot'v [people)
7:37  Bee:                                                    [Someone
7:38  Bee:  said et the end a' the class, couldju plih- please bring
7:39        inna microphone ne(h)x'[time   'h h ]=
7:40  Ava:                         [Mhhh hha ha]['hh
7:41  Bee:                                      [=He got very insu:lt'.

8:01  Ava:  Tou:gh.
8:02        (0.4)
8:03  Bee:  Yeh we[ll y'know it's true we can't hear him::=
8:04  Ava:        [(                        ).
8:05  Ava:  =[ye:ah.
8:06  Bee:  =['nd uh,
8:07  Ava:  Yeah. [hhhh!
8:08  Bee:        ['n:: he wz too much::
8:09  Ava:  [(              ),
8:10  Bee:  ['hh Bu:t uh I hope it gets bettuh. as it goes o:[n.
8:11  Ava:                                                   [Well
8:12        you nevuh know.
8:13  Bee:  Nye::h, en my u- my two ar' classes 'r pretty good I en-
8:14        I'm enjoying them b't=
8:15  Ava:  =W'that's good.
8:16  Bee:  I have so many boo:ks::
8:17  Ava:  [(Really?,)
8:18  Bee:  [Ohhhhh.
8:19  Bee:  I'nna tell you on:e course.
8:20        (0.5)
8:21  Ava:  [(     ).]
8:22  Bee:  [The mah- ] the mah:dern art. The twunnieth century a:rt
8:23        there's about eight books,
8:24  Ava:  Mm [hm,
```

```
8:25  Bee:     [En I wentuh buy a book the other day I [went] ˙hh went=
8:26  Ava:                                              [(mm)]
8:27  Bee:  =downtuh N.Y.U. tuh get it becuz it's the only place thet
8:28        car[ries the book.
8:29  Ava:     [Mmm
8:30  Ava:  Mmh
8:31  Bee:  Tch! En it wz twun::ty do::lliz.
8:32  Ava:  Oh my god.
8:33        (0.4)
8:34  Bee:  Yeuh he- ez he wz handing me the book en 'e tol' me twunny
8:35        dolliz I almos' dro(h)pped i(h)[t ˙hh ˙hh
8:36  Ava:                                 [hhunh.
8:37  Bee:  ˙hhh I said but fer twunny dollars I bettuh hh ˙hh yihknow,
8:38        (0.2)
8:39  Bee:  ˙hhh h[hold o:nto i(h)hh] huhh huh] ˙hh!
8:40  Ava:        [not    drop    it. ] huhh huh]

9:01        (0.2)
9:02  Bee:  Ih wz, (0.2) y'know (fun).=Bud I, I paid it the guy et the
9:03        countuh, (0.4) sorta gay me a discount on it anyway even
9:04        though I didn' go there.
9:05  Ava:  N't's good.
9:06  Bee:  We:ll, (0.7) Ih wz [awright,
9:07  Ava:                     [˙hhh
9:08  Bee:  ˙hhhh
9:09  Ava:  hh[hh!
9:10  Bee:    [B't I still have one more book tuh buy I can't get it,
9:11        (0.8)
9:12  Bee:  °So uh,
9:13        (0.6)
9:14  Bee:  I don'know.The school- school uh, (1.0) bookstore doesn'
9:15        carry anything anymo(h)uh,
9:16  Ava:  Mno?hh
9:17  Bee:  No, I don'know I guess (inna) spring term they don'
9:18        order ez- y'know many books ez they-they- really are
9:19        suppo:se [to. ]
9:20  Ava:           [Yeh.]=
9:21  Bee:  =˙hh en by the time I got tih the bookstore, (0.2) ˙hh
9:22        they were either so:ld ou:t or-or they hadn' come in yet
9:23        or [some]thing. [˙hh
9:24  Ava:     [Myeh.]       [°(I know)/[°(Yeh )
9:25  Bee:  Tch! So [uh,
9:26  Ava:          [°('kay.) ˙hh hh
9:27  Bee:  Ih wz, I don'know what I'm gunnuh do. hEn all the reading
9:28        is from this one book so f(h)ar the(h)t I haven' go(h)t!
9:29  Ava:  hhhhhhhh!
9:30  Bee:  ˙hhhh So she tol' me of a place on Madison Avenue 'n
```

```
9:31           Sevendy Ninth Street.=
9:32  Ava:     =M[mm.
9:33  Bee:       [tuh go en try the:re. Because I als- I tried Barnes
9:34           'n Nobles 'n, (0.6) they didn' have any'ing they don' have
9:35           any art books she tol' me,
9:36  Ava:     Mmm
9:37  Bee:     So,
9:38  (Ava):   ˙hhhh
9:39  Bee:     °That's too bad,
9:40  Ava:     hhhh!

10:01          (0.5)
10:02 Bee:     °(I 'unno )/°(So anyway) ˙hh Hey do you see v- (0.3) fat
10:03          ol' Vivian anymouh?
10:04 Ava:     No, hardly, en if we do:, y'know, I jus' say hello quick'n,
10:05          ˙hh y'know, jus' pass each othuh in th[e hall.]
10:06 Bee:                                           [Is  she] still
10:07          hangin aroun (wih)/(with) Bo:nny?
10:08 Ava:     Ah:::, yeh hh yeh,
10:09 Bee:     Hmh!
10:10          (0.7)
10:11 Ava:     ˙hhh Bud uh I- I- n-like this term I don' have hardly any
10:12          breaks. I made it, up that way.
10:13 Bee:     Mmm.
10:14 Ava:     Like, the only break I have is like t'day. En like, we
10:15          jus' one liddle, g-group? thet stays tuhgethuh.
10:16 Bee:     Tch! Well that's good.=
10:17 Ava:     =En I, don't go in the cafeteria.
10:18 Bee:     Taaff [˙hh stay] clear.]
10:19 Ava:          [I  play-] I    ] go down the gym en fool arou:n,
10:20          yihknow.
10:21 Bee:     [Mmm
10:22 Ava:     [˙hhh
10:23          (0.2)
10:24 Ava:     Bud uh.
10:25          (0.7)
10:26 Ava:     Y'know it jus' doesn' seem wo(h)rth i(h)t hh!
10:27 Bee:     ((Sniff!))
10:28 Bee:     ˙hhh Whad about (0.5) uh:: (0.8) Oh yih go f::- you- How
10:29          many days? you go five days a week. Ri[ght?]
10:30 Ava:                                           [Y e ] ah.
10:31 Bee:     ˙hh Oh gray-˙hhh
10:32 Ava:     ˙hh
10:33 Bee:     °So, ˙hh (then)/(en) yer only (1-)/(w-) in school late on
10:34          Wednesdays then,
10:35 Ava:     Thet's all.

11:01 Bee:     Mm, tch! I wz gonnuh call you. last week someti(h)me
11:02          ˙hhh[hh!
11:03 Ava:         [Yeh my mother a:sked mih I siz I don'know I haven't
```

```
11:04          hea:rd from her.I didn' know what day:s you had.˙h[hh
11:05 Bee:                                                       [eh
11:06          en I[: didn' know w-]
11:07 Ava:       [cla:sses 'r     ] a[nything,
11:08 Bee:                          [I didn'know when you were hh[ome=
11:09 Ava:                                                        [Tch!
11:10 Bee:     =[or-I wz gunnuh k-]
11:11 Ava:      [We l l  M o n d a] y:::,
11:12          (0.2)
11:13 Ava:     Lemme think. ˙hhh Monday::: Wednesday, (0.5) and Friday(s).
11:14          I'm home by one ten.
11:15 Bee:     One ten¿
11:16 Ava:     Two uh'clock. My class ends one ten.
11:17 Bee:     Mm hm,
11:18 Ava:     An:d Wednesdays I go back in the evening(.)/(,)
11:19          (0.5)
11:20 Ava:     [(n) I] take the ca:r so I] le]ave about five uh'clock,
11:21 Bee:     [ Tch!] Oh you come ho:me?] n-]
11:22 Bee:     <Oh that's not ba[d, ]
11:23 Ava:                      [Yeh] en then I go back in again.
11:24 Bee:     (Well ya sh'd)/(Eh least yih) get parking down there that
11:25          t[i-
11:26 Ava:      [Yeh [at that time there's no prob-=Well lately in the=
11:27 Bee:           [at that time
11:28 Ava:     =morning Rosemary's been picking me up. yihknow so I
11:29          (haven' been) even takin a train in [(the morning).
11:30 Bee:                                          [hhOh that's grea:t!
11:31 Ava:     Yeah, t! ˙hhh End uhm, (0.7) Tch! °What else. ˙hhh Oh en-
11:32          Tuesdeh- like Tuesdays I don't go in until two thirdy,
11:33          (0.5)
11:34 Ava:     E[n I'm home by fi:ve.
11:35 Bee:      [hm hmm
11:36          (0.3)
11:37 Ava:     I have- th'class is two thirdy tuh fouh.
11:38          (0.5)
11:39 Bee:     Mm
11:40 Ava:     En then, the same thing is (uh) jus' tihday is like a
11:41          long day cuz I have a break,

12:01          (0.7)
12:02 Bee:     Hm:.
12:03          (0.6)
12:04 Bee:     ˙hh- Not me:, hhuh uh-hhuh ˙hhh! I go in late evry day hh!
12:05 Ava:     Eyeh hh[h!
12:06 Bee:            [No thisz- No I have my early class tihday et four
12:07          thi:rdy.
12:08          (0.2)
12:09 Bee:     [Tch! Except that cl]a-
12:10 Ava:     [(W')that's not bad.]
```

```
12:11 Bee:   That class is suh:: yihknow, this is the indian class 'n-
12:12        ·hhh They stuck us in this cra:zy building thet they juh-
12:13        they're not even finished with it.
12:14 Ava:   Mm hm,
12:15 Bee:   Eh-an', it's called the science building.
12:16 Ava:   Mmhm,
12:17 Bee:   Tch! ·hhhh a-an:d there's no windo:ws,
12:18        (0.2)
12:19 Ava:   Mm[m
12:20 Bee:      [en the doors'r all boarded up en it (s-) hhas signs on
12:21        it please do not entuh, ·hh
12:22 Ava:   Tch!
12:23 Bee:   ·hh yihknow- en there's no way tuh get in the building the
12:24        firs' da:y. ·hh (Bob dropped me) off et schoo:1,
12:25 Ava:   Mmhm
12:26 Bee:   e-en::d, there wz a ha-et-there wz a hole in the wall in
12:27        the back a' the building en, eh-there wz anothuh girl
12:28        walking around she says ·hhh uh-dihyou know where the
12:29        science building is 'n I said- well I said- yihknow, the
12:30        guard jus' told me thet this wz the bui:lding. So she seh-
12:31        ·hh are you goin here fer 'n-·hh fer en in:dian class by
12:32        any chance 'n I said yes.hh So I said c'mon we'll fi:nd
12:33        it tuhgethuh en we craw::led through the hole in the wa:11,
12:34        ·hmhhh tch! We wou:nd up among paint can:s en:d·hh an:::d
12:35        yihknow stucco floo:r, e[n' ·hhh
12:36 Ava:                            [hhhh!
12:37 Bee:   en men's o:veralls work overa(hhh)lls? ·hh[hhh!
12:38 Ava:                                              [hunhh!

13:01 Bee:   En we k- en there wz a liddle o:pening. en we walked out
13:02        en we were by en elevater 'n we- yihknow we pressed the
13:03        button ['n k-so ih wz up on the sekkin floor we couldn'=
13:04 Ava:          [hhh
13:05 Bee:   =find a stairway ·hh[hhh
13:06 Ava:                       [Nhhh!
13:07 Bee:   En w-en: we got i(h)n the elevater en the e(h)levater
13:08        (my )/(like) (h)wasn' even finished yihknow like there wz-
13:09        ·hhhh jih-ih wz, sort'v pa::dded on the side, it had no,
13:10        (0.5) emergency doo[r y-yet (hh)'n hh ·hhh!=
13:11 Ava:                      [hhhhhhh!
13:12 Bee:   =e-en we rode up t(h)ih th's(h)ekkin flo' we di(h)dn' think
13:13        we were gunnuh lea[ve the groun' but we got [up there 'n
13:14 Ava:                     [·hhh!                      [hhhh
13:15 Bee:   ·hhhh en then we had- they had trouble. They ha-they have
13:16        no place for ar cla:ss.
13:17        (0.2)
13:18 Ava:   [ ( O h h.)]
13:19 Bee:   [ That's wh]y they have us in this buildin-we finally got
```

```
13:20          a- 'hhh a roo:m tihday in-in the leh- a lectchuh hall,
13:21           'h[hh=
13:22 Ava:        [ °Mmm
13:23 Bee:     =Because they gave us this cla:ssroom, yihknow. 'hh there's
13:24          abou:t, (0.5) fifty people in the cla:[ss.
13:25 Ava:                                          [Yeh.
13:26 Bee:     En::d, yihknow, (0.2) they tu-they gave us a room they
13:27          said 'hh well during the day this room holds fawty eight
13:28          people. [uh(h)hh!
13:29 Ava:             [(Mmm.)
13:30 Bee:     'hhh It hold about twunny fi:ve.
13:31 Ava:     Mmm.
13:32 Bee:     'T's too muh-they did that with my linguistics class a:lso.
13:33 Ava:     hh[hh!
13:34 Bee:       ['hh they stuck us in a cornuh somepla[ce.
13:35 Ava:                                            [mThat's funny. 'hhh
13:36 Bee:     En this- en::: this guy fuh linguistics lass- lafts et iz
13:37          own: jo:kes (h)yihknow so [it's-
13:38 Ava:                              [mYe:h
13:39 Bee:     'hhh It gets sickening a(hhh)fte(hhh)r aw[hi(h)le- 'hhh]
13:40 Ava:                                              [I   k n o w] I
13:41          know, I know,
13:42 Bee:     'hh But it's not too bad, 'hh

14:01 Ava:     °That's goo[d,
14:02 Bee:                [Dihyuh have any-cl- You have a class with
14:03          Billy this te:rm?
14:04 Ava:     Yeh he's in my abnormal class.
14:05 Bee:     mnYeh [ how-]
14:06 Ava:           [Abnor]mal psy[ch.
14:07 Bee:                         [Still not gettin married,
14:08 Ava:     'hhh Oh no. Definitely not.[married.]
14:09 Bee:                                [No  he's] dicided [defin[itely?]
14:10 Ava:                                                   ['hhh [O h   ]
14:11          no.
14:12 Bee:     'hh Bec'z [las'] time you told me he said no: but he wasn't=
14:13 Ava:               [ No.]
14:14 Bee:     =su:re,
14:15 Ava:     n:No definitely not. He, he'n Gail were like on the outs,
14:16          yihknow¿
14:17          (0.7)
14:18 Ava:     [  S o  ] uh,]
14:19 Bee:     [ They al] way]s are(hh)hhh
14:20 Ava:     Ye:h.
14:21 Bee:     'hhh
14:22 Ava:     In'n out, in'n out.
14:23 Bee:     There's only one time that I r-hh 'hh- thet they really
14:24          looked happy wz the time they were etchor hou(h)se.
```

```
14:25 Ava:    Oh:. Yea:h. Didn' they look ha:ppy.=
14:26 Bee:    =[Uhhh huhh! 'hhh
14:27 Ava:    =[Ho ho ho,
14:28 Bee:    hhhunh [hunhh.hh
14:29 Ava:           [Tha wz about ez happy ez they ge:t. Eh-hu:h,
14:30 Bee:    'hh Really (now)=
14:31 Ava:    =They have a prob'm.
14:32        (0.4)
14:33 Bee:    Mm.
14:34        (0.5)
14:35 Ava:    Definite pro:b'm,
14:36 Bee:    We:ll, 'hh (0.3) I don'know.
14:37 Ava:    YOU HO:ME?
14:38        (0.4)
14:39 Bee:    No,
14:40 Ava:    Oh I didn't think so.

15:01 Bee:    nNo,
15:02        (0.9)
15:03 Bee:    You are, hhnhh [hnhh! 'hhh
15:04 Ava:                  [Y'sounded too fa[r  a-]
15:05 Bee:                                  [Ri:gh]t? hh=
15:06 Ava:    =Yeh.=
15:07 Bee:    =See? hI-I'm doin' somethin right t'ay finally, ['hh
15:08 Ava:                                                     [Mm
15:09 Bee:    I finally said something right. (0.2) You are home. hmfff
15:10 Ava:    Yeh- I believe so. [Physically anyway.
15:11 Bee:                       [°°hhm hhh
15:12 Bee:    Yea-a-h.°Not mentall(h)y (h)though(hh)
15:13 Ava:    °No,
15:14 Ava:    khhhh!
15:15 Bee:    °hmhhh 'hh So yih gonna be arou:n this weeken'¿
15:16 Ava:    Uh::m. (0.3) Possibly.
15:17 Bee:    Uh it's a four day weeken-I have so much work t'do it
15:18        isn' ffunn[y.
15:19 Ava:             [Well, tomorrow I haftuh go in.
15:20        (0.2)
15:21 Bee:    Y'have cla:ss [tomorrow?
15:22 Ava:                 [hhhh
15:23 Ava:    ((breathily)) One cla:ss I have.=
15:24 Bee:    =You mean:: Pace isn't clo:s[ed?
15:25 Ava:                               [No we have off
15:26        Monday [°(b't not) 'hhh
15:27 Bee:           [Mm I have off ts- Monday too. hmfff
15:28 Ava:    A:nd uh:m 'hh I haftuh help- getting some schedules
15:29        t'gether fuh- m-t! [my o:ld Mistuh Ba:rt.
15:30 Bee:                      ['hhhh
```

```
15:31 Bee:    °Hmmm.
15:32 Ava:    A:nd I haftuh get the group tihgethuh fuh him.hh
15:33         (0.5)
15:34 Ava:    t! tch!
15:35 Bee:    BOY YUH BUSY KID! hh ˙hhh
15:36 Ava:    Yeh I know.He gay me [tickets t'the ballet in d- exchange=
15:37 Bee:                         [hh ˙hhh
15:38 Ava:    =fuh that, so it['s not too] bad.
15:39 Bee:                   [ O h  :   ] hh
15:40 Bee:    Busy busy [busy. ]
15:41 Ava:              [°hhhhh]
15:42 Ava:    A::nd,

16:01 Ava:    hhh[hh
16:02 Bee:       [Oh I've been [getting,]
16:03 Ava:                     [S a  t ]ihday I n- I've-g-I haftuh go-
16:04         I think Sunday I'm going ice skating.
16:05         (1.2)
16:06 Ava:    I wz sposetuh go tuh A:lbany. But we'd haftuh leave
16:07         t'morrow morning, so that wen ou:t. the window,
16:08 Bee:    °Mm,
16:09         (1.0)
16:10 Ava:    En I don't know exagly what's going o:n.re[ally.
16:11 Bee:                                              [Well if yer
16:12         arou:nd I'll probably see y(hh)ou hn[hh! ˙hh
16:13 Ava:                                         [Why, whuts (Bob doing)
16:14 Bee:    Uh-u-uh:: goin o:ff::
16:15 Ava:    Where's he goin.
16:16 Bee:    To Wa:shin'ton,
16:17 Ava:    Oh.
16:18         (0.7)
16:19 Bee:    He asn' been there sih-since Christmas [so:. hHe's going.
16:20 Ava:                                           [Mm.
16:21         (0.5)
16:22 Ava:    Yeh w'l I'll give you a call then tomorrow.when I get in
16:23         'r sumn.
16:24         (0.5)
16:25 Bee:    Wha:t,
16:26 Ava:    <I'll give yih call tomo[rrow.]
16:27 Bee:                            [Yeh: ] 'n [I'll be ho:me t'mor]row.
16:28 Ava:                                      [When I-I get  home.] I
16:29 Ava:    don't kno-w- I could be home by-˙hh three, I c'd be home
16:30         by two [I don't] know.]
16:31 Bee:           [ Well  ] when ]ever. I'll poh I-I might go t'the
16:32         city in the mo:rning any[way,
16:33 Ava:                            [It depends on how (tough the)=So
16:34         what time y'leaving f'the city,
```

```
17:01 Bee:   Oh:: probly abou-t te[n=
17:02                         [((ringing sound in background))
17:03 Bee:   =ten thirdy eleven, er-[n-d-ih-] ˙hh          ]
17:04 Ava:                        [O     h ] if you wanna] leave about
17:05        eleven [I'll walk down with ] [you.]°Cz I haftuh go] t'school]
17:06             [((ringing sound in b] [ackg]round))          ]        ]
17:07 Bee:                               [I t ] de p en :d s]how I ro:]l
17:08        outta bed tom(h)orr(h)uh![˙hh!]
17:09 Ava:                      [Well] le'[s see-eh-so ] lemme give=
17:10 Bee:                               [how I fee:l.] hh
17:11 Ava:   =you a call about ten thi:rdy.
17:12 Bee:   ˙hh Yeeuh.
17:13 Ava:   [A'ri:ght?]
17:14 Bee:   [I'll  see] w'ts-
17:15 Bee:   Yeah. [°See   w h a t ' s   g o i n g   o:n.]
17:16 Ava:        [Maybe you wanna come downtuh school] see what the new
17:17        place looks like,
17:18        (0.5)
17:19 Bee:   Yih may:be. (N)a::[h, b't I hadn'-]
17:20 Ava:                     [You c'n come innoo] a cla:ss with m[e.
17:21 Bee:                                                        [I
17:22 Bee:   haven' thought about that la(h)tely hh huh eh-[huh!
17:23 Ava:                                                 [Why
17:24        donch[a I mean you won' haftuh do any]thing,
17:25 Bee:        [.hh   You   know   I   wu-u-u ] I wonder if Do:nna
17:26 Bee:   went back tuh school, i'z [I wz curious tuh know,  ]
17:27 Ava:                            [ I n- Y'know- Fridays is] a funny
17:28        day. mMost a' the people in schoo:l, ˙hh that's why I only
17:29        have classes on Tuesday en Fri:day ˙hh (0.3)°u- one cla:ss,
17:30        because most a' them have o:ff those days. Yih kno[w like=
17:31 Bee:                                                     [Ye::h,
17:32 Ava:   =if yih kuh work yer schedule out that [way=I cuutn't.
17:33 Bee:                                           [Right.
17:34        (0.7)
17:35 Ava:   Tch! But if you wanna-uh:m (0.2) come in en see.
17:36 Bee:   Tch! I wouldn' know wheretuh look fuh her(hh) hnhh-hnh[h!˙hh
17:37 Ava:                                                        [Well
17:38        you know, you know, come along with me,
17:39        (0.7)
17:40 Ava:   A:nd uh:m,

18:01        (0.7)
18:02 Ava:   °Wuhwz I gonnuh say.
18:03        (0.7)
18:04 Ava:   You c'n come in the class with me, it's a logic class=I
18:05        think yih gonna see a pitcher o:n something good
18:06        tomorruh in that class anyway so it's n[o ha:ssle,
18:07 Bee:                                           [°Nnh,
```

```
18:08 Ava:   ˙hh 'T's only f'f'fty minutes anyway,
18:09        (0.6)
18:10 Ava:   [A:nd uh,
18:11 Bee:   [˙hh W'l I'll see. hhYih[know
18:12 Ava:                        [Maybe if yih come down I'll take
18:13        the car (then)/(down).
18:14 Bee:   t! We:ll, uhd-yihknow I-I don' wanna make any- thing
18:15        definite because I-yihknow I jis:: I jis::t thinkin:g
18:16        tihday all day riding on th'trai:ns hhuh-uh
18:17        ˙hh[h!
18:18 Ava:      [Well there's nothing else t'do.<I wz
18:19        thingin[g of taking the car anyway.] ˙hh
18:20 Bee:          [that I would go into the ss-uh-]=I would go into
18:21        the city but I don't know,
18:22 Ava:   Well if I do ta:ke it, this way if- uh-if- y'know uh::
18:23        there's no pa:rking right away I c'n give you the car
18:24        en you c'n look aroun a li'l bit.
18:25 Bee:   Mye::[:m,    ]
18:26 Ava:        [y'know] en see what happens.
18:27        (0.4)
18:28 Bee:   Wel[l I'll see I] don'know ah, yihknow it's just u:n idea,=
18:29 Ava:      [if you want,]
18:30 Bee:   =I n-I wanniduh go to uh-
18:31        (0.7)
18:32 Bee:   t!˙hhhhh the: Hallmark card shop on fifty seventh en fifth,
18:33 Ava:   (Oh:)=/ (Mm:)=
18:34 Bee:   =I wanniduh look aroun fuh some cards,
18:35 Ava:   (Oh:.)/(Right.)
18:36 Bee:   Tch! I'll get some advance birthday cards, hhm hmh!
18:37        (0.6)
18:38 Bee:   ˙hhh A:n:d uh, (0.5) Me:h,
18:39        (0.2)

19:01 Bee:   Oh Sibbie's sistuh hadda ba:by bo:way.
19:02 Ava:   Who¿
19:03 Bee:   Sibbie's sister.
19:04 Ava:   Oh really?
19:05 Bee:   Myeah,
19:06 Ava:   [°(That's nice.)/[°(Sibbie's sistuh.)
19:07 Bee:   [She had it yestihday. Ten:: pou:nds.
19:08 Ava:   °Je:sus Christ.
19:09 Bee:   She ha[dda ho:(hh)rse hh ˙hh ]
19:10 Ava:         [(        b a : b y . )]
19:11 Bee:   hhhuhh! ˙hh (Guess) why-But theh-sh-I-She wz ovuh-She's
19:12        lo:ng-She wz long ovuhdue.
19:13 Ava:   Mmm.
19:14 Bee:   And she, She had gai:ned about fawty pounds anyway. ˙hh
19:15        They said she was treme:ndous.
```

```
19:16        (0.5)
19:17 Bee:   So I'm sure they're happy about that.
19:18 Ava:   Nyeh thet she'[s treme(h)ndous] ˙hhh
19:19 Bee:              [I think uh   hh ]
19:20 Ava:   ˙hh
19:21 Bee:   I think huh hu[sbin wannid a boy anyweh.
19:22 Ava:              [hhhuh!
19:23 Ava:   Oh:.
19:24        (0.2)
19:25 Bee:   They were (0.2) t! deci:ding.
19:26        (0.6)
19:27 Ava:   Y[eh
19:28 Bee:    [°Mmmm. Tch! ˙hh WE:ll, hmff tch!=
19:29 Bee:   [Awright so,
19:30 Ava:   [Well if you wan' me (to) give you a ring tomorrow morning.
19:31 Bee:   Tch! ˙hhh We:ll y-you know, let's, eh- I don'know, I'll
19:32 Bee:   see (h)may[be I woon' even be in,]
19:33 Ava:            [Well when yih go intuh] the city y'gonna haftuh
19:34        walk down t'the train a[n y w a y.]
19:35 Bee:                          [ r-Ri:ght.]
19:36 Ava:   So might ez well walk with some[buddy. ˙hh
19:37 Bee:                                 [Right. So I'll s-Alright.
19:38        so gimme a call,
19:39 Ava:   Bout ten thirdy.
19:40 Bee:   Ri:ght.

20:01 Ava:   Okay th[en.
20:02 Bee:          [[A'right.
20:03 Ava:   [A'ri[ght.
20:04 Bee:   [Tch![ I'll (s-)/(t-) I'll talk tihyou then t'mor[row.
20:05 Ava:                                                   [O:kay.=
20:06 Bee:   =Okay [buh buy,
20:07 Ava:        [Bye bye.
                 -----End call-----
```

References

Atkinson, J. M. 1992. Displaying Neutrality: Formal Aspects of Informal Court Proceedings. In P. Drew and J. Heritage (eds.) *Talk at Work*. Cambridge: Cambridge
University Press, pp. 199–211.

Austin, J. L. 1962. *How to do Things with Words*. Cambridge, MA: Harvard University
Press.

Austin, J. L. 1979. *Philosophical Papers*. Oxford and New York: Oxford University
Press.

Beach, W. A. 1993. Transitional Regularities for "Casual" "Okay" Usages. *Journal of
Pragmatics* 19: 325–52.

Brazil, D., Coulthard, M., and Johns, C. 1980. *Discourse Intonation and Language
Teaching*. London: Longman.

Brown, P. and Levinson, S. C. 1978. Universals of Language Usage: Politeness Phenom-
ena. In E. N. Goody (ed.) *Questions and Politeness Strategies in Social Interaction*.
Cambridge: Cambridge University Press, pp. 56–311.

Brown, P. and Levinson, S. C. 1987. *Politeness: Some Universals in Language Usage*.
Cambridge: Cambridge University Press.

Button, G. 1988/89. Topic initiation: business at hand. *Research on Language and Social
Interaction* 22: 61–92.

Button, G. and Casey, N. 1984. Generating Topic: The Use of Topic Initial Elicitors.
In J. M. Atkinson and J. Heritage (eds.) *Structures of Social Action*. Cambridge:
Cambridge University Press, pp. 167–90.

Button, G. and Casey, N. 1985. Topic Nomination and Topic Pursuit. *Human Studies* 8:
3–55.

Coulthard, M. 1977. *An Introduction to Discourse Analysis*. London: Longman.

Couper-Kuhlen, E. 2004. Prosody and Sequence Organization in English Conversation:
The Case of New Beginnings. In E. Couper-Kuhlen and C. E. Ford (eds.) *Sound
Patters in Interaction: Cross-Linguistic Studies from Conversation*, Amsterdam:
John Benjamins, pp. 335–76.

Davidson, J. 1984. Subsequent Versions of Invitations, Offers, Requests, and Proposals Dealing with Potential or Actual Rejection. In J. M. Atkinson and J. Heritage (eds.) *Structures of Social Action*. Cambridge: Cambridge University Press,
pp. 102–28.

Davidson, J. A. 1990. Modifications of Invitations, Offers and Rejections. In G.
Psathas (ed.) *Interaction Competence*. Washington: International Institute for
Ethnomethodology and Conversation Analysis and University Press of America,
pp. 149–80.

Drew, P. 1984. Speakers' Reportings in Invitation Sequences. In J. M. Atkinson and
J. Heritage (eds.) *Structures of Social Action*. Cambridge: Cambridge University
Press, pp. 152–64.

Drew, P. and Heritage, J. 1992b. Analyzing Talk at Work: An Introduction. In P. Drew and
J. Heritage (eds.) *Talk at Work*. Cambridge: Cambridge University Press, pp. 3–65.

Drew, P. and Heritage, J. (eds.) 1992a. *Talk at Work*. Cambridge: Cambridge University
Press.

Drew, P. and Holt, E. 1998. Figures of Speech: Figurative Expressions and the Management of Topic Transition in Conversation. *Language in Society* 27: 495–523.

Egbert, M. M. 1997. Some Interactional Achievements of Other-Initiated Repair in Multi-Person Conversation. *Journal of Pragmatics* 27: 611–34.

Gardner, R. 1997. The Conversation Object Mm: A Weak and Variable Acknowledging Token. *Research on Language and Social Interaction* 30(2): 131–56.

Gardner, R. 2002. *When Listeners Talk*. Amsterdam and Philadelphia: John Benjamins.

Goffman, E. 1955. On Face-Work: An Analysis of Ritual Elements in Social Interaction. *Psychiatry* 18(3): 213–31. Reprinted in E. Goffman, *Interaction Ritual: Essays in Face to Face Behavior*. Garden City, NY: Doubleday Anchor, pp. 5–45.

Goffman, E. 1963. *Behavior in Public Places: Notes on the Social Organization of Gathering*. New York: Free Press.

Goffman, E. 1964. The Neglected Situation. In The Ethnography of Communication, John J. Gumperz and Dell Hymes (eds.), *Special issue of American Anthropologist* 66(6), part 2: 133–36.

Goffman, E. 1969. *Strategic Interaction*. Philadelphia: University of Pennsylvania Press.

Goffman, E. 1978. Response Cries. *Language* 54: 787–815.

Goldberg, J. A. 1978. Amplitude Shift: A Mechanism for the Affiliation of Utterances in Conversational Interaction. In J. Schenkein (ed.) *Studies in the Organization of Conversational Interaction*. New York: Academic Press, pp. 199–218.

Goodwin, C. 1979. The Interactive Construction of a Sentence in Natural Conversation. In G. Psathas (ed.) *Everyday Language: Studies in Ethnomethodology*. New York: Irvington Publishers, pp. 97–121.

Goodwin, C. 1980. Restarts, Pauses, and the Achievement of Mutual Gaze at Turn-Beginning. *Sociological Inquiry* 50: 272–302.

Goodwin, C. 1981. *Conversational Organization: Interaction Between Speakers and Hearers*. New York: Academic Press.

Goodwin, M. H. 1983. Searching for a Word as an Interactive Activity. In J. N. Deely and M. D. Lenhart (eds.) *Semiotics 1981*. New York: Plenum Press, pp. 129–38.

Goodwin, M. H. and Goodwin, C. 1986. Gesture and Coparticipation in the Activity of Searching for a Word. *Semiotica* 62(1/2): 51–75.

Heritage, J. 1984a. *Garfinkel and Ethnomethodology*. Cambridge: Polity Press.

Heritage, J. C. 1984b. A Change-of-State Token and Aspects of Its Sequential Placement. In J. M. Atkinson and J. Heritage (eds.) *Structures of Social Action*. Cambridge: Cambridge University Press, pp. 299–345.

Heritage, J. C. 1985. Analyzing News Interviews: Aspects of the Production of Talk for an Overhearing Audience. In T. A. Dijk (ed.) *Handbook of Discourse Analysis*, vol. III. New York: Academic Press, pp. 95–119.

Heritage, J. C. 1988. Explanations as Accounts: A Conversation Analytic Perspective. In C. Antaki (ed.) *Understanding Everyday Explanation: A Casebook of Methods*. Beverly Hills: Sage, pp. 127–44.

Heritage, J. C. 1998. *Oh*-Prefaced Responses to Inquiry. *Language in Society* 27: 291–334.

Heritage, J. 2002. The Limits of Questioning: Negative Interrogatives and Hostile Question Content. *Journal of Pragmatics* 34: 1427–46.

Heritage, J. C. and Roth, A. L. 1995. Grammar and Institution: Questions and Questioning in the Broadcast News Interview. *Research on Language and Social Interaction* 28(1): 1–60.

Heritage, J. C. and Sorjonen, M.-L. 1994. Constituting and Maintaining Activities Across Sequences: *And*-Prefacing as a Feature of Question Design. *Language in Society* 1: 1–29.

Hopper, R., Doany, N., Johnson, M., and Drummond, K. 1990/91. Universals and Particulars in Telephone Openings. *Research on Language and Social Interaction* 24: 369–87.

Hopper, R. and Koleilat-Doany, N. 1989. Telephone Openings and Conversational Universals: A Study in Three Languages. In S. Ting-Toomey and F. Kevizing (eds.) *Language, Communication and Culture*. Newbury Park: Sage, pp. 157–79.

Houtkoop-Steenstra, H. 1991. Opening Sequences in Dutch Telephone Conversations. In D. Boden and D. H. Zimmerman (eds.) *Talk and Social Structure: Studies in Ethnomethodology and Conversation Analysis*. Cambridge: Polity Press, pp. 232–50.

Jefferson, G. 1972. Side Sequences. In D. Sudnow (ed.) *Studies in Social Interaction*. New York: Free Press, pp. 294–338.

Jefferson, G. 1978a. Sequential Aspects of Storytelling in Conversation. In J. Schenkein (ed.) *Studies in the Organization of Coversational Interaction*. New York: Academic Press, pp. 219–48.

Jefferson, G. 1978b. What's In a "Nyem"? *Sociology* 1(1): 135–39.

Jefferson, G. 1980. On "Trouble-Premonitory" Response to Inquiry. *Sociological Inquiry* 50(34): 153–85.

Jefferson, G. 1981. *The Abominable "Ne?": A Working Paper Exploring the Phenomenon of Post-Response Pursuit of Response*. Occasional Paper no. 6, Department of Sociology, University of Manchester, England.

Jefferson, G. 1983a. An Exercise in the Transcription and Analysis of Laughter. *Tilburg Papers in Language and Literature* 35.

Jefferson, G. 1983b. Issues in the Transcription of Naturally-Occurring Talk: Caricature versus Capturing Pronunciational Particulars. *Tilburg Papers in Language and Literature* 34.

Jefferson, G. 1984. On Stepwise Transition from Talk About a Trouble to Inappropriately Next-Positioned Matters. In J. M. Atkinson and J. Heritage (eds.) *Structures of Social Action*. Cambridge: Cambridge University Press, pp. 191–221.

Jefferson, G. 1985. An Exercise in the Transcription and Analysis of Laughter. In T. A. Dijk (ed.) *Handbook of Discourse Analysis*, vol. III. New York: Academic Press, pp. 25–34.

Jefferson, G. 1990. List Construction as a Task and Interactional Resource. In G. Psathas (ed.) *Interaction Competence*. Washington: International Institute for Ethnomethodology and Conversation Analysis and University Press of America, pp. 63–92.

Jefferson, G. 1996. A Case of Transcriptional Stereotyping. *Journal of Pragmatics*, 26: 159–70.

Jefferson, G. 2004. Glossary of Transcript Symbols with an Introduction. In G. H. Lerner (ed.) *Conversation Analysis: Studies from the First Generation*. Amsterdam and Philadelphia: John Benjamins, pp. 13–31.

Jefferson, G. and Schenkein, J. 1978. Some Sequential Negotiations in Conversation: Unexpanded and Expanded Versions of Projected Action Sequences. In J. Schenkein (ed.) *Studies in the Organization of Conversational Interaction*. New York: Academic Press, pp. 155–72.

Koshik, I. 2002. A Conversation Analytic Study of Yes/No Questions Which Convey Reversed Polarity Assertions. *Journal of Pragmatics* 34: 1851–77.

Lazaraton, A. L. 1991. A Conversation Analysis of Structure and Interaction in the Language Interview. Ph.D. dissertation, Department of TESL and Applied Linguistics, University of California, Los Angeles.

Lazaraton, A. 1997. Preference Organization in Oral Proficiency Interviews: The Case of Language Ability Assessments. *Research on Language and Social Interaction* 30: 53–72.

Lerner, G. H. 2002. Practice Does Not Make Perfect: Intervening Actions in the Selection of Next Speaker. Plenary Address at the Conference on Language, Interaction and Culture, University of California, Los Angeles.

Lerner, G. H. 2003. Selecting Next Speaker: The Context-Sensitive Operation of a Context-Free Organization. *Language in Society* 32: 177–201.

Lerner, G. (ed.). 2004a. *Conversation Analysis: Studies from the First Generation*. Amsterdam and Philadelphia: John Benjamins.

Lerner, G. H. 2004b. The Collaborative Turn Sequence. In G. H. Lerner (ed.) *Conversation Analysis: Studies from the First Generation*. Amsterdam and Philadelphia: John Benjamins, pp. 225–56.

Levinson, S. 1979. Activity Types and Language. *Linguistics* 17: 365–99. Reprinted in P. Drew and J. Heritage. 1992a. *Talk at Work*. Cambridge: Cambridge University Press, pp. 66–100.

Levinson, S. C. 1980. Speech Act Theory: The State of the Art. *Language and Linguistic Teaching: Abstracts* 13(1): 5–24.

Levinson, S. C. 1981. The Essential Inadequacies of Speech Act Models of Dialogue. In H. Parret, M. Sbisa, and J. Verschueren (eds.) *Possibilities and Limitations of Pragmatics: Proceedings of the Conference on Pragmatics at Urbino, July 8–14, 1979*. Amsterdam: Benjamins, pp. 473–92.

Levinson, S. C. 1983. *Pragmatics*. Cambridge: Cambridge University Press.

Lindström, A. K. B. 1994. Identification and Recognition in Swedish Telephone Conversation Openings. *Language in Society* 22(2): 231–52.

Lindström, A. K. B. 1997. Designing Social Actions: Grammar, Prosody, and Interaction in Swedish Conversation. Ph.D. dissertation, Department of Sociology, University of California, Los Angeles.

Maynard, D. W. 2003. *Bad News, Good News: Conversational Order in Everyday Talk and Clinical Settings*. Chicago: University of Chicago Press.

Mehan, H. 1979. *Learning Lessons*. Cambridge, MA: Harvard University Press.

Mehan, H. 1985. The Structure of Classroom Discourse. In T. A. Dijk (ed.) *Handbook of Discourse Analysis*, vol. III. New York: Academic Press, pp. 120–31.

Merritt, M. 1976. On Questions Following Questions in Service Encounters. *Language in Society* 5(3): 315–57.

Nagel, E. 1961. *The Structure of Science: Problems in the Logic of Scientific Explanation*. New York: Harcourt, Brace & World.

Onions, C. T. (ed. and rev.) 1984. *Shorter Oxford English Dictionary*, 3rd edition, 2 vols. Oxford: Clarendon Press.

Park, Y.-Y. 2002. Recognition and Identification in Japanese and Korean Telephone Conversation Openings. In K. K. Luke and T.-S. Pavlidou (eds.) *Telephone Calls: Unity and Diversity in Conversational Structure Across Languages and Cultures*. Amsterdam: John Benjamins, pp. 25–47.

Peyrot, M. 1994. *Therapeutic Preliminaries: Conversational Context and Process in Psychotherapy*. Paper presented at the Annual Meetings of the American Sociological Association, Los Angeles, CA.

Pomerantz, A. 1978. Compliment Responses: Notes on the Co-operation of Multiple Constraints. In J. Schenkein (ed.) *Studies in the Organization of Conversational Interaction*. New York: Academic Press, pp. 79–112.

Pomerantz, A. 1984. Agreeing and Disagreeing with Assessments: Some Features of Preferred/Dispreferred Turn Shapes. In J. M. Atkinson and J. Heritage (ed.) *Structures of Social Action: Studies in Conversation Analysis*. Cambridge: Cambridge University Press, pp. 57–101.

Psathas, G. 1991. The Structure of Direction-Giving in Interaction. In D. Boden and D. H. Zimmerman (eds.) *Talk and Social Structure: Studies in Ethnomethodology and Conversation Analysis*. Cambridge: Polity Press, pp. 195–216.

Raymond, G. 2000. The Structure of Responding: Type-Conforming and Non-Conforming Responses to Yes/No Interrogatives. Ph.D. dissertation, Department of Sociology, University of California, Los Angeles.

Raymond, G. 2003. Grammar and Social Organization: Yes/No Interrogatives and the Structure of Responding. *American Sociological Review* 68: 939–67.

Raymond, G. 2004. Prompting Action: The Stand-Alone "So" in Ordinary Conversation. *Reseasrch on Language and Social Interaction* 37(2): 185–218.

Roth, A. and Olsher, D. 1997. Some Standard Uses of "What About"-Prefaced Interrogatives in the Broadcast News Interview. *Issues in Applied Linguistics* 8(1): 3–25.

Sacks, H. 1974. An Analysis of the Course of a Joke's Telling in Conversation. In R. Bauman and J. Sherzer (eds.) *Explorations in the Ethnography of Speaking*. Cambridge: Cambridge University Press, pp. 337–53.

Sacks, H. 1975. Everyone Has to Lie. In M. Sanches and B. G. Blount (eds.) *Sociocultural Dimensions of Language Use*. New York: Academic Press, pp. 57–80.

Sacks, H. 1987 [1973]. On the Preferences for Agreement and Contiguity in Sequences in Conversation. In G. Button and J. R. E. Lee (eds.) *Talk and Social Organisation*. Clevedon: Multilingual Matters, pp. 54–69.

Sacks, H. 1992a. *Lectures on Conversation*, vol: I, ed. Gail Jefferson, introduction by Emanuel A. Schegloff. Oxford: Blackwell.

Sacks, H. 1992b. *Lectures on Conversation*, vol. II, ed. Gail Jefferson, introduction by Emanuel A. Schegloff.

Sacks, H. and Schegloff, E. A. 1979. Two Preferences in the Organization of Reference to Persons and Their Interaction. In G. Psathas (ed.) *Everyday Language: Studies in Ethnomethodology*. New York: Irvington Publishers, pp. 15–21.

Sacks, H., Schegloff, E. A., and Jefferson, G. 1974. A Simplest Systematics for the Organization of Turn-Taking for Conversation. *Language* 50: 696–735.

Scheflen, A. E. 1961. *A Psychotherapy of Schizophrenia: Direct Analysis*. Springfield, IL: C. C. Thomas.

Schegloff, E. A. 1968. Sequencing in Conversational Openings. *American Anthropologist* 70: 1075–95.

Schegloff, E. A. 1972. Notes on a Conversational Practice: Formulating Place. In D. N. Sudnow (ed.) *Studies in Social Interaction*. New York: Free Press, pp. 75–119.

Schegloff, E. A. 1979. Identification and Recognition in Telephone Openings. In G. Psathas (ed.) *Everyday Language: Studies in Ethnomethodology*. New York: Erlbaum, pp. 23–78.

Schegloff, E. A. 1980. Preliminaries to Preliminaries: "Can I Ask You a Question." *Sociological Inquiry* 50: 104–52.

Schegloff, E. A. 1986. The Routine as Achievement. *Human Studies* 9: 111–51.

Schegloff, E. A. 1987. Analyzing Single Episodes of Interaction: An Exercise in Conversation Analysis. *Social Psychology Quarterly* 50(2): 101–14.

Schegloff, E. A. 1988a. Goffman and the Analysis of Conversation. In P. Drew and A. Wootton (eds.) *Erving Goffman: Exploring the Interaction Order*. Cambridge: Polity Press, pp. 89–135.

Schegloff, E. A. 1988b. On an Actual Virtual Servo-Mechanism for Guessing Bad News: A Single Case Conjecture. *Social Problems* 35(4): 442–57.

Schegloff, E. A. 1988c. Presequences and Indirection: Applying Speech Act Theory to Ordinary Conversation. *Journal of Pragmatics* 12: 55–62.

Schegloff, E. A. 1988/89. From Interview to Confrontation: Observations on the Bush/Rather Encounter. *Research on Language and Social Interaction* 22: 215–40.

Schegloff, E. A. 1990. On the Organization of Sequences as a Source of "Coherence" in Talk-in-Interaction. In B. Dorval (ed.) *Conversational Organization and its Development*. Norwood, NJ: Ablex Publishing Co., pp. 51–77.

Schegloff, E. A. 1992a. Introduction. In G. Jefferson (ed.) *Harvey Sacks: Lectures on Conversation*, vol. I. Oxford: Blackwell, pp. ix–lxii.

Schegloff, E. A. 1992b. On Talk and Its Institutional Occasions. In P. Drew and J. Heritage (eds.) *Talk at Work*. Cambridge: Cambridge University Press, pp. 101–34.

Schegloff, E. A. 1992c. To Searle on Conversation: A Note in Return. In John R. Searle et al. (eds.) *(On) Searle on Conversation*. Amsterdam and Philadelphia: John Benjamins, pp. 113–28.

Schegloff, E. A. 1995. Discourse as an Interactional Achievement III: The Omnirelevance of Action. *Research on Language and Social Interaction* 28(3): 185–211.

Schegloff, E. A. 1996a. Confirming Allusions: Toward an Empirical Account of Action. *American Journal of Sociology* 104(1): 161–216.

Schegloff, E. A. 1996b. Issues of Relevance for Discourse Analysis: Contingency in Action, Interaction and Co-Participant Context. In E. H. Hovy and D. Scott (eds.) *Computational and Conversational Discourse: Burning Issues – An Interdisciplinary Account*. Heidelberg: Springer Verlag, pp. 3–38.

Schegloff, E. A. 1996c. Some Practices for Referring to Persons in Talk-in-Interaction: A Partial Sketch of a Systematics. In B. A. Fox (ed.) *Studies in Anaphora*. Amsterdam: John Benjamins, pp. 437–85.

Schegloff, E. A. 1996d. Turn Organization: One Intersection of Grammar and Interaction. In E. Ochs, E. A. Schegloff, and S. A. Thompson (eds.) *Interaction and Grammar*. Cambridge: Cambridge University Press, pp. 52–133.

Schegloff, E. A. 1998. Body Torque. *Social Research* 65(3): 535–96.

Schegloff, E. A. 2001. Getting Serious: Joke → Serious "No." *Journal of Pragmatics* 33(12): 1947–55.

Schegloff, E. A. 2002a [1970]. Opening Sequencing. In J. E. Katz and M. Aakhus (eds.) *Perpetual Contact: Mobile Communication, Private Talk, Public Performance*. Cambridge: Cambridge University Press, pp. 321–85.

Schegloff, E. A. 2002b. Reflections on Research on Telephone Conversation: Issues of Cross-Cultural Scope and Scholarly Exchange, Interactional Import and Consequences. In K. K. Luke and T. S. Pavlidon (eds.) *Telephone Calls: Unity and Diversity in Conversational Structure Across Languages and Cultures*. Amsterdam: John Benjamins, pp. 249–81.

Schegloff, E. A. 2003. Conversation Analysis and Communication Disorders. In C. Goodwin (ed.) *Conversation and Brain Damage*. New York: Oxford University Press, pp. 21–55.

Schegloff, E. A. 2004a [1970]. Answering the Phone. In G. H. Lerner (ed.) *Conversation Analysis: Studies from the First Generation*. Amsterdam/Philadelphia: John Benjamins, pp. 63–107.

Schegloff, E. A. 2004b. Putting the Interaction Back into Dialogue (Commentary on Pickering and Garrod: "Toward a Mechanistic Psychology of Dialogue"). *Behavioral and Brain Sciences* 27(2): 207–08.

Schegloff, E. A. 2005. On Integrity in Inquiry . . . of the Investigated, not the Investigator. *Discourse Studies* 7(45): 455–80.

Schegloff, E. A. 2006 [frth]. Interaction: The Infrastructure for Social Institutions, the Natural Ecological Niche for Language, and the Arena in Which Culture is Enacted. In N. J. Enfield and S. C. Levinson (eds.) *Roots of Human Sociality: Culture, cognition and interaction*. London: Berg.

Schegloff, E. A. and Sacks, H. 1973. Opening Up Closings. *Semiotica* 8: 289–327.

Schegloff, E. A., Jefferson, G., and Sacks, H. 1977. The Preference for Self-Correction in the Organization of Repair in Conversation. *Language* 53(2): 361–82.

Searle, J. R. 1969. *Speech Acts*. Cambridge: Cambridge University Press.

Searle, J. R. 1975. Indirect Speech Acts. In P. Cole and J. L. Morgan (eds.) *Syntax and Semantics*, vol. III. New York: Academic Press, pp. 59–82.

Searle, J. R. 1976. The Classification of Illocutionary Acts. *Language in Society* 5: 1–24.

Searle, J. R. and Vanderveken, D. 1985. *Foundations of Illocutionary Logic*. Cambridge: Cambridge University Press.

Sinclair, J. M. and Coulthard, R. M. 1975. *Towards an Analysis of Discourse: The English Used by Teachers and Pupils*. London: Oxford University Press.

Tarplee, C. 1991. *Working on Talk: Interactions Between Adults and Young Children During Picture Book Labelling Sequences*. Paper presented at a Conference on Current Work in Ethnomethodology and Conversation Analysis, Amsterdam.

ten Have, P. 1991. Talk and Institution: A Reconsideration of the "Asymmetry" of Doctor–Patient Interaction. In D. Boden and D. H. Zimmerman (eds.) *Talk and Social Structure: Studies in Ethnomethodology and Conversation Analysis*. Cambridge: Polity Press, pp. 138–63.

Terasaki, A. 2004. Pre-Announcement Sequences in Conversation. In G. H. Lerner (ed.) *Conversation Analysis: Studies from the First Generation*. Amsterdam and Philadelphia: John Benjamins, pp. 174–223. First appeared as Social Science Working Paper 99, School of Social Sciences, Irvine, CA, 1976.

West, C. and Zimmerman, D. H. 1983. Small Insults: A Study of Interruptions in Cross-Sex Conversations between Unacquainted Persons. In B. Thorne, C. Kramarae, and N. Henley (eds.) *Language, Gender and Society*. Rowley, MA: Newbury House, pp. 102–17.

Whalen, M. and Zimmerman, D. H. 1987. Sequential and Institutional Contexts in Calls for Help. *Social Psychology Quarterly* 50: 172–85.

Zimmerman, D. H. 1984. Talk and Its Occasion: The Case of Calling the Police. In D. Schiffrin (ed.) *Meaning, Form, and Use in Context: Linguistic Applications*. Washington, DC: Georgetown University Press, pp. 210–28.

Index

action-formation, xiv, 7
action-projection utterances, 44
action-type sequence series
    generally, 207–13
    offer series, 210–13
    question series, 207
    TG conversation example, 207–8
actions
    action-type sequence series, 207–13
    and adjacency pairs, 10–12
    agreeing. *See* agreements
    analysis, 2–3, 8
    bodily actions, 11, 47
    chicken dinner example, 10
    Chinese dinner example, 11
    confirming, 8
    development of courses of action, 251
    housemates example, 10
    importance, 1
    meaning, 7–12
    multiple actions in one TCU, 9
    successive parts of courses of action, 213–15
    and turns-at-talk, 10
    types, 7
adjacency pairs
    and actions, 10–12
    alternative second pair parts, 16, 58–59
    base pairs, 27
    basic operation, 13–21
    chicken dinner example, 24–26
    closings, 22–24
    collapsed adjacent pairs, 239
    contiguity, 14–16
    counters, 16–19, 21
    dormitory examples, 23–24, 25
    expansion. *See* expansions
    first pair parts, 13, 251
    greetings example, 22
    meaning, 9
    minimal form, 13–14, 22–27, 251
    pair-type relation, 13–14
    progressivity, 15–16
    relevance rules, 19–21, 251–52
    vs. retro-sequences, 9, 217
    second pair parts, 13, 251
    and silence, 19–21
    TG conversation example, 22
agreements
    actions, 8
    agreement tokens, 94, 95

preference organization, 91
    weak agreements, 165
announcements
    multiple preferences, 74–75
    pre-announcements, 37–41
    preference organization, 59, 60–61
    specific pre-sequences, 28
anticipatory accounts, 68–69
aphorisms, 186, 193, 257
Arthur and Rebecca example, 253–62
artificial intelligence, 20
assessments
    Chinese dinner example, 125
    known-answer question sequences, 224
    multiple preferences, 73–74
    personal state inquiry sequences, 124
    preference organization, 59, 70–71
    self-deprecations, 226–28
    sequence-closing sequences, 186
    sequence-closing thirds, 123–26
    TG conversation examples, 124, 126
    used-furniture store example, 126–27
asymmetrical alternatives, 59
Atkinson, J. M., 221–22, 224
Austin, John, 8
auto discussion examples, 71–72, 170, 178–79

BB gun examples
    insert expansions, 111–14
    pre-pre-sequences, 47
    repair sequences, 150–51
    successive sequences, 213–15
Beach, W. A., 120
Berkeley examples, 99, 198, 240–41
blessing example, 5–7
blocking responses
    pre-announcements, 40
    pre-invitations, 30–31, 33–34
    pre-offers, 37
    summons–answer sequences, 51–53
bodily actions, 11, 47
bookstore example, 35–36
Button, G., 169

card party example, 210–13
Casey, N., 169
change-of-state tokens, 118, 132
chicken dinner examples
    actions, 10
    adjacency pairs, 24–26

thematic threads, 246–49
turn-constructional units, 4–5
Chinese dinner examples
  actions, 11
  exchange sequences, 201
  sequence-closing thirds, 120–21, 125, 129, 136
  summons–answer sequences, 50–51
classrooms, 222
coffee chat example, 245–46
collaborative turn sequences, 241
collapsed adjacent pairs, 239
complaints
  adjacency pairs, 14
  incidental sequences, 244
  negative formulations, 131
  preference organization, 61
  summons–answer sequences, 53
compliance markers, 94
compliance tokens, 7
composite sequence-closing thirds
  Chinese dinner example, 129
  college dormitory example, 131–32
  Erhardt example, 127–28
  fishing-trip example, 137–38
  holiday weekend invitation example, 139–40
  MDE-MTRAC example, 138–39
  minimal post-expansions, 127–42
  post-party examples, 132–36
  pre-party example, 131
compression devices, 89
conference pass, 106
confirming, 8
Connie and Dee example, 149–50
continuing states of incipient talk, 26, 35, 115, 193
conversation. *See* talk-in-interaction
conversation analysis
  methodology, 252–63
  transcript symbols, 265–69
counters
  adjacency pairs, 16–19, 21
  vs. insert expansions, 99
  MDE-MTRAC example, 18–19
  psychotherapeutic session example, 17–18
  and reciprocal sequences, 195
  stolen example, 233
  Tarplee example, 17
  used-furniture store examples, 18, 129
courtesy terms, 49
cross-cutting preferences, 76–78

Davidson, J., 76, 121
"Dear Abby" advice column example, 191–92
Debbie and Nick examples, 36–37, 243–44
Debbie and Shelley example, 258
default, preference organization, 66–67
diction, function, 62
dinner-party example, 182–83
disagreements
  dormitory examples, 159–61
  ice-cream sandwich example, 159–61
  other-initiated repairs implying, 151–55
  post-expansions, 169
  post-expansions with second pair parts, 159–61

dormitory examples
  adjacency pairs, 23–24, 25
  post-expansion disagreements, 159–61
  sequence-closing thirds, 131–32
  topic-proffering sequences, 177–78
  topicalization, 155–58
Drew, P., 75, 127, 186, 221

elaboration, 65–66
emergency services example, 108–9
Erhardt examples, 48, 68, 127–28, 144–45
exchange sequences
  and counters, 195
  generally, 195–207
  "how-are-you" sequences, 196, 197–202, 232–33
  "how's school going" examples, 202–4
  MDE-MTRAC examples, 200–2
  normative constraints, 203–4
  TG conversation, 198–200, 203–4
  two brothers example, 196
expansions
  adjacency pairs, 109, 252
  distinctive types, 223–25
  insert expansions. *See* insert expansions
  post-expansions. *See* post-expansions
  pre-expansions. *See* pre-expansions
  topic-proffering sequences, 169
  types, 117, 252

farewells
  alternative second pair parts, 16
  closure of sequences, 115, 258–59
  second pair parts, 58
first pair parts (FPPs)
  function, 257
  meaning, 13, 251
  post-expansion reworkings, 162–68
  preference organization, 81–96
  relevance, 252
fish-tanks examples, 103, 104, 122, 183–86

Gardner, R., 189
generic insertions, 106
generic orders of organization, xiv
generic pre-sequences, 48–53, 58
Gerri and Shirley example, 79–80
go-ahead responses, 30, 92–93, 255
Goethe, J. W. von, 260
Goffman, E., 83, 153, 219
Goodwin, C., 6, 48, 240
Goodwin, M. H., 240
grammar, function, 3, 62
greetings
  See also "how are you" sequences
  alternative second pair parts, 16
  closure of sequences, 115
  exchange sequences, 196, 197–202
  minimal adjacency pairs, 22
  second pair parts, 58
"guess what,", 37, 38

hedging responses, 31–34, 69
Heritage, J., 62, 75, 118, 136, 155, 215, 221, 224

holiday weekend invitation example, 139–40, 153–54
Holt, E., 186
house-burning example, 199
housemates example, 10
"how are you" sequences
    action-type sequence series, 207–210
    assessments, 124
    exchange sequences, 196, 197–202, 232–33
    minimal adjacency pairs, 22
"how's school going" examples, 202–4

ice-cream sandwich example, 75, 159–61
idiomatic formulations, 186
incidental sequences
    Debbie and Nick example, 243–44
    generally, 237–44
    parenthetical sequences, 241–42
    stalled example, 242
    try-marking, 237–39
indexical responses, 189
insert expansions
    BB gun example, 111–14
    vs. counters, 99
    emergency services example, 108–9
    expansion of expansions, 109–11
    extent, 111–14
    function, 81
    generally, 97–114
    generic insertions, 106
    insert sequences, 97
    Missiz Kelly examples, 97, 105
    post-first insert expansions, 100–6
    pre-second insert expansions, 106–9
    presidential race example, 109–10
    promissory character, 99
    regulation of growth, 181
    repair sequences, 100–6
    service encounters, 108–9
    stalled example, 99
    types, 100
inter-turn gaps, 67–68
interaction
    interactional projects, 244–49
    nature, xiv–xv
    terminology, 251
interrogative sequences, 109
intonation, 136, 238
invitations
    declining, 127
    pre-invitations, 29–34
    pre-second insert expansions, 107
    preference organization, 59, 61
    sequence-closing thirds, 125
    specific pre-sequences, 28

Jefferson, Gail, 42, 56, 100, 106, 153, 155, 181, 183, 207, 219, 221, 262, 265
Jewish boy example, 126
jokes, 186, 218–19

known-answer questions, 223–25
Koshik, I., 62

Lazaraton, A., 226–28, 229–30
legal proceedings, sequence-closing thirds, 221–2
Lerner, G. H., 161, 241
Levinson, S. C., 109, 223–24
Lindström, A. K. B., 94

Maynard, D. W., 38, 157
MDE-MTRAC examples
    See also stolen examples
    counters, 18–19
    exchange sequences, 200–2
    non-canonical forms, 231–34
    pre-tellings, 42–43
    recognition, 88
    sequence-closing thirds, 138–39
medical consultations, 222
Mehan, H., 222, 224
Merritt, M., 109
methodology
    Arthur and Rebecca example, 253–62
    generally, 252–63
    re-beginning, 263–64
Missiz Kelly examples, 97, 105, 218
mitigation, 64–65
multiple pre-expansions, 53–57
musings, 142–48

negative formulations, 131
negative polarity markers, 62
news interviews, 221
news marks, 155
non-canonical forms
    generally, 231–37
    stolen example, 231–34
noticeables, 86–87
noticing, 219

offers
    adjacency pairs, 14
    multiple preferences, 75–76
    offer series, 210–13
    pre-offers. *See* pre-offers
    preference organization, 59, 60, 85
    specific pre-sequences, 28
"oh"
    Chinese dinner example, 129
    sequence-closing thirds, 118–20, 128–30, 135
"oh-okay,", 127–28, 135–37
"okay"
    Chinese dinner example, 120–21
    sequence-closing thirds, 120–23, 135
    used-furniture store examples, 121, 141
Olsher, D., 209
other-initiated repairs
    BB gun example, 150–51
    Connie and Dee example, 149–50
    disagreement-implicated, 151–55
    insert expansions, 101–4, 105–6, 116–17
    non-minimal post-expansions, 149–51
    retro-sequences, 218
    TG conversation example, 152–53
    therapy session example, 155
out-louds, 143

parenthetical sequences, 241–42
personal state inquiry sequences, 124
Peyrot, M., 17
phonetics, function, 3
Pomerantz, A., 59–60, 63, 71, 73–74, 78–81, 94, 129, 146, 165, 225–26, 228, 230
positioning
  anticipatory accounts, 68–69
  Erhardt example, 68
  inter-turn gaps, 67–68
  pre-emptive reformulation with preference reversal, 70–73
  preference organization, 67–73
  pro-forma agreements, 69–70
  TG conversation examples, 67, 68
  turn-initial delays, 68
post-completion musings
  Erhardt example, 144–45
  minimal post-expansions, 142–48
  pre-party examples, 143–44, 145–46
  Virginia example, 147–48
post-expansions
  assessments, 123–26
  composites, 127–42
  disagreements, 169
  distinctive types, 223–25
  first-pair part reworkings, 162–68
  generally, 117–68
  minimal post-expansions, 118–48, 221–23
  non-minimal post-expansions, 148–68
  other-initiated repairs, 149–51
  post-completion musings, 142–48
  preference organization, 117
  regulation, 181
  second-pair part challenges, 159–61
  sequence-closing thirds, 118–27, 221–23
  topicalization, 155–58
post-mortems, 142–48
post-party examples
  preference organization, 83
  sequence-closing thirds, 132–36
practice
  framework, 249
  incidental sequences, 237–44
  interactional projects, 244–49
  non-canonical forms, 231–37
  sequence organization, 231–50
  thematic threads, 244–49
  try-marking, 237–39
pre-announcements
  blocking responses, 40
  generally, 37–41
  pre-empting responses, 41
  recurrent turn formats, 38
  Schenkein examples, 38, 39, 40, 41
  Terasaki examples, 38, 40
pre-conditions, 45–47
pre-disagreements, 69, 70, 85, 102–4, 151
pre-emptive questions, 232–34
pre-emptive reformulation, 70–73
pre-emptive responses
  pre-expansions, 41, 56
  preference organization, 90

pre-expansions
  Arthur and Rebecca example, 255–56, 259–60
  backgrounds, 46
  generally, 28–57
  generic pre-sequences, 48–53
  multiple pre-expansions, 53–57
  nature, 81
  pre-announcements, 37–41
  pre-invitations, 29–34
  pre-offers, 34–37
  pre-pre-sequences, 44–47
  pre-sequences, 28
  pre-telling, 41
  preference organization, 90–93
  regulation, 181
  specific pre-sequences, 29
  summons–answer sequences, 48–53
  transition to base sequence, 36–37
pre-invitations
  blocking responses, 30–31, 33–34
  generally, 29–34
  go-ahead responses, 30
  hedging responses, 31–34
  telephone call examples, 30
pre-mentions, 45–47
pre-offers
  blocking responses, 37
  bookstore example, 35–36
  Debbie and Nick example, 36–37
  generally, 34–37
  preference organization, 85, 91
pre-party examples
  post-completion musings, 143–44, 145–46
  post-expansions, 115–16
  sequence-closing thirds, 131
pre-pausals, 68
pre-pre-sequences
  BB gun example, 47
  born-again Christian example, 46–47
  generally, 44–47
  pre-conditions, 45–47
  pre-mentions, 45–47
  preliminaries, 46–47
  Sugihara example, 46
pre-rejections, 102–4
pre-requests, 62, 90–91
pre-sequences
  Arthur and Rebecca example, 256
  generic pre-sequences, 48–53, 58
  meaning, 28
  nature, 81, 250
  specific pre-sequences, 29
  thematic threads, 245
  transition to base sequence, 36–37
pre-tellings
  generally, 41
  insert expansions, 108, 109, 110
  MDE-MTRAC example, 42–43
  non-canonical forms, 234
  pre-telling sequences, 42
  TG conversation example, 40
prefaces, 41–44

preference organization
    alternative second pair parts, 16
    Arthur and Rebecca example, 255
    asymmetric alternatives, 59
    cross-cutting preferences, 76–78
    default, 66–67
    elaboration, 65–66
    first pair parts, 81–96
    generally, 58–96
    mitigation, 64–65
    multiple preferences, 73–78
    positioning, 67–73
    post-expansions, 117
    practices, 63–81
    pre-expansions, 90–93
    second pair parts, 81, 179–80
    self-deprecation, 225–30
    terms, 58–63
    type conformity, 78–81
    variations, 225–30
    "yes/no" questions, 78–81
preliminaries, 46–47
presidential race example, 109–10
pro-forma agreements, 69–70
pro-repeats, 155
prosody, 62
Psathas, G., 107
psychotherapeutic session example, 17–18

questions
    known-answer questions, 223–25
    pre-emptive questions, 232–34
    question series, 207
    "yes/no" questions, 78–81, 170, 172

Raymond, G., 66, 78–79, 80, 246, 257
re-beginning, 263–64
reciprocal exchanges, 195–207
recognition, 88–89
recognitional reference forms, 237
rejections
    post-expansions, 159–61
    pre-rejections, 102–4
relevance rules
    adjacency pairs, 19–21, 251–52
    conditional relevance, 20
    function, 21
repair sequences
    fish-tanks examples, 103, 104
    insert expansions, 100–6
    Missiz Kelly examples, 97, 105
    other-initiation of repair, 101–4, 105–6, 116–17,
        149–51, 218
    other-repair, 101
    pre-disagreements, 102–4, 151
    retro-sequences, 217–19
    self-initiation of repair, 101
    self-repair, 101
    specificity, 101
    TG conversation examples, 102, 106
    Virginia example, 103–4
requests
    deferred requests, 94

free goods, 83
immediate requests, 94
mock requests, 25–26
pre-requests, 62, 90–91
preference organization, 59, 83–86, 94, 95–96
specific pre-sequences, 28
response cries, 219
responses
    alternative responses, 59
    blocking, 30–31, 33–34, 37, 40, 51–53
    go-ahead responses, 30, 92–93, 255
    hedging, 31–34, 69
    indexical responses, 189
    pre-empting, 41, 56, 90
    topic-proffering sequences, 173–79
    trouble-premonitory responses to inquiry, 207
resumption searches, 24
retro-sequences
    vs. adjacency pairs, 9, 217
    generally, 217–19
    noticing, 219
    other-initiated repairs, 218
    sources, 217
right-hand parenthesis markers, 98
Rossano, Federico, 116
Roth, A., 209, 221

Sacks, Harvey, xii, xiv, 2, 18, 26, 28, 40, 41, 59, 64, 67,
    69, 71, 77, 100, 115, 124, 151, 153, 169, 183, 204,
    217, 219, 221, 237, 257, 260, 264
Saunders example, 109–10
Scheflen, A. E., 17
Schegloff, Emanuel, 1, 2, 9, 18, 26, 40, 44, 45, 49, 59, 62,
    64, 72, 86, 88, 98, 100, 102, 105, 107, 113, 115, 125,
    131, 143, 148, 153, 154, 178, 179, 183, 197, 202,
    204, 217, 221, 232, 237, 243, 248, 257, 260, 264
Schenkein, J., 38, 39, 40, 41, 106, 181
Searle, John, 8
second pair parts (SPPs)
    challenging post-expansions, 159–61
    meaning, 13, 251
    preference organization, 81, 179–80
    relevance, 252
self-deprecation, 225–30
self-identification, 88–90
self-praise, 146
sequence closing
    adjacent pairs, 22–24
    dormitory example, 23–24
    examples, 258–59
    generally, 115–17
    Syracuse trip example, 23–24
sequence-closing sequences
    aphorisms, 186, 193
    basic form, 186–87
    collaboration, 187, 189, 190–91
    "Dear Abby" advice column example, 191–92
    dedicated sequences, 186–94
    dinner-party example, 182–83
    fish-tanks examples, 183–86
    generally, 181–94
    indexical responses, 189
    initial turns, 186

resistance, 187
second turns, 186–87
silence, 194
TG conversation examples, 184, 187–91
third turns, 187
unilateral and foreshortened endings, 181–86
sequence-closing thirds
Arthur and Rebecca example, 257
assessments, 123–26
Chinese dinner examples, 120–21, 136
composites, 127–42
dormitory example, 131–32
fish-tanks examples, 122
fishing-trip example, 137–38
generally, 118–27
holiday weekend invitation example, 139–40
Jewish boy example, 126
legal proceedings, 221–22
MDE-MTRAC example, 138–39
news interviews, 221
"oh", 118–20, 128–30, 135
"oh-okay,", 127–28, 135–37
"okay,", 120–23, 135
post-party example, 132–36
pre-party example, 131
repeats, 126–27
turn types, 126–27
used-furniture store examples, 121, 126–27, 129–30, 141
variations, 221–23
working-out example, 119–20
sequence organization
framework, 249
meaning, xiv, 1–3, 9
non-canonical forms, 231–37
practice. *See* practice
vs. sequential organization, 2
summary, 251–52
variations, 220–30
sequences
base sequences, 29
insert sequences. *See* insert expansions
interrogative sequences, 109
meaning, xi, 3, 9
pre-sequences. *See* pre-sequences
pre-telling sequences, 42
repair. *See* repair sequences
side sequences, 56
succession. *See* successive sequences
vs. topicality, 113–14
types, 251
service encounters, 108–9
side sequences, 56
silence
and adjacency pairs, 19–21
and self-deprecations, 226
sequence-closing sequences, 194
Smith-Thanksgiving example, 162
Sorjonen, M.-L., 215
speech act theory, 8
speech-exchange systems, xiv
stalled example
incidental sequences, 242

insert expansions, 99
mitigation, 64–65
recognition, 88
stew dinner examples, 84, 94–95
stolen examples
See also MDE-MTRAC examples
non-canonical forms, 231–34
topic-proffering sequences, 171, 176–77
story-telling, 9, 41–44
structural organization, xiv
successive sequences
action-type sequence series, 207–13
BB gun example, 213–15
card party example, 210–13
generally, 195–16
"how-are-you" sequences, 196, 197–202, 207–10
multi-part tellings, 215–16
offer series, 210–13
question series, 207
reciprocal/exchange sequences, 195–207
relevance ties, 195
successive parts of courses of action, 213–15
Sugihara example, 46
summaries, sequence-closing sequences, 186
summons–answer sequences
alternative responses, 59
blocking responses, 51–53
Chinese dinner example, 50–51
function, 58
generic pre-sequences, 48–53
go-ahead responses, 62
used-furniture store examples, 51–53, 56
symbols, transcript symbols, 265–69
Syracuse trip example, 23–24

talk-in-interaction, meaning, xiii
Tarplee, C., 17
taxonomy, 252
tellings
multi-part tellings, 215–16
multiple preferences, 74–75
non-canonical forms, 234
pre-tellings. *See* pre-tellings
ten Have, P., 222
Terasaki, A., 37, 38, 39, 40
TG conversation
action-type sequence series, 207–8
assessments, 124, 126
default, 66–67
elaboration, 65
exchange sequences, 198–200, 203–4
hedging responses, 32–33
minimal adjacency pairs, 22
multi-part tellings, 215–16
positioning, 67, 68
post-expansion reworkings, 164–68
pre-tellings, 40
preference organization, 62
recognition, 88
repair sequences, 102, 106, 152–53
sequence-closing sequences, 184, 187–91
sequence-closing thirds, 140

TG conversation (*cont.*)
   topic-proffering sequences, 170, 171–76
   transcript, 270
Thanksgiving example, 95–96
thematic threads
   chicken dinner examples, 246–49
   coffee chat example, 245–46
   generally, 244–49
therapy session example, 155
topic-proffering sequences
   assertion format, 170
   auto discussion examples, 170, 178–79
   dormitory example, 177–78
   expansions, 169
   generally, 169–80
   meaning, 169–70
   recipient-oriented topics, 170
   responses, 173–79
   second tries, 173–76
   stolen examples, 171, 176–77
   TG conversation examples, 170, 171–76
   turn organization, 171–72
   "yes/no" questions, 170, 172
topicality, vs. sequence, 113–14
topicalization, 155–58
touched-off stories, 219
transcript symbols, 265–69
transition-relevance place, 4
trouble premonitory responses to inquiry, 207
trouble problem, meaning, xiv
try-marking, 237–39
turn-constructional units (TCUs)
   chicken dinner example, 4–5
   meaning, 3–7
   multiple actions in one TCU, 9
   shapes, 3–4
   Virginia example, 5–7
turn-initial delays, 68
turn-initial markers, 69
turns
   and actions, 10
   Arthur and Rebecca example, 257
   clumps, 1–2, 113
   double functions, 169

   meaning, xi, xiv, 3–7
   organization, xiv–xv
   sequence-closing sequences, 186–87
   topic-proffering sequences, 171–72
two brothers example, 196
type conformity, 78–81

used-furniture store examples
   assessments, 126–27
   counters, 18, 129
   multiple pre-expansions, 53–56
   preference organization, 91–92
   sequence-closing thirds, 121, 129–30, 141
   summons–answer sequences, 51–53

variations in sequence organization
   classrooms, 222
   distinctive sequence and expansion types, 223–25
   English as second language, 226–28, 229–30
   generally, 220–30
   known-answer questions, 223–25
   legal proceedings, 221–22
   medical consultations, 222
   news interviews, 221
   preference organization, 225–30
   self-deprecation, 225–30
   sequence-closing thirds, 221–23
   work settings, 222
Virginia examples
   clumps, 2
   post-completion musings, 147–48
   repair sequences, 103–4
   turn-constructional units, 5–7

waterbed examples, 36–37, 243–44
West, C., 105
Whalen, M, 202
word selection, meaning, xiv
work settings, 222
working-out example, 119–20

"yes/no" questions, 78–81, 170, 172

Zimmerman, D. H., 105, 109, 202